Please note

We believe accurate, plain-English legal information should help you solve many of your own legal problems. But this text is not a substitute for personalized advice from a knowledgeable lawyer. If you want the help of a trained professional—and we'll always point out situations in which we think that's a good idea— consult an attorney licensed to practice in your state.

12th edition

Everybody's Guide to

Small Claims Court

by Attorney Ralph Warner

NOLO

Twelfth Edition	MARCH 2008
Editor	EMILY DOSKOW
Production	SARAH HINMAN
Proofreading	MARK NIGARA
Index	BAYSIDE INDEXING SERVICE
Printing	DELTA PRINTING SOLUTIONS, INC.

Warner, Ralph E.
　Everybody's guide to small claims court / by Ralph Warner and Emily Doskow. -
- 12th ed.
　　　p. cm.
　Includes index.
　ISBN-13: 978-1-4133-0762-7 (pbk.)
　ISBN-10: 1-4133-0762-0 (pbk.)
　1. Small claims courts--United States--Popular works.　I. Doskow, Emily. II.
Title.
KF8769.Z9W37 2008
347.73'28--dc22

　　　　　　　　　2007038828

For information on bulk purchases or corporate premium sales, please contact the Special Sales department. For academic sales or textbook adoptions, ask for Academic Sales. Call 800-955-4775 or write to Nolo at 950 Parker St., Berkeley, CA, 94710.

Thank You

Nolo is as much family as business. Without the help of many Nolo family members, there would be no books such as this one. Over the years, a number of talented friends have read the manuscript of this book and made helpful suggestions for improvement. With enough help, even a tarnished penny can be made to shine. Thanks to Natasha Kaluza, Jeanne Stott, Ella Hirst, Nick Aquino, Mary Alice Coleman, Scott Reep, and Susan Cornell. Thanks also to Jennifer Wedel, who made significant improvements to the 11th edition that will last long beyond that version of the book. Many thanks also to the small claims court clerks and legal advisors whose input keeps this book fresh.

Ella Hirst, Stanley Jacobsen, Beth Laurence, and Alayna Schroeder compiled the research for earlier editions; for the 12th edition thanks go to Terry McGinley and Alayna Schroeder. Their thorough, patient, and dedicated work has made this a better book.

For the 11th and 12th editions, a very warm thank you goes to Judge (Ret.) Roderic Duncan and Commissioner Douglas G. Carnahan, whose perspectives "from the bench" on the small claims court process are an invaluable contribution. Another sincere thanks goes to John Lamb for assistance with consumer protection laws.

For Toni,

the light, the heart, and the love of my life.

Table of Contents

8 Who Can Be Sued?

9 Where Can You Sue?

10 Plaintiff's and Defendant's Filing Fees, Court Papers, and Court Dates

Your Small Claims Court Companion

Filing a case in small claims court is a highly cost-effective strategy for resolving all kinds of disputes. In most states, the maximum amount you can sue for has increased substantially in recent years, and court judgments have become far easier to collect. In addition, many states have implemented innovative mediation programs for small claims, which can spare you the time and tension of presenting your case to a judge. So, although more can and should be done to make small claims court a true people's court, it is an efficient forum that gives participants an opportunity to resolve many personal consumer and small business disputes.

The goal of this book is to give people bringing a case and those defending one all the information necessary to make the best possible use of small claims court. From deciding whether you have a case through gathering evidence, arranging for witnesses, planning your courtroom presentation, and collecting your money, you will find everything you need here.

TIP

From the bench. *Everybody's Guide to Small Claims Court* is the only such guide to include practical suggestions from two former small claims court judges. You'll see their comments throughout the book.

Everybody's Guide to Small Claims Court has now been in print for more than 25 years. The current edition has been completely updated to reflect literally hundreds of recent practical and legal changes. My goal is to make it the best possible tool to help you answer such questions as:

- How does small claims court work?
- Do I have a case worth pursuing or defending?
- How do I prepare my case to maximum advantage?
- What witnesses and other evidence should I present?
- What do I say in court?
- Can I appeal if I lose?
- How do I collect my judgment?

Proper presentation of your small claims action can often mean the difference between receiving a check and writing one. This isn't to say that I can tell you how to take a hopeless case and turn it into a blue-ribbon winner. It does mean that with the information contained here, and with your own creativity and common sense, you will be able to develop and present your legal and factual position as effectively as possible. In short, this book really will show you how a case with a slight limp can be set on four good legs.

Just as important as knowing when and how to bring your small claims court action is knowing when not to. Clearly, you don't want to waste time and energy dragging a hopeless case to court. And even if your case is legally sound, you won't want to pursue it if your chances of collecting from the defendant are poor.

As with any book, I have had to make a number of decisions as to the order in which I cover small claims issues and the depth the book goes into on each topic. For example, the question of whether an oral contract is valid is discussed in Chapter 2 but not again in Chapter 16 on automobile repairs, where it may also be relevant. So please take the time to read, or at least skim, the entire book before you focus on the chapters that interest you most. A very good way to get an overview of the entire small claims process is to read the Table of Contents.

In addition to studying the information you'll find here, it's important that you review the materials made available by your state's small claims court. Crucial technical details such as when and where court is held, what types of evidence are allowed and prohibited, and how much it will cost to collect a judgment are covered in more detail in these materials than I can possibly do in this 50-state guide. Fortunately, accessing this material is easy—it's usually available online as well as in free pamphlets available at your small claims court clerk's office. You'll find the URL for your state's small claims website in the Appendix.

Now a few words about two potentially sensitive subjects. First, when grappling with the ever-tricky personal pronoun, I have decided to simply take turns rather than using the cumbersome "he or she" and "his or her." Please bear with me if I inadvertently use one or the other too many times in a single chapter.

Second, it's appropriate to say a few words about my many referrals to other Nolo self-help law books and Nolo's website. Lest you think my only goal is to try to sell you another book, let me make three points. First, Nolo is by far the most comprehensive publisher of self-help law materials in the United States. As a result, there are many legal areas where Nolo publishes the only decent materials aimed at nonlawyers. Second, because a huge variety of legal issues can be litigated in small claims court, information in many other Nolo books and in Nolo's free online Legal Encyclopedia may be useful (and is far too voluminous to repeat here). Third, as Nolo's books are available at most American libraries, it shouldn't be hard to look up any needed information at no cost. ●

In the Beginning

First Things

Small claims procedures are established by state law. This means there are differences in the operating rules of small claims courts from state to state, including the maximum amount for which you can sue; who can sue; and the what, where, and when of filing papers. There are even differences in what small claims court (or its equivalent) is called in the different states, with "justice," "district," "municipal," "city," "county," and "magistrates" court among the names commonly used.

Although the details of using small claims courts vary from state to state, the basic approach necessary to prepare and present a case is remarkably similar everywhere. But details are important, and you should do three things to make sure you understand how small claims court works in your state:

- Look up the summary of your state's rules in the 50-state Appendix to this book.
- Obtain your local small claims rules from your small claims court clerk's office.
- Check out your state's small claims rules online. You'll find the URL for your state's small claims court in the Appendix.

The purpose of small claims court is to hear disputes involving modest amounts of money, without long delays and formal rules of evidence. Disputes are normally presented directly by the people involved. Lawyers are prohibited in some states, including Michigan and California (except to argue their own disputes), but are allowed in most. However, the limited dollar amounts involved usually make it economically unwise to hire a lawyer. The maximum amount of money for which you can sue (in legal jargon, the "jurisdictional amount") is set by state law, too. For example, the limit is $5,000 in the District of Columbia, $5,000 in New York, and $7,500 in Minnesota. These amounts are typical, although there is considerable variation. Some states allow small claims court cases of up to $15,000, while others limit cases to no more than $2,000. (See the Appendix.)

There are three great advantages of small claims court:

- You get to prepare and present your own case without having to pay a lawyer more than your claim is worth.

- Filing, preparing, and presenting a small claims case is relatively easy. The gobbledygook of complicated legal forms and language found in other courts is kept to a minimum. To start your case, you need only fill out a few lines on a simple form (for example, "Defendant owes me the sum of $4,000 because the 2004 Neon they sold me on January 1, 2004, in supposedly 'excellent condition' died less than a mile from the car lot"). When you get to court, you can talk to the judge in plain English without any legal jargon. Even better, if you have helpful documents or witnesses, you can present them to the judge without complying with the thousand years' accumulation of rusty, musty procedures, habits, and so-called rules of evidence of which the legal profession is so proud.

- Small claims court doesn't take long. Most disputes are heard in court within two or three months from the time the complaint is filed. The hearing itself seldom takes more than 15 minutes. The judge announces a decision either right there in the courtroom or mails it within a few days.

But before you decide that small claims court sounds like just the place to bring your case, you will want to answer a basic question: Will the results you expect to achieve balance out the effort you will have to expend? Even in small claims court, a successful case will probably take ten to 20 hours to prepare and present and, depending on your personality, may actually cause a few sleepless nights.

In order to assess whether your dispute is worth the effort of bringing to court, you will want to understand the details of how small claims court works. Being clear about who can sue, where, and for how much is a good start. You will also want to learn a little law to answer such important questions as whether you are likely to win and, if so, how much. And, of course, even if you conclude you do have a winning case, you'll want to understand how best to prepare and present it. Finally, and most importantly, comes the detail that so many people overlook, to their later dismay. Assuming that you prepare and present your case brilliantly and get a judgment for everything you request, can you collect the money? The ability to get paid seems a silly thing to overlook, doesn't it? Unfortunately, many plaintiffs who go through the entire small claims procedure and come out winners have no chance of collecting a dime because they have sued a person who has neither money nor any reasonable prospect of getting any.

The purpose of the first dozen chapters of this book is to help you decide whether or not you have a case worth pursuing. These are not the chapters where grand strategies are brilliantly unrolled to baffle and confound the opposition—that comes later. Here I am more concerned with such mundane tasks as locating the person you want to sue, suing in the right court, filling out the necessary forms, and properly delivering the forms to the person you're suing.

Occasionally throughout this book we reproduce forms used in California small claims court. Forms used in other states may look somewhat different, but you will find that the differences are usually more a matter of graphics than of substance. The basic information requested—who is suing whom about what—is very similar everywhere. Blank copies of all forms are available at your local small claims clerk's office and often online (see the Appendix for your state's small claims website).

Things to Think About Before Initiating or Defending Your Case

Here is a preliminary checklist of things you will want to think about at this initial stage. As you read further, we will go into each of these areas in more detail. But if you haven't already gotten a copy of your local small claims court rules, do it now.

Questions a Plaintiff Needs to Answer

☐ 1. Do you have a good case? That is, can you establish or prove all the key pieces of your claim? (See Chapter 2 for a discussion of what is needed to win contract, debt, property damage, and other common types of cases.)

☐ 2. How many dollars is your claim for? If it is for more than the small claims maximum, do you wish to waive the excess and still use small claims court? (See Chapter 4.)

☐ 3. Have you made a reasonable effort to contact the other party to offer a compromise? (See Chapter 6.)

☐ 4. Are you within the deadline by which you must file your suit? (See Chapter 5.)

☐ 5. Whom do you sue and how do you identify this person or business on your court papers? In some types of cases, especially those involving businesses and automobiles, this can be a little more technical and tricky than you might have guessed. (See Chapter 8.)

☐ 6. Which small claims court should you bring your suit in? (See Chapter 9.)

☐ 7. If mediation is offered or encouraged by your small claims court, do you understand how it works and how best to use it? (See Chapter 6.)

☐ 8. Can you prove your case? That is, do you understand what evidence you need to bring to court to convince a judge you are in the right? (See Chapters 14–22.)

☐ 9. Can you make a convincing courtroom presentation? (See Chapter 15.)

☐10. And, the most important question: Assuming you can win, is there a reasonable chance you can collect? (See Chapters 3 and 24.)

Questions a Defendant Needs to Answer

☐ 1. Do you have legal grounds for a countersuit against the plaintiff? Or put another way, does the plaintiff really owe you money instead of the other way around? (See Chapters 10 and 12.)

☐ 2. Do you have a partial or complete defense against the plaintiff's claim? Or put another way, has the plaintiff filed a bogus lawsuit? (See Chapters 2 and 12.)

☐ 3. Is the plaintiff's money demand reasonable or excessive? (See Chapter 4.)

☐ 4. Has the plaintiff brought the suit within the proper time limit? (See Chapter 5.)

☐ 5. Has the plaintiff followed reasonably correct procedures in bringing suit and delivering the court papers to you? (See Chapters 11 and 12.)

☐ 6. If mediation is offered or encouraged by your small claims court, do you understand how it works and how to use it? (See Chapter 6.)

☐ 7. Have you made a reasonable effort to contact the plaintiff in order to arrive at a compromise settlement? (See Chapters 6 and 12.)

☐ 8. Assuming you'll fight the case in court, you'll normally need proof that your version of events is correct. Can you collect evidence and witnesses to accomplish this? (See Chapters 13–15.)

☐ 9. Are you prepared to present your side of the case convincingly in court? (See Chapter 15.)

TIP

Defendants may want to file their own lawsuit. In addition to their right to defend themselves, defendants also have the opportunity to file their own case against the plaintiff. (See Chapters 10 and 12.) Do this if you believe that you lost money due to the same events the plaintiff is complaining about and the plaintiff is legally responsible for your loss. Defendants' claims commonly develop out of a situation in which both parties are negligent (for example, in a car accident) and the question is who was more at fault. If your claim is for less than the small claims court maximum, you can file there. But if it is for more, you will want to check your state's rules. Typically, you'll learn that you should file your case in a different court (and have your opponent's case transferred there), but your state may use a different system. (See Chapter 10.)

Legal Jargon Defined

Mercifully, there is not a great deal of technical language used in small claims courts. But there are a few terms that may be new to you and that you will have to become familiar with. Don't try to learn all of these terms now. Refer back to these definitions when you need them.

Abstract of Judgment: An official document you get from the small claims court clerk's office that indicates that you have a money judgment in your favor against another person. Filing it with the County Recorder places a lien on real property owned by the judgment debtor. (For more information about property liens, see Chapter 24.)

Appeal: In the small claims context, a request that the superior court rehear the case from scratch and reverse the decision of the small claims court. Some states allow only a defendant to appeal; others allow the parties to appeal based only on law—not facts. Many require you to post a bond when you file an appeal. (See Chapter 23 and the Appendix.)

Calendar: A list of cases to be heard by a small claims court on a particular day. A case taken "off calendar" is removed from the list. This usually occurs because the defendant has not received a copy of the plaintiff's lawsuit or because the parties jointly request that the case be heard on another day.

Claim of Exemption: A procedure by which a "judgment debtor" can claim that, under federal or state law, certain of his money or other property is exempt from being grabbed to satisfy a debt.

Conditional Judgment: When a court issues "equitable relief" (such as the return of a piece of property), it has power to grant a conditional judgment. A conditional judgment consists of certain actions or requirements that are contingent on other actions (for instance, return the property in ten days or pay $2,000).

Continuance: A court order that a hearing be postponed to a later date.

Counterclaim: When a defendant responds to a plaintiff's lawsuit by countersuing the plaintiff for damages arising from the same act or failure to act that the plaintiff's lawsuit is about, also known as a Claim of Defendant or a Cross Complaint.

Default Judgment: A court decision in favor of the plaintiff (the person filing suit) when the defendant fails to show up (that is, defaults).

Defendant: The person or "party" being sued.

Defendant's Claim: A claim by a defendant that the plaintiff owes him money. The claim is filed as part of the same small claims action that the plaintiff started.

Dismissed Case: A dismissal usually occurs when a plaintiff drops her case. If the defendant has not filed a counterclaim, the plaintiff simply files a written request for dismissal. If the defendant has filed a counterclaim, both plaintiff and defendant must agree in writing before the court will allow a dismissal. A judge may also dismiss a case if a defendant successfully claims that a case was filed in the wrong court. (See Chapter 9.) Also, if a plaintiff does not show up in court on the appointed day, the judge may dismiss the case. Most cases are dismissed "without prejudice," which is legal jargon meaning they can be refiled. But if a case is dismissed "with prejudice," it means that it can't be refiled unless the plaintiff successfully appeals the dismissal.

Equitable Relief: There are several areas in which a small claims court judge has the power to issue judgment for something other than money damages—that is, to order a party to return unique property, end a fraudulent contract, fix a mistaken contract, or do one or more of the acts discussed in more detail in Chapter 4. This type of judgment is called "equitable relief" (as opposed to "monetary relief").

Equity: The value of a particular piece of property that you own. For example, if a car has a fair market value of $10,000 and you owe a bank $8,000 on it, your equity is $2,000.

Eviction: See Unlawful Detainer Proceeding, below.

Exempt Property: Under federal and state law, certain personal and real property is exempt from being taken to pay ("satisfy") court judgments if the debtor follows certain procedures. (See Chapter 24.)

Formal Court: As used here, this term refers to the regular state courts other than small claims court. The states call their trial courts by all sorts of names (municipal, superior, district, circuit, supreme, civil, and so on.). In California, for example, claims too large to qualify for small claims court are heard in superior court. All of these courts require considerable attention to often confusing legal language and procedure, and you will want to do some homework if you decide to bring a case there. If your claim really is too big for small claims court, see *Represent Yourself in Court: How to Prepare & Try a Winning Case,* by Paul Bergman and Sara Berman-Barrett (Nolo). Or, if you choose to hire a lawyer, see *The Lawsuit Survival Guide: A Client's Companion to Litigation,* by Joseph Matthews (Nolo), available only as an eBook at www.nolo.com. With or without a lawyer, you'll find guidance on certain important pretrial procedures in *Nolo's Deposition Handbook,* by Paul Bergman and Albert Moore (Nolo).

Garnish: To attach (legally take) money—usually wages, or commissions, or a bank account—for payment of a debt.

Hearing: The court trial.

Homestead: Homestead laws allow homeowners to protect a certain amount of the equity in their homes from attachment and sale to satisfy most debts. Homestead laws can work in one of two ways. In some states, the homeowner must file a paper called a Declaration of Homestead. In other states, simply owning a home (and having the deed recorded) is enough to entitle the homeowner to homestead protection. (See Chapter 24.)

Judge Pro Tem: A lawyer who pinch-hits for a regular judge on a temporary basis. Because this person isn't an elected or officially appointed judge, she can only hear your case with your written consent, which will normally be requested on the day you go to court.

Judgment: The decision given by the court. A judgment must be written down and signed by a judge.

Judgment Creditor: A person to whom money is owed under a court decision.

Judgment Debtor: A person who owes money under a court decision.

Jurisdiction: A court's authority to hear and decide a case. To properly hear a case, a court must have jurisdiction over the type of dispute and over the parties. A small claims court has jurisdiction to hear cases involving money damages up to a certain amount—for example, $10,000 in Alaska, $4,000 in Kansas. (This is often called the "jurisdictional amount" or "jurisdictional limit.") Some small claims courts also have jurisdiction over certain types of nonmoney cases, such as unlawful detainer (eviction) actions, and some may award nonmoney remedies (equitable relief), as discussed in Chapter 4. Generally, small claims courts have jurisdiction over parties who live in the state, were present in the state when the dispute arose, or who purposefully do business in the state. (For more information about the courts' jurisdiction over people, see Chapter 8.)

Jury Trial: All small claims cases and appeals are heard by judges or commissioners—you're generally not entitled to a jury. Some small claims courts allow jury trials, although most do not. (See the Appendix for your state's rules.)

Levy: A legal method to seize property or money for unpaid debts under court order. For example, a sheriff can levy on (take and sell) your automobile if you refuse to pay a judgment.

Lien: A legal right to an interest in the real estate (real property) of another for payment of a debt. To get a lien, you first must get a court judgment and then take proper steps to have the court enter an Abstract of Judgment. To establish the lien, you then take the abstract to the County Recorder's office in a county where the judgment debtor has real estate.

Magistrate: Another word for judge.

Mediation: A process encouraged in many small claims courts by which the parties to a dispute meet with a neutral person (the mediator) who attempts to help them arrive at their own solution to the problem. If mediation succeeds, it's normally not necessary to argue the case in court; if it fails, the dispute can still go to court to be decided on by a judge.

Motion to Vacate Judgment: The motion the defendant must file to reopen a proceeding in which the judge entered a default judgment because the defendant didn't show up. (See Chapter 15.)

Order of Examination: A court procedure allowing a judgment creditor to question a judgment debtor about the extent and location of assets.

Party: Lawyer-talk for a participant in a lawsuit. Thus the plaintiff or defendant may be referred to as a party—and both together as the parties—to a small claims suit.

Plaintiff: The person or "party" who starts a lawsuit.

Prejudice: A term used when a case is dismissed. A case dismissed "without prejudice" can be refiled at any time as long as the statute of limitations period has not run out (see Chapter 5). However, a case dismissed "with prejudice" is dead (can't be refiled) unless the dismissal is first successfully appealed.

Process Server: The person who delivers court papers to a party or witness. (See Chapter 11.)

Recorder (Office of the County Recorder): The county office that makes and files important legal documents, such as deeds to real property. The County Recorder's office is usually located in the main county courthouse.

Release: A written agreement in which a person agrees to waive a right or responsibility, for example, a "release of liability."

Replevin: A type of legal action in which the owner of movable goods is given the right to recover them from someone who shouldn't have them. It is commonly used in relation to buyers and sellers; for example, a seller might bring a replevin action if the seller delivered goods to a buyer who then failed to pay for them. Some states' small claims courts allow replevin actions.

Satisfaction of Judgment: A written statement filed by the judgment creditor when the judgment is paid. (See Chapter 23.)

Service: The formal delivery of court papers to a party or witness, which must be done in a manner specified by statute. Also called "service of process."

Statute of Limitations: The time period during which you must file your lawsuit. It normally starts on the date the act or failure to act giving rise to the lawsuit occurred, and ends one or more years later, with the number of years depending on the type of suit. (See Chapter 5.)

Stay of Enforcement: When a defendant appeals a small claims court judgment to the superior court, enforcement (collection) of the judgment is stayed (stopped) until the time for appeal has expired.

Stipulation: An agreement on any topic relevant to a case, entered into by the parties and then presented to the judge.

Submission: When a judge wants to delay deciding a case until a later time, she "takes it under submission." Some judges announce their decision as to who won and who lost right in the courtroom. More often, they take the case under submission and mail out a decision later.

Subpoena: A court order requiring a witness to appear in court. It must be delivered to the person subpoenaed to be valid. (See Chapter 14.)

Subpoena Duces Tecum: A court order requiring that certain documents be produced in court.

Substituted Service: A method by which court papers may be delivered to a defendant who is difficult to reach by other means. (See Chapter 11.)

Transfer: The procedure by which the defendant can have a small claims case transferred to a "formal court." In most states this can be done when the defendant has a claim against the plaintiff for an amount greater than the small claims maximum. In a few states, the defendant can transfer a case simply to get out of small claims court. In many states, a defendant who wants a jury trial can also transfer to formal court. See the Appendix for details.

Trial de Novo: The rehearing of a small claims case from scratch after a defendant appeals. In this situation, the previous decision by the small claims judge has no effect, and the appeal takes the form of a new trial (trial de novo). This is allowed only in some states. Check the Appendix.

Unlawful Detainer Proceeding: Legalese for "eviction." Also known as "summary dispossess" and "forcible entry and detainer" in some states. Unlawful detainer proceedings may be brought in small claims court in some states but are not allowed in most. Check the Appendix.

Venue: This basically refers to the proper location (courthouse or county) in which to bring a suit and is discussed in detail in Chapter 9. If a suit is brought in the wrong county or court (one that is too far from where the defendant lives or a key event in the case occurred), it can be transferred to the right court or dismissed. If it is dismissed, the plaintiff must refile in the right court. However, the case can be heard even in the wrong court if both parties appear and agree to it.

Wage Garnishment: After a judgment has been issued (and the defendant's time to appeal has elapsed), the small claims court clerk will issue a Writ of Execution on the judgment creditor's request. This may be turned over to a sheriff, marshal, or constable with orders to collect (garnish) a portion of the judgment debtor's wages directly from an employer.

Writ of Execution: An order by a court to the sheriff, marshal, or constable to collect a specific amount of money due.

How to Use This Book

This guide covers the procedures that both plaintiffs and defendants should use to successfully bring or defend a small claims case. Unlike other guides, it also contains step-by-step instructions for preparing particularly common small claims cases, along with examples from real cases.

Chapters 2 and 3 help you answer the basic question of whether you should sue in the first place by asking two crucial questions: Do you have a good case? Can you collect any money from the defendant if you win? If your answer to either of these questions is "no," then you should read Chapter 6 to see whether you might be able to settle your dispute without going to court, or you should consider dropping the idea of a lawsuit.

Chapters 4–9 walk you through the procedural details. Small claims court is meant to be easy, but it still has rules about how much money you can sue for, who you can sue, what court you should bring your lawsuit in, and so forth.

Chapters 10 and 11 are about the actual paperwork: How do you fill out your papers and deliver them to the defendant once you've decided to bring a small claims lawsuit?

Chapter 12 is for the defendant. You've just been sued; what do you do?

Chapters 13–15 get you ready for your day in court. In Chapters 23 and 24 you'll find out how the judge issues a ruling, how to appeal, and how to collect your money if you're successful.

In Chapters 16–22, we look at the most common types of cases and discuss strategies to handle each. Even if your fact situation doesn't fit neatly into one of these categories, I recommend that you read this material. By picking up a few hints here and a little information there, you should be able to piece together a good plan of action. For example, many of the suggestions I make to handle motor vehicle repair disputes can also be applied to cases involving problems with fixing major appliances such as televisions, washers, and expensive stereos. ●

Do You Have a Good Case?

Stating Your Claim on Your Court Papers

One of the advantages of small claims court is that when you file your case you are not required to present theories of law—instead, you simply state the facts of the dispute and rely on the judge to fit them into one or another legal theory of recovery. All you really need to know is that you have suffered monetary loss and that the person or business you are suing caused your loss.

To illustrate how this works, let's jump ahead and take a look at the form you will fill out when you file your case. Turn to Chapter 10 and find the form entitled Sample Plaintiff's Claim (this form may be called by another name, such as "complaint," in your state). Look at Section 3a. As you can see, there is no space to state a lengthy legal argument. Indeed, there is barely room to briefly describe your dispute and list the date on which it occurred or began. Depending, of course, on the facts of your case, you will state your claim more or less like this:

- "John's Dry Cleaners ruined my jacket on December 13, 20xx."
- "His dog bit me on the corner of Rose and Peach Streets in West Covina, California, on April 27, 20xx."
- "The car repairs that Joe's Garage did on my car on July 11, 20xx, were done wrong, resulting in an engine fire."
- "Landlord refused to return the cleaning deposit when I moved out of my apartment on August 11, 20xx, even though I left it clean."
- "The used car I purchased from her on January 26, 20xx, in 'tiptop condition,' blew a gasket the next day."
- "The $5,000 I lent defendant has not been repaid by November 12, 20xx, as promised."

> 💡 **TIP**
>
> **Don't argue your case until you get to court.** When you state your case on the court papers, your goal is to notify the other party and the court of the issue in dispute. You don't need or want to try to list your evidence or otherwise try to convince anyone that you are in the right or that the law is on your side. Your chance to do this will come later in court.

Time to Get Organized

Even before you file your case, you should set up a good system to safeguard key papers and evidence. It's no secret that more than one case has been won (or lost) because of good (or bad) recordkeeping. One excellent approach is to get a couple of manila envelopes or file folders and label them with the name of your dispute (*Lincoln vs. Williams*). Use one folder to store all documentary evidence, such as receipts, letters, names and addresses of potential witnesses, and photographs. The other is for your court papers. Once organized, make sure you conscientiously store your folders in a safe place.

But Is My Case Really Any Good?

If you read the little pamphlets small claims court clerks hand out, you will learn pretty much what I have just outlined. You will be told to:

- briefly state the nature of your dispute
- organize any evidence and witnesses you think will help back up your version of events
- come to court on time
- be polite, and
- let the judge decide if your case is any good.

At a very primitive level, this is decent advice—you expend little effort or thought and rely on the judge to do the heavy legal lifting. The big problem with this approach—and something the little pamphlet won't tell you—is that the judge will not decide your case based on who she believes is morally "right" (although it never hurts to seize the high moral ground) or on whose presentation and witnesses are more convincing. Instead, the judge must apply exactly the same legal rules to your case as would be followed if your dispute was heard in a formal court.

 JUDGES' TIPS

"Unfair" doesn't automatically mean "illegal." Unfortunately, the mere fact that you have suffered a trauma at the hands of another person does not automatically entitle you to a legal judgment. The law must support your contention that you were harmed by the *illegal* actions of another. —Commissioner Douglas G. Carnahan

Obviously this means there are a number of problems with this "stay ignorant and trust the judge" approach. Here are the biggies:

- If you don't understand the legal rules the judge will apply to decide your case, you may waste time and energy pursuing an obvious loser.

- If you don't understand the legal realities that underlie your case, you may prepare irrelevant arguments. In a worst-case scenario, you may not even understand—and therefore fail to fulfill—the key legal requirements necessary to have a judgment entered in your favor.

- If you win—and especially if you lose—you won't know why.

If none of this sounds good to you, perhaps you are open to considering a more informed approach. This consists of taking the time to understand the basic legal—as well as the moral—issues that underlie your case. Or put another way, it means looking at your case in the same way a judge will ultimately view it.

> **TIP**
>
> **Defendants need the same legal knowledge as plaintiffs.** To defend a case well, a defendant needs to understand the essential legal elements of the case the plaintiff is attempting to prove. Once armed with this information, the defendant will be in good shape to try to convince the judge that at least one essential legal requirement is missing.

Assuming you are game, start by reading the rest of this chapter. It contains a discussion of the legal theories most commonly used to establish legal liability in small claims court. In many instances, this information will be all you need to prepare your case. But occasionally, you will want to do additional legal research, as would be true if the exact wording of a statute or key court decision has a direct bearing on your case. (See Chapter 25 for more on how to do legal research.)

> **CAUTION**
>
> **Check your state's small claims court rules.** Many small claims courts limit the types of cases they will decide in addition to restricting the dollar amount of damages you can claim. For example, Rhode Island's small claims court only allows breach of contract claims and claims by consumers for damages connected with retail products or services. Ask your small claims court clerk or review your small claims court's rules to make sure your type of case can be heard. (See the Appendix for contact information.)

Below is a list of the most common legal theories and what you need to prove to establish each one. The rest of this chapter reviews each key legal theory in detail, so you can see whether the facts of your case fit the requirements of at least one of them.

Bad Debt: A type of contract case. To prevail, you need to prove the debt exists, its amount, when payment was due, and that the person you are suing hasn't paid it or has only partially paid it.

Breach of Contract: One or more terms of a valid contract (written, oral, or implied) has been broken by the person you are suing. As a result, you have suffered a monetary loss.

Breach of Warranty: A written or implied warranty (assurance) extended to you by a merchant has been breached and, as a result, you have suffered a monetary loss—for example, a new or used car suffers mechanical problems while still covered by warranty.

Failure to Return a Security Deposit: Another variety of contract case that commonly arises between tenants and landlords. As discussed in more detail in Chapter 20, you need to prove that a deposit was made, that it was not returned (or only partially returned), and that the premises were sufficiently clean and undamaged when you left that the landlord owes you some or all of the amount withheld.

Libel or Slander (Defamation): To prove a libel or slander case, you must show that the other party said or wrote something untrue about you or your business, that others heard or read it and understood it was about you, and that it really did damage your reputation. (Public figures must also show that the person defaming them knew the offending statement or writing was false or was made in "reckless disregard of the truth.")

Nuisance: Someone's conduct creates a health or safety hazard to you (and perhaps to other neighbors or nearby property owners) or interferes with your ability to use and enjoy your property—for example, a factory makes so much noise that you and other nearby residents are kept awake all night.

Personal Injury: The negligent (careless) or intentional behavior of the person you are suing has caused you to suffer personal injury.

Product Liability: You or your property were injured by a defective product. If so, you qualify for recovery under the legal doctrine of "strict liability," which holds the manufacturer responsible for the damages you suffered, without your having to prove negligence.

Professional Malpractice: A lawyer, doctor, or other professional's failure to use the ordinary skills of members of that profession results in you, as a client or patient, being harmed (in the case of a lawyer or accountant, you must suffer a monetary loss).

Property Damage: The negligent (careless) or intentional behavior of the person you are suing has damaged your personal property.

> **CAUTION**
> **Other legal theories exist.** Because the legal theories listed above are involved in more than 99% of small claims cases, I do not list the technical legal requirements for the dozens of more obscure types of lawsuits. However, if your case isn't covered here, you may sensibly want to do some additional research to determine whether it meets the qualifications of some other legal theory.

Now, before we consider each of these legal theories individually, here is an example of why it's so important to establish not only that you have suffered a loss, but also that the defendant really is legally required to compensate you.

EXAMPLE: One night, someone entered the garage in Sue's apartment complex, smashed her car window, and stole her custom car stereo worth $600. Upon discovery of the theft, and after reporting it to the police, Sue promptly filed suit against the landlord in small claims court. As part of preparing for her day in court, Sue got several witnesses to the fact that her car had been vandalized and obtained a copy of the police investigation report. She also got several estimates as to the cost of repairing the damage to the car window and replacing the stereo.

Sue only overlooked one thing. Unfortunately for her, it was a crucial one. Under the circumstances the building owner wasn't liable. He had never promised (either orally or in writing) to keep the garage locked. In addition, he had never locked the garage or otherwise led Sue to believe that he would do so. The judge determined that all the tenants knew or should have known that anyone could gain access to the garage, either from inside or outside the building, and that there had been no previous crimes committed there. The judge concluded that, in failing to lock the garage, the building owner was neither in violation of a contract nor guilty of any negligent behavior. As he explained to Sue when he ruled for the landlord, the legal situation she faced was little different than it would have been if her car had been damaged on the street.

Now let's take this same situation, but change a few facts. Let's assume the lease Sue signed with the landlord stated that Sue would be assigned a parking place in a "secure garage." Let's also assume that the garage had always been locked until the lock broke seven days before the theft occurred. Finally, let's assume that Sue and other tenants had asked the owner to fix the lock the day after it broke, but that he hadn't "gotten around to it." In this situation, Sue should win. The landlord made a contractual promise to the tenants (to keep the garage locked) and then failed to keep it though he'd had plenty of time to fulfill his obligation. The breach of contract allowed the thief access to the car.

How to Approach a Breach of Contract Case

A contract is any agreement between individuals or businesses in which one side agrees to do something for the other in exchange for something in return. For example, A asks B to paint his kitchen for $3,000 and B agrees. The agreement can be written or oral (in most situations), or implied from the circumstances. Contracts made by minors can be found invalid if they are made before the minor turns 18. However, in most states, if a minor makes a contract and then honors it after turning 18, the contract is valid and can no longer be annulled.

All contracts come with an obligation that each party carry out its terms in "good faith." This means each contracting individual or business will deal with the other fairly and honestly under the circumstances so that the common purpose set out in the agreement can be achieved. On the other side of the coin, courts have found "bad faith" when one party does something that evades the spirit of the agreement or violates community standards of fairness and reasonableness. Practically, it's important to understand that all contracts contain an unwritten good faith requirement, because it means that a small claims judge often won't find in favor of a party who sues based on a highly technical—but obviously unfair or unreasonable—interpretation of contract language. For example, if X agrees to landscape Y's yard in two weeks, but on the last afternoon doesn't quite finish because she is called to the bedside of a sick child, a court will not agree with Y's contention that he doesn't have to pay for any of the work because X technically missed the 14-day deadline. Instead, a judge will almost surely rule that Y's duty to carry out the agreement in good faith requires him to allow X to finish the job a few days late.

Common Contract Rules

Here is a short summary of basic contract principles designed to help you understand whether you've got a valid contract in the first place:

- A gift is not a contract. As every law student learns on the first day of contracts class, a promise to make a gift is not a contract. The reason is simple: The gift's recipient hasn't promised to do anything in return. Or put another way, an enforceable contract absolutely depends on an exchange—or a promise to exchange—something of value, such as money for services.

EXAMPLE 1: Marcia tells Steve she is in a bad way financially, so Steve promises to give Marcia $750 on January 1. Later, Steve changes his mind, because he decides he doesn't like Marcia after all. Can Marcia sue Steve for the $750? No. This is not a contract, because Marcia has not promised to do anything for Steve in return for his promise to make a loan. Steve had only indicated that he would give Marcia a gift in the future. A promise to make a gift is not an enforceable contract because there is no reciprocal promise or "quid pro quo," sometimes also called "consideration."

- A loan is a contract. In contrast to Example 1, above, a loan, or a promise to make a loan, is normally a valid contract. That's because each party provides the other something of value: The lender agrees to advance the borrower the money, and the borrower agrees to pay it back.

- An agreement to exchange goods, services, or money is a contract. The most common type of contract occurs when A agrees to pay money to B in exchange for B agreeing to work for A or provide A with valuable goods.

EXAMPLE 2: Steve promises to pay Marcia $750 on January 31 in exchange for Marcia's promise to tutor Steve's oldest son. This is a valid contract because each person has promised to do something for the other. If Steve fails to pay Marcia on January 31 and Marcia has kept her part of the bargain, then Marcia can go to court, claiming breach of contract.

- Most oral contracts are valid if proven. The great majority of spoken agreements are valid and enforceable, assuming their existence can be established to the satisfaction of a judge. But there are several major exceptions to this rule. Generally speaking, oral contracts are not valid if they: (1) can't be accomplished within a year, (2) are for the sale of real estate, or (3) involve the sale of goods or property worth more than $500. (But this third type of transaction needs very little written proof—a faxed order or a letter confirming a deal will be enough.) Because the great majority of oral consumer contracts— whether to fix a kitchen, repair a car, or deliver a bed—can easily be carried out in less than a year (even if it actually takes longer), most oral contracts that can be proven to the satisfaction of a judge can be enforced in small claims court.

• Someone's unjust enrichment can prove a contract. A contract can be implied where one party has obviously benefited from the other and the other expects to be paid for goods or services. This is a tricky area of contract law that occasionally surfaces in small claims cases. The judge will be particularly interested in evidence that the party who received the benefit knew that the service provider expected to be paid.

EXAMPLE 3: Paul asked Barbara if she wants her house painted. Barbara says "Yes," and Paul paints her house. After he's done with the work, Barbara refuses to pay, claiming that because they never agreed on a price, there was no contract. Barbara is wrong. A contract exists when one person does work for another in circumstances where payment is normally expected and the second person accepts it. Consent can be stated, as in this example, or even implied, as would be the case if Barbara simply watches Paul paint her house. In other words, even though one or more technical parts of a contract is missing, when work is involved the law will require that a person who knowingly benefits from another person's work pay for it, unless it is absolutely clear the work was donated.

Unpaid Debts

Often a contract that has not been honored involves a failure to pay money. Hardly a day goes by in any small claims court when someone isn't sued for failing to pay the phone company, the local hospital, a friend (former, probably), a relative, or even late fines to the public library. (See Chapter 18 for more on small claims suits where money is owed.) In many situations, getting a judgment for an unpaid debt involves no more than stating that the defendant made a commitment to buy certain goods or services, that they were, in fact, provided, and that a legitimate bill for X dollars has not been paid.

As a plaintiff, you must normally prove:

• the identity of the debtor

- the existence of a contract with the debtor
- that you kept your promises under the deal (normally that you provided the goods, services, or loan), and
- that the debt hasn't been paid.

If you are a defendant and believe you have a good defense, you'll normally need to prove:

- the goods or services you were supposed to receive were delivered late or not at all or were seriously defective
- the plaintiff never lent you the money in the first place
- you already paid back some or all the money the plaintiff lent you, or
- the plaintiff agreed to a subsequent contract to forgive the debt or give you more time to pay.

If you are sued because you owe money to a company from which you bought consumer goods or consumer services, research your state's consumer protection laws. (See Chapter 25 on painless methods of legal research.) Also, if a seller of consumer goods or services violates a consumer protection law, then you may be able to get your money back or cancel your deal with no obligation to pay.

- If fraud is present as part of a transaction, the deal can be canceled and your money refunded. Fraud can be:
  - intentional misrepresentation (a deliberate, false statement about a product or service)
  - negligent misrepresentation (a statement about a product or service made without investigating its truth)
  - fraudulent concealment (suppression of the truth) or,
  - a false promise (a promise with no intention to perform), or any other act designed to deceive.
- If you make certain types of purchases, you have a "cooling-off" period under federal law during which you can cancel the contract or sale. (See "The Cooling-Off Rule," below.)

The Cooling-Off Rule

If you buy a product or service worth more than $25 at a location that's not the seller's permanent place of business, you have three business days during which you can change your mind and cancel the sale. (16 C.F.R. Part 429.)

The Cooling-Off Rule applies if you buy something from a door-to-door salesperson (even if you invited the salesperson to make the presentation), at work, and at temporary sales locations like convention centers, fairgrounds, and restaurants.

The Cooling-Off Rule does not apply to sales of real estate, insurance, securities, motor vehicles sold at temporary locations as long as the seller has at least one permanent place of business, or arts or crafts sold at fairs, shopping malls, civic centers, and schools. The Cooling-Off Rule also doesn't apply to goods or services that:

- cost less than $25
- are not primarily intended for personal, family, or household use
- are sold entirely by mail or telephone
- are sold after prior negotiations at the seller's permanent business location
- are needed to meet an emergency, or
- are made as part of your request for the seller to do repairs or maintenance on your personal property.

The Cooling-Off Rule requires the salesperson to tell you about your cancellation rights at the time of sale and give you two copies of a cancellation form and a copy of your contract or receipt. The contract or receipt must be in the same language used in the sales presentation, be dated, show the name and address of the seller, and explain your right to cancel.

Failure to Perform a Contract

Sometimes a breach of contract suit results, not from a refusal to pay a bill, but because one party claims that the other failed to carry out one or more of the terms of a contract. Such would be the case if:

- A tenant sued an apartment owner who agreed to rent her an apartment but instead rented it to someone else. (Leases and rental agreements are discussed in more detail in Chapter 20.)

- A small business sued a caterer who showed up four hours late with the food and drink for an important party.

- A customer sued a tattoo artist who began an elaborate skull pattern on his back but couldn't find the time or inspiration to finish it— leaving the customer with what looked like a lumpy potato tattoo and the prospect of paying someone else to finish or remove it.

- A freelance writer hired to write an annual report sued the business involved when it failed to provide essential financial information, making it impossible to do the job.

TIP

In court, you'll need to convince the judge that the contract existed. If the contract is in writing, bring it to court. If it's oral, be prepared to prove its existence through witnesses and circumstantial evidence. Be creative—if you lent money to a debtor using a check, bring a copy. Along with your own testimony that the borrower promised to repay you, this should be all you need to establish the existence of a contract.

Damages resulting from a breach of contract are normally not difficult to prove. After you show that the contract existed and that the other party failed to meet its terms, you should testify as to the dollar amount of damages you have suffered as a result. And when appropriate, you'll also need to introduce evidence to convince the judge that you really did lose this amount.

EXAMPLE 4: Justine and Bob planned a June wedding. Since the families of both prospective spouses were widely dispersed, this was to be a combination family reunion and wedding. As a result, the couple planned a large reception with a meal and arranged to have it catered by Top Drawer Deli. The deli prepared a written list of all food and drink orders, and Justine signed it. When the big day arrived, everything went swimmingly until the 200 guests arrived at the reception to find that, while the band was playing cheerfully, Top Drawer Deli had not shown up with the food and bubbly. The best man hopped into his SUV, drove to the nearest liquor store, and was back in less than 20 minutes with ten cases of champagne. (Clearly there was a reason he was picked as best man.) Someone else had the presence of mind to order 30 pizzas. Two hours later, Top Drawer Deli showed up full of apologies. (A key employee called in sick, and their van broke down.) Justine and Bob accepted the cake and turned down everything else. When the bill came for the whole works, they paid for the cake and told Top Drawer to eat the rest. Top Drawer sued the newlyweds for $4,000 for breach of contract. Bob and Justine countersued for $5,000 for emotional distress. The judge agreed with the newlyweds that by being two hours late to a time-sensitive event, Top Drawer had breached its contract and, as a result, Bob and Justine owed them nothing. But the judge also dismissed Bob and Justine's emotional distress claim after remarking that the reception obviously turned into an unforgettable party.

The fact that many contract cases are easy to win doesn't mean that all result in victory. In fact, a good number of plaintiffs lose cases that they assumed were open and shut. Why? Usually because they:

- failed to show that a contract existed (see Examples 1 and 5)
- failed to show that a contract was broken (see Example 6)
- failed to sue the right defendant (again, see Example 5), or
- failed to establish that they really suffered a monetary loss (see Example 4).

EXAMPLE 5: Ben, a landlord, sued John, the parent of one of his tenants, for damage John's daughter and her roommates did to their rental unit. John was sued because he had cosigned his daughter's lease. Ben easily convinced the judge that the damage had, in fact, occurred, and the judge seemed disposed toward giving him a judgment for the $980 requested, until John presented his defense. He showed that the lease between his daughter and the landlord had been rewritten three times after he originally cosigned it and that he had not added his signature to any of the revised versions, one of which involved replacing several of his daughter's original roommates with others. The judge agreed that because John had not cosigned any of the subsequent leases, he wasn't liable. The reason was simple: There was no longer a contract between Ben and John. (Leases and rental agreements, including a detailed discussion of the rights and responsibilities of cosigners, are discussed in more detail in *Every Landlord's Legal Guide,* by Marcia Stewart, Ralph Warner, and Janet Portman (Nolo).)

EXAMPLE 6: Sid sued Acme Dry Cleaners for $650, the cost of replacing a pigskin suede jacket that was ruined (it shrank dramatically) by Acme. Sid established that he had taken the jacket to Acme for cleaning and had agreed to pay Acme $80. Acme, by accepting the jacket, clearly implied it would properly clean it, so there was no question that a contract existed. Sid was very sure of his loss. He stood in the courtroom and slowly tried to wriggle into the jacket. The sleeves barely came to Sid's elbows, and the coat itself didn't reach his waist. The whole courtroom burst out laughing—including the judge, who almost choked trying to keep a straight face. So far so good, from Sid's point of view. By putting on the shrunken jacket, he made his point more effectively than he could have with ten minutes of testimony.

Unfortunately for Sid, he also overlooked two key things. Sid's first mistake was asking for the full $650, which is how much he paid for the jacket. However, by the time Acme got ahold of it, the jacket was eight months old and had been worn almost every day. Valuation is a common problem in clothing cases. (It's discussed in detail in Chapters 4 and 21.) Sid's jacket was probably worth no more than $400 (and probably less) in its used condition. Whenever property is damaged or destroyed, the amount of money you're entitled to will be limited to the fair market value of the goods at the time the damage occurred—not their replacement value.

Sid's other mistake was failing to anticipate what Acme might say in its defense. Vijay, Acme Dry Cleaner's owner, testified that he was amazed when he saw the jacket after cleaning. His cleaning shop specialized in leather goods, and the cleaning process should not have resulted in such shrinkage. He also testified that he had examined a number of other items in the same cleaning batch and found no similar problem. He then sent the jacket to an "independent testing laboratory." Their report, which he presented to the court, stated that it was the jacket itself, not the cleaning, that was the problem. According to the report, shrinkage occurred because the leather had been severely overstretched prior to assembly.

The judge was convinced by the testing lab report and felt that Acme had breached no contract as far as the cleaning was concerned. However, the judge also felt that Acme, as a leather cleaning specialist, had some responsibility to notify Sid that the jacket should not have been cleaned in the first place. Therefore, the judge held mostly for Acme but did award Sid $100. He also suggested that Sid might want to consider suing the store that sold the jacket. The judge explained that Sid could claim the store breached an implied warranty by selling clothing made from seriously defective material. He could use as evidence the very lab report that lost him his original case.

CROSS-REFERENCE

More material concerning contracts:

- How much you should sue for in breach of contract cases (how to value your damages) is discussed in Chapter 4.
- Breach of warranty—based on a written or oral contract—is covered below.
- Leases and rental agreements—a specialized type of contract—are covered in Chapter 20.
- How to collect on contracts involving unpaid bills is covered in Chapter 18.
- If your contract involves fraud, undue influence, or a simple mistake ($2,000 was mistakenly written as $20,000), you may have a right to have the contract ended or rewritten or to get your goods back under the legal doctrine of "equitable relief." (See Chapter 4.)

How to Approach a Property Damage Case

Another big category of small claims disputes involves a plaintiff's claim that a defendant negligently (carelessly) damaged her property. Less often, the plaintiff claims that the defendant intentionally damaged her belongings.

Negligence

A technical definition of negligence could—and does—fill entire law texts. But I don't recommend your reading one. I remember thinking in law school that the more scholarly professors tried to be in writing about negligence, the more mixed up they got. Like good taste or bad wine, negligence seems to be easy to recognize but hard to define.

So let's breeze right past the "ifs," "ands," and "wherefores" and focus on a plain English definition of negligence. If your property is harmed as a result of another person's conduct, and that person didn't act with reasonable care under the circumstances, you have a valid legal claim based on his negligence.

> **EXAMPLE:** Jake knows the brakes on his ancient Saab are in serious need of repair but does nothing about it. One night, when the car is parked on a hill, the brakes fail and the car rolls across the street and destroys Keija's persimmon tree. Keija sues Jake for $225, the reasonable value of the tree. Jake will lose because he did not act with reasonable care under the circumstances.

Negligence can also occur when a person with a duty or responsibility to act fails to do so. For example, an electrician who promises and then fails to check the wiring in a room where you tell him you saw some frightening sparks would be negligent.

Another obvious situation involving negligence would be one where a car or bus swerves into your traffic lane and sideswipes your fender. The driver of the offending vehicle has a duty to operate the car in such a way as not to damage other cars. By swerving into your lane, it is extremely likely that he has failed to do so. On the other hand, a situation in which negligence could be difficult to show would involve your neighbor's tree that falls on your car while it is properly parked in your driveway. Here you have to be ready to prove that the tree was in a weakened condition for some reason (such as age, disease, or a bad root system), and the neighbor knew about it but was negligent in failing to do something about it. If the tree looked to be in good health, your neighbor probably wasn't negligent, as he had no reason to remove it or prop it up.

Here are some additional examples in which a person or business failed to act with reasonable care and as a result was negligent:

- While playing with his kids in his small backyard, Kevin hits a ball over the fence, smashing a neighbor's window.
- While upgrading Eddie's computer, Bill carelessly installs the wrong chip, which crashes Eddie's hard drive and ruins the computer.

• RapidMail Inc., a local courier service, loses several time-sensitive messages and fails to notify the sender of the problem.

"Compound negligence" exists where more than one person is responsible for the damages you suffer—for example, if two coworkers borrow a priceless Ming vase from your office and break it into smithereens while playing keepaway. When dealing with a situation such as this, in which more than one person may have contributed to your loss, Rule Number One is to sue them all.

EXAMPLE 1: Sandy comes home from work one day to find her new fence knocked over and Fred's Chevy Blazer in the middle of her herb garden. Fred admits his vehicle knocked over the fence when his brakes failed. To Sandy, this may at first seem like a simple case against Fred. But what if Fred had just picked up his car from Atomic Auto Repair, where he had his brakes worked on? Fred's liability may be minimal if Atomic is only 50 feet away and Fred just left the shop with the assurance that the brakes were fixed. Or, it may be extensive if Atomic is located across town and at the last two stop signs Fred's brakes acted "funny" but he continued to drive anyway. Although Sandy may not know all these details, if she learns that Fred recently had his brakes worked on, she would be well advised to sue both Fred and Atomic and let the judge sort out who is more at fault.

EXAMPLE 2: Now suppose that Fred's brakes are fine, but he claims he was rear-ended at the stop sign by Dana, whose pickup truck pushed his vehicle through Sandy's fence. Again, Fred's liability may be minimal (Dana was drunk and speeding), or it may be extensive (Fred ran a stop sign while turning and was rear-ended by Dana, who had the right of way). Again, Sandy would be wise to sue both parties and let the judge sort out who was more at fault.

TIP

Negligence concepts are tricky: Don't try to be a judge. There is often no foolproof way to determine in advance whether someone will be judged to be negligent. In fact, when it comes to accidents, it's often so close a question that lawyers regularly fail to predict the outcome. So if you have suffered a real loss and think someone else caused it, bring your case, present as much evidence supporting your point of view as possible, and let the judge decide.

To help you determine whether you have a good case based on someone else's negligence, answer the following questions:

• Did the person whose act (or failure to act) damaged your property behave in a reasonable way? Or to put it another way, would you have behaved differently if you were in that person's shoes?

• Was your own conduct a significant cause of the injury?

If the person who damaged your property behaved in an unreasonable way (ran a red light when drunk) and you were acting sensibly (driving at 30 mph in the proper lane), you probably have a good case. If you were a little at fault (slightly negligent) but the other fellow was much more at fault (very negligent), you can probably still recover most of your losses, because most courts follow a legal doctrine called "comparative negligence." This involves subtracting the percentage of your negligence from 100% to find out how legally responsible the other party is. Thus, if a judge finds that one person (drunk and speeding) was 80% at fault, and the other (slightly inattentive) was 20% at fault, the slightly inattentive party can recover 80% of her loss.

RESOURCE

How to get more information about negligence. If, despite my advice to keep it simple, you want to get into the gory details of negligence theory, go to your nearest law library and get any recent hardbound legal text on "torts" (wrongful acts or injuries). Or, even easier, if you are near a law bookstore, buy a copy of one of the several competing paperback course summaries covering torts that law students rely on to get through their torts exams. One good one is *Gilbert Law Summaries: Torts,* also available at local law libraries or from online bookstores.

Intentional Acts

Not all injuries to property are accidents. You also have the right to recover money damages if someone intentionally damages your personal property.

> **EXAMPLE:** Basil and Shirley are neighbors who can't stand the sight of each other, despite, or perhaps because of, the fact that both are prize-winning rose growers. When Basil took first place in the local exotic rose contest, Shirley was angry, frustrated, and jealous. She left her hose running on purpose and drowned Basil's roses. By bringing a small claims case, Basil should be able to recover the value of his rose bushes from Shirley. He might even get some money for emotional distress (see below).

In theory, at least, it may be possible to recover punitive damages— money given to you solely for the purpose of punishing the other person—if your property is damaged by the malicious conduct of someone else. However, in part because public sentiment is running strongly against punitive damage awards, they are seldom awarded in small claims court.

CROSS-REFERENCE

More material concerning property damage. To determine how much to sue for, see Chapter 4.

How to Approach a Personal Injury (and Mental Distress) Case

I treat personal injury cases in this separate section because so many people look at them as being a different kind of lawsuit. In fact, most personal injury cases are based on a claim that someone has been negligent (careless), and a few are based on claims of intentional injury. The legal theories involved are the same as those set out in the section just above. To prevail, you must show that your injury was caused by someone's negligent or intentional behavior (unless your injury was caused by a defective product, in which case a different legal doctrine applies—see "How to Approach a Case When You Are Injured by a Defective Product," below).

CAUTION

Check your state's rules. Remember, in some states you cannot file a personal injury case in small claims court, even if the amount of damages is less than the maximum.

Start by understanding that most personal injury cases involve amounts of money that are clearly over the small claims maximum and should therefore be pursued in formal court. However, occasionally a minor personal injury case will be appropriate for small claims.

EXAMPLE 1: Jenny and Karen are playing softball in a picnic area of a park, where many families are enjoying their lunches in the sun. Jenny, never a star fielder, misses a batted ball that hits seven-year-old Willie in the face and chips his tooth. With the help of his parents, Willie sues Jenny and Karen for the $500 it will cost to repair his tooth. Jenny and Karen claim they were just playing a game and shouldn't be held liable. How will a judge decide this case? Almost surely in favor of Willie, who was eating lunch in a picnic area where he had a right to be. By contrast, Jenny and Karen almost surely were careless (negligent). Why? Because as a society, we have decided that picnic areas are for picnickers—not ballplayers—and since Jenny and Karen's game was inappropriate and dangerous to others, they are going to have to pay for their negligence.

EXAMPLE 2: Now, assume that Jenny and Karen move over to a nearby ball field. Their skills haven't improved and Jenny again misses the ball. And again it hits poor Willie—who has escaped his parents and wandered onto the field unobserved—in the mouth. Are Jenny and Karen still liable to pay to fix Willie's tooth? Probably not. Jenny and Karen took reasonable precautions to avoid hitting picnickers by playing on the ball field. Although they may have a responsibility to get little Willie off the field if they spot him, they are probably not legally responsible—that is, negligent—in a situation where he wanders onto the field unnoticed.

TIP

Consider not only your loss but also whether the other party acted reasonably under the circumstances. Before you sue someone for an injury, consider whether it was really caused by negligence. If so, the person is legally liable to make good for your loss. If not (you trip and fall down a perfectly safe set of stairs), you have no right to recover, no matter how serious your injury (again, there's one major exception to the rule that you must demonstrate the other side's negligence—when you are injured by a defective product). If in doubt, go ahead and sue, but be prepared to deal with the negligence question as well as prove the extent of your injury. In Chapters 14 and 15 you'll find some practical advice on how to prove your case.

As discussed in more detail in Chapter 4, you do not have to suffer a physical injury to recover in court based on someone else's negligent or intentionally harmful behavior. Intentional or negligent infliction of mental distress are lawsuits that can be based on nonphysical injuries.

EXAMPLE: Suppose your landlord enters your apartment without notice, permission, or good legal reason. You make it clear that this behavior is highly upsetting and ask her to cease invading your privacy. She nevertheless persists in entering your apartment with no good reason, causing you to become genuinely upset and anxious. You file a small claims case based on the intentional infliction of mental distress. Assuming you can convince the judge that you were truly and seriously upset, your chances of winning are good.

Obviously, not every act of another person that upsets you merits a lawsuit. Generally, to support a court case, the other person's behavior must:

- be negligent, violate a law, be outrageous, be intended to cause you harm, or be done in "reckless disregard" of whether it will cause you harm, and
- cause you emotional distress that is serious (for a negligence case) or severe (for a case where you claim the person's actions were intentional).

This second element is sometimes the hardest to prove in a mental distress case. Proving that you suffered emotional harm can be difficult and often more expensive than a small claims case would warrant. But if you have seen a doctor or therapist and you can get a written statement that you've suffered emotional distress, you could use that for evidence. Of course, your own testimony will probably be your primary form of proof.

One area in which the number of small claims cases is growing involves sexual harassment in the workplace, which is illegal under both federal and state law. Small claims court is a particularly helpful option for people having trouble finding an attorney because their cases will be hard to prove or not worth much in damages. Before going to court, you must file a formal complaint, with either the federal Equal Employment Opportunity Commission (EEOC) or your state's equivalent. Wherever you file, your object before going to small claims court is to get a "right to sue" letter, meaning that the agency will not pursue the matter on its own—a likely outcome, given that these agencies get numerous complaints. Once you've got that letter, you can proceed to court.

RESOURCE
More information on personal injury cases generally. Check out *How to Win Your Personal Injury Claim*, by Joseph Matthews (Nolo).

RESOURCE
More information on sexual harassment or discrimination. Take a look at *Your Rights in the Workplace*, by Barbara Kate Repa (Nolo).

CROSS-REFERENCE
More material on personal injuries. To figure out how much to sue for in personal injury cases, see Chapter 4.

How to Approach a Case When You Are Injured by a Defective Product

If your vacuum cleaner, hair dryer, steam iron, lawn mower, or other product malfunctions and you are injured as a result, you are entitled to recover from the manufacturer or other defendant (usually the person you bought or rented the product from) without proving that the defendant was negligent.

When an injury is serious, product liability cases are always filed in formal court. Now and then, however, a defective product will cause a more minor injury, in which case a small claims court lawsuit may be appropriate. It's best to sue both the manufacturer and seller of the defective product. Be prepared to prove:

- the product really did malfunction

- you were using the product as the manufacturer or seller intended or as they should have foreseen, and

- you were injured as a result.

How to Approach a Breach of Warranty Case

CROSS-REFERENCE

Car warranties. Chapter 17 discusses warranties as they apply to problems with new and used cars.

In simplest terms, a warranty is a promise by the manufacturer or seller of a product that the product is of a certain quality or that they will repair the product for a stated period of time. The manufacturer or seller is legally obligated to live up to its promise if the product turns out to have a defect that's covered by the warranty. Warranty law is extremely confusing, even to lawyers. A principal reason for this is that three separate warranty laws can apply to the retail sale of consumer goods. The unhappy result is that, short of presenting you with a major legal treatise, it's impossible to thoroughly explain warranty law. The best I can do in this short space is to review the basic rules.

Types of Warranties

There are a number of different types of warranties that might apply to your defective product.

Express Written Warranty

If a new or used consumer product comes with an express written warranty, you have the right to rely on what it says. The express warranty may be the seller's written description of the product that you relied on when deciding to purchase it (for example, a promise that a car is defect free). Or, the express warranty may be the manufacturer's or retailer's written promise to maintain the performance of the product (for example, a promise to repair or replace defective parts for a stated period).

Warranty Law: Where Does It Come From?

The Magnuson-Moss Warranty Federal Trade Commission Improvement Act (15 USC § 2302) is a federal law that applies in every state. In addition, every state has a commercial code, which includes similar laws regulating retail sales and warranty protections for consumers. Some states have enacted separate consumer protection and warranty laws that go beyond the Magnuson-Moss Act and these commercial codes. For example, in California, a warranty or guarantee is still good even if the buyer doesn't fill out and return the manufacturer's form (Cal. Com. Code § 2801), and in Kansas an implied warranty exists even for goods sold "as is," unless the consumer has knowledge of the exact defects in the merchandise (Kan. Stat. Ann. § 50-639). To find out about your state's warranty laws, search your state statutes for "commercial code," "consumer protection," or "warranty" (see Chapter 25 for more on how to do this), or get in touch with your state consumer protection agency.

Express Oral Warranties

If a seller makes an oral statement describing a product's features (for example, "these tires will last at least 25,000 miles" or "this car is in running condition") or what it will do ("it will work for two years"), and you rely on them in deciding to purchase the product, you have the right to rely on those statements. It is important to understand that this is true even though a more limited written warranty printed on the package states there are no other warranties. You must be able to prove that the seller made the oral statement; if you can't, the written warranty and its limitations may be effective.

Implied Warranties

In most retail sales of consumer products, an implied warranty exists stating that the product is fit for the ordinary purposes for which it is used (for example, that a lawn mower will cut grass, a tire will hold air, and a calculator will add and subtract). This warranty exists in addition to any express written and oral warranties to maintain the product's performance. This applies even if there is a statement (often called a "warranty disclaimer") printed on the product or packaging saying no warranties exist beyond the express written warranty, or that no warranty exists at all, or that all implied warranties are specifically disclaimed.

If the Seller Breaches a Warranty

If you believe any warranty has been breached—for example, a DVD player with a six-month warranty on parts and labor breaks the day after the purchase—you should notify the seller and manufacturer in writing, keeping copies of both letters. Give them a reasonable chance to make necessary repairs or replace the defective product. Thirty days to accomplish this is usually considered reasonable. If they fail to do so, it's time to think about filing in small claims court.

In considering whether and how to pursue a breach of warranty case, realize that small claims court judges tend to evaluate warranty disputes based on their own broad view of what is fair under the circumstances. In other words, if you purchase goods that are clearly defective or do not accomplish the task the seller claimed they would accomplish (either in an advertisement or a personal statement to you), and you have made and documented a good faith effort to give the seller or manufacturer a chance to either fix or replace the goods or refund your money, your chances of winning are excellent—as long as you can prove:

- the warranty existed in the first place
- the defect is "substantial" (for example, a nonfunctioning disc drawer in the DVD player would be substantial, but a small chip in the chrome nameplate would not be), and
- you did not cause the defect by misusing the product.

However, realize that proving the existence of a warranty can be difficult when the promises were made orally and the other party will likely deny he ever made them.

EXAMPLE: Alan purchases a computer and some expensive accounting software from ABC Computer. He thoroughly explains his specialized bookkeeping needs to the salesperson and is assured that the computer and software will do the job. The computer contains a written warranty against defects in parts and labor for 90 days. The warranty statement says that all implied warranties are disclaimed. The software contains no written warranty statement. It is apparent to Alan after a couple of days' work that the software simply is not sophisticated enough to meet the bookkeeping needs he had explained to the salesperson and that the salesperson didn't know what he was talking about when he said it was "perfect for the job."

Two days later the computer has a major crash. Alan calls ABC and asks for the computer to be fixed or replaced and for his money back on the software. When ABC ignores him, Alan sues in small claims court. Alan should have no problem recovering for the price of the computer—it failed within the written warranty period. But the software raises a tougher problem. Alan is claiming a breach of an express oral warranty (the salesperson's statement that the software would meet his needs), and a breach of the implied warranty of general fitness or merchantability. To succeed on the first claim, he must prove that the salesperson did in fact assure him that the software was right for his needs, which may be difficult. Proving the second claim will be even harder, however, because Alan must somehow prove that the software falls below the reasonable standard for sophisticated small business accounting packages. ABC is likely to counter Alan's claim with evidence that the software is in wide use and is generally considered to be adequate to accomplish most accounting tasks. In short, Alan would be smart to focus on trying to prove that in making his decision to purchase the software, he relied on the salesperson's oral statements that the software would meet his specific bookkeeping needs.

How should he do this? If Alan gave the salesperson a written specification detailing his accounting needs and still has a copy, he should show it to the judge. Even better, if he has a witness who heard the salesperson's overly optimistic promises, he should ask this person to testify in court or at least write a letter stating what happened. Unfortunately, if Alan has no convincing evidence as to the salesman's statements, the small claims hearing is likely to come down to his word against the salesperson's, with the judge left to decide who appears to be telling the truth.

How to Approach a Professional Malpractice Case

An increasing number of small claims cases are being filed against doctors, lawyers, accountants, and other professionals. The main reason is that it can be difficult or impossible to get lawyers to represent you in a formal court action. (Lawyers accept only one in 20 medical malpractice cases, according to one study.) As a result, the injured person must decide to either file without a lawyer in formal court or scale down the dollar amount of her claim to fit into small claims court.

To succeed with a malpractice claim, you must establish all of the following facts:

- **Duty.** The lawyer, doctor, dentist, or other professional owed you a duty of care. This is automatic as long as you were a patient or a client.

- **Carelessness.** The professional failed to use at least ordinary professional skills in carrying out the task (unless the person claimed to be a specialist, in which case the standard is higher). This one can be tougher to prove, because unless the mistake is breathtakingly obvious, you'll normally need to get the opinion of one or more other professionals (experts) that your professional screwed up. In theory, you can do this via a letter, but since the professional you are suing will almost surely be in court denying all wrongdoing, far better to have your expert witness testify in person.

- **Causation.** The professional's carelessness directly caused the harm or injury you suffered. For most types of malpractice, showing that the professional caused your injury isn't a problem (if a dentist stuck a drill through your cheek, for example). But in the legal field, the causation issue can be tricky. That's because you typically will need to show not only that the professional's mistake caused you to lose but also that you would have won if no mistake had been made. In other words, you need to convince the judge your underlying lawsuit was a winner.

- **Damages.** The harm you suffered at the hands of the professional resulted in actual economic loss to you.

EXAMPLE: You consult a lawyer about an injury you suffered when you tripped and fell at a store. The lawyer agrees to file a lawsuit on your behalf but forgets to do so before the two-year statute of limitations runs out. Several malpractice lawyers you consult won't represent you in suing the incompetent lawyer because your injuries were fairly minor and they aren't sure that even if malpractice is established, you will be able to prove that you would have won your case against the store. (In other words, they believe you may not have been harmed by your lawyer's mistake in failing to file your case on time because your case wasn't so hot in the first place.) You sue your lawyer in small claims court. His failure to file your case on time is clearly an act of carelessness (a lawyer using ordinary legal skills would have filed on time), but to win you'll also have to show that your lawyer's careless act resulted in monetary harm to you. This means convincing the judge that, in fact, your case against the store was a winner and that your injuries were serious enough to qualify for at least the amount of money you are requesting.

RESOURCE
Further reading on malpractice cases. *Represent Yourself in Court: How to Prepare & Try a Winning Case,* by Paul Bergman and Sara Berman-Barrett (Nolo), explores how to bring a malpractice case in formal court.

How to Approach a Nuisance Case

In legal theory, what's called a "private nuisance" occurs whenever someone prevents or disturbs your use or enjoyment of your property. For example, if your neighbor lets his dog bark all night, preventing you from sleeping, that's a private nuisance. If the barking persists and causes you real discomfort after you ask that the dog be kept quiet, you can sue.

To successfully sue someone for causing a private nuisance, you must prove that:

- you own, rent, or lease property
- the defendant created or maintained a condition that was
  - harmful to your health
  - indecent or offensive, or
  - obstructed your free use of your property
- you did not consent to the person's conduct
- the person's conduct interfered with your use or enjoyment of your property
- the conduct would be reasonably annoying or disturbing to an ordinary person
- you were, in fact, harmed (for example, your sleep was disturbed) by the person's conduct, and
- the seriousness of the harm outweighs the public benefit of the conduct.

A "public nuisance," by contrast, means that someone is acting in a way that causes a group of people to suffer a health or safety hazard or lose the peaceful enjoyment of their property. For example, lots of noisy airplanes suddenly begin flying low over a residential area or a chemical plant lets toxic fumes drift over a neighboring property. Public nuisance suits are often initiated by groups of individuals who all file small claims suits at more or less the same time.

To successfully sue a person or group of people for creating a public nuisance, you must prove all the facts listed above relating to private nuisance and also that:

- the condition affected a substantial number of people at the same time
- any social usefulness of the offending conduct is outweighed by the seriousness of the harm, and

• the harm you suffered was different from the harm suffered by the general public (for example, if a chemical plant's fumes are noticeable from the nearby freeway but ashes from the plant's smokestack fall into your swimming pool).

One fairly common example of this phenomenon involves the filing of multiple small claims lawsuits against drug-selling neighbors or their landlords. (See Chapter 20 for more about these types of cases.)

TIP

Try mediation before filing a lawsuit against a neighbor. It is very difficult to put a dollar value on lawsuits against neighbors for antisocial acts, no matter how annoying. In addition, filing suit usually makes long-term relationships worse. For these reasons, disputing neighbors should always try mediation before turning to small claims court. (See Chapter 6 for more on mediation.)

Can You Collect Your Money If You Win?

This is the shortest chapter in the book but one of the most important. It asks you to focus on a very simple question: If I win my small claims case, can I collect the judgment? Unfortunately, it is easy to get so caught up in thinking about suing the bastard who did you wrong that you forget to think about how you'll collect. This mistake can compound your original loss by wasting your valuable time for the dubious satisfaction of hearing the judge say, "You win."

Collecting from solvent individuals or businesses isn't usually a problem, because most will routinely pay any judgments entered against them. If they don't, there are a number of legal ways you can force them to do so. But unfortunately, a goodly number of people and businesses sued in small claims court are either broke (lawyers say "judgment-proof") or so adept at hiding their assets that collecting your winnings may prove impossible. And if a deadbeat debtor won't pay voluntarily, collecting your judgment can be difficult. For example, debtor protection laws prevent you from seizing many types of property, including the food from the debtor's table, the clothing from her closet, the TV from her living room, or even, in most states, the car from the driveway. (State laws exempt about $1,500–$4,000 of equity in a motor vehicle from being used to pay debts.)

What should these facts mean to you? A significant percentage of people who are not homeless or even "poor" are nevertheless "judgment-proof." You can sue and get judgments against these deadbeat defendants until red cows dance on a pink moon, but you won't be able to collect a dime.

To investigate whether your debtor is a likely deadbeat, start by finding out whether the defendant has a job. If he does, that's good news—when a person fails to pay a judgment voluntarily, the easiest way to collect is to garnish his wages. But you can't garnish a welfare, Social Security, unemployment, pension, or disability check. So if the person sued gets her income from one of these sources, red flags should definitely be flying unless you can locate other nonexempt assets.

Wage Garnishments in a Nutshell

In most states, a creditor with a judgment can't take more than 25% of a judgment debtor's net earnings, or the amount by which the debtor's net earnings exceed 30 times the federal minimum wage, whichever is less. (Net earnings are total earnings minus all mandatory deductions for such items as withheld income taxes and unemployment tax.)

The sheriff or marshal's office in your area can supply you with your state's rules. If you're a defendant, strategies to cope with wage garnishment are covered in *Solve Your Money Troubles: Get Debt Collectors Off Your Back & Regain Financial Freedom*, by Robin Leonard and John Lamb (Nolo).

What about other collection sources? Can't a judgment be collected from assets other than wages? Sure. Real estate, bank accounts, stocks and bonds, and motor vehicles are other common collection sources. And if you've sued a business, you can often collect by ordering the sheriff or marshal to take the amount of the judgment right out of the debtor's cash register.

But remember, as mentioned above, many types of personal property are legally exempt from attachment. In New York, for example, among a long list of exemptions we find "all stoves kept for use in the judgment debtor's dwelling house" and a "pew occupied by the judgment debtor or the family in a place of public worship."

Most states exempt household goods and appliances necessary for everyday living (such as a stove, refrigerator, dishes, or TV set); sentimental items and family keepsakes (such as photos, jewelry, or works of art); and tools or machinery the debtor uses to make a living (such as a computer, professional library, or power saw). A debtor's retirement account, life insurance, pension, and certain types of savings accounts are also protected. Even more significant in terms of assets, a portion or all of the equity in a debtor's home is exempt.

What does all this boil down to? Simply this. Before you file your small claims court case, make sure that at least one of the following is true:

- The person or business you wish to sue is solvent and likely to voluntarily pay a court judgment.

- The person is broke now but is very likely to be solvent in the future. Judgments can be collected for ten years (this period can usually be renewed) and accrue interest as long as they are not paid. In short, if you are willing to take a chance that a destitute college student will eventually get a job, win the lottery, inherit money, win a personal injury lawsuit, or otherwise become solvent sometime in the next few years, go ahead and sue. You'll have to sit on the judgment for awhile, but eventually it should be collectible.

- The defendant has a decent-paying job or is likely to get one in the not-too-distant future, as might be the case with a student. Most states allow a judgment to be collected for five to 20 years from the date it is entered, and you can apply to have this period extended. (See Chapter 24.)

- You can identify other assets—not protected by debtor exemption laws—that you can levy on, such as a bank account or real property (preferably other than the place where the person lives).

- If the defendant is a business that may not voluntarily pay its debts, you can identify a readily available cash source you can collect from—the best source is a cash register. Another good one is a valuable piece of equipment or machinery owned by the judgment debtor, which you can order sold to pay off your judgment.

- Your lawsuit is based on a motor vehicle accident. In some states, a nonpaying defendant can have her license suspended for a period of time. Depending on how much the judgment is for and whether you were injured, a nonpaying defendant can have her license suspended for various lengths of time by the State Department of Motor Vehicles. Just the threat of a license suspension causes most judgment debtors to pay. (See Chapter 24.)

> **CAUTION**
>
> **Beware of bankruptcy.** If a person or a business declares a straight bankruptcy (under Chapter 7 of the federal Bankruptcy Act) and lists you as a creditor, your right to recover a small claims court judgment is cut off, along with most other debts (unless your judgment was based on a secured loan, in which case you do have the right to recover the property pledged as security). There are, however, exceptions to this general rule, such as if your claim arose because you or your property were injured by the fraudulent or malicious behavior of the defendant. In this situation, your right to collect your judgment should survive the bankruptcy, but you may need to intervene in the bankruptcy proceeding. For more information, see *How to File for Chapter 7 Bankruptcy*, by Stephen Elias, Albin Renauer, and Robin Leonard (Nolo).

Now let's look at some situations where you are likely to have a problem collecting:

- The defendant has no job or prospect of getting one.
- You can't identify any property to use as a collection source (for example, your opponent has no real estate, valuable car, or investments).

- If a business is involved, it's a fly-by-night outfit with no permanent address or obvious collection source, such as a cash register or owned fixtures or equipment. (Remember, many businesses lease equipment or take out a secured loan to purchase it, which means you're out of luck.)

- A contractor you want to sue is unlicensed and hard to track down.

 CROSS-REFERENCE

More information on collecting a judgment. In Chapter 24, we deal in detail with the mechanics of collecting after you get your judgment. If you still think that collection may pose a problem, please skip ahead and read this chapter before deciding to sue. ●

How Much Can You Sue For?

The maximum amount for which you can sue—or be sued—in small claims court varies from state to state. For example, it's $7,500 in Minnesota, $1,500 in Kentucky, and $5,000 in Texas. You'll find the limits for other states in the Appendix, but because these are increased periodically, you'll always want to check by calling your local small claims court clerk or, better yet, obtaining a copy of your local court rules. With some exceptions, small claims courts do not hear cases unless they are for money damages. Thus, you can't use small claims court to get a divorce, stop the city from cutting down your favorite oak tree, change your name, or do many of the thousands of other things that require a solution other than one side paying money to the other.

One exception to the "money only" rule involves equitable relief. This is legalspeak for a court's power to order a person or business to do something specific, such as return a uniquely valuable piece of property or change a contract that contains an obvious mistake. These remedies are discussed in "Equitable Relief," below.

Another exception to the money-only rule involves evictions. In some states, a landlord can use small claims court to evict tenants in certain situations. (See Chapter 20 and the Appendix for more information.)

Cutting Down a Claim to Fit Under the Limit

It is legal to reduce an excessive claim so that it will fit into small claims court. Thus, you could take a $5,300 debt and bring it into small claims court in Oregon (where the dollar limit is $5,000) asking for only $5,000. (Again, costs for filing and serving papers are always recoverable in addition to the dollar limit. See "Don't Forget to Ask for Your Costs" in Chapter 15.) But if you do this, you forever waive the $300 difference between $5,000 and $5,300. In legal parlance, this is called "waiving the excess." Why might you want to do this? Because the alternative to small claims court involves filing your suit in formal court with dozens of complicated rules and the likelihood that you'll need to hire a lawyer, who will surely charge considerably more than $300 to represent you.

It is possible to represent yourself in formal court, but doing so requires a good bit of homework and the fortitude to walk into an unfamiliar and sometimes hostile arena. If you do plan to go it alone, by far the best book ever published on handling your own case is *Represent Yourself in Court: How to Prepare & Try a Winning Case,* by Paul Bergman and Sara Berman Barrett (Nolo).

TIP

Check out the court just above small claims. In most states, there are several levels of courts with different monetary limits. A case that doesn't fit into small claims court may be appropriately filed in an intermediate level court (possibly called "circuit," "district," or "county" court, depending on the state). In recent years, these courts, which typically hear cases worth between $10,000 and $25,000, have gradually begun to be "delawyered" and become more user-friendly as more and more people represent themselves.

Splitting Small Claims Court Cases

It is not legal to split an over-the-limit claim into two or more pieces to fit each into small claims court. Taking the $5,300 figure we used above, this means you couldn't sue the same person separately for $3,500 and $1,800 based on the same claim. (Defendants' claims that are over the small claims limit are discussed in Chapters 10 and 12.) As with most rules, however, a little creative thought can sometimes point the way to an exception. Start by understanding that it's perfectly okay to bring multiple suits against the same person, as long as they are based on different claims, and that there is often a large gray area in which it is genuinely difficult to differentiate between one divided claim and several independent ones. This, of course, is where the creativity comes in.

If you can reasonably argue that a $5,300 case actually involves two or more separate contracts or injuries to your person or property, you may as well try dividing it. The worst that will happen is that a judge will disagree and tell you to choose between taking the entire claim to formal court or waiving any claim for money in excess of $5,300 and staying in small claims court.

> **CAUTION**
>
> **Some states limit the number of small claims cases you can bring in a year.** If you're thinking of splitting a small claims case into two cases below the maximum dollar amount, first check your court's rules (see the Appendix) to make sure that your state doesn't limit the number of cases you can bring each year. California, for example, allows only two claims of over $2,500 each year.

EXAMPLE 1: One morning, a man in the private telephone business came into small claims court with two separate lawsuits against the same defendant for a combined total of $8,100. One claim, he said, was for failure to pay for the installation of a number of new phones, and the other was for failure to pay for moving phones to a different location. The man claimed that each lawsuit was based on a separate contract. The judge, after asking a few questions, told the man that he was on the borderline between one divided (not acceptable) and two separate (acceptable) claims. Nevertheless, the judge decided to give the man the benefit of the doubt and allowed him to present each case. The man won both and got one judgment for $4,600 and a second for $3,500.

EXAMPLE 2: Another morning, a woman alleged that she had lent a business acquaintance $4,000 on two separate occasions and was therefore bringing two separate suits, each for $4,000. The defendant objected, claiming that she had borrowed $8,000 to be repaid in two installments. A different judge, after briefly listening to each side of the argument, agreed with the defendant. The judge told the plaintiff that only one claim was involved and that if she didn't want to waive all money over $5,000, she should go to municipal court, which had a top dollar limit of $25,000.

 JUDGES' TIPS

Even the experts are challenged by "claims splitting." Claims splitting is complex, and small claims judges are sensitive to the issue. It's a good idea to seek some kind of advice, either from the court clerk, the small claims advisor, or a lawyer before making a final decision on what to do about filing multiple claims. —Commissioner Douglas G. Carnahan

How to Calculate the Exact Amount of Your Claim

Usually, determining the amount to sue for is fairly easy. But for some types of cases it can be a little tricky. Before we get to the tricky part, let's start with a basic rule: When in doubt, always estimate your damages a little on the high side. Why? Because the court has the power to award you less than you request, but can't give you more, even if the judge feels that you are entitled to it. But don't go overboard—if you sue for $2,500 on a $1,000 claim, you are likely to spur your opponent to furious opposition, ruin any chance for an out-of-court compromise, and lose the respect of the judge. But if you can reasonably increase your claim amount, it's not a bad idea to do so.

> **TIP**
>
> **Ask to amend your claim if you belatedly discover you should have requested more.** If you find yourself in court and realize you have asked for too little, ask the judge to allow you to amend your claim on the spot. Some judges will do this and, at the same time, offer the defendant extra time to prepare to defend against the higher claim. Other judges will allow you to dismiss your original case and start over, which is fine as long as your time to file hasn't run out. (See Chapter 5.)

Calculating the Exact Amount—Contract Cases

To arrive at the exact figure to sue for in contract cases, compute the difference between the amount you were supposed to receive under the contract and what you actually received. For example, if Jeannie Goodday agrees to pay Homer Brightspot $4,200 to paint her house but then pays him only $3,000, Homer has a claim for $1,200, plus the cost of filing suit and serving Jeannie with the papers. (Court costs that can be added to your judgment are discussed in more detail in Chapter 15.) The fact that Jeannie and Homer made their agreement orally does not bar Homer from suing. As discussed in Chapter 2, oral contracts are generally legal as long as they can be carried out in a year and don't involve either the sale of real estate or goods (personal property) worth $500 or more. (Also see Chapter 22 for a discussion of the relatively relaxed written contract requirements for the sale of goods.)

> **TIP**
>
> **Write it down.** Because people who are embroiled in a dispute almost always remember the details of any oral contract differently, oral contracts can be hard to prove in court. This is one of several good reasons why it is always wise to reduce agreements to writing, even if only by use of an informal note or letter agreement dated and signed by both parties.

Unfortunately, some claims based on breach of contract are harder to reduce to a dollar amount. This is often due to a legal doctrine known as "mitigation of damages." Don't let the fancy term throw you. As with so much of law, the concept behind the mumbo jumbo is simple. "Mitigation of damages" means that the person bringing suit for breach of contract must, himself, take all reasonable steps to limit the amount of damages he suffers.

EXAMPLE: Tillie Tenant moves out three months before the end of her lease (remember, a lease is a contract). Her monthly rent is $950. Can Larry Landlord recover the full $2,850 ($950 x 3 months) from Tillie in small claims court? Maybe not. In many states, Larry must try to limit (or mitigate) his damages by taking reasonable steps to attempt to find a new tenant. If Larry can immediately rerent the apartment to someone else for $950 or more per month, he has suffered little or no damage (he has fulfilled his responsibility to "mitigate damages"). More typically, it might take Larry several weeks or months (unless he had plenty of advance notice, or Tillie herself found a new tenant) to find a suitable new tenant. For example, if it took Larry one month and $75 worth of newspaper ads, he could recover approximately $1,025 (one month's rent + $75) from Tillie, assuming the judge found that Larry had taken reasonable steps to find the new tenant.

The mitigation of damages concept applies to most contracts in which the person damaged has the opportunity to take reasonable steps to limit her losses. In the earlier house painting example, if Jeannie Goodday had agreed to pay Homer Brightspot $300 per day for seven days to paint her house and then had canceled after the first day, Homer would be eligible to sue her for the remaining $1,800, based on Jeannie's violation of the contract. However, in court, Homer likely would be asked whether he had earned any other money during the six days. If he had, it would be subtracted from the $1,800. But what if Homer refused other work and slept in his hammock all week? If Jeannie could show that he had turned down other jobs or had refused to make reasonable efforts to seek available work, the judge would likely consider this a failure to mitigate damages and reduce Homer's recovery accordingly.

Loan Contracts

How much should you sue for if you lent money to a person who promised to repay it but failed to do so? Bring suit for the total you are currently owed, including any unpaid interest (assuming it doesn't result in your claim exceeding the small claims maximum). I have seen several disappointed people sue for the exact amount of the debt (say, $500) and not include interest (say, $50), thinking they could have the judge add the interest when they got to court. This normally can't be done—in most states, the judge doesn't have the power to make an award larger than the amount you request.

TIP

Don't invent interest if none was provided as part of the loan. As a general rule, you can only recover interest when it is called for in a written or oral contract. For example, if you loaned a friend $1,000 but never mentioned interest, you can sue only for the return of the $1,000.

CAUTION

Understand special rules for installment loans. If you are owed money under the terms of a promissory note (contract) that calls for repayment to be made in installments, you are normally only entitled to recover the amount of the payments that have already been missed (that is, what you are currently owed) and not those that aren't yet due. And this is true even if you are sure future installments will never be paid. But there is an important exception to this rule: You can sue for the entire loan amount plus any interest your contract calls for if your installment contract contains what lawyers call an "acceleration clause"—language that states that the entire amount of the loan is immediately due if one payment is missed.

Extra Damages for Bad Checks

In some situations, a statute (law) establishes your right to receive extra compensation, over and above the amount of the financial loss. The most common of these involves a bad check (or a check on which the writer stops payment in bad faith).

The majority of states have bad check laws, which allow you to recover the amount of the check plus a penalty of two or three times the amount of the check if the person giving it to you does not make it good within the time period allowed by the statute—usually within 30 days of your written demand to do so. In some states, such as California, this law is mandatory—the judge must award the penalty.

In addition, there are usually some minimum and maximum penalties allowed:

- You can usually sue for some minimum amount in damages, no matter how small the bad check. Thus, in California, which has a minimum penalty of $100, if you get a $25 bad check, you can sue for $125.

- There is usually a top limit on the damages you can sue for, no matter how large the check. Thus, in California, where the maximum penalty is $1,500, for a $600 bad check, the most you can sue for is $2,100 (the amount of the check plus the $1,500 maximum).

TIP

Don't forget to demand payment before you sue. If someone gives you a bum check or stops payment on a check and you want to try to collect the triple damages, start by sending a letter by certified mail demanding payment of the amount of the bad check, plus any applicable service charge and your mailing costs. Wait at least 30 days before filing suit to give the check writer time to pay.

RESOURCE

Further reading. *Solve Your Money Troubles: Get Debt Collectors Off Your Back & Regain Financial Freedom*, by Robin Leonard and John Lamb (Nolo), contains the details of every state's bad check law.

TIP

Watch your back if you stop payment on a check. If you write a check and then stop payment because you believe the service or goods you purchased were substandard (or never provided), write a letter to the other party stating in detail why you were dissatisfied. If you are later sued in small claims court, bring a copy of your letter to court and show it to the judge as part of your defense.

Calculating the Exact Amount—Property Damage Cases

When your property has been damaged by the negligent or intentional act of someone else, you usually have a right to recover the amount of money it would take to fix the damaged item.

EXAMPLE: John Quickstop plows into Melissa Caretaker's new BMW, smashing the left rear fender. How much can Melissa recover? Melissa is entitled to recover the amount it would cost to fix, or if necessary, replace, the damaged part of her car if John won't pay voluntarily. Melissa should get several estimates from responsible body and fender shops and sue for the amount of the lowest one. (For more on proving car accident cases, see Chapter 19.)

There is, however, a big exception to this rule, which comes up when the cost of fixing the item exceeds its total value. You are not entitled to a new or better object than the one that was damaged—only to have your loss made good. Had Melissa been driving a ten-year-old car, the cost to fix the fender might have exceeded the value of the entire car. In this situation, she would be entitled to the value of the car, not what it would cost to repair it. In short, the most you can recover is the fair market value of a damaged item (the amount you could have sold it for) figured one minute before the damage occurred. From this amount, you have to subtract the item's scrap value, if any.

TIP

Give yourself the benefit of the doubt when putting a value on property. No one knows exactly how much any piece of used property is worth. Recognizing that reasonable minds can differ, it makes sense to place a fairly aggressive value on property that has been destroyed. But don't demand a ridiculous amount, or you'll likely offend the judge and perhaps even weaken your case.

EXAMPLE: Let's return to Melissa from our last example, assuming now that her BMW is ten years old. If several used car price guides indicated the car was worth $2,800 and it would cost $3,000 to repair the fender, she would be limited to $2,800 compensation, minus what the car could be sold for in its damaged state. If she could only sell the car for $800 for scrap, she would be entitled to $2,000. However, if Melissa had installed an expensive rebuilt engine a few weeks before the accident, she might legitimately argue that the car was worth $3,800. Assuming the judge agreed, Melissa would legally be entitled to recover the entire $3,000 to replace the fender, because the car is worth more than replacing the fender.

Unfortunately, knowing what something is worth and proving it are quite different. A car that you are sure is worth $4,000 may look like it's only worth $3,000 to someone else. In court, you will want to be prepared to show that your piece of property is worth every bit of the $4,000. The best way to do this is to get some estimates (opinions) from experts in the field (like a used car dealer if your car was totaled). One way to present this type of evidence is to have the expert come to court and testify, but in small claims court you can also have the expert prepare a written estimate, which you then present to the judge. Depending on the type of property involved, you may also want to check newspaper and flea market ads for the prices asked for comparable goods and submit these to the judge. And of course, there may be other creative ways to establish the dollar amount of the damage you have suffered. For tips on proving the dollar amount of damage in particular types of cases, see Chapters 16–21.

 CAUTION
Replacement costs aren't relevant when figuring how much you are owed when property is destroyed. Many people insist on believing they can recover the cost of getting a replacement object when theirs has been totaled. As you should now understand, this isn't necessarily true. If Melissa's $1,200 car was totaled and she claimed she simply couldn't get another decent car for less than $2,000, she would still be limited to recovering $1,200.

Calculating the Exact Amount—Cases Involving Damage to Clothing

Clothing is property, so why treat it separately here? First, because disputes involving clothing are extremely common in small claims court. Second and more important, judges seem to apply a logic to them that they apply to no other property damage cases. The reason for this is that clothing is personal to its owner and often has little or no value to anyone else, even though it may be in good condition. It follows that if a judge strictly applied the rules we just learned (that you are limited to recovering no more than the current market value of a damaged item), plaintiffs would often get little or no compensation. Recognizing this, most judges are willing to bend the rules a little to arrive at a value for damaged clothing that is based on the item's original cost and how long it had been worn.

When suing for damage to new or almost-new clothing, it follows that you should sue for the amount you paid. If the damaged item has already been worn for some time, sue for the percentage of its original cost that reflects how much of its useful life was used up when the damage occurred. For example, if your two-year-old suit that cost $900 new was destroyed, sue for $450 if you feel the suit would have lasted another two years.

To summarize, in clothing cases, most judges want answers to these questions:

• How much did the clothing cost originally?

• How much of its useful life had already passed at the time the damage occurred?

• Does the damaged item still have some value to the owner, or has it been ruined?

EXAMPLE 1: Wendy took her new $250 coat to Rudolph, a tailor, to have alterations made. Rudolph cut part of the back of the coat in the wrong place and ruined it. How much should Wendy sue for? $250, because the coat was almost new. She could probably expect to recover close to this amount.

EXAMPLE 2: The same facts as in Example 1, but the coat was two years old and had been well worn, although it was still in good condition. Here, Wendy would be wise to sue for $175 and hope to recover between $100 and $150.

EXAMPLE 3: This time let's return Wendy's coat to its almost new condition but have Rudolph damage it only slightly. I would still advise Wendy to sue for the full $250. Whether she could recover that much would depend on the judge. Most would probably award her a little less on the theory that the coat retained some value. Wendy should argue that she didn't buy the coat expecting to not be able to wear it in public, and as far as she was concerned, the coat was ruined.

Calculating the Exact Amount—Personal Injury Cases

Because so much money is usually at stake, lawyers quickly take over the great majority of cases in which someone is injured. However, some small personal injury cases do end up in small claims court. Dog bite cases are one common example.

 CAUTION

Some small claims courts don't allow personal injury lawsuits. Another reason personal injury cases are usually filed in formal court is that many states don't allow these cases to be filed in small claims court. In other states, a small claims judge can award an injured party only the dollar amount of the person's out-of-pocket losses (doctors' bills, lost time from work), but doesn't have the power to award an additional amount to cover the injury victim's pain and suffering, no matter how legitimate. So before filing even a minor personal injury case in small claims court, be sure you check your local rules.

> **TIP**
>
> **Try to settle or mediate your personal injury claims.** If you are seriously injured, you'll almost always want to sue for more than the small claims maximum. But to gain a fair recovery, you may not need to sue at all. Many people successfully negotiate or mediate a satisfactory settlement with an insurance company. For information on how to do this without being skinned, see *How to Win Your Personal Injury Claim*, by Joseph L. Matthews (Nolo).

To determine how much to sue for, add up the dollar amount of the following losses:

- out-of-pocket medical costs,
  including medical care providers $ _____

- loss of pay, or paid time off,
  for missing work $ _____

- pain and suffering $ _____

- damage to property $ _____

TOTAL $ _____

Let's look at each of these categories in a little more detail.

Medical/Hospital bills. The amount of your medical and hospital bills, including transportation to and from the doctor, is routinely recoverable as long as you have established that the person you are suing is at fault. However, if you are covered by health insurance and the insurance company has already paid your medical costs, you will find that your policy says that any money you recover for these costs must be turned over to the company. Often, insurance companies don't make much effort to keep track of, or recover, small claims court judgments, as the amounts of money involved don't make it worthwhile. Knowing this, many judges are reluctant to grant judgments for medical bills unless the individual can show he personally paid out of pocket for the money. But if you had uninsured expenses or deductible payments, by all means include them.

Loss of pay. Loss of pay or paid time off as a result of an injury is viewed in a similar way. Assume the cocker spaniel down the block lies in wait for you behind a hedge and grabs a piece of your derriere for breakfast, and as a result you miss a day of work getting yourself patched up. You are entitled to recover any lost pay, commissions, or vacation time. However, if your job offers unlimited paid sick time, and therefore you suffer no loss for missing work, you have nothing to recover.

Pain and suffering. The third area of recovery is for what is euphemistically called "pain and suffering." When you read about big dollar settlements, a good chunk of the recovery almost always falls into this category. No question, recovering from some injuries really is a painful, miserable ordeal for which compensation is reasonable. It is also true that in the hands of an aggressive lawyer, "pain and suffering" can become an excuse for an inflated claim.

But suppose that you have suffered a minor, but painful, injury and you do want to attempt to recover compensation for your discomfort in small claims court. How much should you ask for? There is no one right answer. When valuing a client's pain and suffering, a lawyer will typically sue for three to five times the amount of the out-of-pocket damages (medical bills and loss of work). Therefore, if you were out of pocket $500, you might wish to ask for $1,500, the overage being for "pain and suffering." To get this, you'll have to convince the judge that you have suffered real pain and inconvenience. The best way to do this is to present bills for medical treatment. If the judge concludes you suffered a real injury, she will be more likely to add an amount for "pain and suffering." This is why lawyers routinely encourage their clients to get as much medical attention as is reasonably possible.

EXAMPLE 1: Mary Tendertummy is drinking a bottle of pop when a mouse foot floats to the surface. She is immediately nauseated, loses her lunch, and goes to the doctor for medication. As a result, she incurs a medical bill of $150 and loses an afternoon's pay of an additional $150. She sues the soda pop company for $900, claiming that the extra amount is to compensate her for pain and suffering. This may well be considered to be reasonable and, depending on the judge, she will probably recover most of this amount.

EXAMPLE 2: The same thing happens to Roy Toughguy. But instead of losing his lunch, he just tosses the soda pop away in disgust and goes back to work. A few weeks later he hears about Mary's recovery and decides to sue—after all, he could use $900. How much is Roy likely to recover? Probably not much more than the price of the soda pop—because he didn't see a doctor and wasn't too upset by the incident, the judge is likely to conclude he suffered little or no injury.

Property damage. Often a personal injury is accompanied by injury to property. Thus, a dog bite might also ruin your pants. If so, include the value of your damaged clothing when you determine how much to sue for.

> ### Don't Count on Recovering Punitive Damages in Small Claims Court
>
> Formal trial courts have the power to award extra damages (over and above out-of-pocket losses and pain and suffering) if an injury is caused by the malicious or willful misconduct (often a fraudulent or criminal act) of the defendant. When the defendant is wealthy, these damages—which are designed to punish the defendant—can run into the millions. About half the states do not allow punitive damages (sometimes called "exemplary damages") to be awarded in small claims. But even in those states where it is theoretically possible to receive punitive damages, small claims court's low dollar limit largely rules them out, except in a few instances where specific dollar amounts are established for bad checks or failure to return a tenant's security deposit on time (see Chapter 20). If you believe you have been injured by conduct wretched enough to support a claim for hefty punitive damages, see a lawyer.

Calculating the Exact Amount—Emotional or Mental Distress

There are all sorts of ways we can cause one another real pain without even making physical contact, especially in increasingly crowded urban environments. For example, if I live in the apartment above you and pound on my floor (your ceiling) for an hour at 6:00 a.m. every day, I will probably quickly reduce you to a raving maniac. What can you do about it short of slashing my tires?

One remedy is for you to sue me in small claims court based on the fact that my actions constitute the intentional infliction of emotional distress. (You could also sue me for causing a nuisance; see Chapter 2.) But how much should you sue for? Unfortunately, it's impossible to provide a formula. It depends on how obnoxious my behavior is, how long it has gone on, and how clearly you have asked me to cease it (this should be done several times in writing). And if this isn't vague enough, it will also depend greatly on the personality of the judge, who may be very skeptical of all neighbor disputes, thinking they don't belong in court in the first place. At the very least, you'll need to convince the judge you are an extremely reasonable person and your neighbor is a true boor before you will be eligible for any compensation.

One way to try to convince the judge you aren't a hypersensitive complainer is to sue for a reasonable amount. Thus, I would normally advise against suing for your state's small claims maximum, or anything close to it, unless the other person's behavior clearly makes her out to be first cousin to Attila the Hun.

TIP

Choose mediation when neighbors are involved. As discussed in Chapter 6, the process of filing, preparing, and arguing a lawsuit tends to make both sides even madder than they were previously. And, of course, the losing side is likely to stay mad for a long, long time. This may be fine if you are suing a large company or someone you are never likely to interact with again, but given the high value most people place on good relations with neighbors, it's usually best to at least try to settle your case through mediation before going to court.

Calculating the Exact Amount—Malpractice Cases

In theory, most malpractice cases are worth far more than can be sued for in small claims court. But because legal rules (what it takes to prove liability, for example) are usually tilted to favor professionals and these cases are expensive to bring, it's often hard to find a lawyer to represent you on a contingency-fee basis (meaning that the lawyer doesn't charge you up front but takes a percentage of the settlement). That means that quite a few malpractice cases end up being scaled down to fit into small claims court.

For most types of malpractice you simply need to prove that the doctor's malpractice harmed you financially as well as physically, and then you can sue for that amount (assuming it is below the small claims court maximum). Thus, if a doctor negligently misdiagnosed an illness and as a result you experienced serious medical problems, you would present the court with:

- all medical, hospital, and drug bills you paid that occurred after the misdiagnosis that you claim could have been avoided

- the opinion of a second doctor that the first doctor's handling of your problem did not measure up to accepted medical standards (or, in plain language, that the first doctor screwed up)

- an estimate for your pain and suffering, and

- proof of loss of any pay or vacation time as a result of the misdiagnosis.

> **CAUTION**
>
> **Special rules for legal malpractice.** As discussed in Chapter 2, if your suit is based on a lawyer's having failed to handle your case properly, you have to be able to prove not only that the lawyer was a bungler but that you would likely have won your original case if the lawyer had done a reasonably competent job. And you must also show that you would have won at least as much money as you are suing for in small claims court.

Equitable Relief (or, Money Can't Always Solve the Problem)

Nearly half the states allow judges to grant relief (provided you ask for it) in ways that do not involve the payment of money, if equity (fairness) demands it. In small claims court, "equitable relief" is usually limited to one or more of four categories: "rescission," "restitution," "reformation," and "specific performance." Let's translate these into English.

> ⓘ **CAUTION**
>
> **You may need to do more research.** If you think you may want to sue "in equity," you'll need to look up your state's small claims court law. (You'll find the citation for the law in the Appendix; see Chapter 25 for tips on easy legal research.)

Rescission. This is a remedy that is used to wipe out a grossly unfair or fraudulent contract under any of the following conditions:

- it was based on a mistake as to an important fact,
- it was induced by duress or undue influence, or
- one party simply didn't receive what was promised, through the fault of the other.

EXAMPLE: If a merchant sues you for failure to pay for aluminum siding, the quality of which you contend the merchant seriously misrepresented, you could ask that the contract be rescinded and that any money you paid be returned to you. Don't hesitate to ask for this remedy whenever you feel you have been unfairly treated in a contract dispute.

Restitution. This is an important remedy. It gives a judge the power to order that a particular piece of property be transferred to its original owner when fairness requires the contracting parties be restored to their original positions. It can be used in the common situation in which one person sells another a piece of property (say a motor scooter) and the other fails to pay. Instead of simply giving the seller a money judgment that might be hard to collect, the judge has the power to order the scooter restored to its original owner. If money has been paid under a contract that is rescinded, the judge can order it to be returned, plus damages. Thus, if a used car purchase was rescinded based on the fraud of the seller, the buyer could get a judgment for the amount paid for the car, plus money spent for repairs and alternate transportation.

Reformation. This remedy is somewhat unusual. It has to do with changing (reforming) a contract to meet the original intent of the parties in a situation where some term or condition the parties agreed to was left out or misstated and where fairness dictates the contract be reformed. Reformation is commonly used when an oral agreement is written down incorrectly.

EXAMPLE: Arthur the Author and Peter the Publisher orally agree that Peter will publish Arthur's 200-page book. They then write a contract, inadvertently leaving out the number of pages. If Arthur shows up with a 3,000-page manuscript and demands that it be published in its entirety, a court would very likely "reform" the contract to include the 200-page provision, assuming the judge was convinced that it should have been included in the first place.

Specific performance. This is an important remedy that comes into play when a contract involving an unusual or one-of-a-kind object has not been carried out. Say you agree to buy a unique antique jade ring for your mother's birthday that is exactly like the one she lost years before, and then the seller refuses to go through with the deal. A court could cite the doctrine of "specific performance" to order that the ring be turned over to you. "Specific performance" will only be ordered in situations where the payment of money will not adequately compensate the person bringing suit.

TIP

The small claims dollar maximum applies to cases involving equitable relief. In filling out your court papers for a case in which you want one of the types of equitable relief discussed here, you are still required to indicate that the value of the item in question is under the small claims maximum. Thus, you might describe the nature of your claim as follows: "I want the delivery of my 'one-of-a-kind' antique jade ring, worth approximately $4,000, according to my contract with defendant."

Conditional judgments and equitable relief. In some states, judges have the power to issue conditional judgments in cases involving equitable relief. That is, they can order a party to perform, or stop, a certain act or else pay a money judgment. For example, you agree to sell your baby grand piano for $3,000. The buyer fails to pay, and you sue. The judge orders the buyer to either return the piano or fork over the $3,000. If the piano isn't returned within a short period of time (determined by the judge), then you can enforce the money judgment. (See Chapter 24.)

When Can You Sue?

Each state's legislature sets up time limits within which lawsuits must be filed. These are called statutes of limitations. Time limits are different for different types of cases. If you wait too long, your right to sue will be barred by these statutes.

Why have a statute of limitations? Because unlike wine, lawsuits don't improve with age. Memories fade, witnesses die or move away, and once-clear details become blurred. In other words, disputes are best settled relatively soon after they develop.

Statutes of limitations are almost always at least one year, so if you file promptly, you should have little to worry about.

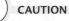 **CAUTION**

Act fast for claims against a government agency. To sue a city, county, state, or governmental agency (for example, a school district), you first must promptly file a claim with the people in charge (for example, the school board, county board of supervisors, city council). Once your claim is rejected—and it usually will be—you can file in small claims court. Often, your administrative claim must be filed within three to six months after your loss occurred, or you are out of luck.

Statute of Limitations Periods

Following is a chart of statutes of limitation periods for four of the most common types of lawsuits. But you will probably need to do further legal research to learn about time limits that might affect your specific situation. Even the time limits specified in the following chart can be affected by things like the "discovery rule"—see "How the Discovery Rule Works," below. Also, the time limits in the chart may not cover every situation. For example, claims involving medical malpractice, eviction, child or spousal support, fraud, product liability, consumer

Statutes of Limitations

These statutes explain when (in years) you must sue for specific types of claims. However, some states have separate rules for particular situations or injuries. Carefully read your state's statutes, or consult an attorney, to learn the rule for your situation.

State	Statute	Contracts Written	Oral	Personal Injury	Property Damage
Alabama	Ala. Code § 6-2-30 et seq.*	6	6	2	6
Alaska	Alaska Stat. § 09.10.010 et seq.	3	3	2	2
Arizona	Ariz. Rev. Stat. Ann. § 12-541 et seq.	6	3	2	2
Arkansas	Ark. Code Ann. § 16-56-101 et seq.	5	3	3	3
California	Cal. Civ. Proc. Code § 335 et seq.	4	2	2	3
Colorado	Colo. Rev. Stat. § 13-80-101 et seq.	6	6	2	2
Connecticut	Conn. Gen. Stat. Ann. § 52-575 et seq.	6	3	3	3
Delaware	Del. Code Ann. tit. 10, § 8101 et seq.	3	3	3	2
D.C.	D.C. Code § 12-301 et seq.	3	3	3	3
Florida	Fla. Stat. Ann. § 95.11 et seq.	5	4	4	4
Georgia	Ga. Code Ann. § 9-3-20 et seq.	6	4	2	4
Hawaii	Haw. Rev. Stat. § 657-1 et seq.	6	6	2	2
Idaho	Idaho Code § 5-201 et seq.	5	4	2	3
Illinois	735 Ill. Comp. Stat. 5/13-201 et seq.	10	5	2	5
Indiana	Ind. Code Ann. § 34-11-2-1 et seq.	10[1]	6	2	2[2]
Iowa	Iowa Code Ann. § 614.1 et seq.	10	5	2	5
Kansas	Kan. Stat. Ann. § 60-501 et seq.	5	3	2	2
Kentucky	Ky. Rev. Stat. Ann. § 413.080 et seq.	15	5	1	2[3]
Louisiana**	La. Civ. Code Art. 3492 et seq.	10	10	1	1
Maine	Me. Rev. Stat. Ann. tit. 14, § 751 et seq.	6	6	6	6
Maryland	Md. Code Ann. [Courts & Jud. Proc.] § 5-101 et seq.	3	3	3	3
Massachusetts	Mass. Ann. Laws ch. 260, § 1 et seq.	6	6	3	3
Michigan	Mich. Comp. Laws § 600.5801 et seq.	6	6	3	3
Minnesota	Minn. Stat. Ann. § 541.01 et seq.	6	6	2	6
Mississippi	Miss. Code. Ann. § 15-1-1 et seq.	3	3	3	3

* Et seq. means "and the next sections following in sequence."
** Louisiana: Statute of limitations known as a "liberative prescription," personal injury known as "delictuel action."
1 For all cases other than payment of money, which is six years.
2 For personal property; statute is six years for damage to real property.
3 For personal property; statute is five years for damage to real property.

Statutes of Limitations (cont'd)		Contracts		Personal	Property
State	Statute	Written	Oral	Injury	Damage
Missouri	Mo. Rev. Stat. § 516.097 et seq.	5[4]	5	5	5
Montana	Mont. Code Ann. § 27-2-201 et seq.	8	5	3	2
Nebraska	Neb. Rev. Stat. § 25-201 et seq.	5	4	4	4
Nevada	Nev. Rev. Stat. Ann. § 11.190 et seq.	6	4	2	3
New Hampshire	N.H. Rev. Stat. Ann. § 508:1 et seq.	3	3	3	3
New Jersey	N.J. Stat. Ann. § 2a:14-1 et seq.	6	6	2	6
New Mexico	N.M. Stat. Ann. § 37-1-1 et seq.	6	4	3	4
New York	N.Y. C.P.L.R. Law § 201 et seq.	6	6	3	3
North Carolina	N.C. Gen. Stat. § 1-46 et seq.	3	3	3	3
North Dakota	N.D. Cent. Code § 28-01-01 et seq.	6	6	6	6
Ohio	Ohio Rev. Code Ann. § 2305.03 et seq.	15	6	2	4
Oklahoma	Okla. Stat. Ann. tit. 12, § 91 et seq.	5	3	2	2
Oregon	Or. Rev. Stat. § 12.010 et seq.	6	6	2	6
Pennsylvania	42 Pa. Cons. Stat. Ann. § 5521 et seq.	4	4	2	2
Rhode Island	R. I. Gen. Laws § 9-1-12 et seq.	10	10	3	10
South Carolina	S.C. Code Ann. § 15-3-510 et seq.	3	3	3	3
South Dakota	S.D. Codified Laws Ann. § 15-2-1 et seq.	6	6	3	6
Tennessee	Tenn. Code Ann. § 28-3-101 et seq.	6	6	1	3
Texas	Tex. Civ. Prac. & Rem. Code § 16.001 et. seq.; Tex. Bus & Com. Code § 2725	4	4	2	2
Utah	Utah Code Ann. § 78-12-22 et seq.	6	4	4	3
Vermont	Vt. Stat. Ann. tit. 12, § 461 et seq.	6	6	3	3
Virginia	Va. Code Ann. § 8.01-243 et seq.	5	3	2	5
Washington	Wash. Rev. Code Ann. § 4.16.005 et seq.	6	3	3	3
West Virginia	W. Va. Code § 55-2-1 et seq.	10	5	2	2
Wisconsin	Wis. Stat. Ann. § 893.40 et seq.	6	6	3	6
Wyoming	Wyo. Stat. § 1-3-102 et seq.	10	8	4	4

4   For all cases but payment of money or property transfer, which is ten years.

Current as of October 2007

sales contracts, or faulty work by builders may all have different statutes of limitations. And some states distinguish between different types of property (usually real and personal property) when establishing statutes of limitations.

You can find your state's laws online at www.nolo.com/statute/state .cfm and on your state's Internet home page, and you will find a printed set at a law library or a large public library. (See Chapter 25 for more on how to do legal research.)

Calculating the Statute of Limitations

Okay, now let's assume you have found out what the relevant limitations period is. How do you know what date to start your counting from? That's easy. Start with the day the injury to your person or property occurred, or, if a contract is involved, start with the day the contract was broken. When a contract to pay in installments is involved, start with the day each payment was missed. (See "Tricky Rules for Installment Contracts," below.)

How the Discovery Rule Works

With some types of cases, such as medical malpractice, the limitations period starts from the date the harm was discovered or reasonably should have been discovered. This rule protects people who don't know they have a problem until well after it has occurred.

EXAMPLE: During an operation, a doctor leaves a small clamp in your abdomen. It isn't until a year later that you experience extreme pain and see a different doctor, who orders an X-ray that shows the clamp. In most states, the statute of limitations for suits based on medical malpractice (often three years) begins from the date you learn of the problem, not the date of the original operation. However, if you walked around in pain for several years before seeing a second doctor and getting an X-ray, chances are a court would rule that the limitations period would start before actual discovery, based on the theory that you could and should have discovered the problem sooner.

Tricky Rules for Installment Contracts

When an installment contract is involved, the statute of limitations (four years on a written contract) normally applies separately to each installment. For example, assume you loan Larry $5,000 and he agrees in writing to pay back the loan in five installments of $1,000 each beginning on January 1, 2006, and continuing on January 1 of each following year through 2010. If Larry fails to make his first payment, then you can sue him in small claims court until January 1, 2010. (Note that you can sue him for only the $1,000 payment he missed, not for the entire $5,000.)

From Larry's point of view, if you don't sue by January 1, 2010, then you cannot sue him for the first missed $1,000 payment because the lawsuit is barred by the statute of limitations.

Because Larry's second installment payment isn't due until January 1, 2007, you have until January 1, 2011 to sue him if he misses that payment, and so on.

There is, however, one important exception to this rule: If the written contract contains an "acceleration clause" stating that if one installment payment is missed, all immediately become due, the statute of limitations expires for a lawsuit to collect all installments on January 2, 2007.

Voluntary Payment After Limitations Periods

I am frequently asked to explain the legal implications of the following situation: After the statute of limitations runs out (say two years on an oral contract to pay for having a fence painted), the debtor voluntarily starts to make payments. Does the voluntary payment have the effect of creating a new two-year statute of limitations period, allowing the person who is owed the money to sue if the debtor again stops paying?

In most states, the answer is no. Simply starting to pay on an obligation after the time to sue has passed doesn't create a new period for suit. All the creditor can do is to keep his toes crossed and hope that the debtor's belated streak of honesty continues. However, if the debtor signs a written agreement promising to make the payments, this does reinstate the contract and create a new statute of limitations period. In legal slang, this is called "reaffirming the debt."

EXAMPLE: Doolittle borrows $1,000 from Crabapple in 1998 under the terms of a written promissory note. The next month he loses his job and never pays back a penny. Crabapple doesn't file a lawsuit within the four-year statute of limitations. In 2003, Doolittle experiences a burst of energy, gets a job, and resolves to pay off all of his old debts. He sends Crabapple $50. A week later, suffering terrible strain from getting up before noon, Doolittle quits his job and reverts to his old ways of waking up a few minutes before race time. Is the four-year statute of limitations allowing Crabapple to sue reinstated by Doolittle's payment? No. As we learned above, once the four-year limitation period for written contracts runs out, it can't be revived by simply making a payment. However, if after Doolittle sent Crabapple the $50, Crabapple coaxed him into sending a letter saying that he would pay the remainder of the debt, Crabapple would again be able to sue and get a judgment if Doolittle failed to pay. Why? Because a written promise to pay a debt that would otherwise be barred by the statute of limitations has the legal effect of reestablishing the debt.

! CAUTION

Debtors—Beware of waiving statutes of limitations.

If a creditor and debtor discuss an unpaid bill and the debtor asks the creditor to give her more time to pay, to lower payments, or to make some other accommodation, the creditor, assuming he is willing to agree, will almost always require that the debtor waive the statute of limitations in writing. This means that if the debtor fails to pay, the creditor will have more time to sue.

Suspending the Statute of Limitations

In a few situations, the statute of limitations is suspended for a period of time (lawyers say "tolled" instead of "suspended"). This can occur if the person sued is in prison, living out of the state, insane, or a minor, or occasionally for other reasons. If one of these events suspends the statute of limitations, then the time period that the event lasts doesn't count towards the statute of limitations, and the counting begins again when the event (prison term, absence from state, and so on) ends.

EXAMPLE 1: Jack borrows money from Tim under a written contract. Jack fails to pay the money back on the day required. Six months later, Jack is sentenced to a year in jail. The four-year statute of limitations would be suspended during this period and Tim would still have three-and-one-half years after Jack gets out of jail to file suit.

EXAMPLE 2: Ed, age 12, stars in a TV series. Just before Ed turns 18, an accountant for the show tells Ed's family that Ed wasn't paid all the money due under his contract. Ed wonders if he can still sue the TV production company. The answer is yes. Ed's time to sue is measured from his 18th birthday (that is, the statute of limitations period would be suspended or tolled while he was a minor). And because most states have a four-year statute of limitation for disputes based on written contracts, this means that Ed could file suit at least until his 22nd birthday.

Defendant Should Tell the Judge If the Statute of Limitations Has Run Out

What should a defendant do if he believes that the statute of limitations period on the plaintiff's lawsuit has run out? Tell the judge. Do this in court as part of stating your defense. Or, if your state is one of the few that requires a defendant to make a written response to the plaintiff's claim before the hearing date (see the Appendix), then include in your response a statement that the statute of limitations bars the plaintiff's claim. Sometimes a judge will figure this out without a reminder, but often she won't. Don't ever assume that because the clerk has filed the papers and you have been properly served, this means that the plaintiff started her suit on time. Clerks rarely get involved in statute of limitations questions. ●

How to Settle Your Dispute

L awsuits should be a last, not a first, resort. In addition to being time-consuming and emotionally draining, lawsuits—even the small claims variety—tend to polarize disagreements into win-all or lose-all propositions where compromise is difficult. It's not hard to understand how this happens. Most of us, after all, are terrified of making fools of ourselves in front of strangers. When forced to defend our actions in a public forum, we tend to adopt a self-righteous view of our own conduct and to attribute the worst motives to our opponents. Many of us are willing to admit in private that we have been a bit of a fool—especially if the other person does, too—but in public, we tend to stonewall, even when it would be to our advantage to appear a little more fallible.

> **CAUTION**
>
> **In most states, you are required to at least ask for the money owed you before filing a small claims lawsuit.** For example, in California the form you fill out to start a small claims lawsuit states, "You must ask the Defendant (in person, in writing, or by phone) to pay you before you sue. Have you done this? If no, explain why not."

Although I am a strong advocate of resolving disputes in small claims court, I have nevertheless witnessed many otherwise sensible people litigate cases that never should have been filed in the first place. In some instances, the amount of money was too small to bother with. In others, the problem should have been talked out over the back fence. And there were some situations in which the practical importance of maintaining civil personal or business relationships between the parties made it silly to go to court over a few hundred or even thousands of dollars.

Let me make this last point in a slightly different way: It is almost always wise to first look for a noncourt solution when the other party is someone you'll have to deal with in the future. Typically, this would include a neighbor, a former friend, or a relative. Similarly, a business owner will almost always benefit by working out a compromise settlement with another established local business, a long-term customer, or a client. For example, an orthodontist who depends on referrals for most new customers should think twice before suing a patient who has refused to pay a bill in a situation where the patient is genuinely upset (whether rightly or wrongly) about the services she received. Even if the orthodontist wins in court, he is likely to turn the former patient into a vocal enemy—one who may literally bad-mouth him from one end of town to the other and in the end cost him a lot more than he won in court.

Try to Talk Out Your Dispute

It is rarely a waste of time to try to negotiate a compromise with the other party. Indeed, many states all but require you to make the attempt. For tips on writing demand letters, see "Write a Formal Demand Letter," below.

But, first things first. Before you reach for pen and paper, try to talk to the person with whom you are having the dispute. The wisdom of trying to talk out a dispute may seem obvious. But apparently it isn't, since I am frequently consulted by someone with an "insurmountable dispute" who has never once tried to discuss it calmly with the other party. I suspect the reason for this is that many of us have a strong psychological barrier to contacting people we are mad at, especially if we have already exchanged heated words. If you fall into this category, perhaps it will be easier to pick up the phone if you remind yourself that a willingness to compromise is not a sign of weakness. After all, it was Winston Churchill, one of the 20th century's greatest warriors, who said, "I would rather jaw, jaw, jaw than war, war, war."

💡 TIP

A compromise offer is not binding. It's important to know that an offer of compromise—whether made orally or in writing—does not legally bind the person making it to sue for that amount if the compromise is not accepted. Thus, you can make an oral or written demand for $2,000, then offer to compromise for $1,500, and, if your compromise offer is turned down, still sue for $2,000. If the person you are suing tries to tell the judge you offered to settle for less, the judge will not consider this to be relevant.

In an effort to help you arrive at a good compromise, here are a few of my personal negotiation rules, which, of course, I modify to fit the circumstances:

- If you are the potential plaintiff, start by offering to settle for about 20% less than your original written demand. Why 20%? If you offer a smaller discount, chances are you won't be taken seriously. Offer a bigger discount and you're giving away too much too soon.

- If you are the potential defendant, and you conclude that the plaintiff probably has a decent case, start by offering to pay about 50% of the amount demanded. This should be enough to start negotiations without conceding too much too soon. Many plaintiffs will ultimately agree to knock as much as one third off their original demand, in order to save the time and trouble of going to court.

- Money isn't always at the root of the problem. If you pay close attention to the other party's concerns, you may find that the key to arriving at an agreement can be found elsewhere. For example, a print shop owner who refuses to repay you $2,000 for a screwed-up job might agree to do the disputed job over and give you a discount on the next one, in exchange for an agreement to continue to work together and speak well of each other in the future.

- The patient negotiator has the edge. Many Americans are in such a big hurry to arrive at a solution that they agree to a bad one. Take your time. If you make a lowball offer and the other person gets mad and hangs up, you can always wait a few days and call back with a slightly sweetened one.

• Good negotiators rarely change their position quickly, even if the other side does. Instead, they raise or lower their offer in very small increments. For example, if your opponent counters your original offer of a 20% reduction in exchange for a settlement by offering to pay 50% of what you originally asked for, you'll do best by not jumping to accept or even agreeing to split the difference. Instead, counter by reducing your original demand by an additional 5%–10%. Often this will result in your opponent further improving her offer. And even if she doesn't, you haven't lost anything, because once she has made the 50% offer, she is unlikely to withdraw it.

TIP

Why it's rarely wise to split the difference. Often, an inexperienced negotiator will quickly agree to the other party's offer to split the difference or settle a claim for 50¢ on the dollar. It's rarely wise to do this. After all, by proposing to split the difference, your opponent has all but conceded she'll pay that amount. Better to counter by reducing your first offer by a smaller amount and leave the next move up to your opponent.

• Estimate how much money a compromise settlement is worth to you, given the fact that a settlement eliminates the time and aggravation of going to court. I do this by putting a dollar value on my time and then multiplying by the number of hours I estimate a court fight will take. Also, based on the facts of your case, take into consideration the chances that you might lose or get less than you ask for. In a study of 996 small claims cases that actually went to trial, only 32% resulted in the plaintiff receiving 100% of the amount claimed; 22% resulted in the plaintiff getting between 50% and

100% of the amount claimed; 20% resulted in the plaintiff getting less than half; and in 26% of the cases, the plaintiff got nothing at all. (See "Small Claims and Traffic Courts," by John Goerdt (National Center for State Courts).)

EXAMPLE: In a recent dispute my business, Nolo, had with a phone company, Nolo originally asked for $5,000. The phone company admitted some liability and offered to compromise. After considering the value of the time Nolo would invest bringing the dispute to court, we decided that it would make sense to compromise for $3,500. And although we were sure we had a strong case, we had to admit that there was some possibility the judge would not agree, so we decided to subtract another $500 and accept a settlement for $3,000. Unfortunately, after several conversations and letters, the phone company wouldn't offer a dime more than $2,000. Since this was too low, we decided to go to court. As it happened, the small claims judge awarded us the entire $5,000. But then the phone company appealed and received a new trial. After the case was presented over again, the second judge reduced our final award to $3,500. Considering that it was easier to prepare the case the second time, we still probably came out ahead of the game, as compared to accepting the $2,000. In truth, however, given the time needed to prepare for two court presentations, we probably netted only about $500 more.

TIP

If you settle, sign a written agreement, pronto. If you talk things out with your opponent, write down your agreement as soon as possible. Oral settlement agreements, especially between people who have little confidence in one another, are often not worth the breath used to express them. And writing down an agreement gives each party a chance to see whether they really have arrived at a complete understanding. Often one or more details must still be hashed out. (In "Write Down the Terms of Any Settlement," below, I show you how to reduce a compromise agreement to writing.)

RESOURCE

Learn more about negotiating. On several occasions when I have been involved in important negotiations, I've gotten help by rereading *Getting to Yes: Negotiating Agreements Without Giving In*, by Roger Fisher and William Ury (Penguin). I also like *Getting Past No: Negotiating Your Way From Confrontation to Cooperation*, by William Ury (Bantam). *Neighbor Law: Fences, Trees, Boundaries & Noise*, by Cora Jordan and Emily Doskow (Nolo), has excellent advice on negotiating neighborhood quarrels.

Mediate Your Dispute

If you and the opposing party can't seem to resolve matters one on one, mediation is the next best settlement technique. Mediation is a procedure in which the disputants voluntarily meet with a neutral third party who helps them discuss the issues and arrive at their own solution. For small claims disputes, mediation is available right in the courthouse in many counties. In others, it's provided by community-based mediation programs.

Why Mediate?

Many people ask why they should waste any time at all mediating with an opponent who they believe is unreasonable. My best answer is that when the parties to a small claims court case voluntarily agree to mediate, the majority of disputes are settled. Settlement is especially likely when, deep down, one or both parties realize they have an interest in arriving at a solution that's at least minimally acceptable to the other party. This is particularly common in disputes between neighbors or businesspeople who live or work in the same geographical area and who really don't want the dispute to fester.

Studies have shown that people who agreed to have their cases mediated were more likely to be satisfied with the outcome of the case than litigants who went to trial. One reason for this is that people who arrive at a mediated settlement are more likely to pay up than are people who have a judgment imposed on them after losing a contested trial.

Is entering into mediation always a good idea? No. If you are determined to get the total amount you are asking for, and you will have no ongoing relationship with the other party (for example, your dispute is with a large corporation or government agency), bypassing mediation and going directly to court makes more sense.

EXAMPLE: John rented an apartment from Frontier Arms, Inc. When he moved out and left the unit undamaged and spotless, the Frontier Arms manager made up a bogus reason to avoid refunding his $1,500 deposit. John decided that proposing mediation was a waste of time, because he was pretty sure a judge would enter a judgment for his entire $1,500, plus $3,000 punitive damages as provided by his state's law when a landlord keeps a tenant's deposit without a good reason. (See Chapter 20.)

Arbitration

In addition to mediation, a few states also offer binding arbitration before a volunteer lawyer as an alternative to having a case heard in small claims court. Typically, the arbitrator and the parties sit down at a table and discuss the case. If the parties don't arrive at their own solution, the arbitrator renders a decision just as a judge would. The only advantage of arbitration over going before a small claims judge or a commissioner is that, in some areas, it's faster to meet with the arbitrator.

Unfortunately, arbitration also comes with a big built-in disadvantage: The arbitrator is likely to be a volunteer lawyer, who is far less knowledgeable than a judge about the broad range of laws that apply to consumers and small businesses. For this reason, I usually recommend against this procedure.

New York Note. In New York state, where volunteer lawyer arbitrators are routinely used, this disadvantage is compounded by the fact that you can't appeal from the decision of an arbitrator as you could from a judge's decision.

Nonbinding Arbitration. In a few areas, a procedure called nonbinding arbitration is available. This is much like mediation, in the sense that both parties must agree to any settlement. The only difference is that, unlike a mediator, who doesn't make a formal recommendation, the arbitrator will recommend—but not compel—a solution. Especially if it's more easily available than mediation, it's often a good idea to try nonbinding arbitration; the arbitrator's recommendation can be a pretty good indication of what will happen if the case ends up going to court.

How Does the Mediation Process Work?

A small claims mediation session typically lasts between 30 minutes and three hours. Although many mediators are ex-attorneys or even ex-judges, they have no power to impose a decision on you. The result is that mediation sessions tend to be much more relaxed than court proceedings, and they often result in compromises that both parties are better able to live with.

You can't force the other party into mediating—both of you must agree to engage in the process. However, many states now "strongly encourage" small claims litigants to mediate before they head into the courtroom, including telling them that the judge may look more favorably upon parties who willingly try to mediate. Your small claims court appointment may even be scheduled to include an extra block of time before the hearing so that you and the other party can meet with the mediator. Your discussions during the mediation session are confidential—if the mediation fails, the judge won't be told what went on.

Although it makes sense to approach mediation with an open mind and be ready to agree to a reasonable compromise, nothing requires you to agree on anything at this stage. It's your right to have your case presented to a judge if you wish. You can even call off the mediation in the middle, which is particularly appropriate if, despite your spirit of compromise, the other party refuses to realize that he's in the wrong or will only settle for a ridiculously low amount. Also watch out for result-oriented mediators who make you feel like you have to give up a large chunk of your claim just to reach a settlement. Being reasonable doesn't mean giving away the farm.

Assuming you do want to mediate, how can you get a reluctant opponent to the table? Often you can get help from your local court-sponsored or community mediation program. Typically, as soon as you notify a mediation program that you have a dispute and would like to try mediation, an employee or volunteer with the mediation program will contact the other party or parties and try to arrange a mediation session.

If you and the other party do agree on a mediated settlement, it will normally be recorded by the mediator on a form called a "Mediated Agreement," or something similar. The agreement, signed by both parties, will spell out the terms of the settlement and the deadlines for payments or other actions. If the mediation occurs after the plaintiff has already filed a small claims case, some counties will add the agreement into the court record in a sealed envelope.

Should Defendants Mediate?

Suppose now that you are a defendant in a small claims case or have received a letter threatening a lawsuit. Should you ask for mediation? The answer is almost always a resounding yes, assuming you have a defense to all or part of the plaintiff's claim or believe the plaintiff is asking for too much money even though he's got a decent case. Mediation will give you a great opportunity to present your side of the dispute and try to arrive at an acceptable compromise. It can also allow you to bring up other issues that may be poisoning your relationship with the plaintiff but would not be considered relevant in court.

RESOURCE

Learn to be a good mediator. People who are well prepared to engage in mediation are likely to achieve far better results than those who take a more casual approach. The best source of information on how to mediate successfully is *Mediate, Don't Litigate: Strategies for Successful Mediation*, by Peter Lovenheim and Lisa Guerin, available as a downloadable eBook at www.nolo.com. If you read it before you mediate, you will almost certainly achieve better results than would otherwise have been possible.

If Your Opponent Violates the Agreement

Assuming both parties honor the agreement you reached in mediation, that's the end of the case—no court judgment is ever entered by the judge or reported to a credit agency. Some states will automatically set a second court date in case the agreement isn't honored. If your agreement is honored, however, then you can either advise the court to cancel the second date or simply not show up.

If your opponent doesn't honor her obligations under the mediated agreement by the deadline, you must go back to court and obtain a judgment. That's easy in the states where a second court date was scheduled automatically. In other states, you will need to request a new court date or simply request a judgment, either of which can often be done by mail. Ask the court whether they have forms for such follow-up—if not, write a letter similar to the "Sample Letter Requesting Judgment" shown below.

> **TIP**
>
> **In case the mediated settlement agreement is broken, protect your right to ask for the full amount.** Most disputes that are successfully mediated result in a compromise, as would occur where A sues B for $2,000 and agrees to accept $1,200. But if B fails to pay within the time allowed by the written mediation agreement, A may want a judgment for the full $2,000. After all, A no longer has an incentive to compromise if B isn't willing to end the dispute without a day in court. Add a sentence or two to your mediated agreement stating that if the other party doesn't meet her settlement obligations, you reserve the right to make your full, original claim in court. Even if you forget to add this, ask the judge for the full amount when you write your letter requesting judgment or when you get to court.

EXAMPLE: Elena rents a filthy apartment from MNO Realty. She does her best to clean it up, but after two months decides the place is hopeless. She provides a proper 30-day notice and moves out. MNO refuses to refund her $1,000 security deposit, claiming the unit is dirty. Elena sues in small claims, asking for $3,000, the extra $2,000 being for punitive damages (see Chapter 20). The day of the court hearing, she and MNO's owner agree to mediate. Worried that she may have trouble proving that she left the apartment cleaner than when she moved in, Elena agrees to accept her $1,000 deposit back with no damages. In the Mediation Agreement, the parties forget to specify what happens if MNO fails to pay. When MNO does, in fact, fail to pay Elena under the terms of the mediation agreement, she sends a short letter to the court, as follows:

Sample Letter Requesting Judgment

Patruska vs. MNO Realty

Small Claims # _____

Dear Judge:

I sued MNO Realty for failure to return my security deposit after I moved out of their duplex at 111 Maple Street, Santa Cruz, California, giving proper 30-day notice and leaving the unit cleaner than when I moved in. It has now been more than six months since I moved out. On November 23, 20xx, Peter Vargas of MNO and I participated in a mediation conference at Santa Cruz Small Claims Court, at which I agreed on a compromise settlement of $1,000. I did this primarily to get the case over with and to receive my $1,000, which I badly need. Had I realized that MNO would not pay me, I would never have agreed to waive the $600 punitive damages to which I believe I am fully entitled.

Accordingly, I am requesting that you enter a judgment for the $2,000 I sued for, not just the $1,000 I agreed to in mediation.

Sincerely,

Elena Patruska

Elena Patruska

Write a Formal Demand Letter

If your efforts to talk out your problems fail (or despite my urging you refuse to try) and you decide not to propose or agree to mediation, your next step is to send your adversary a letter.

Why Send a Demand Letter?

Many courts require you to make a formal "demand" for payment. But even where writing a formal demand letter isn't legally required, there are two reasons why doing so makes great sense. First, in as many as one-third of all disputes, your demand letter will serve as a catalyst to settlement. Second, even if no settlement results, setting out your case in a formal letter affords you an excellent opportunity to lay your case before the judge in a carefully organized way. Or, put another way, it allows you to "manufacture" evidence that you will likely be permitted to use in court if your case isn't settled.

EXAMPLE: Sunita purchases a designer dress on eBay from Maya. When it arrives, she realizes that the dress was meant to come with a jacket and is too skimpy to be worn without it. Maya refuses to take the dress back. She hangs up the phone whenever she hears Sunita's voice on the line. Sunita writes a demand letter outlining all of this and sends it via certified mail. Maya doesn't respond. In court, Maya feigns complete surprise, claiming, "I had no idea you had a problem with the dress—why didn't you say something before?" Sunita's demand letter, with its complete account of events, can now be used as evidence to back up Sunita's account of the dispute—and it will make Maya look less believable on the whole.

> ⊙ **CAUTION**
>
> **You can be sued without first being sent a formal letter stating that a lawsuit is imminent.** Some people believe they can't be sued until they receive a formal letter asking for payment and saying that a lawsuit will be filed if it isn't forthcoming. This is not necessarily true. A simple past-due notice form from a creditor, stating that if the account isn't paid promptly court action will be pursued, is usually sufficient. In addition, a judge has the power to conclude that an oral demand for payment is adequate.

In the 20-some years since I wrote the first edition of *Everybody's Guide to Small Claims Court,* readers have sent in hundreds of small claims success stories. One thing has consistently delighted me: Many self-proclaimed winners never had to file their small claims case in the first place. These readers took my advice and wrote the other party a clear, concise letter demanding payment. As a result of either the letter itself or conversations it engendered, they received all, or at least a significant part, of what they asked for.

That a simple letter can be so effective may at first seem paradoxical, especially if you have already unsuccessfully argued with your adversary in person or over the phone. To understand why the written word can be so much more effective, think about the times you have found yourself embroiled in a heated consumer dispute. After angry words were exchanged—maybe even including your threat of a lawsuit—what happened next? The answer is often "nothing." For any number of reasons, you didn't follow up on your "I'll sue you" threat. And, of course, you aren't the only one who hasn't made good on a declaration of intent to file a lawsuit. In fact, so many people who verbally threaten to sue don't actually do it that many potential defendants don't take such threats seriously.

But things often change if you write a letter, laying out the reasons why the other party owes you money and stating that if you fail to get satisfaction, you plan to go to small claims court. Now, instead of being just another cranky face on the other side of the counter or a voice on the phone, you and your dispute assume a sobering realness.

Really for the first time, the other party must confront the likelihood that you won't simply go away, but plan to have your day in court. And he must face the fact that he will have to expend time and energy to publicly defend his position and that you may win. In short, assuming your position has at least some merit, the chances that the other party will be willing to pay at least a portion of what you ask go way up when you make your case in writing.

How to Compose Your Letter

When writing your demand letter, here are some pointers to keep in mind:

Use a typewriter or computer. If you don't have a typewriter or computer, check your public library. Many have typewriters or computers that you can use for free or for a minimal charge.

Concisely review the main facts of the dispute. At first it may seem a bit odd to outline these details; after all, your opponent knows the story. But remember—if you end up in court, the letter will be read by a judge, and you want the judge to understand what happened. Now is a good chance to make a record not only of the initial dispute, but of any subsequent phone conversations, unanswered calls, or inappropriate conduct by the defendant.

Be polite. Absolutely avoid personally attacking your adversary (even one who deserves it). The more you attack, the more you invite the other side to respond in a similarly angry vein.

Write with your goal in mind. The letter should encourage your opponent to make a businesslike analysis of the dispute and ask herself such questions as:

- What are my risks of losing?
- How much time will a defense take?
- Do I want the dispute to be decided in public?

Ask for exactly what you want. For example, if you want $2,000, don't beat around the bush—ask for it (or possibly a little more to allow some negotiating room). Explain how you arrived at this figure. And be sure to set a deadline. One week (two weeks at the outside) is usually best; anything longer and your opponent has less motivation to deal with you right away. Supply the actual date, to remove any doubt.

Conclude by stating you will promptly pursue your legal remedies if your demand is not met. Remind the defendant that a court judgment could adversely affect his or her credit rating.

Make and keep copies. Make a copy of each letter before you send it, and keep a copy of the receipt for sending the letter certified mail with a return receipt requested. Keep all correspondence from your adversary, also.

Use certified mail. It's worth the hassle of standing in line at the post office to have proof that you sent the demand letter via certified mail with a return receipt requested. If you do end up in small claims court, you can use the receipt to counter your opponent's claim that she never received any demand letter.

TIP

Make sure you can prove the letter arrived. It's a good idea to send the demand letter by both certified mail with a return receipt and by regular mail. That way if the case does go to court, you can show the judge the certified mail receipt as proof that the defendant got your letter. Even if the defendant refuses to accept the certified mailing, the fact that you also sent the letter by regular mail and it wasn't returned to you will probably incline the judge to believe that the defendant received it.

A Real Small Claims Case—Bad Letters and Better Letters

Now let's consider a real small claims case. The facts (with a little editorial license) are simple: Jennifer moved into Peter's house in August, agreeing to pay $550 per month in rent. The house had four bedrooms, each occupied by one person. The kitchen and other common areas were shared. Things went well enough until one chilly evening in October, when Jennifer turned on the heat. Peter was right behind her to turn it off, explaining that heat inflamed his allergies.

As the days passed and fall deepened, heat became more and more of an issue, until one cold, late November night Jennifer returned home from her waitress job to find her room "about the same temperature as the inside of an icicle." After a short cry, she started packing and moved out the next morning. She refused to pay Peter any additional rent, claiming that she was within her rights to terminate her month-to-month tenancy without giving notice because the house was uninhabitable. It took Peter one month to find a suitable tenant and to have that person move in. Therefore, he lost rent in the amount of $550.

After calling Jennifer several times and asking her to repay the $550, only to have her slam down the phone in disgust, Peter wrote her the following letter:

61 Spring Street
Detroit, MI
January 1, 20xx

Jennifer Tenant
111 Lake Street
Detroit, MI

Dear Jennifer:

You are a real idiot. Actually, you're worse than that: you're malicious—walking out on me before Christmas and leaving me with no tenant when you know that I needed the money to pay my child support. You know that I promised to get you an electric room heater. Don't think I don't know that the real reason you moved out was to live with your boyfriend.

Please send me the $550 I lost because it took me a month to rerent the place. If you don't, I will sue you.

In aggravation,

Peter Landperson
Peter Landperson

To which Jennifer replied:

---

111 Lake Street
Detroit, MI
January 4, 20xx

Peter Landperson
61 Spring Street
Detroit, MI

Dear Mr. Landperson:

You nearly froze me to death, you cheap bastard. I am surprised it only took a month to rent that iceberg of a room—you must have found a rich polar bear (ha ha). People like you should be locked up.

I hope you choke on an ice cube.

Jennifer Tenant
Jennifer Tenant

Both Peter and Jennifer made the same mistake. Instead of being businesslike, each deliberately set out to annoy the other, reducing any chance of compromise. In addition, they each assumed that they were writing only to the other, forgetting that the judge would be privy to their sentiments. Thus, both lost a valuable chance to present the judge with a coherent summary of the facts as they saw them. As evidence in a subsequent court proceeding, both letters were worthless.

Now let's interrupt these proceedings and give Peter and Jennifer another chance to write sensible letters. You might want to interrupt your own proceedings and have a trusted friend read your letter before you send it.

Jennifer Tenant
61 Spring Street
Detroit, MI
January 1, 20xx

Jennifer Tenant
111 Lake Street
Detroit, MI

Dear Jennifer:

As you will recall, you moved into my house at 61 Spring Street on August 1, 20xx, agreeing to pay me $550 per month rent on the first of each month. On November 29, you suddenly moved out, having given me no advance notice whatsoever.

I realize that you were unhappy that the house was a little on the cool side, but I don't believe that this was a serious problem, as the temperature was at all times over 60 degrees and I had agreed to get you an electric heater for your room by December.

I was unable to get a tenant to replace you (although I tried every way I could and asked you for help) until January 1, 20xx. This means that I am short $550 rent for the room you occupied. If necessary, I will take this dispute to court because, as you know, I am on a very tight budget. I hope that this isn't necessary and that we can arrive at a sensible compromise.

I am also willing to try to mediate this dispute, if you agree. I have tried to call you with no success. Perhaps you can give me a call in the next week to talk this over.

Sincerely,

Peter Landperson
Peter Landperson

To which our now enlightened Jennifer promptly replied:

January 4, 20xx
111 Lake Street
Detroit, MI

Peter Landperson
61 Spring Street
Detroit, MI

Dear Peter:

I just received your letter concerning the rent at 61 Spring Street and am sorry to say that I don't agree either with the facts as you have presented them, or with your demand for back rent.

When I moved in August 1, 20xx, you never told me that you had an allergy and that there would be a problem keeping the house at a normal temperature. I would not have moved in had you informed me of this.

From early October, when we had the first cool evenings, all through November (almost two months), I asked that you provide heat. You didn't. Finally, it became unbearable to return from work in the middle of the night to a cold house, which was often below 60 degrees. It is true that I moved out suddenly, but I felt that I was within my rights under Michigan law, which clearly allows tenants to sue landlords for constructive eviction when the landlord fails to provide a necessity such as heat. In fact, you are lucky that I am not suing you for damages for constructive eviction.

Since you mentioned the nonexistent electric heater in your letter, let me respond to that. You first promised to get the heater over a month before I moved out and never did. Also, as I pointed out to you on several occasions, the heater was not a complete solution to the problem, as it would have heated only my room and not the kitchen, living room, or dining areas. You repeatedly told me that it would be impossible to heat these areas.

Peter, I sincerely regret the fact that you feel wronged, but I believe that I have been very fair with you. I am sure that you would have been able to rerent the room promptly if the house had been warm. I don't believe that any compromise is possible, so mediation does not make sense. If you wish to go to court, I'll be there with several witnesses who will support my position.

Sincerely,

Jennifer Tenant
Jennifer Tenant

As you can see, while the second two letters are less fun to read, they are far more informative. In this instance, the goal of reaching an acceptable compromise or agreeing to mediation was not met, but both parties have prepared a good outline of their positions for the judge. Of course, in court, both Peter and Jennifer will testify and present witnesses and possibly other evidence that will tell much the same story as is set out in the letters. However, court proceedings are often rushed and confused, and it's nice to have a written statement for the judge to fall back on. Be sure the judge is given a copy of your demand letter when your case is presented. The judge won't be able to guess that you have it; you will have to let her know and hand it to the clerk. (For more about how to conduct yourself in court, see Chapters 13–15.)

Sample Demand Letters

Below are letters a consumer might write to an auto repair shop after being victimized by a shoddy repair job and to a contractor who botched a remodeling contract.

Sample Letter: Car Repair

June 16, 20xx

Tucker's Fix-It-Quick Garage
9938 Main Street
Houston, TX

Dear Mr. Tucker,

On May 21, 20xx, I took my car to your garage for servicing. Shortly after picking it up the next day, the engine caught fire because of your failure to properly connect the fuel line to the fuel injector. Fortunately, I was able to douse the fire without injury.

As a direct result of the engine fire, I paid the ABC garage $1,281 for necessary repair work. I enclose a copy of their invoice.

In addition, I was without the use of my car for three days and had to rent a car to get to work. I enclose a copy of an invoice showing the rental cost of $145.

In a recent phone conversation, you claimed that the fire wasn't the result of your negligence and would have happened anyway. And you said that even if it was your fault, I should have brought my car back to your garage so you could have fixed it at a lower cost.

As to the first issue, Peter Klein of the ABC Garage is prepared to testify in court that the fire occurred because the fuel line was not properly connected to the fuel injector, the exact part of the car you were working on.

Second, I had no obligation to return the car to you for further repair. I had the damage you caused repaired at a commercially reasonable price and am prepared to prove this by presenting several higher estimates by other garages.

Please send me a check or money order for $1,426 on or before July 15. If I don't receive payment by that date, I'll promptly file this case in small claims court. And assuming I receive a judgment, which will be part of the public record available to credit agencies, I will promptly follow all legal avenues to collect it.

You may reach me during the day at 555-2857 or in the evenings until 10 p.m. at 555-8967.

Sincerely,

Marsha Rizzoli

Marsha Rizzoli

Sample Letter: Home Contractor

June 20, 20xx

Beyond Repair Construction
10 Delaney Avenue
Seattle, WA

Dear Sirs:

You recently did replacement tile work and other remodeling on my downstairs bathroom at 142 West Pine Street, here in Seattle. As per our written agreement, I paid you $4,175 upon completion of the job on May 17, 20xx.

Only two weeks later, on June 1, I noticed that the tile in the north portion of the shower had sunk almost half an inch, with the result that our shower floor was uneven and water pooled in the downhill corner before eventually going down the drain.

In our telephone conversations, you variously claimed that the problem:

- was in my imagination
- was my fault, because the floor was uneven to begin with, or
- was too minor to bother with.

Sorry, but I paid for a first-class remodeling job, and I expect to receive it. Please contact me within ten days to arrange to pay me $1,200 (the cost of redoing the work per the enclosed estimate from ABC Tile) or to arrange to redo the work yourself. If I don't hear from you by June 15, 20xx I will promptly file in small claims court.

Sincerely,

Ben Price
Ben Price

Write Down the Terms of Any Settlement

If you and the other party agree to a settlement, either on your own or with the help of a mediator, it's important to promptly write it down. When a mediator is involved, preparing a written agreement is usually the last step in the mediation process. If you and your opponent negotiate your own settlement, you'll need to cooperate to reduce it to writing. Lawyers call an agreement to settle a dispute a "release," because in exchange for some act (often the payment of money), one person gives up (or releases) her claim against another. For instance, if the paint on John's building is damaged when Sandra, a neighboring property owner, spray-paints her building on a windy day, John might agree to release Sandra from liability (that is, not sue Sandra) if she agrees to pay $2,000 to have the damaged area of John's building repainted.

A written release is valid if it is signed by both parties; is fair, in the sense that neither party was tricked into signing on the basis of a misrepresentation; and provides each party with some benefit (if you pay me $500, I won't sue you and I'll keep my dog out of your yard). If either party later violates the terms of the settlement, the other can file a lawsuit and receive a court judgment for appropriate damages.

It's important to understand that settlement agreements are powerful legal documents. If you completely release someone who damaged your car for $500, only to later find out that the damage was more extensive, you'll be stuck with the $500 unless you can convincingly claim that the other party was guilty of misrepresentation or fraud in getting you to sign the settlement agreement. Of course, in most situations, where the details of a dispute are all well known, a settlement can be comfortably signed with the knowledge that the dispute will finally be laid to rest.

Get the Court's Stamp of Approval

Assuming a small claims case has actually been filed, you may have a choice as to whether your agreement is presented to a judge and made part of a court order or is simply written as a binding contract between you and the other party. Especially if it's less trouble (sometimes getting a court order involves an extra trip to court), you may be tempted to accept a contract and not bother with a court order. Generally, I recommend against this unless you are sure the other party really will honor the agreement. A court order (judgment) is far easier to enforce than a contract. Especially if you suspect that the other side may not do what they promise, it is definitely worth a little extra effort to have your settlement contract incorporated into a judgment of a court. (This obviously won't be possible if the dispute is settled before a small claims lawsuit is even filed.)

Below we provide a sample release ("Sample General Release") adopted from Nolo's book, *101 Law Forms for Personal Use,* by Robin Leonard and Ralph Warner. That book contains a number of specialized releases adapted to auto accidents, property damage, and personal injuries that I don't have space to reprint here. It also contains mutual release forms for use when both parties are giving up claims. In addition, release forms are often available from office supply stores that carry legal documents and from lawyers' form books, available at law libraries.

No matter where you get your release, it should contain the following information:

- The names and addresses of the party being released (the potential defendant) and the party granting the release (the potential plaintiff).

- A brief description of the "what," "when," and "where" of the dispute or issue to which the release pertains. (The release below provides several blank lines for your use in briefly describing the events giving rise to the need for the release.)

- A statement of what the person giving up a claim is getting in return. As mentioned, for a release to be a valid and enforceable contract, the person signing the release (releasor) must receive something of benefit (called "consideration" by lawyers) in exchange for agreeing to give up the right to sue. The release below provides a space for this "consideration" to be described. Typically, it is money. If so, simply enter the amount. If it is an agreement by the releasee to perform or not perform some act (for example, stop his dog from barking at night), describe the act.

- A statement that the release applies to all claims arising from the dispute or issue, both those known at the time the release is signed and those that may come along later. This provision is very common in releases; without it they wouldn't be worth much.

- A statement that the release binds all persons who might otherwise have a legal right to file a claim on behalf of the releasor (for example, the releasor's spouse or heirs). Although I have included this provision in my releases for caution's sake, it is rare that it will ever prove relevant. In fact, such persons are usually bound by the release anyway.

- The date the release is signed.

- The signatures of the parties. Legally, only the person granting a release needs to sign it, but we think it is a better practice for both parties to do so—after all, this important document contains statements that affect both of their rights. In the case of mutual releases, which occur when both parties give up a claim against the other, both must sign.

TIP

Use witnesses. There is no legal requirement for a release to be witnessed, but if you don't completely trust the other person and think he may later claim "it's not my signature," a witness can be a good idea. If a release involves a lot of money or a potentially large claim, you may want to bolster the chances of its being upheld (should it ever be challenged later) by signing it in front of a witness or two who can later testify, if the issue arises, that the other party was under no duress and appeared to know what he was doing. If your release involves a small claim, it is not necessary to do this.

Sample General Release

1.   _[person signing release and agreeing not to sue]_   , Releasor, voluntarily and knowingly executes this release with the express intention of eliminating Releasee's liabilities and obligations as described below.

2.   Releasor hereby releases   _[person being released]_   , Releasee, from all claims, known or unknown, that have arisen or may arise from the following occurrence: _[description of events giving rise to release, including location and date if appropriate—see box for sample language]_   .

> Sample Language:
>   a.   "Repair work incompletely done to Releasor's boat at the Fixmeup Shipyards on 5/6/04."
>   b.   "Agreement by Releasee made during the week of June 6, 20xx, to deliver the fully laid out and pasted-up manuscript for the book *Do Your Own Brain Surgery* to Releasor's address no later than July 6, 20xx, which Releasee failed to keep."
>   c.   "A tree growing on Releasee's property at 1011 Oak Street fell into Releasor's backyard at 1013 Oak Street on August 7, 20xx. It damaged Releasor's fence, which had to be replaced. The tree itself had to be removed."

3.   Releasor understands that, as to claims that are known to the parties when the release is signed, any statutory provisions that would otherwise apply to limit this general release are hereby waived. Releasor also understands that this release extends to claims arising out of this incident that are not known by Releasor at the time this release is signed.

4.   In exchange for granting this release Releasor has received the following payment or other consideration: _[amount of money, or description of something else of value that person signing release received from other party—see box for sample language]_   .

> Sample Language:
>   a.   "$150 cash."
>   b.   "A used RCA television set."
>   c.   "An agreement by   _[Releasee's name]_   to desist from further activities as described in Clause 3 of this release."
>   d.   "An agreement by   _[Releasee's name]_   to repair Releasor's Apple Macintosh computer by January, 20xx."

Sample General Release (cont'd)

5. By signing this release Releasor additionally intends to bind his or her spouse, heirs, legal representatives, assigns, and anyone else claiming under him or her. Releasor has not assigned any claim covered by this release to any other party. Releasor also intends that this release apply to the heirs, personal representatives, assigns, insurers, and successors of Releasee as well as to the Releasee.

This release was executed on _____, 20__, at ____*[city and state]*____

_____   _____
Releasor's signature   Date

_____   _____
Releasor's name (print)   County of residence

_____
Releasor's address

_____   _____
Releasor's spouse's signature   Date

_____   _____
Releasor's spouse's name (print)   County of residence

_____   _____
Releasee's signature   Date

_____   _____
Releasee's name (print)   County of residence

_____
Releasee's address

_____   _____
Releasee's spouse's signature   Date

_____   _____
Releasee's spouse's name (print)   County of residence

_____   _____
Witness's signature   Date

_____   _____
Witness's name (print)   County of residence

_____
Witness's address

_____   _____
Witness's signature   Date

_____   _____
Witness's name (print)   County of residence

_____
Witness's address

Agreement Just Before Court Hearing

Occasionally, disputes are settled while you are waiting for your case to be heard. Even on the day you go to court, it is proper to ask the other person to step into the hall for a moment to talk the matter over. If you can agree on a last-minute compromise, wait until the courtroom clerk calls your case by name and then tell the judge the amount you have agreed upon and whether the amount is to be paid all at once, or over time. Typically, the judge will order that the case be dismissed if one person pays the other the agreed-upon amount on the spot, or, if payment is to be made later, she will enter a judgment for the amount that you have agreed on.

Another possibility is that you and your opponent will agree to a last-minute attempt to mediate. If so, you will want to explain this to the judge, who in turn will normally delay ("continue," in legalese) your case until the mediation session takes place. If mediation works and your case settles, you and the other party should jointly notify the court clerk. Again, unless the agreed-upon amount is immediately paid, the debtor will normally want to return to court and have the settlement amount made part of an official court order (judgment). ●

Who Can Sue?

Who can sue in small claims court? The answer is easy. You can—as long as you:

- are 18 years of age or an emancipated minor,
- have not been declared mentally incompetent in a judicial proceeding, and
- are suing on your own claim.

 CAUTION

Special requirements for some plaintiffs. Some states do not let unlicensed contractors and other businesspeople who work without required licenses to bring suit on claims related to their business. Prisoners are allowed to sue in some states but not in others. In states where they can sue, their cases must usually be presented in writing. (In a few states, prisoners can name an adult representative to appear on their behalf.) Check your state's small claims rules before bringing suit.

What If You Want to Sue but Can't Appear in Court?

People who will find it difficult or impossible to show up in small claims court to present their case often ask whether there is another way to proceed. For people in certain categories—prisoners, business owners, landlords, and certain military personnel stationed out of state—the answer may be yes (check your state's rules for details). Even if you don't fit into an approved category, a small claims judge has the discretion to hear your case through a nonlawyer representative if you convince the judge that for some good reason, such as bad health or advanced age, you need assistance and the person you send to court is familiar with what happened. To see whether this procedure will work in your situation, talk to your county's small claims court advisor.

Married Couples

What if you and your spouse co-own a car that is vandalized by your neighbor's teenager? What if you and your spouse are both listed as payees on a bad check? These are called "joint claims" and you and your spouse can and should sue together. If you are a married couple with a joint claim, you should both list your names as plaintiffs. It is usually okay for one spouse to appear at the hearing on behalf of both spouses as long as:

- the claim is joint
- the represented spouse has given written consent, which you should bring to court, and
- the court determines the interests of justice would be served.

Employees May Appear on Behalf of a Business

States used to require the owner of a business to show up in small claims court personally. This discouraged the owners of many small unincorporated businesses from using small claims court. For example, a dentist who wished to sue on an overdue bill would have had to show up in court.

These days, a number of states are more understanding of business time pressures. If a business (incorporated or unincorporated) wishes to sue on an unpaid bill, it can often send an employee to court to testify about the debt as it is reflected in the written records of the business. For instance, in many states, a landlord suing for unpaid rent can send a property manager to court to establish the fact that the rent was unpaid (but see cautions about bringing eviction cases in small claims court in Chapter 20). For a business owner to invoke this time-saving procedure, the employee sent to court must be familiar with the company's books and able to testify about how the debt was entered in them.

Make sure that anyone who goes to small claims court on behalf of your business has firsthand knowledge about the dispute. For example, if your rug store is suing a customer who refuses to pay because a carpet was improperly installed, you will probably lose if you send to court only your bookkeeper, who knows nothing about what happened on the particular job. In this situation, some judges may postpone the case for a few days to allow the business owner to show up with the carpet installer and present testimony about the quality of the repair, but don't count on it—try to send the appropriate person the first time.

Sole Proprietorships

If you own a small business and are the sole proprietor, you will list both your name and the name of your business on your court papers. Generally, a sole proprietor must appear personally at the court hearing.

> **CAUTION**
> **Does your business use a fictitious name?** Most states require companies that use a fictitious name (such as Tasty Donut Shop) to file a declaration stating that you have properly executed, filed, and published a fictitious business name statement as required by your state's law. Check with the small claims clerk.

Business Partnerships

If you are filing a claim on behalf of a partnership, you should sue on behalf of the individual partners and the partnership itself. When it comes to appearing in court, most states allow either a partner or a regular employee to do so.

Corporations

If you are filing a claim on behalf of a corporation, whether profit or nonprofit, list the corporation itself as the plaintiff. The corporation may be represented at the hearing by either:

- an officer or director of the corporation, or
- an employee who is authorized to file claims on behalf of the corporation by the corporation's board of directors. If a nonofficer of a corporation signs the forms, the court clerk may want to see some documentation that the person suing is properly authorized.

Limited Liability Companies

List the limited liability company (LLC) as the plaintiff. Most states allow any member to appear in court. But check your local rules; LLCs are fairly new, so procedures are still in flux in many states.

Nonprofits and Unincorporated Associations

If you are suing on behalf of a nonprofit corporation or an unincorporated association, the Plaintiff's Claim should list the name of the corporation or association and the name of an officer or director who will appear in court (such as, "ABC Canine Happiness Society, by Philip Pup, Executive Director"). An officer may represent the nonprofit or unincorporated association at the hearing.

Motor Vehicle Claims

When a claim arises out of damage to a motor vehicle, the registered owner(s) of the vehicle must file in small claims court. So, if you are driving someone else's car and get hit by a third party, you can't sue for damage done to the car. The registered owner must file the lawsuit.

Government Agencies

If you are suing on behalf of a government agency such as a public library, city tax assessor's office, or county hospital, you should list the organization's official name as the plaintiff. When you file the papers, you must show the court clerk proper authorization to sue.

Special Rules for Prisoners and Military Personnel Transferred Out of State

In some states, prisoners are not allowed to bring small claims lawsuits. Other states have special procedures for prisoners who want to sue in small claims court. In California, for example, a prisoner who wants to sue in small claims court must file papers by mail and then either submit testimony in the form of written declarations or have another person appear on his or her behalf in court (Cal. Civ. Proc. Code § 116.540(f)).

In some states, military personnel who have been transferred out of state are also allowed to bring small claims court cases without having to appear in court personally. Check your state rules for information on how to do this.

Suits by Minors

If you are under 18 years old, your parent or legal guardian must sue for you. The exception is that, in some states, emancipated minors can sue on their own. When your parents or guardians sue on your behalf, they must fill out a form asking to have one of them appointed your guardian ad litem and have the form signed by the judge. "Guardian ad litem" means "guardian for the purposes of the lawsuit." Ask the court clerk for the rules in your state.

Class Actions (Group Lawsuits)

In small claims court there is no such thing as a true class action lawsuit, where a number of people in a similar situation ask a court's permission to join together in one lawsuit against the same defendant. However, as many community and advocacy groups have discovered, if a large number of people with a particular grievance (pollution, noise, drug sales) sue the same defendant at the same time in small claims courts, something remarkably like a class action is created.

This technique was pioneered in the early 1980s by a group of determined homeowners who lived near the San Francisco airport. Several times, the group won more than 100 small claims court judgments against the City of San Francisco, based on excessive noise. They hired expert witnesses, did research, ran training workshops, and paid for legal advice when needed, as part of a coordinated effort to efficiently present their cases. The City of San Francisco tried to fend off these cases by arguing that the homeowners were, in effect, involved in a class action lawsuit and such suits are not permitted in small claims court. A California court of appeals disagreed, saying, "Numerous 'mass' actions against the City alleging that noise from the City airport constituted a continuing nuisance were neither too 'complex' nor had such 'broad social policy import' that they were outside the jurisdiction of Small Claims Court…." (*City and County of San Francisco v. Small Claims Div., San Mateo Co.,* 190 Cal.Rptr. 340 (1983).)

A similar strategy has been widely used in many cities to shut down drug houses. Neighbors organize to sue landlords who rent to drug-selling tenants, claiming the legal theory of nuisance (use of property that unreasonably interferes with the rights of others—Chapter 2). In these cases the neighbors claimed the nuisance was the emotional and mental distress that accompanied living near a drug house. Typically, each neighbor sues for the maximum amount. Thus, 30 neighbors who coordinate their small claims filings can, together, bring what amounts to a $225,000 case. A number of drug house cases have resulted in large judgments, and problems that had dragged on for months or years were quickly cleaned up.

Successful mass small claims lawsuits based on legal nuisance have also been brought against polluting refineries and factories.

JUDGES' TIPS

Group lawsuits can lend credibility and weight to a "neighborhood quarrel." One of the purposes of the small claims court is to provide a neighborhood forum to resolve group lawsuits that might otherwise clog up the higher courts. If neighbors can band together to address problems of barking dogs, rock bands, drug houses, and so on, each individual's case will be that much more credible to the judge.

—Commissioner Douglas G. Carnahan

TIP

Select a small committee to coordinate your lawsuits. When a good-sized group of plaintiffs all sue the same defendant based on the same grievance, it's wise to coordinate strategy. This typically involves creating an informal plaintiffs' organization to organize intergroup communications, find witnesses and, if needed, expert witnesses (see Chapter 14), conduct a training session for everyone who will testify in court, discuss settlement offers, and, if requested, meet with the judge to plan how to efficiently and effectively present your multiple cases in court.

CAUTION

Losing defendants have the right to a new trial on appeal. People who sue and beat corporations, governmental entities, and other defendants with deep pockets in small claims court are likely to be faced with a tougher battle on appeal. That's because all losing small claims defendants have the right to appeal to superior court, where both sides have the right to be represented by a lawyer. (See Chapter 23.)

Participation by Attorneys and Bill Collectors

In the majority of states, you are permitted to be represented by an attorney in small claims court. In some states, attorneys are allowed only if the judge consents, and in still other states attorneys required if the party is a corporation. Some states don't allow representation by attorneys at all. (See the Appendix for your state's rules.)

Even in states that don't allow lawyers in small claims court, it is still perfectly legal to get an attorney's advice about your small claims case.

Many states, including Arkansas, California, Colorado, Kentucky, Michigan, Missouri, Montana, Nebraska, New York, Ohio, Oklahoma, and Texas, forbid the use of small claims court by "assignees" (a fancy term that usually refers to collection agencies). In other words, in these states you cannot hire someone to sue for an unpaid debt. But the majority of states still allow suits by collection agencies. Check with your small claims court clerk for information.

TIP

Attorneys can always bring suits on their own behalf. Even in states that don't allow attorneys to represent someone else in small claims court, attorneys are allowed to sue on or defend their own claims. ●

Who Can Be Sued?

You are allowed to sue just about any defendant—person, sole proprietorship, partnership, corporation, LLC, or government entity—in small claims court. Under certain circumstances, you can even sue out-of-staters. Indeed, figuring out where to sue (see Chapter 9) is often more difficult than figuring out who to sue.

CAUTION

No suits against the federal government in California courts. To sue the United States government, you must file in federal, not state, court. Contact the nearest federal district court clerk's office for information.

How to Sue One Person

If you are suing an individual, simply name the person on the form, using the most complete name that you know for that person. If the person calls himself J.R. Smith and you don't know what the J.R. stands for, simply sue him as J.R. Smith. However, if with a little effort you can find out that J stands for James, it's better to sue him as James R. Smith.

TIP

What to do if a person uses several names. Lots of people use two or more names. Thus Jason Graboskawitz may also use J.T. Grab. When in doubt, list the name the person uses most often for business purposes first, followed by the words "also known as" (or "a.k.a.") and any other names. Thus you might sue Jason Graboskawitz, a.k.a. J.T. Grab.

How to Sue Two or More People

If you are suing more than one person on a claim arising from the same incident or contract, list the complete names of all defendants. Then you must "serve" (deliver copies of court papers to) each of them to bring them properly before the court. (See Chapter 11.) Listing both names is also required when the defendants are husband and wife: List the defendants as John Randolph Smith and Jane Smith, husband and wife. Or, if you don't know the name of one spouse: John Randolph Smith and Mrs. John Randolph Smith, husband and wife.

> **EXAMPLE:** J.R. and June Smith, who are married, borrow $1,200 from you to start an avocado pit polishing business. Unfortunately, in the middle of the polishing, the seeds begin to sprout. J.R. and June get so furious that they refuse to repay you. If you wish to sue them and get a judgment, you should list them as James R. Smith and June Smith—not Mr. and Mrs. Smith. But now suppose that J.R. borrowed $1,200 for the avocado pit business in January, June borrowed $1,000 to fix her motorcycle a month later, and neither loan was repaid. In this situation, you would sue each in separate small claims actions.

TIP

Two defendants are better than one, and three are better than two. If two or more people are responsible for your loss (for example, if three tenants damaged your apartment), sue them all. This will enable you to get judgments against several people. You'll be glad you did when you try to collect—if one defendant turns out to be an artful dodger, you can go after the others. (For more information on collecting your judgment, see Chapter 24.)

How to Sue an Individually Owned Business

List the name of the owner and the name of the business (Ralph C. Jones, individually and doing business as [d.b.a.] Jones's Texaco). But never just assume that the name of the business is really the same as the name of the owner. For all you know, Jim's Garage may be owned by Pablo Garcia Motors, Inc. (On suing a corporation, see below.) If you get a judgment against Jim's Garage and there is no Jim, it will be worthless unless you take steps to have the judgment changed to reflect the correct name. This can take extra time and trouble. Far better to be sure you sue the right person in the first place.

A few states have liberalized their rules and do not penalize plaintiffs who incorrectly state the business defendant's name. New York allows a plaintiff to sue a defendant under any name used in conducting business if it is impossible to find out the defendant's true name. California allows a plaintiff to correct a defendant's name at the time of the hearing and, in some cases, after judgment, when the defendant is a business person using a fictitious name.

How to Find Out Who Owns a Business

Many states require that all people who do business using a name other than their own file a fictitious business name statement with the county clerk in the county or counties in which the business operates. This is public information that you can get from the county clerk. Another way to figure out who owns a business is to check with the business tax and license office in the city where the business is located. (If the business is not located in an incorporated city, try the county.) The tax and license office will have a list of the owners of all businesses paying taxes in the city. They should be able to tell you, for example, that the Garden of Exotic Delights is owned by Rufus Clod. Once you find this out, you sue Rufus Clod, individually and d.b.a. The Garden of Exotic Delights.

 If for some reason the tax and license office or the county clerk can't help, you may want to check with the state. Millions of people, from exterminators to embalmers, must register with one or another office in their state. So, if your beef is with a teacher, architect, smog control device installer, holder of a beer or wine license, or member of another profession that must register, you will very likely be able to learn who and where the person or business is with a letter or phone call. Check for the name of the profession in the phone book under the state government listings, or search your state's official website for the name of the profession. When you find an agency that looks like it should have jurisdiction over the type of business you wish to sue, call its public information number and explain your problem. It may take a little persistence, but eventually you should get the help you need.

How to Sue a Partnership

All partners in a general partnership business are individually liable for all the acts of the business. It follows that you should list the names of all the business partners, even if your dispute is only with one (Patricia Sun and Farah Moon, d.b.a. Sacramento Gardens). See below for information on how to learn who owns a particular partnership.

> **EXAMPLE:** You go to a local cleaners with your new sky blue suit. They put too much cleaning fluid on it, which results in a small gray cloud that settles on the right rear shoulder. After unsuccessfully trying to get the cleaners to take responsibility for improving the weather on the back of your suit, you start thinking about a different kind of suit. When you start filling out your court papers (see Chapter 10), you realize that you know only that the store says "Perfection Cleaners" on the front, and that the guy who has been so unpleasant to you is named Bob. You call the city business tax and license people and they tell you that Perfection Cleaners is owned by Robert Johnson and Sal De Benno. You should sue both and also list the name of the business (Robert Johnson and Sal De Benno, d.b.a. Perfection Cleaners).

> **CAUTION**
>
> **Special procedures to sue limited partnerships.** Limited partnerships normally consist of one or a few general partners who are subject to being sued, and a number of limited partners who, as investors, normally can't be sued. So if you are suing a limited partnership, list the name of the partnership itself and the general partner or partners. Do not list the limited partners. Limited partnerships must register with the secretary of state. For information on who to sue and serve with papers, contact the secretary of state.

How to Sue a Corporation or Limited Liability Company (LLC)

Corporations and limited liability companies (LLCs) are legal people. This means that you can sue, and enforce a judgment against, the business entity itself. You should not sue the owners, officers, or managers of the corporation or LLC as individuals, unless you have a personal claim against them that is separate from their role in the corporation or LLC. That's because in most situations, the real people who own or operate the corporation or LLC aren't themselves legally liable to pay the corporation's or LLC's debts. This concept is called "personal limited liability" and is one big reason why many people choose to incorporate or form an LLC in the first place.

Be sure to list the full name of the corporation or LLC when you file suit (John's Liquors, Inc., a Corporation, or John's Liquors, LLC). Here again, the name on the door or on the stationery may not be the organization's real name, as corporations and LLCs sometimes use fictitious names. To be sure, check with the city or county business license people where the corporation or LLC is headquartered. Information is also usually available from either the secretary of state or the corporations commissioner's office, located in your state capital.

You may sue a corporation or LLC in your state if it does business there, even if its headquarters are in another state.

How to Name Defendants in a Motor Vehicle Accident Case

Special rules apply when it comes to motor vehicle accidents. In most states, if your claim arises from an accident with an automobile, motorcycle, truck, or RV, you should name both the driver of the vehicle and the registered owner as defendants. This is because the vehicle's owner may be liable even if she wasn't driving. Most of the time, you will obtain this information at the time of the accident. If the police make an accident report, it will contain this information. You can get a copy of any police report from the police department for a modest fee. If there was no police report—and assuming you have the license number of the offending vehicle—contact the Department of Motor Vehicles. Tell them you want to find out who owns a vehicle and her address, for purposes of filing and serving a lawsuit based on a motor vehicle accident. This is a legitimate reason in most states, and you will get the information you need. However, in some states, the owner of the car will be notified of your request.

Remember, when you sue more than one person (in this case the driver and the owner, if they are different), serve papers on both. When a business owns a vehicle, sue both the driver and the owners of the business. If a minor child is driving the car, find out the names of her parents and, if possible, whether they gave her permission to drive. (See "How to Sue Minors," below.)

EXAMPLE: You are involved in a car accident, and the driver of the other car is a young woman who first identifies herself as "Suzie Q" and then tells the police that her name is Suzanne Quigley. When you try to talk to Suzie about paying to replace your smashed headlight, she blows you off. You request a copy of the accident report from the police and find out that Suzanne is 17 and was driving a car owned by her parents, whose names are George and Mary Quigley. You strike out when you ask Suzanne's parents to pay for the damage but find out she was driving the car with their permission. When you sue, you list the defendants as follows: Suzanne Quigley, also known as Suzie Q, a minor; and George Quigley and Mary Quigley, husband and wife and parents of defendant Suzanne Quigley and co-owners of the motor vehicle.

How to Sue Minors

It is very difficult to succeed when you sue a minor for breach of contract, because minors can disavow (back out of) any contract they sign as long as they do it before they turn 18, unless the contract was for a necessity of life—for example, food—in which case the minor's parents are probably responsible. You can sue "emancipated minors," that is, people under 18 who are legally treated as adults. This includes minors who are on active duty in the armed services, are married, or have been emancipated (freed from parental control) by court order.

What about damage caused by minors? Although it is legal to sue minors for injuring you or damaging your property, it's rarely worthwhile, because most are broke and therefore can't pay the judgment. (There are exceptions, of course.) However, if you do wish to sue someone under 18, do it like this: "John Jeffrey, a minor, and William Jeffrey, his father."

But what about suing the offending kid's parents? Normally, a parent is not legally responsible to pay for damages negligently caused by his children. However, there are some exceptions to this rule. In virtually all states, if a child is guilty of "malicious or willful misconduct," a parent may be liable up to a certain dollar amount per act for all property damage ($10,000 in some states; often a lot more if a gun is involved) and sometimes for personal injuries. Parents may also be liable for damage done by their minor children in auto accidents, if they authorized the child to drive. (Check the index to your state's laws under "Minors," "Children," or "Parent and Child" for your rules.)

EXAMPLE 1: John Johnson, age 17, trips over his shoelace while delivering your newspaper and crashes through your glass door. Can you recover from John's parents? Probably not, as John is not guilty of "willful misconduct."

EXAMPLE 2: John shoots out the same glass door with a slingshot after you have repeatedly asked his parents to disarm him. Can you recover from the parents? Probably.

How to Sue Government Agencies

Many states have special rules and procedures that must be followed before a suit can be brought against a state or local government agency. Often, you have to act very quickly or you lose your right to sue. Your local small claims court clerk will be able to advise you as to the procedures you must follow and time limits you must meet.

Let's look at the rules of a state we will call Typical. Before you can sue a city because your car was illegally towed away, a city employee damaged your property or injured you, or the city did anything else to you involving personal injury or property damage, you must first file a claim with the city and have it denied. To do this, get a claim form from the city clerk. For cases involving a personal injury or damage to property, your claim must be filed within six months of the date of the incident. For claims involving breach of contract or damage to real property, you have one year in which to file your claim. The city attorney will review your claim and make a recommendation to the city council. Sometimes the recommendation will be to pay you, but most often it will be to deny your claim, no matter how meritorious. Once the city council acts, you will receive a form letter. If it's a denial, you have six months in which to file your small claims case. Attach a copy of the denial letter to your small claims complaint; the small claims clerk will want to see it.

The rules for suits against counties and districts (for example, school districts) are basically the same. Get a complaint form from the clerk of the county board of supervisors (or the board governing the district). Complete and file it promptly (six months for personal injury or property damage; one year for breach of contract or damage to real property). Within a month or so after filing, you will be told whether your claim is approved or denied. If your claim is denied, you can then proceed to file in small claims court within six months.

Claims against a department of the State of Typical must also be filed within six months for personal injury and property damage, and one year for breach of contract or damages to real property.

> ⓘ **CAUTION**
>
> **No lawsuits against the U.S. government in small claims court.** You can't bring a small claims suit against the federal government, a federal agency, or even against a federal employee for actions relating to his or her employment. The federal government may not be sued in any state court without its consent. Suits against the federal government normally must be filed in federal district court.

How to Sue the Estates of Deceased People

Death does not prevent lawsuits from being brought or judgments from being collected against the deceased's estate. However, it does present a number of technical legal hurdles.

Assuming the defendant made a will (or died without a will or other estate-planning device such as a living trust), a probate proceeding will be held. All claims against the estate should be made promptly, in writing, to the personal representative of the deceased person's estate and directly to the probate court. If the personal representative knows about the debt owed to you, you should receive a formal notice to file your claim—but this won't happen if your debt isn't known. If you don't receive notice promptly after a person who owes you money dies, and you don't know who the personal representative is (usually it's a surviving spouse, adult child, or other close relative), check court probate filing records in the county where the defendant lived at the time of his death. If the personal representative doesn't honor your claim, you will need to file suit within three months.

It's possible that in some instances you may check for a probate filing and not find one. That's because these days, many people use living trusts and other devices to transfer the property of a deceased person directly to the inheritors. Your best bet is to present your claim to the deceased person's spouse, child, or close relative. If it is denied or ignored, you have the right to file suit against anyone who inherits from the deceased. Do it as soon as possible. ●

Where Can You Sue?

S mall claims courts are local. This makes sense, because the dollar amounts involved aren't large enough to justify people traveling great distances to go to court. A small claims court judicial district is the same as a county. The next county will have its own similar, but separate, small claims court. Normally, your dispute will be with a person or business located nearby. If so, all you really need to know is that you can sue in the county in which the defendant lives or, if a business is involved, where its main place of business is located.

Occasionally, however, the person or business you want to sue resides at a considerable distance from where you live. How you should proceed in this situation depends primarily on whether the defendant is located in your state or a different state.

Where to Sue Out-of-State Defendants

Skip ahead to "Suits Against Out-of-State Businesses," below, if you're planning to sue a business. Otherwise, read on.

Suits Against Out-of-State Individuals

The basic rule is that state courts—including small claims courts—only have the power (lawyers call this jurisdiction) to hear cases involving individuals who live in or are present in the state. If you want to sue someone who lives in another state and doesn't travel to your state, you will have to sue in the state where the person lives, not in the state where you live. Often you can file papers by mail, but normally you'll need to show up in person on court day. (Some states allow people on active duty in the military and occasionally others to present their case entirely in writing.)

There are, however, three circumstances under which you can use your state's small claims court to sue an out-of-state resident:

1. Out-of-state residents can successfully be sued in-state if you manage to serve them with court papers while they're physically within your state's borders *and* if the dispute arose in your state. For example, you live in Florida and a nonresident injures you or damages your property while he or she is in Florida, or a contract with a nonresident was negotiated, performed, or violated in Florida. (On serving court papers, see Chapter 11.)

2. A nonresident who has a vehicle accident in your state may be sued in your state's small claims court no matter where he lives. Similarly, a nonresident owner of a vehicle may be sued no matter where he lives if his car was being driven in your state by another person and was involved in an accident. Contact your small claims court clerk for details.

3. The out-of-state owner of real property (including owners of apartments and other rental housing) located in your state may be sued here on claims relating to that property.

Suits Against Out-of-State Businesses

When it comes to suing a business in small claims court, you may sue any business that is organized (incorporated or established as an LLC) in your state.

In addition, you may bring suit against any business—whether incorporated or not—if one of the following conditions is true:

- the business was responsible for injuring you or damaging your property in your state *and* you can find a way to serve your court papers on the business in your state (see Chapter 11 on serving court papers)

- the business breaches a contract with you that was negotiated or was to be performed in your state *and* you can find a way to serve your court papers on the business in your state (see Chapter 11 on serving court papers)

- the business has an office, warehouse, retail establishment, restaurant, or other physical facility here, even if that business is headquartered or organized elsewhere, or
- the business does regular business in your state by selling products or services, employing a sales rep who calls on you personally or by phone to solicit business, sending you a catalog to solicit your business, or placing advertising in your state's media.

> **TIP**
>
> **The short story about suing out-of-state businesses.** What it comes down to is that most large national businesses can be sued in any state, but smaller businesses that are headquartered in another state, do no business in your state, and have no physical presence in your state can be sued only in the states where they operate.

EXAMPLE 1: While on vacation in Florida, you slip and fall in the ticket office of a small locally owned commuter airline that operates only in Florida. When you return home to Maine, you file suit against the airline for your injuries in small claims court. The judge will toss out your case, because Maine courts do not have the power (jurisdiction) to hear a case involving a defendant that doesn't operate, advertise, or solicit business in Maine. The only place you can sue the little airline is in Florida.

EXAMPLE 2: You're at home in Maine and planning your vacation to Florida, and you slip and fall in the ticket office of a national airline that has its headquarters in Florida. This time, you can sue the airline for your injuries in small claims court. The fact that the airline does business in Maine gives this state's courts the power to hear your case, even though the airline has its headquarters elsewhere.

EXAMPLE 3: You own a small graphic design company in Maine and negotiate a contract over the phone and via email with a clothing designer in New York to design business cards and signs for a new store that the clothing designer plans to open in Maine. You complete the work on time but the designer refuses to pay you. Can you sue the designer in Maine's small claims court? Yes. It's arguable whether the contract was negotiated in Maine, but it's a fact that you performed the work in Maine. Thus, you can sue the designer in Maine small claims court *if* you can serve your court papers on the designer within Maine's borders.

Where to Sue Defendants in Your State

If the person or business you want to sue resides or does business in your state, you have to decide which small claims court should hear your suit.

Of all the aspects of small claims court that differ from state to state, the rules on where to sue seem to be the most variable. Some states let you sue only in the district or county where the defendant resides. Others also allow you to sue where an accident occurred, a contract was broken or originally signed, merchandise was purchased, a corporation does business, and so on.

On the very first page of the first chapter, I asked you to get a copy of the rules for your local small claims court. Refer to them now to determine where to sue (also look at your state's listing in the Appendix). The first thing you will want to look at is what type of political subdivisions (judicial district, precinct, city, county) your state uses to define the geographical boundaries of its small claims courts. Next, you will want to carefully study your local rules in order to understand the criteria used to define which district a particular lawsuit should be brought in (for example, suits can always be brought where a defendant lives). If this information is not set out in the information sheet, call the clerk of the court and ask. Often you may be eligible to sue in more than one judicial district (for example, where a defendant lives or where a traffic accident occurred). If you have a choice, you'll obviously want to pick the court that is most convenient for you.

TIP

In a few states you can sue for larger amounts in some areas. In some states, such as New York, Pennsylvania, and Tennessee, you can sue for higher amounts in certain counties. Obviously, if yours is a larger claim, you'll want to see whether you are eligible to sue in one of these locations. (The rules for all states are set out in the Appendix.)

General Rules on Where You Can Sue

Depending on the specific rules of your state, you can generally sue in any one of the following political subdivisions:

- the judicial district in which the defendant resides or has a place of business at the time you file your lawsuit
- the judicial district in which the contract underlying your lawsuit was supposed to be carried out
- the judicial district in which the injury underlying your lawsuit occurred, or
- the judicial district in which the rental property is located (for landlord-tenant security deposit disputes or evictions).

Now let's consider some typical rules about where you can sue within a state.

You Can Sue Where the Defendant Lives or Has Its Principal Place of Business

Because most small claims disputes are local, most plaintiffs follow the simplest provisions of the rules about where you can sue. They sue individual defendants in the judicial district where they live or business defendants (corporations, LLCs, or unincorporated businesses) in the judicial district where they do business.

> **EXAMPLE:** Downhill Skier lives in City County, but also owns a mountain cabin in Snowy County, where he spends several months a year. Late one snowy afternoon, Downhill drives his new Porsche from the ski slopes to his ultramodern, rustic cabin. Turning into his driveway, he executes a bad slalom skid right into Woodsey Carpenter's elderly but much-loved pickup. Where can Woodsey properly sue? Obviously, Woodsey can sue in City County where Downhill has his permanent address, and he can probably also sue in Snowy County where the cabin is located, on the theory that Downhill also lives there. In many states, Woodsey is also eligible to sue Downhill in Snowy County because small claims cases may also be filed where damage occurred.

You Can Sue Where the Relevant Contract Was Entered Into

Most states assume that the place where a written contract is signed is also where it will be carried out. Therefore, you can usually sue where the contract was signed, if a problem develops.

Arizona, California, Indiana, and a few other states are more thorough. (See the Appendix.) In these states, a suit can be brought either where the contract was signed or where the contract was to be performed. This is good common sense, as the law assumes that, if people enter into a contract to perform something at a certain location, it is probably reasonably convenient to both. If, for example, Downhill gets a telephone installed in his mountain cabin, or has the fender on his Porsche fixed by a Snowy County mechanic, or has a cesspool put in at his cabin, or agrees to sit (and pay) for a portrait in Snowy County, he can be sued in Snowy County if he fails to keep his part of the bargain. Of course, as we learned above, Downhill can also be sued in City County, where he resides permanently.

EXAMPLE: John Gravenstein lives in Sonoma County, California, where he owns an apple orchard. He signs a contract to buy spare parts from Acme Mechanical Apple Picker Co., an international corporation with offices in San Francisco, New York, Paris, and Guatemala City. John signs the contract in Sonoma County. The parts are sent to John from San Francisco via UPS. They turn out to be defective. After trying and failing to reach a settlement with Acme, John wants to know if he can sue them in Sonoma County. Yes. Even though Acme doesn't have a business office in Sonoma County and they performed no action there in connection with their agreement to sell John the spare parts, the contract was signed there.

TIP

If you have a choice of judicial districts, pick the most convenient one. As you should now understand, there may be two, three, or more judicial districts in which you can properly file your case. In this situation, simply choose the one that serves you best. As long as that district is proper, you have no obligation to pick one the defendant prefers.

Unfortunately, it isn't always easy to determine the location where a contract was "entered into"—particularly when the people who made the contract did so from different locations. If you enter a contract over the phone or online, for example, there could be an argument that the contract was entered into either where you are or where the other party is. Rather than trying to learn and apply all the intricacies of contract law, your best bet is probably to sue in the place most convenient to you, claiming that the contract was made there. On the other hand, if someone sues you at the wrong end of the state and you believe there is a good argument that the contract was formed where you live (that is, where you accepted the other party's offer), write to the court as soon as you have been served and ask that the case be dismissed. (See "What Happens If You Are Sued in the Wrong Small Claims Court?" below.)

In Most States, You Can Sue Where the Injury to Your Person or Property Occurred

Most states allow you to sue in the judicial district where the act or omission underlying the lawsuit occurred (see the Appendix). "Act or omission" is a shorthand term that lumps together things that lead to lawsuits like automobile accidents, warranty disputes, and landlord-tenant disputes, for the purpose of deciding where you're allowed to sue. This means that if you are in a car accident, a dog bites you, a tree falls on your head, or a neighbor floods your cactus garden, you can sue in the judicial district where the event or injury occurred, even if this is a different district from the one in which the defendant resides.

EXAMPLE: Addison is returning to his home in Indianapolis from Bloomington, Indiana, following an Indiana University basketball game. At the same time, Lenore is rushing to Bloomington from her home in Brown County, Indiana, more than 40 miles west of Bloomington. Lenore runs a red light and demolishes Addison's Toyota near the Indiana University gym in downtown Bloomington, which is in Monroe County. After parking his car and taking a bus home, Addison tries to figure out where he can sue Lenore if they can't work out a fair settlement. Unfortunately for him, he can't sue in Indianapolis, as Lenore doesn't reside there and the accident didn't happen there. Addison would have to sue either in Monroe County, where his property was damaged, or in Brown County, where Lenore lives. Luckily for Addison, Monroe County is just an hour from Indianapolis.

What Happens If You Are Sued in the Wrong Small Claims Court?

The sometimes complicated rules as to where you can sue and be sued, discussed above, occasionally mean that people and businesses are sued in the wrong court. If you are served with court papers that list an improper judicial district for the hearing, you have two choices.

1. Show up and go ahead with the case. Although the court has independent authority to transfer a case to a correct court, the judge is likely to go ahead with your trial if both parties show up ready to proceed. Doing this may be a good choice if the court you are sued in is reasonably convenient.

2. Challenge the location in which the case is filed (called "challenging venue"). You can challenge venue by:

   • promptly writing a letter to the court explaining the reasons why you believe the case has been filed in the wrong place, and sending a copy of the letter to all other parties, or

   • showing up on the court date and challenging the location in person. See the sample letter below.

If a court determines that the suit has been filed in the wrong court, it will either dismiss the case or transfer it to a proper court. A dismissal shouldn't be a problem as long as the plaintiff sued reasonably promptly after the loss occurred, because the plaintiff still has plenty of time to refile, with no worries that too much time will have passed. (See Chapter 5 for information about statutes of limitations.) If the defendant challenges venue with a letter but the court rules that, in fact, the suit was brought in the correct court, then the judge will probably delay the hearing for a few days to give the defendant time to make arrangements to appear.

Sample Letter by Defendant Challenging Venue

2100 Coast Drive
Beachtown, FL
December 12, 20xx

Small Claims Court
600 Washington
Tallahassee, FL

Re: *Upton vs. Downey*
   # 987 321

Dear Judge:

I am the defendant in this case. Because I have been sued in the wrong court and will be highly inconvenienced if I have to defend myself there, I request that you please dismiss this court action.

My request is based on the fact I live in Beachtown, FL, and the car accident that gave rise to this case occurred in Orange County. The fact that plaintiff later moved to Tallahassee and chose to file suit in your court does not amount to a valid legal reason to have it heard there.

Sincerely,

Fred Downey

Fred Downey

Plaintiff's and Defendant's Filing Fees, Court Papers, and Court Dates

How Much Does It Cost?

Fees for filing a case in small claims court are very moderate—usually not much more than $50. In some states, people with very low incomes can ask to have court filing fees waived. Normally, a defendant doesn't have to pay anything unless the defendant files a claim against the plaintiff (often called a counterclaim). There is usually an additional fee for serving papers on the opposing party, unless you are in a state that allows personal service to be carried out by a nonprofessional process server and you have a friend who will do it for you without charge. (See Chapter 11.) Most states allow service by certified or registered mail, which doesn't cost much. In a few situations, you may have to hire a professional process server. This will probably cost at least $25, but the fee will be higher if the person you are suing is hard to locate. You can get your filing fees and service costs added to the court judgment if you win. (See Chapter 15.)

Filling Out Your Court Papers and Getting Your Court Date

Now let's look at the initial court papers themselves to be sure that you don't trip over a detail. This book uses California small claims court forms as examples, but you will find that your local forms will require similar information. You should have little trouble filling out your papers by following the examples printed here, but if you do, simply ask the clerk for help. It's best to type the forms if you can. Small claims clerks are required by law in most states to help you fill out forms. It should go without saying that adopting a friendly, courteous approach towards the clerk will usually produce the best results.

Fill Out the Plaintiff's Claim

To start your case, obtain and complete the form entitled Plaintiff's Statement. (In some states, slightly different terminology is used, such as General Claim or Plaintiff's Claim.) All you need to do is properly name the defendant(s), as discussed in Chapter 8, and briefly state what happened, as outlined in Chapter 2. Some courts require that you fill this out at the courthouse, with the clerk's help. (See "Sample Plaintiff's Claim," below, for an example from California.)

 CROSS-REFERENCE

Be sure you sue the correct defendant in the right place. Chapter 7 has details about the correct way to list yourself or your business as the plaintiff. In Chapter 8, we discussed how to properly name the defendant. In Chapter 9, you learned about the rules that establish the proper judicial district in which to file your small claims case.

 TIP

Fill out your court papers online. Some states' court systems have jumped on the Internet bandwagon and allow you to fill out your small claims court forms online. (See the Appendix for your state's small claims court website.) If you fill out your forms online, you will still probably have to print out the forms, sign them, and deliver them to the small claims court clerk.

File Your Papers With the Small Claims Court Clerk

After you've completed your Plaintiff's Claim, sign the original and make several copies of all pages of the form. Take the original and the copies to the small claims court clerk at the courthouse where you're filing your case. The clerk will assign your case a number, stamp the

Sample Plaintiff's Claim

<table>
<tr><td>

SC-100   **Plaintiff's Claim and ORDER to Go to Small Claims Court**

Notice to the person being sued:

- You are the Defendant if your name is listed in ② on page 2 of this form. The person suing you is the Plaintiff, listed in ① on page 2.
- You and the Plaintiff must go to court on the trial date listed below. If you do not go to court, you may lose the case.
- If you lose, the court can order that your wages, money, or property be taken to pay this claim.
- Bring witnesses, receipts, and any evidence you need to prove your case.
- Read this form and all pages attached to understand the claim against you and to protect your rights.

Aviso al Demandado:

- Usted es el Demandado si su nombre figura en ② de la página 2 de este formulario. La persona que lo demanda es el Demandante, la que figura en ① de la página 2.
- Usted y el Demandante tienen que presentarse en la corte en la fecha del juicio indicada a continuación. Si no se presenta, puede perder el caso.
- Si pierde el caso la corte podría ordenar que le quiten de su sueldo, dinero u otros bienes para pagar este reclamo.
- Lleve testigos, recibos y cualquier otra prueba que necesite para probar su caso.
- Lea este formulario y todas las páginas adjuntas para entender la demanda en su contra y para proteger sus derechos.

</td><td>

Clerk stamps date here when form is filed.

Fill in court name and street address:

Superior Court of California, County of
Alameda
600 Washington Street
Third Floor
Oakland, CA 94607

Clerk fills in case number and case name:

Case Number:

Case Name:

</td></tr>
</table>

Order to Go to Court

The people in ① and ② must go to court: *(Clerk fills out section below.)*

Trial Date	Date	Time	Department	Name and address of court if different from above
	1._____	_____	_____	_____
	2._____	_____	_____	_____
	3._____	_____	_____	_____

Date: _____   Clerk, by _____, Deputy

Instructions for the person suing:

- You are the Plaintiff. The person you are suing is the Defendant.
- *Before* you fill out this form, read Form SC-150, *Information for the Plaintiff (Small Claims),* to know your rights. Get SC-150 at any courthouse or county law library, or go to: *www.courtinfo.ca.gov/forms*
- Fill out pages 2 and 3 of this form. Then make copies of **all** pages of this form. (Make 1 copy for each party named in this case and an extra copy for yourself.) Take or mail the original and these copies to the court clerk's office and pay the filing fee. The clerk will write the date of your trial in the box above.
- You must have someone at least 18—not you or anyone else listed in this case—give each Defendant a court-stamped copy of all 5 pages of this form and any pages this form tells you to attach. There are special rules for "serving," or delivering, this form to public entities, associations, and some businesses. See Forms SC-104, SC-104B, and SC-104C.
- **Go to court on your trial date listed above.** Bring witnesses, receipts, and any evidence you need to prove your case.

Judicial Council of California, www.courtinfo.ca.gov
Revised January 1, 2008, Mandatory Form
Code of Civil Procedure, §§ 116.110 et seq.,
116.220(c), 116.340(g)

Plaintiff's Claim and ORDER to Go to Small Claims Court (Small Claims)

SC-100, Page 1 of 5 →

American LegalNet, Inc.
www.FormsWorkflow.com

Sample Plaintiff's Claim (cont'd.)

Case Number:

Plaintiff *(list names)*: Andrew Printer

(1) The Plaintiff (the person, business, or public entity that is suing) is:

Name: Andrew Printer   Phone: (510) 827-7000

Street address: 1000 Marilee Street Fremont CA 94536
      Street   *City*   *State*   *Zip*

Mailing address *(if different)*: n/a
      Street   *City*   *State*   *Zip*

If more than one Plaintiff, list next Plaintiff here:

Name: n/a   Phone: ( )

Street address:
      Street   *City*   *State*   *Zip*

Mailing address *(if different)*:
      Street   *City*   *State*   *Zip*

☐ *Check here if more than 2 Plaintiffs and attach Form SC-100A.*

☐ *Check here if either Plaintiff listed above is doing business under a fictitious name. If so, attach Form SC-103.*

(2) The Defendant (the person, business, or public entity being sued) is:

Name: Acme Illusions, Inc   Phone: (510) 555-1212

Street address: 100 Primrose Path Oakland CA 94602
      Street   *City*   *State*   *Zip*

Mailing address *(if different)*:
      Street   *City*   *State*   *Zip*

If more than one Defendant, list next Defendant here:

Name: n/a   Phone: ( )

Street address:
      Street   *City*   *State*   *Zip*

Mailing address *(if different)*:
      Street   *City*   *State*   *Zip*

☐ *Check here if more than 2 Defendants and attach Form SC-100A.*

☐ *Check here if any Defendant is on active military duty, and write his or her name here:* _____

(3) The Plaintiff claims the Defendant owes $ 950.00 **.** *(Explain below):*

a. Why does the Defendant owe the Plaintiff money? Defendant failed to pay me for a printing and typesetting job that was completed on March 15, 20xx.

b. When did this happen? *(Date):* March 15, 20xx

  If no specific date, give the time period: *Date started:* _____ *Through:* _____

c. How did you calculate the money owed to you? *(Do not include court costs or fees for service.)* _____

  Based on our written agreement and the actual costs of the work.

☐ *Check here if you need more space. Attach one sheet of paper or Form MC-031 and write "SC-100, Item 3" at the top.*

Sample Plaintiff's Claim (cont'd.)

Plaintiff *(list names)*: Andrew Printer

Case Number:

(4) You must ask the Defendant (in person, in writing, or by phone) to pay you before you sue. Have you done this? ☒ Yes ☐ No

If no, explain why not: _____

(5) Why are you filing your claim at this courthouse?
This courthouse covers the area *(check the one that applies)*:

a. ☒ (1) Where the Defendant lives or does business.   (4) Where a contract (written or spoken) was made,
    (2) Where the Plaintiff's property was damaged.   signed, performed, or broken by the Defendant *or*
    (3) Where the Plaintiff was injured.   where the Defendant lived or did business when the Defendant made the contract.

b. ☐ Where the buyer or lessee signed the contract, lives now, or lived when the contract was made, if this claim is about an offer or contract for personal, family, or household goods, services, or loans. *(Code Civ. Proc., § 395(b).)*

c. ☐ Where the buyer signed the contract, lives now, or lived when the contract was made, if this claim is about a retail installment contract (like a credit card). *(Civil Code, § 1812.10.)*

d. ☐ Where the buyer signed the contract, lives now, or lived when the contract was made, or where the vehicle is permanently garaged, if this claim is about a vehicle finance sale. *(Civil Code, § 2984.4.)*

e. ☐ Other *(specify)*: _____

(6) List the zip code of the place checked in (5) above *(if you know)*: 94602

(7) Is your claim about an attorney-client fee dispute? ☐ Yes ☒ No
If yes, and if you have had arbitration, fill out Form SC-101, attach it to this form, and check here: ☐

(8) Are you suing a public entity? ☐ Yes ☒ No
If yes, you must file a written claim with the entity first. ☐ *A claim was filed on (date):* n/a
If the public entity denies your claim or does not answer within the time allowed by law, you can file this form.

(9) Have you filed more than 12 other small claims within the last 12 months in California?
☐ Yes ☒ No   *If yes, the filing fee for this case will be higher.*

(10) I understand that by filing a claim in small claims court, I have no right to appeal this claim.

(11) I have not filed, and understand that I cannot file, more than two small claims cases for more than $2,500 in California during this calendar year.

I declare, under penalty of perjury under California State law, that the information above and on any attachments to this form is true and correct.

Date: 4/15/20xx   Andrew Printer   ▶ Andrew Printer
    Plaintiff types or prints name here   *Plaintiff signs here*

Date: _____   ▶
    Second Plaintiff types or prints name here   *Second Plaintiff signs here*

Requests for Accommodations
Assistive listening systems, computer-assisted, real-time captioning, or sign language interpreter services are available if you ask at least 5 days before the trial. Contact the clerk's office for Form MC-410, *Request for Accommodations by Persons With Disabilities and Response. (Civil Code, § 54.8.)*

original and the copies with the case number, keep the original form with your signature, and return the copies to you. (See Chapter 11.)

> ! CAUTION
>
> **Filing papers by mail is possible but not recommended.** Small claims clerks will accept cases filed by U.S. mail. Although some small claims courts encourage this practice, I recommend it only if you are a long distance from the court in which you must sue. The problem with filing by mail is that there is no one on the spot to answer questions. The details of getting a small claim properly filed can be confusing, and it often helps to review them with a real live person. However, if you do wish to file by mail, contact the court clerk or check your court's website to find the exact procedures.

Supply Documentary Evidence

In most small claims courts, you don't need to provide written evidence until you get to court. Some small claims courts, however—such as those in Washington, DC—require that certain types of evidence (such as copies of unpaid bills, contracts, or other documents on which the claim is based) be provided at the time you file your first papers.

Whether or not your state's rules require written documentation of certain types of claims, it is wise to spend a little time thinking about how you will prove your case. I discuss this in detail in the later chapters of this book. You should read ahead and figure out exactly what proof you will need and how you will present it before you file your first court papers. Being right is one thing—proving it is another.

Getting Your Hearing Date

One of the great advantages of small claims court is that disputes are heard quickly. This is important. Many people avoid lawyers and the regular courts primarily because they can take what seems like forever.

Businesspeople, for example, increasingly rely on private mediation or arbitration, caring more about resolving a dispute promptly than winning a complete victory. Anyone who has had to wait more than a year for a case to be heard in one or another constipated formal trial court knows the truth of the old cliché, "Justice delayed is justice denied."

When you file your papers, you should also arrange with the clerk for a court date. Select a date that is convenient for you. You need not take the first date the clerk suggests. Be sure to leave yourself enough time to get a copy of the claim form served on the defendant(s). (See Chapter 11 for service information.) If you fail to properly serve your papers on the defendant in time, there is no big hassle—just notify the clerk, get a new court date, and try again.

In New York and some other states, an "early" hearing is required, but no maximum number of days is set. Many other states require that the case be set for trial within a certain number of days.

Small claims court cases are most often heard beginning at 9 a.m. Monday through Friday. Larger courts are also required to hold evening or Saturday sessions.

The Defendant's Forms

In most states, a defendant doesn't have to file any papers to defend a case in small claims court unless the defendant wants the case transferred to formal court. However, in a few states, including Arizona and Connecticut, a defendant must respond in writing. (See the Appendix for your state's rules.) In the majority of states, the defendant simply shows up for the hearing on the date and at the time indicated, ready to tell her side of the story. (If you need to get the hearing delayed, see "Changing a Court Date," below.) It is proper, and advisable, for a defendant to call or write the plaintiff and see whether a fair settlement

Sample Defendant's Claim

SC-120

Defendant's Claim and ORDER to Go to Small Claims Court

Clerk stamps date here when form is filed.

Notice to the person being sued:

- You are being sued by the person you are suing.
- You must go to court on the trial date listed below. If you do not go to court, you may lose the case.
- If you lose, the court can order that your wages, money, or property be taken to pay this claim.
- Bring witnesses, receipts, and any evidence you need to prove your case.
- Read this form and all pages attached, to understand the claim against you and to protect your rights.

Aviso al demandado:

- La persona que ha demandado lo está demandando a usted.
- Tiene que presentarse a la corte en la fecha de su juicio indicada a continuación. Si no se presenta, puede perder el caso.
- Si pierde el caso la corte puede ordenar que le quiten de su sueldo, dinero u otros bienes para pagar este reclamo.
- Lleve testigos, recibos y cualquier otra prueba que necesite para probar su caso.
- Lea este formulario y todas las páginas adjuntas, para entender la demanda en su contra y para proteger sus derechos.

Fill in court name and street address:

Superior Court of California, County of
Alameda
600 Washington Street
Third Floor
Oakland, CA 94607

Fill in case number and case name:

Case Number:
002006

Case Name:
Printer v. Acme Illusions, Inc.

Order to Go to Court

The people in ① and ② must go to court: *(Clerk fills out section below.)*

Trial Date	→ Date	Time	Department	Name and address of court if different from above
1.				
2.				
3.				

Date: _____ Clerk, by _____, Deputy

Instructions for the person suing:

- *Before* you fill out this form, read Form SC-150, *Information for the Plaintiff (Small Claims)*, to know your rights. Get SC-150 at any courthouse or county law library, or go to: *www.courtinfo.ca.gov/forms*
- Fill out pages 2 and 3 of this form. Then make copies of **all** pages of this form. (Make 1 copy for each party named in this case and an extra copy for yourself.) Take or mail the original and these copies to the court clerk's office and pay the filing fee. The clerk will write the date of your trial in the box above.
- You must have someone at least 18—not you or anyone else listed in this case—give each Plaintiff a court-stamped copy of all 3 pages of this form and any pages this form tells you to attach. There are special rules for "serving," or delivering, this form to public entities, associations, and some businesses. See Forms SC-104, SC-104B, and SC-104C.
- **Go to court on your trial date listed above.** Bring witnesses, receipts, and any evidence you need to prove your case.

Judicial Council of California, www.courtinfo.ca.gov
Revised July 1, 2007, Mandatory Form
Code of Civil Procedure, § 116.110 et seq.

Defendant's Claim and ORDER to Go to Small Claims Court
(Small Claims)

SC-120, Page 1 of 3 →

Sample Defendant's Claim (cont'd.)

Defendant *(list names):* Acme Illusions, Inc.

Case Number:
002006

① **The Plaintiff (the person, business, or public entity that sued first) is:**

Name: Andrew Printer   Phone: (510) 827-7000

Street address: 1000 Marilee Street   Fremont   CA   94536
       Street   *City*   *State*   *Zip*

Mailing address *(if different):*   n/a
             Street   *City*   *State*   *Zip*

If more than one Plaintiff, list next Plaintiff here:

Name: n/a   Phone: ( )

Street address: _____
       Street   *City*   *State*   *Zip*

Mailing address *(if different):* _____
             Street   *City*   *State*   *Zip*

☐ *Check here if more than 2 Plaintiffs and attach Form SC-120A.*

☐ *Check here if any Plaintiff is on active military duty and write his or her name here:* _____

② **The Defendant (the person, business, or public entity suing now) is:**

Name: Acme Illusions, Inc   Phone: (510) 555-1212

Street address: 100 Primrose Path   Oakland   CA   94602
       Street   *City*   *State*   *Zip*

Mailing address *(if different):* n/a
             Street   *City*   *State*   *Zip*

If more than one Defendant, list next Defendant here:

Name: _____   Phone: ( )

Street address: _____
       Street   *City*   *State*   *Zip*

Mailing address *(if different):* _____
             Street   *City*   *State*   *Zip*

☐ *Check here if more than 2 Defendants and attach Form SC-120A.*

☐ *Check here if either Defendant listed above is doing business under a fictitious name. If so, attach Form SC-103.*

③ **The Defendant claims the Plaintiff owes $** 300.00 **.** *(Explain below):*

a. Why does the Plaintiff owe the Defendant money? Because of delays and poor workmanship in a printing job he performed for me.

b. When did this happen? *(Date):* 3/15/20xx

     If no specific date, give the time period: *Date started:* _____ *Through:* _____

c. How did you calculate the money owed to you? *(Do not include court costs or fees for service.)* _____
Based on our written agreement.

☐ *Check here if you need more space. Attach one sheet of paper or Form MC-031 and write "SC-120, Item 3" at the top.*

Sample Defendant's Claim (cont'd.)

Defendant *(list names):* Acme Illusions, Inc.

Case Number:
002006

(4) **You may ask the Plaintiff (in person, in writing, or by phone) to pay you before you sue. Have you done this?** ☒ Yes ☐ No

(5) **Is your claim about an attorney-client fee dispute?** ☐ Yes ☒ No
If yes, and if you have had arbitration, fill out Form SC-101, attach it to this form, and check here: ☐

(6) **Are you suing a public entity?** ☐ Yes ☒ No
If yes, you must file a written claim with the public entity first. ☐ *A claim was filed on (date):* n/a
If the public entity denies your claim or does not answer within the time allowed by law, you can file this form.

(7) **Have you filed more than 12 other small claims within the last 12 months in California?**
☐ Yes ☒ No *If yes, the filing fee for this case will be higher.*

(8) I understand that by filing a claim in small claims court, I have no right to appeal this claim.

(9) If I do not have enough money to pay for filing fees or service, I can ask the court to waive those fees.

(10) I have not filed, and understand that I cannot file, more than two small claims cases for more than $2,500 in California during this calendar year.

I declare, under penalty of perjury under California State law, that the information above and on any attachments to this form is true and correct.

Date: 4/15/20xx   Waldo Fergus, President   ▶ *Waldo Fergus*
                Defendant types or prints name here   *Defendant signs here*

Date:_____
          Second Defendant types or prints name here   *Second Defendant signs here*

Requests for Accommodations
Assistive listening systems, computer-assisted, real-time captioning, or sign language interpreter services are available if you ask at least five days before the trial. Contact the clerk's office or go to *www.courtinfo.ca.gov/forms* for *Request for Accommodations by Persons With Disabilities and Response* (form MC-410). (Civil Code, § 54.8.)

Need help?
Your county's Small Claims Advisor can help for free.

Or go to "County-Specific Court Information" at:
www.courtinfo.ca.gov/selfhelp/smallclaims

can be reached without going to court, or to propose mediation. (See Chapter 6.)

Sometimes a party you planned to sue sues you first (for example, over a traffic accident where you each believe the other is at fault). As long as your grievance stems from the same incident, you can file a defendant's claim (sometimes called a counterclaim) for up to the small claims court maximum and have it heard by a judge at the same time that the plaintiff's claim against you is considered. However, if you believe that the plaintiff owes you money as the result of a different injury or breach of contract, you may have to file your own separate case. (See "Sample Defendant's Claim," above, for an example of a counterclaim.)

All states require you to file any defendant's claim (counterclaim) in writing within a certain time period after being served with the plaintiff's claim (usually ten to 30 days). When you file a defendant's claim, you become a plaintiff as far as this claim is concerned. In a few states, such as California, where only the defendant can appeal, this means that if you lose your defendant's claim, you can't appeal that part of the case. Of course, even in these states, if you lose on the original plaintiff's claim, you can normally appeal that portion of the judgment. Appeal rules vary a great deal from state to state and can be complicated. (See Chapter 23 and the Appendix.)

In most states, if a defendant's claim is for more than the small claims maximum, the case will be transferred to a formal court. Some states allow transfers only at the discretion of a judge, who may inquire whether the defendant's claim is made in good faith. Check your court rules and your state's listing in the Appendix. A defendant who does not want to cope with the procedures of formal court may be wise to scale down the claim to fit under the small claims limit. (See Chapter 4.)

! CAUTION

A defendant may be required to file a defendant's claim or lose the right to do so. A defendant who has a claim against a plaintiff arising out of the incident underlying the plaintiff's lawsuit will almost always want to promptly file it. Some states require defendants to file a counterclaim as part of the plaintiff's lawsuit; others allow defendants to file their own lawsuit later. If this is an issue for you, check your state's rules.

Jury Trials

Jury trials are not available in small claims court in the great majority of states. Plaintiffs know this when they file and can usually opt for a different court if they want trial by jury. Defendants, of course, don't have this up front choice. To compensate, some states allow a defendant who wants a jury trial to transfer a case to a formal court no matter how small the claim. Others allow transfer only when the defendant's claim exceeds the small claims court maximum. Normally, a defendant must request a jury trial (or a transfer to a court where a jury is permitted) promptly after being served with court papers. And jury fees (often ranging from $100 to $500) must typically be paid in advance. Fees are normally recoverable if you win. Asking for a jury trial also tends to delay proceedings, and some people will make the request for this reason.

Changing a Court Date

It is sometimes impossible for a defendant to be present on the day set by the court for the hearing. It can also happen that the plaintiff will select a court date and serve the defendant, only to find that an unexpected emergency makes it impossible for him to be present.

It is normally not difficult to get a case postponed. To arrange this, call the other party and try to agree on a mutually convenient date. Don't start by calling the clerk, who doesn't know what days the other party has free. Yes, sometimes it is difficult to talk to someone with whom you are involved in a lawsuit, but try to swallow your pride and treat this as a routine business transaction. Once all parties have agreed to a new date, send the court clerk a notice in writing signed by both parties. Here is a sample:

Sample Joint Request for Postponement

11 South Street
Denver, CO.
January 10, 20xx

Clerk of the Small Claims Court
Denver, CO

Re: SC 4117 (*Rodriguez v. McNally*)

Mr. Rodriguez and I agree to request that you postpone this case to a date after March 1, 20XX. If possible, we would prefer that it not be scheduled on March 27 or 28.

John McNally
John McNally

John Rodriguez
John Rodriguez

If for any reason you can't or won't communicate with the other party, make your written request directly to the court clerk, sending a copy to the other party on the same day (it's a good idea to have a friend mail the letter so you have a witness, if needed). Here is a sample:

Sample Letter Requesting Postponement

37 Birdwalk Boulevard
Trenton, NJ
January 15, 20xx

Clerk
Small Claims Court
Trenton, NJ
Re: Small Claims No. 374-628

Dear Clerk:

I have been served with a complaint (No. 374-628) by John's Laundry, Inc. The date set for a hearing, February 15, falls on the day of my son's graduation from Nursing School in Oscaloosa, Oklahoma, which my husband and I plan to attend.

I called John's Laundry and asked to have the case delayed one week. They did not return my call.

I feel that I have a good defense to this suit. Please delay this case until any date after February 22, except March 13, which is my day for a medical checkup.

Thank you,

Sally Wren

Sally Wren
cc: John's Laundry

What if an emergency occurs just a few days before a scheduled hearing? The court still has the power to reschedule your case if the judge is convinced that circumstances warrant it (for example, a key witness has left town to attend a funeral). Immediately hand-carry a written request for a postponement to the court clerk and send a copy to the other party. If you are out of town, call the clerk, explain the problem, and ask for guidance.

 CROSS-REFERENCE

What if your opponent doesn't show up? For detailed instructions on how to proceed if your opponent (whether you're the plaintiff or defendant) doesn't show up to the court hearing, see Chapter 15. ●

Serving Your Papers

After the plaintiff files her Plaintiff's Claim with the small claims clerk, she must deliver a copy of the Plaintiff's Claim to the defendant(s). This is called "service of process," and no lawsuit is complete without it. The reason that you must serve the other side is obvious: The defendant(s) deserve to know about your claims against them and need to be notified of the day, time, and place that they can show up to defend themselves. Any defendant who files a Defendant's Claim against the plaintiff(s) must also serve copies of the Defendant's Claim on all plaintiffs. Also, you may need to know about the service of process rules if you need to deliver a subpoena to a witness. (See Chapter 14.) A Proof of Service form must be filed with the small claims court clerk for every party or witness that papers are served on.

CAUTION

Check to be sure your papers were served. Never show up in court on the day of the court hearing on the assumption that your certified mail service has been accomplished. If the defendant didn't sign for the paper, you will be wasting your time. Call the court clerk a couple of days in advance and verify that the service of process has been completed. This means the certified letter has been signed for by the defendant, not by someone else at the address.

Who Must Be Served

All defendants on the Plaintiff's Claim or all plaintiffs on the Defendant's Claim must be served. It is not enough to serve one defendant or plaintiff and assume that he will tell the other(s). This is true even if the parties are married, live together, or do business together.

! CAUTION

If you don't serve a party, the judge will postpone the hearing or dismiss your case against that party. If you sue only one person and don't serve that person according to the rules, then the judge will probably postpone the hearing until after you're able to serve that person. If you sue more than one person and serve only one properly, the judge cannot enter a judgment against those people you didn't serve and will dismiss your action against those parties. Some states will allow you to refile your claim against those parties if you wish.

Where Can Papers Be Served?

Normally, papers must be served in the state where you filed your lawsuit. Thus, you can't sue someone in a Massachusetts court and serve papers on them in Oklahoma. An exception involves suits having to do with motor vehicle accidents or lawsuits against out-of-state owners of real estate located in-state. Many states allow out-of-state service on this type of claim. Your small claims court clerk will show you how this is handled in your state.

Assuming the person you want to sue resides or does business in your state, you can serve papers anyplace in the state. (See Chapter 9.)

How to Serve an Individual

There are several ways to serve papers on individual defendants. (See "How to Serve Papers on a Business," below, for information on serving a business.) All depend on your knowing where the defendant is. If you can't find the defendant personally and do not know where she lives or works, you can't serve her, and it probably makes little sense to file a lawsuit.

Serving Someone With a Post Office Box

If you know nothing more than the individual defendant's post office box, you'll need to get her street address in order to serve her. To do this, you must give the post office a written statement saying that you need the address solely to serve legal papers in a pending lawsuit. (See "Sample Request to Post Office for Boxholder's Address," below.) This should work, but if it doesn't, refer the post office employee to the Post Office's Administrative Support Manual § 352.44e(2). There is no fee for the Post Office providing this information. 39 CFR § 265.6(d)(4)(ii).

Sample Request to Post Office for Boxholder's Address

June 1, 20xx
Postmaster
Minneapolis, MN

<u>REQUEST FOR BOXHOLDER INFORMATION NEEDED
FOR SERVICE OF LEGAL PROCESS</u>

Please furnish the name and street address of the following post office box holder:

<u>Don Defendant</u>
<u>P.O. Box 0000</u>
<u>Minneapolis, MN 55405</u>

1. Capacity of requester (e.g., process server, attorney, party representing self): <u>Party representing self.</u>

2. Statute or regulation that empowers me to serve process (not required when requester is an attorney or a party acting pro se—except a corporation acting pro se must cite statute): <u>I am a party representing myself.</u>

Sample Request to Post Office for Boxholder's Address (cont'd.)

3. The names of all known parties to the litigation: <u>Peggy Plaintiff and Don Defendant.</u>

4. The court in which the case has been or will be heard: <u>Hennepin County Small Claims Court, City Hall, Room 306, Minneapolis, MN 55415.</u>

5. The docket or other identifying number if one has been issued: <u>Case Number 000000.</u>

6. The capacity in which this individual is to be served (e.g., defendant or witness): <u>Defendant.</u>

WARNING: THE SUBMISSION OF FALSE INFORMATION TO OBTAIN AND USE BOXHOLDER INFORMATION FOR ANY PURPOSE OTHER THAN THE SERVICE OF LEGAL PROCESS IN CONNECTION WITH ACTUAL OR PROSPECTIVE LITIGATION COULD RESULT IN CRIMINAL PENALTIES INCLUDING A FINE OF UP TO $10,000 OR IMPRISONMENT OF NOT MORE THAN 5 YEARS, OR BOTH (TITLE 18 U.S.C. SECTION 1001).

I certify that the above information is true and that the address information is needed and will be used solely for service of legal process in conjunction with actual or prospective litigation.

Peggy Plaintiff

Peggy Plaintiff
123 Maiden Lane
Minneapolis, MN

Personal Service

Personal service means that someone hands the defendant the relevant papers. You have various options regarding who performs this task. Of course, if you use someone who doesn't personally know the defendant, the server will need to be particularly careful to serve the right person. These are your options for who can serve the defendant.

- **Sheriff, marshal, or constable.** All states allow personal service to be made by law officers, although not all officers will serve civil subpoenas. Using this method is often valuable for its sobering effect. The fee can be added to your judgment if you win.

- **Private process servers.** Many states also allow service by private process servers, whom you will find listed in the yellow pages. Fees charged are usually based on how long the service takes. See your state's listing in the Appendix to find out whether your state allows service by private process servers.

- **Service by disinterested adult.** California, Colorado, Washington, and some other states (see the Appendix) allow service by any person who is at least 18 years old, except the person bringing a suit. Any person means just that—a relative or a friend is fine. However, many states require that this person be approved by the court.

CAUTION

A mailbox isn't personal enough. No matter who serves the papers, if personal service is used, the claim and a summons must be handed to the defendant. You can't simply leave the paper at the defendant's job or home or in the mailbox. If the process server locates the right person, but the person refuses to take the paper, acts hostile, or attempts to run away, the process server should simply put the paper down and leave. Valid service has been accomplished. The process server should never try to use force to get a defendant to take any papers.

How to Find a Good Process Server

Unfortunately, sheriff's offices in some states are getting out of the process-serving business. This means that you may have to hire a private person or company. Some of these are truly fly-by-night—they've figured out that process serving is a quick way to make a buck. You may even see them cruising around the courthouse looking for business. To make sure you're dealing with a business that backs up its promises, do a little research first. One indicator of trustworthiness is how long the process server has been in business—ask to see a business license or look in the phone book for process servers who list the date their business was founded. You can also ask the small claims court clerk for a list of registered process servers. If you know any lawyers, you can ask them for a recommendation.

Certified Mail

In the majority of states, you can serve papers by sending them to the defendant(s) via certified mail with a return receipt requested. In some states, service by certified (or registered) mail is onc among several ways you may serve papers, whereas other states require you to try service by certified mail first, before any other method of service. (See the Appendix.) Normally, the court clerk does the mailing for you and charges a small fee. This is recoverable if you win. (See Chapter 15.) The mail method is both cheap and easy, but in most states the defendant must sign for the letter for this type of service to be effective. (In a few states, including Alaska, service is accomplished even if a certified letter is rejected by the defendant.) Most businesses and many individuals routinely sign to accept their mail. However, some people never do, knowing instinctively, or perhaps from past experience, that nothing good ever comes by certified mail. The consensus in an informal survey of court clerks is that about 50% of court papers served by certified mail are accepted. If you try using the mail to serve your papers and fail, and you end up having to pay a process server, tell the judge about it as part of your presentation and chances are your costs will be added to the judgment.

Serving Someone in the Military

It is proper to serve someone who is on active duty in the armed forces. If the person shows up, fine. If not, however, you have a problem. Although you can usually get a default judgment against a properly served defendant who fails to show up, this is not true if the person you are suing is in the military (other than the reserves).

Default judgments cannot normally be taken against people on active duty in the armed forces, because Congress has given our military personnel special protections. To get a default judgment, you will probably have to file a statement under penalty of perjury that the defendant is not in the military. This declaration is available from the clerk. Clerks almost always accept a Declaration of Nonmilitary Service signed by the plaintiff, as long as the plaintiff reasonably believes that the defendant is not on active duty. This constitutes a lenient interpretation of the law by clerks, but no one seems to be complaining.

Regular First-Class Mail

A minority of states, including Connecticut and New York, allow papers to be served by first-class mail. The states differ, however, on what you must do if the defendant doesn't answer your complaint within the time limit. New York, for example, presumes that the defendant received the papers unless the envelope comes back as "undeliverable." Connecticut, on the other hand, requires you to back up unanswered regular mail service with personal service by the sheriff. Check with your court clerk to see if this method is available in your area.

Substituted Service (or "Nail and Mail")

It can be difficult to serve certain individuals. Some have developed their skill at avoiding process servers into a high art. In some states, avoiding service no longer works, as there is now a procedure that allows "substituted service" if you make "reasonable efforts" to serve a defendant and fail. Often the slang for this type of service is "nail and mail," because in several states, if you are unable to serve the defendant personally, you do not have to leave the claim with a live person but can simply tack one copy to the defendant's door and mail the second copy.

In a typical state, substituted service works like this:

1. Small claims papers may be served by an adult who is not named in the lawsuit by leaving a copy at the person's dwelling place in the presence of a competent member of the household who is at least age 18 (and who must be told what the papers are about) or at the person's workplace during normal business hours with the person in charge (who must be told what the papers are about).

2. On the same day, a copy of the papers must also be mailed to the defendant by first-class mail.

Service is complete ten days after mailing. Be sure that all steps, including mailing the extra copy, are carried out by an adult who is not named in the lawsuit.

How to Serve Papers on a Business

When you sue a business, the same methods of service discussed just above can be used. However, if you use the personal service or certified mail service methods, you'll need to know how the business is legally organized in order to determine who you must serve. (See "Who Should

Be Served," below.) And if you know only a business defendant's post office box, you'll normally want to get its street address. (See "Serving Someone with a Post Office Box," above.)

Who Should Be Served?

No matter which method of service you choose, whom you must serve depends on how the business is organized.

Sole proprietorship. Serve the owner.

Partnership. Serve at least one partner.

Limited partnership. Serve the partner who runs the business (the general partner) or the agent for service of process.

Corporation (profit or nonprofit). Serve an officer (president, vice-president, secretary, or treasurer) or the agent for service of process.

Limited liability company. Serve an officer (president, vice-president, secretary, or treasurer) or the agent for service of process.

Who to Serve When Suing a Business

When suing a business, you need to serve your court papers on the owner, a partner, the president, vice-president, secretary, treasurer, or the business's agent for service of process. How do you find out who this person is?

One simple approach is to call the business and ask who, and where, they are. If they won't tell you, the city or county tax and license people where the business is located should be able to do so. (See Chapter 8.) Or, for a corporation, limited partnership, or LLC organized in your state, you should be able to get this information from the office of the Secretary of State for your state.

Substituted or Personal Service

If you need to serve papers on a business with a local office, store, or other physical location, personal service or substituted service is best if your state allows this type of service. (See the Appendix.). Have a process server or "disinterested adult" attempt to deliver the papers personally to the proper person at the business address. If the person is unavailable, the process server should leave the papers at the defendant's business during usual business hours with the person in charge (this is the first step in "substituted service"). Then, mail a copy of the summons and complaint, via certified mail, to the person to be served at the same address.

Certified Mail Service

Service via certified mail is probably your best bet if the business doesn't have a local office, store, or other physical location and if your state allows this type of service. (See the Appendix.). To serve a business via certified mail, ask the court clerk to send the court papers to the proper person and address and pay the small fee. You can serve:

- the proper person as listed in "Who Should Be Served," above, or
- the business's registered agent for service of process, if the business has its only address outside of your state.

How to Serve a Government Agency

As discussed in Chapter 8, before you can sue a city, county, or other government agency you must first file an administrative (in-house) claim against that agency within a specified number of days after the incident that gave rise to your claim. (The fact that you have done this must be stated in your Plaintiff's Claim.) After your claim is denied—or if it is ignored—you can go ahead and sue in small claims court. To serve your papers, call the governmental body in question and ask who should be served. Then proceed, following the rules set out in "How to Serve an Individual," above.

Time Limits in Which the Plaintiff's Claim Must Be Served

The plaintiff in a small claims case is responsible for making sure that the defendant receives copies of the lawsuit before the hearing date. Every state has its own rule about the deadline by which the defendant must be served; some states require as few as five days before the hearing, whereas others require as many as 30 days. Check with your small claims court clerk for the rules in your state.

If the defendant is served fewer than the required number of days before the trial date, he can either go ahead with the trial anyway or request a postponement. If you're the defendant and it's impossible for you to show up in person to ask for a delay, call the court clerk. Point out that you weren't served in the proper time and that you want the case postponed. The clerk should see to it that a default judgment is not entered against you. (See Chapter 10.) But just to be sure, get the clerk's name and take thorough notes about your conversation.

To count the days to see whether service has been accomplished in the correct time, do not count the day the service is made, but do count the day of the court appearance. Also count weekends and holidays, unless the last day falls on a weekend or holiday. If so, the period extends to the next day that is not a holiday.

> **EXAMPLE:** Jack serves Julie on July 12 in Los Angeles, California, with court papers listing a July 22 court date. California's rules require Jack to serve Julie with the court papers at least 15 days before the hearing. July 13 is a Sunday. To count the days you do not count July 12, the day of service, but you would count July 13, 14, 15, 16, 17, 18, 19, 20, 21 and 22, for a total of ten days. Ten days is not enough time before the hearing date. Julie can either request a postponement because she wasn't served according to the rules, or she can choose to go ahead with the hearing.

If you are unable to serve the defendant(s) within the proper time, simply ask the court clerk for a new court date and try again.

How to Notify the Court That Service Has Been Accomplished ("Proof of Service")

If you have asked the court clerk to serve your papers by certified mail, you need do nothing else. The court clerk sends out the certified mail for you, and the signed post office receipt comes back directly to the clerk if service is accomplished. It's as simple as that.

However, a court has no way of knowing whether or not papers have been successfully filed by personal, substituted service, or first-class mail unless you tell them. So, you are required to do so. Notification is accomplished by filing a form known as a Proof of Service with the court clerk after the service has been made. (See "Sample Proof of Service," below.) The Proof of Service form must be signed by the person actually making the service. A Proof of Service is used both by the plaintiff and by the defendant if the defendant files a Defendant's Claim. It must be returned to the clerk's office.

How and When to Serve a Defendant's Claim

As you will remember from our discussion in Chapter 10, a Defendant's Claim is the form that the defendant files when he wishes to sue the plaintiff for money damages. A Defendant's Claim should be filed with the clerk and served on the plaintiff within the proper number of days before the hearing. Days are counted in the same way as discussed above.

If you are a defendant who has filed a claim and you are unable to serve the plaintiff, simply show up on the court hearing date with your papers and serve the plaintiff in the hallway (not in the courtroom). Then explain to the judge why it was impossible to locate the plaintiff earlier. The judge will normally delay the case for a few days, unless both you and the plaintiff agree to proceed with your claim that day. Either way, the judge should accept your Defendant's Claim as having been validly served.

Sample Proof of Service

SC-104 **Proof of Service**

Use this form to serve a **person**, **business**, or a **public entity**. To learn more about proof of service, read *What Is "Proof of Service"?*, Form SC-104B. To learn more about how to serve a business or entity, read *How to Serve a Business or Public Entity*, Form SC-104C.

To serve a **business**, you must serve **one** of the following people:
• Owner (for a sole proprietorship)
• Partner (for a partnership) or general partner (for a limited partnership)
• Any officer or general manager (corporation or association)
• Any person authorized for service by the business (corporation, association, general partnership, limited partnership)
• Any person authorized for service with the Secretary of State (corporation, association, limited liability company (LLC), limited liability partnership (LLP), limited partnership)

To serve a **public entity**, you must first file a claim with that entity, then serve **one** of the following people:
• Clerk (of a city or county)
• Chief Officer or Director (of a public agency)
• Any person authorized for service by the entity

(1) a. If you are serving a **person**, write the person's name below:

_____

b. If you are serving a **business** or **entity**, write the name of the business or entity, the person authorized for service, and that person's job title:

<u>Acme Illusions, Inc.   Waldo Fergus, President</u>
Business or Agency Name   Person Authorized for Service   Job Title

(2) **Instructions to Server:**
You must be at least 18 years old and **not be named in this case**. Follow these steps:
Give a copy of all the documents checked in **(3)** to:
• The person in **(1)**, *or*
• A competent adult (at least 18) living with, and at the home of the person in **(1)**, *or*
• An adult (at least 18) who seems to be in charge at the usual workplace of the person in **(1)**, *or*
• An adult (at least 18) who seems to be in charge where the person in **(1)** receives mail, (but not a U.S. post office box), if there is no known physical address for the person in **(1)**.
THEN,
• Mail a copy of the documents to the person in **(1)**,
• Complete and sign this form, and
• Give or mail your completed form to the person who asked you to serve these court papers.

(3) **I served the person in (1) a copy of the documents checked below:**
a. ☒ SC-100, *Plaintiff's Claim and ORDER to Go to Small Claims Court*
b. ☐ SC-120, *Defendant's Claim and ORDER to Go to Small Claims Court*
c. ☐ Order for examination *(This form must be personally served. Check the form that was served):*
   *Note: The court can issue a civil arrest warrant if the served party does not come to court **only** if the order for examination was personally served by a registered process server, sheriff, marshal, or someone appointed by the court.*
   (1) ☐ SC-134, *Application and Order to Produce Statement of Assets and to Appear for Examination*
   (2) ☐ AT-138/EJ-125, *Application and Order for Appearance and Examination*
d. ☐ Other *(specify):* _____

Clerk stamps date here when form is filed.

Fill in court name and street address:
Superior Court of California, County of
Alameda
600 Washington Street
3rd Floor
Oakland, CA 94607

Fill in case number, case name, hearing date, day, time, and department below:
Case Number:
002006
Case Name:
Printer v. Acme Illusions, Inc.
Hearing Date: 6/15/20xx
Time: 9:00 a.m. **Dept.:** 304

Judicial Council of California, www.courtinfo.ca.gov
Revised January 1, 2007, Optional Form
Code of Civil Procedure, §§ 116.340, 415.10, 415.20

Proof of Service
(Small Claims)

SC-104, Page 1 of 2
→
American LegalNet, Inc.
www.FormsWorkflow.com

Sample Proof of Service (cont'd.)

Case name: _Printer v. Acme Illusions, Inc._

Case Number: _002006_

(4) **Fill out "a" or "b" below:**

a. ☐ **Personal Service:** I personally gave copies of the documents checked in ③ to the person in ①:

On _(date):_ _____ At _(time):_ _____ ☐ a.m. ☐ p.m.

At this address: _____

City: _____ State: _____ Zip: _____

b. ☒ **Substituted Service:** I personally gave copies of the documents checked in ③ _(a, b, or d)_ to _(check one):_

☐ a competent adult (at least 18) at the **home** of, and living with the person in ① , or

☐ an adult who seems to be in charge where the person in ① usually **works**, or

☒ an adult who seems to be in charge where the person in ① **receives mail**, or has a private post office box (not a U.S. post office box), if there is no known physical address for the person in ①.

I told that adult, "Please give these court papers to (name of person in ①) ."

I did this on _(date):_ _May 10, 20xx_ At _(time):_ _10:15_ ☒ a.m. ☐ p.m.

At this address: _100 Primrose Path_

City: _Oakland_ State: _CA_ Zip: _94602_

Name or description of the person I gave the papers to: _Donna Doolittle_

After serving the court papers, I put copies of the documents listed in ③ in an envelope, sealed the envelope, and put first-class prepaid postage on it. I addressed the envelope to the person in ① at the address where I left the copies.

I mailed the envelope on _(date):_ _5/11/20xx_ from _(city, state):_ _Fremont, CA_ by leaving it _(check one):_

a. ☐ At a U.S. Postal Service mail drop, or

b. ☒ At an office or business mail drop where I know the mail is picked up every day and deposited with the U.S. Postal Service, or

c. ☐ With someone else I asked to mail the documents to the person in ① and I have attached that person's completed Form SC-104A.

(5) **Server's Information**

Name: _Margaret Middleman_ Phone: _510-703-2220_

Address: _123 Treelined Way_

City: _Fremont_ State: _CA_ Zip: _94536_

Fee for service: $ _-0-_

If you are a registered process server:

County of registration: _____ Registration number: _____

(6) I declare under penalty of perjury under California state law that I am at least 18 years old and not named in this case and that the information above is true and correct.

Date: _5/11/20xx_

Margaret Middleman ▶ _Margaret Middleman_

Type or print server's name | _Server signs here after serving_

Revised January 1, 2007

Proof of Service
(Small Claims)

SC-104, Page 2 of 2

How and When to Serve Subpoenas

In Chapter 14, we discuss subpoenaing witnesses and documents. The rules as to who can do the serving are the same as those set forth in "How to Serve an Individual," above, with one important difference: Any person, including the person bringing the suit, can serve the subpoena. In addition, in many states, the person making the service must be ready to pay the person subpoenaed a witness fee on the spot if it is requested. This is often a flat fee (normally $40–$100), plus a mileage fee based on the distance to the courthouse. If you hire a sheriff or marshal to do the service, he or she will ask you to pay this fee, plus the service fee, in advance. In many states, if the witness doesn't ask for the fee, it will be returned to you. (See Chapter 14 for details.)

A witness must be served with a subpoena far enough in advance of the court hearing date to give the witness "reasonable time" to prepare for and travel to the hearing.

Costs of Service

Professional process servers commonly charge from $20–$75 per service, depending on how far they must travel. You can usually get these costs of service added to your judgment if you win, but be sure to remind the judge to do this when you conclude your court presentation. However, a few courts will not give the successful party an award to cover a process server's costs unless she first tried to have the papers served by the cheaper certified mail approach. Other courts prefer that you don't use the mail approach at all, because they feel that it wastes time because too often the mail isn't accepted. Ask the small claims clerk or small claims advisor in your district how the court prefers that you accomplish service and how much the judge will allow as a service of process fee. ●

The Defendant's Options

This chapter is devoted to a review of the concerns of small claims defendants. Most of this material has already been discussed in the first 11 chapters, but because the plaintiff, as the initiator of a lawsuit, has so far gotten more than half the attention, let's now look at a small claims case exclusively from the point of view of the person being sued.

How should a defendant approach a small claims case? Start by understanding that there is no one correct course of action—it all depends on the facts of the dispute and your personal desires.

 CAUTION

A response may be required. In some states the defendant is required to make a written response to the plaintiff's claim to avoid having a default judgment entered against her. The deadline for submitting the response differs from state to state. Check the Appendix for your state's rules.

Claim That You Weren't Properly Served With Court Papers

You may conclude that you were not properly (legally) served with the plaintiff's court papers. (See Chapter 11.) Perhaps the Plaintiff's Claim was left with your neighbors, or maybe you weren't given the correct number of days in which to respond. Because there are one or more procedural defects in the plaintiff's case, you may be tempted to not show up in court. This would be a mistake. The judge may be unaware of or overlook the problem and issue a default judgment against you. If this happens, you will have to go to the trouble of requesting that the default be vacated. (See Chapter 15.)

When the plaintiff fails to have court papers properly served on you or makes some other procedural error, your best course of action is to contact the court in writing, explain the problem, and ask that the case be dismissed. If the court can't or won't help, show up on the day in question and make your request in person. If the problem involves a failure to serve papers on you properly, chances are the plaintiff will re-serve you at this time, but at least the case should be delayed (continued) to give you a chance to prepare your defense.

Claim You Were Sued in the Wrong Small Claims Court

If you think the plaintiff has filed suit in the wrong small claims court or, in legal lingo, "in the wrong venue" (see Chapter 9), you can challenge the court's right to hear the case (challenge the venue).

As discussed in Chapter 9, you can do this in two ways. First, you can go to court on the day your case is scheduled and request that the case be dismissed. If the judge disagrees with you, she will simply go ahead and hear the case. However, if the judge agrees that the location is improper, she will either dismiss the case or transfer it to a court in the appropriate judicial district, unless for some reason you volunteer to have it heard right then—perhaps just to get it over with.

Your second, and probably easier, option is to write to the court, explaining why you think the claim was brought in the wrong place. Send a copy of your letter to each of the other parties. If the judge agrees that the suit was brought in the wrong place, she will dismiss it. If she disagrees, she will postpone the hearing to give you an opportunity to appear. You will receive notification of the court's decision by mail.

> **TIP**
>
> **Out-of-state defendants should ask for a dismissal.** As discussed in Chapter 9, if you don't live—or do business—in the state in which you are sued, the small claims court normally doesn't have power ("jurisdiction") to enter a valid judgment against you, unless court papers are served on you while you happen to be in the state. Exceptions to this rule exist for out-of-staters sued because of a dispute involving their real property located in the state or because of a traffic accident that occurred in the state. If you are an out-of-state resident and receive small claims papers via the mail, promptly write a letter to the court explaining that you do not believe you are subject to the court's jurisdiction. Send a copy of your letter to each of the other parties. Stay in touch with the court until you are sure the case has been dismissed.

Claim You Were Sued After the Statute of Limitations Expired

Plaintiffs do not have an indefinite period of time in which to sue someone for a perceived wrong. If the event the plaintiff is suing you over happened in the hazy past, check Chapter 5 to see whether the plaintiff has missed the deadline (statute of limitations) by which she must sue. The statutes of limitations are different for different types of lawsuits but are never less than one year from the date of the incident. The main exception to this rule is if the plaintiff is suing a government agency, in which case the plaintiff must file an administrative claim form with the government within a shorter period of time. (See Chapter 5.)

You Have a Partial Defense—Try to Compromise

If you feel that perhaps the plaintiff has some right on his side but that you are being sued for too much, your best bet is to try to work out a compromise settlement. (See Chapter 6 for more on how to negotiate.) One good approach is to call or write the plaintiff and make a settlement offer. How much to offer depends on the relative merits of your case as compared to the plaintiff's, and whether the plaintiff is asking for a reasonable or inflated amount. Assuming the plaintiff has a pretty strong legal position (you probably are legally liable) and is asking the court for an amount that's, broadly speaking, reasonable, a good starting point is to make an initial offer to pay about half of the request. Remember, even with a strong case, the plaintiff may be motivated to accept your offer if for no other reason than to save the time and trouble it takes to prepare for and appear in court. More likely, your initial offer will set in motion a little dance of offer and counteroffer, ending with the plaintiff accepting a compromise of somewhere between 65% and 80% of the original demand. Obviously, if the plaintiff is asking for way too much, or you are not sure that a judge would find that you are liable in the first place, you'll want to offer less or fight the case.

Any settlement you make should be set down in writing along the lines outlined in Chapter 6.

> ⚠ **CAUTION**
>
> **Don't rely on being judgment-proof.** Some defendants who have at least a partial defense to the plaintiff's claim are tempted not to show up and defend a case in small claims court because they have no money and figure that, even if they lose, the plaintiff can't collect. If you have a decent defense, this is just plain dumb. Judgments are good for anywhere from five to 20 years, depending on the state (see "Time Limits to Collect Court Judgments," in Chapter 24) and can be renewed, if necessary. Hopefully, you'll get a job or otherwise put a few dollars together sometime in the

future and, if so, you probably won't want them immediately taken away to satisfy a small claims judgment that you believe shouldn't have been entered in the first place. So wake up and defend yourself while you can. One possible exception to this "always fight back if you have a decent case" advice occurs when you plan to declare Chapter 7 bankruptcy. Bankruptcy wipes out most debts, including small claims judgments.

CROSS-REFERENCE

More information on personal bankruptcy. See *How to File for Chapter 7 Bankruptcy*, by Stephen Elias, Albin Renauer, and Robin Leonard (Nolo).

You Want to Avoid Conflict—Try to Mediate

In Chapter 6, I discuss mediation in some detail. Please reread this material. As you do, consider that engaging in mediation is frequently beneficial to the defendant, because mediation tends to encourage a compromise settlement for a lower amount than the plaintiff has demanded. In addition, mediation gives the defendant a chance to raise issues that would not be considered relevant by a small claims court judge. For example, in a dispute between neighbors, local businesspeople, or relatives, mediation affords an opportunity for both legal and emotional concerns to be raised and dealt with.

TIP

Ask the small claims clerk for help setting up mediation. Mediation of small claims cases works in various ways in different states. In many it can take place in the courthouse itself and is encouraged by the small claims court. In others it's available at a nearby community mediation project. Ask the small claims court clerk where mediation is available in your area. Then, if necessary, contact the mediation project and enlist their help in bringing the plaintiff to the table.

You Have Absolutely No Defense

Now let's assume that you were properly served with the plaintiff's papers in a proper court before the deadline, you have no valid defense to the merits of the case, and neither you nor the plaintiff want to compromise. Perhaps you borrowed money under the terms of a written contract and haven't been able to pay it back. Because you know you'll lose, you may conclude that it makes little sense to defend yourself in court. Your decision not to show up will very likely result in a default judgment against you. This judgment will most probably be for the dollar amount demanded by the plaintiff, plus the amount of the filing fee and any reasonable costs to serve the papers on you. (In Chapter 15 you can read about default judgments and how you can probably get one vacated if you act immediately.)

 TIP

Even if you owe 100% of the plaintiff's demand, it never hurts to make an offer. Especially if you have the money, why not offer to pay 75%–90% of what the plaintiff requests. To save the trouble of going to court—or for some other reason you may never guess—the plaintiff may accept, even though if he went to court he would almost surely win a judgment for the whole amount.

You Want to Pay the Plaintiff in Installments

If you do not dispute the amount of the plaintiff's claim but you want to make payments in installments rather than all at once, your best bet is to show up on the day your case is scheduled and explain your situation to the judge. Tell the judge how much you can afford to pay each month. The judge has the discretion to allow you to pay the judgment in installments.

Explain why it would be difficult or impossible to pay any judgment all at once. For example, if you are on a fixed income, have recently been unemployed and have a lot of debts, or have a low or moderate income and a large family, just state these facts—there is no need to tell a long sob story. (See Chapter 23 for more on paying a judgment in installments.)

If You, Not the Plaintiff, Were Wronged— File a Defendant's Claim

Finally, some defendants will not only want to dispute the plaintiff's claim but will also want to sue the plaintiff back. Perhaps you are outraged that the plaintiff sued first, because you are the person who was wronged. To assert your own claim against the plaintiff, promptly file a Defendant's Claim (sometimes called a counterclaim) for up to the dollar limit for your state's small claims court. (See the Appendix.) If you want to sue for a greater amount, ask the small claims clerk how to transfer the case to formal court.

 CROSS-REFERENCE

Defendant's claim. For more on what to do if you wish to sue the plaintiff, see Chapters 10 and 11.

Assuming your case stays in small claims court, both your claim and the plaintiff's will be heard together. You should prepare and present your case just as you would if you had filed first—that is, understand the legal basics that underlie your case, make a practical and convincing oral presentation, and back it up with as much hard evidence as you can find.

Have Your Case Transferred to Formal Court

Depending on state law and the facts of your case, you may be able to have your case transferred out of small claims court to a formal court. This may be called municipal, superior, district, county, justice, circuit, city, or civil court. Whatever the name used in your state, this court will allow lawyers and require formal rules of evidence and procedure, including far more paperwork than is required in small claims court.

Transfer rules vary greatly from one state to the next. Some states allow any defendant to transfer any case, while others allow it only if the defendant files his or her own claim (a counterclaim) for an amount greater than the small claims limit or makes a request for a jury trial. Still other states allow a case to be transferred only with the discretionary approval of a judge. And some states don't allow transfers at all.

If you are interested in transferring your case, look at the brief summary for your state in the Appendix to see if it's possible. Then, you absolutely need to consult your state's rules. But first it makes sense to ask yourself why you would want to transfer a case out of small claims court. My answer is that it is rarely a good idea. Because small claims court is cheaper, more user-friendly, and far less time-consuming than formal court, you'll usually want to defend your case right there, unless, of course, you want to file a defendant's claim (counterclaim) for an amount significantly over the small claims limit. Here are some other situations in which it might make sense to transfer your case:

- To get a jury trial (in states where transfer for this reason is allowed). In my view, nonlawyers are almost always better off trying a case before a judge under relaxed small claims rules than submitting to the extra level of formality a jury trial adds to the already fussy rules of formal court. But I know people who disagree, believing that there is no justice without a jury.

- Because you know how to navigate in formal court far better than the plaintiff—or are willing to hire a lawyer to represent you. Yes, this approach may be a tad cynical, but given the opportunistic nature of many plaintiffs, why not take full advantage of every possible edge you have.

Fight Back

Suppose now you feel you don't owe the plaintiff a dime and you want to actively fight the case filed against you. To do this, file a response to the plaintiff's claim if required (see the Appendix), then show up in court on the date stated in the papers served on you, ready to present your side of the story.

Before you even think about the merits of the plaintiff's case, your first job is to check to be sure the plaintiff has brought it within the time allowed by the statute of limitations. (See Chapter 5.) If not, tell the judge at the beginning of your presentation and request that the plaintiff's case be dismissed.

To successfully present your defense, you'll want to be prepared to make a well-organized, convincing oral statement, backed up with as much evidence as possible. Good case presentation strategies, including how to present witnesses, estimates, diagrams, and other evidence, are discussed in Chapters 13–22 and apply both to defendants and plaintiffs. If the plaintiff has asked for too much money, you'll also want to be sure you tell the judge exactly why it is too much. (See Chapter 4.)

Take apart your opponent's case. To do this, you will normally want to focus on any facts that show you are not legally liable. To do this, reread Chapter 2 to see what the plaintiff must prove for all the common types of small claims cases and see whether you can disprove any key points. If after doing this you conclude the plaintiff arguably does have a winning case, next consider whether he has asked for the right dollar amount. Obviously, if you can convince a judge that you only owe a couple of hundred, not several thousand, dollars, you will have won a substantial victory. (On calculating damages, see Chapter 4.)

EXAMPLE 1: The plaintiff sues you for a breach of contract. You reread Chapter 2 to understand what the plaintiff must prove to win her case. Then, assuming the facts support your position, you might present evidence that no contract existed in the first place or that, even if a contract did exist, the plaintiff violated its terms so thoroughly that you were justified in considering it void. And even if you have to admit that you broke a valid contract, you might claim the plaintiff is asking for far too much money.

EXAMPLE 2: You are sued by someone claiming your negligent conduct resulted in his property being damaged (as would be the case in a fender bender). To successfully defend, you want to convince the court that you were not negligent (careless), or, if you were, that the plaintiff was more negligent. And even if the judge decides that the accident was your fault, you might want to claim that the plaintiff paid far more than was necessary to have the car fixed.

Gather evidence. As emphasized in Chapters 13 and 14, the key to winning (or not losing) in small claims court is very often to convince the judge that your version of the facts is correct. To do this, you'll normally need to back up your oral presentation with convincing evidence. One good approach is to present the testimony of an eyewitness (if you are lucky enough to have one) or an expert witness who agrees with your position (for example, a mechanic who can explain how the plaintiff damaged your engine). In addition, you will want to show the judge any available documentary evidence such as letters, photos, and opinions of experts—or sometimes even damaged property—that back up your version of events. For example, if you are a computer repair person sued by someone who claims you ruined her PC, you may want to get a written opinion from another repair shop that the current problem with the computer has nothing to do with the defect you fixed. In addition, it would make sense to present any advertisements or trade pricing data that tend to show that the plaintiff is placing an inflated value on her ruined but very old computer. And don't forget that you can also bring along physical evidence. Suppose, for example, you are sued for nonpayment on a handmade ceramic tea service that you commissioned from the plaintiff. If you can bring that teapot into court and show the judge that it doesn't pour properly, your defense may be in the bag.

Be prepared to make a convincing courtroom presentation. The plaintiff gets to talk first. Patiently and quietly wait until it's your turn. When the plaintiff is done, be prepared to make a short and logical presentation of why the plaintiff should receive little or nothing. As mentioned several times in this book, once you have your arguments thought out, it is an extremely good idea to practice exactly what you plan to say in front of a friend or family member until it is perfect. One trick to getting and keeping the judge's attention is not to repeat uncontested facts presented by the plaintiff; instead, immediately focus on why the plaintiff's case is misguided.

EXAMPLE: Tom, the landlord, listens patiently as Evie, the tenant, spends five minutes presenting a rambling, sometimes incorrect history of their landlord-tenant relationship as an introduction to her main point that she should have gotten her security deposit back because she left the rental unit clean and undamaged. When it's finally Tom's turn, he ignores Evie's inconsequential mistakes. Instead, he focuses on the exact point of the dispute by saying, "Your Honor, the key to my defense is that the plaintiff left the rental at 127 Spring Street in a dirty and damaged condition. I have pictures to demonstrate this and a reliable witness to back it up. But first I would like to briefly list the three worst problems." ●

Getting Ready for Court

Once you've filed papers with the small claims clerk and properly served the other party, the preliminaries are over and you are ready for the main event—your day in court. Movies, and especially TV (yes, even Court TV), have done much to create false impressions of court proceedings. Ask yourself what a trial might have been like before every lawyer fancied himself Raymond Burr, Charles Laughton, or even Johnnie Cochran, and judges acted "parental," or "stern," or "indignantly outraged," in the fashion of Judge Judy.

I mention this "movie-itis" because it is a particularly common ailment in small claims court. Cases that should be easily won are sometimes lost because one party or the other goes marching around the courtroom antagonizing everyone with comic opera imitations of television attorneys. And don't assume you are immune. Movie-itis can often be a stealth disease, with few people realizing they have it. To find out whether you are infected, ask yourself a few self-diagnostic questions:

- Have you frequently watched courtroom scenes on TV or in the movies?

- Have you ever imagined that you were one of the lawyers?

- How many times have you watched a real court case in person as compared to watching a trial that was staged for the media?

I'm sure you get the idea. Chances are good that, like most of us, your idea of what a court proceeding is like comes mostly from Hollywood. If so, the best advice I can give you is to put aside everything you think you have learned by watching the media and just be yourself. To succeed in small claims court, you don't need fancy clothes, words, or attitudes. Just use plain English to tell the judge what happened and why you are right.

Movie-itis aside, most people who present or defend small claims cases do pretty well. But it's also true that only a few make outstanding presentations. It's fair to ask, what set this elite group apart? I bet you know what I'm going to say. That's right—practice and preparation. The people who do best are those who prepare carefully enough that they are able to make a clear, concise presentation, backed up by the orderly introduction of convincing evidence.

The rest of this chapter and Chapters 14 and 15 contain basic information about how small claims court works and how to prepare.

JUDGES' TIPS

Watch small claims court in action before your own hearing. If you're nervous about your court date or if you want to get a taste of how the court might approach your type of dispute, feel free to visit the court while it is in session and observe how the judges digest and then rule on the cases that are presented to them. You may see an example of your type of case! —Commissioner Douglas G. Carnahan

TIP

Language problems? Look for help from the court or from community organizations. Some courts have interpreters available to translate the court proceedings. Call in advance if this service is needed. If no court interpreter is available, many ethnic and cultural organizations offer interpreter services to low-income persons free of charge. Be sure to contact the appropriate organization well in advance of your court date to ask for help.

Getting Help From a Private Lawyer

Many states allow lawyers to represent clients in small claims court, although some states do not. Even in states that allow lawyers, however, the amount of money at stake often doesn't justify paying a lawyer's legal fees. It may be cost-effective, though, to hire a lawyer to give you advice only. If you are worried about some legal aspect of your case and can't get an answer from the court clerk or by doing your own research (see Chapter 25), it can be sensible to discuss the problem with a lawyer. It should not cost more than $100–$200 for a short consultation. Make sure you negotiate the fee in advance.

JUDGES' TIPS

It's perfectly proper to get assistance from a lawyer. A lawyer can be extremely helpful in preparing your case, especially if it's complicated. —Commissioner Douglas G. Carnahan

Mediation

As discussed in considerable detail in Chapter 6, free or low-cost mediation services are available in many communities. Normally the choice of whether to mediate is yours. However, the courts in some judicial districts so strongly encourage the parties to mediate, it may seem like it's required. Ask any small claims clerk for information on how to contact local mediation programs.

Mediation programs are designed to help people settle their own disputes—not to impose a decision, as is done in small claims court. Especially if you will inevitably have a continuing relationship with the person with whom you have a dispute—as is the case with a neighbor, family member, or many business relationships—trying to achieve a compromise settlement is almost always wiser than fighting it out in court.

Even if your opponent previously has been reluctant to engage in mediation, you can again raise this possibility with the judge just before your case is heard by telling the judge you are still willing to mediate. The judge, who has the power to postpone the case to allow the parties to try to settle it, may attempt to talk the other party into giving mediation a try. As part of doing so, the judge will probably point out that if the case is settled, the amount of the judgment will not appear on the loser's credit record.

Practice, Practice, Practice

Once you are pretty sure your case can't be settled and you will need to go to court, your best approach is to practice presenting it. Line up an objective, tough-minded friend and run through your entire case just as you plan to on court day. Ask your friend for suggestions, not compliments. For example, she may tell you that you need a witness or written documentation, a better grasp of the legal technicalities involved, or a better-organized presentation. Take her advice to heart and make all possible improvements. Then, practice again.

The four key phrases to remember as you prepare and practice your courtroom presentation are:

- **Be polite** to the judge, your opponent, the clerk, and the bailiff.
- **Bring evidence** from witnesses or documents to supplement your own verbal statement of the facts.
- **Organize your presentation** to include only necessary facts in a logical way.
- **Keep it short.**

Remember that the person who is deciding your case has heard thousands of similar stories and will get bored or annoyed if you are needlessly repetitive. Finally, don't let the robe and other trappings of judicial office obscure the fact that you are dealing with a human being who, like anyone else, is far more likely to be sympathetic to your point of view if you can convince him that you occupy the moral high ground (for example, you are honest, kind, and pay your debts) and that your opponent is the bad guy (tricky, hard-hearted, and fails to keep his promises).

Getting to the Courthouse

Before you locate the right courtroom, you obviously have to get to
the right building. Sometimes doing this can be tricky, because small
claims courts are often not in the main courthouse. Like a half-forgotten
relative, many are housed wherever the city or county has an empty
room. In short, don't assume that you know where your small claims
court is unless you've been there before or have asked the court clerk for
specific directions. Plaintiffs have already had to find the clerk's office
to file their papers, so they probably know where the courtroom is, but
defendants should check this out in advance. Be sure, too, that your
witnesses know exactly where and when to show up. And do plan to be
a few minutes early—people who rush in flustered and late start with a
strike against them.

Court Times

Small claims cases are most often scheduled either at 9 a.m or early in
the afternoon. Usually a number of cases are set for the same time and
heard in turn. In other words, your case may be scheduled for 9 a.m.
but won't actually start until about 10 a.m. Arrive a few minutes before
9 a.m. and use any wait time to watch other cases before your own
begins. In larger cities, Saturday or evening sessions may also be held.
If it is not convenient for you to go to court during business hours and
night court is an option, request that your case be scheduled at one of
these other sessions.

Understanding the Courtroom and Basic Procedure

Most small claims proceedings are conducted in standard courtrooms
also used for regular trials.

> (!) **CAUTION**
> **Leave sharp metal objects at home.** This may seem like common sense, but remember that all visitors to courthouses must pass through metal detectors these days, and if you have scissors, metal knitting needles, a knife, or any other weaponlike object with you, it will be confiscated or held for you by security.

Most judges still sit on little elevated wooden throne (called "the bench") boxes and wear black robes. In addition to the judge, a clerk and a bailiff will normally be present. They usually sit at tables immediately in front of or next to the judge. The clerk's job is to keep the judge supplied with necessary files and papers and to make sure that proceedings flow smoothly. The bailiff is there to keep order in the courtroom if tempers get out of hand.

Courtrooms are divided about two-thirds of the way toward the front by a little fence (known to initiates as the "bar"). The public must stay on the opposite side of the bar from the judge, clerk, bailiff, and parties, unless asked to come forward. This invitation occurs when the clerk calls your case by name (*Smith vs. Jones* or *Abercrombie vs. Lee*). At this point you and any witnesses will normally be asked to step to the front of the room and sit at a table (known as the "counsel table"). You will then face the judge with your back to the spectator section of the courtroom. In a few courtrooms, judges try to hurry things along by asking everyone to stand while their case is being heard. The idea seems to be that if people can't sit down, they will present their cases faster.

In small claims courts, you must swear (or affirm, if you wish) to tell the truth. Often this oath is administered before the first case is heard, to everyone who will testify at that entire session. However, occasionally the oath will be administered to participants separately as each case is called.

In the great majority of small claims courts, you, your opponent, and your witnesses will present the entire case from the counsel table. This means that neither you nor your witnesses sit in the witness box next to the judge.

Courtroom Etiquette 101

From watching television, most of us know that lawyers often dress in expensive, formidable-looking suits. No such formal dress is required for your appearance in small claims court. Although it's polite to dress in a neat and professional manner, it's not required, and if you are coming directly to court from your work as a housepainter, for example, the judge will probably understand and excuse your paint-splattered appearance.

It is also polite—but not required—for parties and witnesses to stand when they address the judge. The respectful and recommended way to address the judge directly is "Your Honor." If you need to refer to the judge in the third person, say "Her Honor" (for example, speaking to the bailiff, "Please give Her Honor these documents").

Other suggestions for showing respect to the court and the other litigants come from Commissioner Douglas G. Carnahan:

- Don't walk in the "well" of the courtroom, which is the area between the lawyers' table and the judge's bench. This is a security zone, and the bailiff will prevent you from entering it, sometimes rather aggressively.

- Turn off your cell phones and pagers before you enter the courtroom.

- Keep courtroom chitchat to a minimum. Many judges find it distracting.

- Even while you are waiting for your case to be called, an attentive, pleasant demeanor will make a good impression on the judge. This means pay attention, don't read the newspaper, don't chew gum, and don't listen to your iPod.

JUDGES' TIPS

Be nice to the clerk and the bailiff. The clerk organizes the paperwork, and the bailiff keeps order, although sometimes each person shares some of the other's work. Don't antagonize them; they will often report their (positive or negative) impressions to the judge.
—Commissioner Douglas G. Carnahan

Normally, the plaintiff will be asked to present her case first and introduce any witnesses, who will also get a chance to have their say. When the plaintiff is done, it will be the defendant's turn to speak and present witnesses. Both sides should have any papers or other evidence that backs up their story carefully organized to present to the judge. This can include bills, receipts, estimates, photographs, contracts, letters to or from your opponent, and other types of documentation or physical evidence. At the appropriate place in your presentation, tell the judge you have evidence you want her to see, and then hand it to the clerk, who in turn will give it to the judge. As I emphasize often in this book, appropriate documentation can be a huge aid to winning your case. But don't go overboard: Judges are a little like donkeys—load them too heavily and they are likely to become uncooperative and possibly even ornery.

TIP

Copies of documents. It is courteous but not required to bring at least three copies of each document you plan to show the judge: one for you, one for the judge, and one for your opponent. You can highlight or otherwise make notes on your copies to remind yourself why the particular document is important.

Dealing With Your Opponent

As you plan your courtroom strategy, give thought to your opponent. What sort of presentation will she make? And even more important, how can you best counter her arguments? Figuring out how to cope with your opponent's best points is not only an effective way to flesh out your case, but it can be a good way to turn the negative energy you probably feel (frustration, annoyance, anger) into something creative.

Once in court, always be polite when presenting or defending your case. If you are hostile or sarcastic, you run the considerable risk of losing the respect of the judge. Never interrupt your opponent when she is speaking—you will get your chance. When you do, lay out the key facts that support your position directly to the judge; don't get into an argument with the other side. It's the judge you need to convince, not your opponent.

TIP

How to cope with the big lie. Although not an everyday occurrence, big lies definitely are told in small claims court and can sometimes strongly influence the judge in your opponent's favor if you aren't prepared to poke holes in them. If your adversary tells a whopper, your best approach is to wait calmly for your turn to speak and then say something like this: "Your Honor, almost everything defendant (or plaintiff) has said about __ X __ is simply not true. Please let me prove this to you with facts." Then present your testimony and evidence—or if you have already shown the judge key evidence, remind the judge of how it demonstrates that your opponent's story is totally false. For example, if your former landlord who failed to return your security deposit swears you left the apartment filthy, you will totally destroy his credibility if you can show the judge photos that demonstrate how clean it really was. Fortunately, if you can demonstrate that your opponent has told one big lie, the judge will distrust and hopefully disbelieve the rest of what he says.

Dealing With the Judge or Commissioner

The person who hears your case may be a regular court judge who also presides over many other types of cases. But, increasingly, full-time commissioners and referees are being hired to handle small claims cases. Commissioners are attorneys trained to preside over small claims cases but who are paid lower salaries and benefits than are paid to judges (a bit like colleges hiring nontenured instructors instead of full professors). By and large, commissioners and referees—who usually hear small claims cases on a daily basis—do a very competent job, sometimes better than judges, who have other duties and occasionally act as if they are too important to hear such small disputes.

Temporary Judges (Judge Pro Tem)

In addition to commissioners and regular judges, volunteer lawyers are also routinely appointed when a judge or commissioner is ill or on vacation. The legal slang for a temporary judge is "judge pro tem." If your case comes up on a day when only a pro tem judge is present, you will be given a choice as to whether you want to go ahead or have your case rescheduled on a day when a regular judge or commissioner will be present. Especially if your case is contested and you feel it involves fairly complicated legal issues, you may not want to accept a pro tem judge—unless you're in an area where you know that none of the full-time judges are up to par. Pro tem judges are not paid, and often do not have much practical experience in the legal areas that are commonly heard in small claims court. They receive some training, but nothing like what a regular judge or commissioner has. Although some are excellent, too many are seriously substandard, meaning that as a group they are best avoided. Perhaps it will really bring this point home if I tell you that in the 20 years I have authored this book, I've received more complaints about lousy pro tem judges than about any other aspect of small claims court.

CAUTION

Sometimes an attempt is made to hide your right to reject a temporary judge. In some courtrooms, before court begins for the day, a clerk will ask you to sign a form accepting a particular judge, without clearly explaining that the judge is a local lawyer serving on a temporary (pro tem) basis and that you have the right to say no. Don't fall for this. Whenever you are asked to approve a judge, you can be sure the person is a substitute for the real judge, and you have the right to say no.

CAUTION

You can't appeal from an arbitrator's decision in New York. To save time, residents of the Empire State are often encouraged to have their cases heard by a volunteer lawyer arbitrator instead of a small claims court judge. But beware of this alternative. In addition to getting a less experienced decision maker, there is no right to appeal from an arbitrator's decision, as there is from the decision of a regular small claims judge.

Disqualifying a Prejudiced Judge

What if your case will be heard by a regular judge or commissioner who you don't like, either because you know the person or because you have been put off by the way she has handled other cases? For example, you might live in a small town or city and be convinced a particular judge, whose reputation you know, is likely to be hard on you (for example, you are a landlord and the judge is known to be pro-tenant). Laws exist in nearly all states that allow you to "disqualify" a regular judge simply on your honest belief that the judge is "prejudiced" against you. No one will ask you to prove it. To disqualify a judge, in some states you can simply say, when your case is called (after you've been "sworn in"), something like this: "Your Honor, I believe you are prejudiced against my interest, and I request a trial before another judge." In other states, you need to put your disqualification request in writing and file it in advance. If you think you may want to take advantage of a disqualification procedure, check with the small claims clerk before your court date to be sure you understand the rules.

Especially for cases where a lot is at stake—for example, a group of people file nuisance cases based on drug dealing or noise (see Chapter 20)—it often makes sense to do some research on the judge who is likely to be assigned your case. Start by asking the small claims court clerk for a list of the judges who may be assigned to your case. One good way to check them out is to have someone in your group (or perhaps a friend or relative) who has the necessary contacts talk to several local lawyers who have practiced before the listed judges. Many lawyers will readily share their opinions, especially if they consider a particular judge to be obnoxious or incompetent. If you discover reliable information about a particular judge that makes you doubt her ability to be fair, be prepared to challenge her.

JUDGES' TIPS

If you're going to reject a temporary or regular judge, you must do it before the judge does anything with your case. You cannot "test" a judge's opinion about the case, decide you don't like it, then try to reject him. This is not only ineffective but also rude.
—Commissioner Douglas G. Carnahan

JUDGES' TIPS

You don't have to say why you believe a judge is prejudiced. After you state your challenge, the judge may have you take the oath again and ask you to repeat your challenge. You aren't expected to say why you challenged the judge, just that you believe she is prejudiced against you or your cause. —Judge (Ret.) Roderic Duncan

Organizing Your Testimony and Evidence

It's essential that you organize what you have to say and the physical evidence you wish to show the judge. Do this by dividing your testimony into a list of the several main points you want to make. Under each heading, note any items of physical or documentary evidence you wish to show the judge. If your evidence consists of a number of items, make sure that you put them in order and can find each item quickly.

> **EXAMPLE (from the plaintiff's point of view):** Let's assume your case is based on a hotel's failure to return your deposit when you canceled a wedding reception three months before the event was to be held. Your list of key points—and the evidence to back them up—might look like this:
>
> - Valley View Hotel refused to return my $500 deposit when I canceled my wedding reception.
> - This was true even though I canceled 83 days before the event.
> - The contract I signed with the hotel allowed a full refund if cancellation occurred more than 60 days before the event. (Show contract to the judge.)
> - When I canceled, Valley View told me (and claims they sent me a letter stating) that their cancellation policy had been changed the previous month to require 90 days' notice in order to get a refund.
> - I never received a letter and had no idea of the policy change until I canceled and asked for my money back.
> - Even if Valley View did send me a letter, the change should not affect my contract, which was signed before the policy change. The key point here is, because I never signed a new contract, the existing contract was still valid.
> - In any event, the hotel has a duty to try and rerent the banquet room to minimize (mitigate) any damages they suffered. And they had plenty of time (83 days) to do so. (See Chapter 4 for a discussion of the mitigation of damages point.)

- Ninety days is an unreasonably long cancellation policy.
- Here is a list of the cancellation policies of five other hotels in the area, all of which allow a full refund on much shorter notice than 83 days. (Give list to the judge.)

EXAMPLE (from the defendant's point of view): Because Valley View goes second, their representative can't know in advance what the plaintiff will say and what evidence it will present. It follows that Valley View will need to adopt a little more flexible approach. Still, chances are that Valley View reps have talked to the plaintiff or exchanged letters, so they probably have a pretty good idea of what to expect. Accordingly, Valley View's list might look something like this.

- True, we didn't refund the $500. The reason was we turned down two other receptions for that same day before the plaintiff canceled. Because we ended up with no other function, we lost at least $500.
- Although it is true that the written contract allowed cancellation prior to 60 days before the event, plaintiff was notified that this policy had been changed to 90 days before the contract was signed in two ways:
  - A sign on the reservations desk where the plaintiff sat to sign the contract. (Show sign to judge.)
  - Testimony of Angie Ells, who booked the reservation. Angie will testify that she included a written notice of the change with the contract package. (Show judge a copy of the notice.) ●

Witnesses

I t can be extremely helpful to have someone in court with you who knows the facts of your case firsthand and can support your point of view. In many types of cases, such as car accidents or disputes over whether or not a tenant left an apartment clean, witnesses are particularly valuable. However, in other fact situations, witnesses aren't as necessary. For example, if a friend borrowed $500 and didn't pay it back, you don't need a witness to prove that your now ex-friend's signature on the promissory note is genuine, unless you expect him to claim that it was forged.

Who Makes a Good Witness

A good witness should have firsthand or personal knowledge of the facts in dispute. This means either she saw something that helps establish your case (for example, the car accident, dog bite, or dirty apartment) or is an expert you have consulted about an important aspect of your case (for example, a car mechanic who testifies that your engine wasn't fixed properly). The judge will not be interested in the testimony of a person who is repeating secondhand or generalized information such as "I know Joe is a good, safe driver and would never have done anything reckless," or "I didn't see Joe's apartment before he moved out, but both Joe and his mother, who couldn't be here today, told me that they worked for two days cleaning it up."

Above all, a good witness is believable. This isn't always an easy quality to define. For example, a police officer may be a symbol of integrity to some people, but others will automatically discount much of what she says. But remember, it's the judge you are trying to convince, and judges tend to be fairly establishment folk. They make comfortable salaries, own their own homes, and generally tend to like the existing order of things, and most judges would be likely to believe a police officer.

In many types of cases, such as a car accident, you won't have much choice as to witnesses. You will be lucky to have one person who saw what happened. Often this will be a close friend or family member. There is no rule that says you can't have these people testify for you. Indeed, a person's spouse, roommate, or close friend can often give very convincing testimony. But given a choice, it is usually better to have a witness who is neither buddy nor kin. That's because a judge may discount the testimony of people to whom you are close on the theory that they would naturally be biased in your favor.

 TIP

One little trick to dispel a judge's cynicism about friends or family who are witnesses. Have a closely related witness bend over backward to treat the other side as fairly as possible. Thus, if your brother is your only witness to the fact that ABC Painting splashed paint on your boat, he might point out to the judge not only that he saw ABC employees screw up, but that it was a very windy day and the painter was understandably having a hard time keeping the paint on the dock where it belonged.

In some types of disputes, such as whether your house was properly painted or the work on the car engine was completed competently, you have an opportunity to plan ahead to locate witnesses. That's because the type of witness you need is usually not an eyewitness who saw the work in progress but instead an expert in the field who can convincingly explain what went wrong. Obviously this type of witness is only valuable if she really does have good credentials and relevant knowledge so that a judge is likely to believe what she says. Thus, in a dispute over whether or not car repairs were properly done, it's preferable to bring a letter from a car mechanic with 20 years' experience who has completed a load of training courses rather than one from your neighbor "who knows a lot about cars."

Selecting and Preparing Witnesses

- Educate your witness thoroughly about your legal and factual position and what your opponent is likely to say. In court, the witness will be on her own, and you want to be sure that the story comes out right. It is completely legal to thoroughly discuss the case with your witness beforehand, as long as you do not coach or encourage the witness to lie or exaggerate.

- Never ask a witness to testify in court unless you know exactly what he will say. This sounds basic, but people have lost cases because their witnesses got mixed up, and in one instance, the witness actually supported the other side.

- Never use a subpoena to require a witness to be present unless you make sure that it is okay with the witness, as might be the case if she needs a good reason to take off a few hours from her job. (For more about subpoenas, see "Subpoenaing Witnesses," below.) Otherwise you may end up making the person so mad he will testify against you.

- Do not offer to pay an eyewitness to testify on your behalf (except for the small witness fee he is entitled to by law). If discovered, your payment will likely be seen as a bribe.

- On the other hand, it's proper and perfectly legal to pay an expert witness—say a car mechanic who has examined your engine—a reasonable fee for her time in court in addition to the time she spent checking your car. As a cheaper and easier alternative, however, the expert can simply write a letter to the judge explaining her findings, which you can then present as part of your case.

For tips on selecting and preparing witnesses for specific types of cases, see Chapters 16–22.

As with your own presentation, the best way to be sure your witness really will be able to explain the key facts to the judge succinctly and concisely is to have her practice her testimony in advance. As long as she sticks to the truth, rehearsing the exact words she will say in court is completely legal. I suggest meeting with your witness and a friend you have asked to act as a mock judge. Start by presenting your case to the pretend judge exactly as you plan to do it in court. Then ask your witness to stand and explain her version of what happened. Have the other friend ask the witness questions about anything that's unclear in the presentation, as a judge would do.

If at first your witness is a little disorganized or unsure, work with her to develop a coherent presentation that covers all key points. When she says something that sounds good, help her write it down and ask her to practice several times before your court date.

Subpoenaing Witnesses

In small claims court, you should almost never use a subpoena to compel a witness to come to court and testify unless the witness has already agreed to testify. This is because the very act of dragging someone into court who doesn't want to come may set her against you. Why use a subpoena at all then?

Why Use a Subpoena

Your witness may need proof that she is testifying for you in court on a specific day in order to get approval to miss work. Or, in rare cases, you may really need testimony from a reluctant witness, in which case you can compel the witness to show up by using a subpoena and informing the witness that the court may fine her if she fails to appear.

How to Subpoena a Witness

In most states, you can require that a witness with firsthand knowledge of what happened be present if that person resides within a certain distance from the courthouse. (The distance varies from state to state. It is often about 150 miles, but in some states subpoenas reach only within county boundaries.)

Expert witnesses cannot be subpoenaed. For this reason they often submit their opinions in writing, a practice that is allowed in most courts.

Below is the standard California subpoena form. The one in your state will probably look quite similar. You will probably need to prepare an original and two copies. Once prepared, take the subpoena form to the clerk, who will issue it. Service must be made personally, and you must return the proof of service, which is probably on the back of the subpoena, to the clerk's office. (Rules for service are discussed in Chapter 11.)

Witness Fees

A subpoenaed witness is usually entitled to a modest fee upon demand. You must pay your witness this fee ahead of time if the witness asks you to. If you win your case, you will probably be able to recover your witness fees from the other side.

TIP

Get a receipt. When you pay your witness's transportation fee as required by law, write a short receipt so that you can prove how much you paid when it comes time to ask the judge to reimburse you for the expense.

The judge has discretion as to whether or not to reimburse you for witness fees. Most judges are strict about this, making the loser pay the winner's witness fees only if they find that the subpoenaed witness was essential to the case. This means that if your case is so strong that you don't need a witness to appear in person but you subpoena one anyway, you may well have to pay the witness fee even though you win the case. (For more information on recovering costs associated with your small claims lawsuit, see Chapter 15.)

Sample Small Claims Subpoena

Name and Address of Court:
Municipal Court, County of Alameda
Berkeley-Albany Judicial District
2000 Center Street

SC-107

SMALL CLAIMS CASE NO. **(123456)**

PLAINTIFF/DEMANDANTE *(Name, address, and telephone number of each):*	DEFENDANT/DEMANDADO *(Name, address, and telephone number of each):*
Public Library **100 Allston Way** **Berkeley, CA 94704**	**John O'Gara** **100 Scenic Drive** **Berkeley, CA 94702**

Telephone No.:   Telephone No.:

Telephone No.:   Telephone No.:

☐ See attached sheet for additional plaintiffs and defendants.

SMALL CLAIMS SUBPOENA
FOR PERSONAL APPEARANCE AND PRODUCTION OF DOCUMENTS
AND THINGS AT TRIAL OR HEARING AND DECLARATION

THE PEOPLE OF THE STATE OF CALIFORNIA, TO *(name, address, and telephone number of witness, if known):*

Jane Doe

1. **YOU ARE ORDERED TO APPEAR AS A WITNESS in this case at the date, time, and place shown in the box below UNLESS your appearance is excused as indicated in box 4b below or you make an agreement with the person named in item 2 below.**

   a. Date: Time: ☐ Dept.:   ☐ Div.:   ☐ Room:
   b. Address:

2. **IF YOU HAVE ANY QUESTIONS ABOUT THE TIME OR DATE YOU ARE TO APPEAR, OR IF YOU WANT TO BE CERTAIN THAT YOUR PRESENCE IS REQUIRED, CONTACT THE FOLLOWING PERSON BEFORE THE DATE ON WHICH YOU ARE TO APPEAR:**

   a. Name of subpoenaing party: *John O'Gara*   b. Telephone number: *510-555-1212*

3. **Witness Fees:** You are entitled to witness fees and mileage actually traveled both ways, as provided by law, if you request them at the time of service. You may request them before your scheduled appearance from the person named in item 2.

PRODUCTION OF DOCUMENTS AND THINGS
(Complete item 4 only if you want the witness to produce documents and things at the trial or hearing.)

4. YOU ARE *(item a or b must be checked)*:

   a. ☒ Ordered to appear in person and to produce the records described in the declaration on page two. The personal attendance of the custodian or other qualified witness and the production of the original records are required by this subpoena. The procedure authorized by Evidence Code sections 1560(b), 1561, and 1562 will not be deemed sufficient compliance with this subpoena.

   b. ☐ Not required to appear in person if you produce (i) the records described in the declaration on page two and (ii) a completed declaration of custodian of records in compliance with Evidence Code sections 1560, 1561, 1562, and 1271. (1) Place a copy of the records in an envelope (or other wrapper). Enclose the original declaration of the custodian with the records. Seal the envelope. (2) Attach a copy of this subpoena to the envelope or write on the envelope the case name and number; your name; and the date, time, and place from item 1 in the box above. (3) Place this first envelope in an outer envelope, seal it, and mail it to the clerk of the court at the address in item 1. (4) Mail a copy of your declaration to the attorney or party listed at the top of this form.

5. **IF YOU HAVE BEEN SERVED WITH THIS SUBPOENA AS A CUSTODIAN OF CONSUMER OR EMPLOYEE RECORDS UNDER CODE OF CIVIL PROCEDURE SECTION 1985.3 OR 1985.6 AND A MOTION TO QUASH OR AN OBJECTION HAS BEEN SERVED ON YOU, A COURT ORDER OR AGREEMENT OF THE PARTIES, WITNESSES, *AND* CONSUMER OR EMPLOYEE AFFECTED MUST BE OBTAINED BEFORE YOU ARE REQUIRED TO PRODUCE CONSUMER OR EMPLOYEE RECORDS.**

DISOBEDIENCE OF THIS SUBPOENA MAY BE PUNISHED AS CONTEMPT BY THIS COURT. YOU WILL ALSO BE LIABLE FOR THE SUM OF FIVE HUNDRED DOLLARS AND ALL DAMAGES RESULTING FROM YOUR FAILURE TO OBEY.

[SEAL]   Date issued:

Clerk, by _____, Deputy

(See reverse for declaration in support of subpoena)   **Page one of three**

Form Adopted for Mandatory Use Judicial Council of California SC-107 [Rev. January 1, 2000]	**SMALL CLAIMS SUBPOENA AND DECLARATION**	Code of Civil Procedure, § 1985 et seq.

Sample Small Claims Subpoena (cont'd.)

PLAINTIFF/PETITIONER: Public Library, 100 Allston Way, Berkeley	CASE NUMBER:
DEFENDANT/RESPONDENT: John O'Gara, 100 Scenic Dr., Berkeley	123456

**DECLARATION IN SUPPORT OF
SMALL CLAIMS SUBPOENA FOR PERSONAL APPEARANCE
AND PRODUCTION OF DOCUMENT AND THINGS AT TRIAL OR HEARING**
(Code Civil Procedure sections 1985, 1987.5)

1. I, the undersigned, declare I am the ☐ plaintiff ☒ defendant ☐ judgment creditor
☐ other *(specify)*: in the above entitled action.

2. The witness has possession or control of the following documents or other things and shall produce them at the time and place specified on the *Small Claims Subpoena* on the first page of this form.

    a. ☒ For trial or hearing *(specify the exact documents or other things to be produced by the witness)*:

      Book inventory information collected by the main branch of the public library during the calendar year 20xx.

      ☐ Continued on Attachment 2a.

    b. ☐ After trial to enforce a judgment *(specify the exact documents or other things to be produced by the party who is the judgment debtor or other witness possessing records relating to the judgment debtor)*:

      (1) ☐ Payroll receipts, stubs, and other records concerning employment of the party. Receipts, invoices, documents, and other papers or records concerning any and all accounts receivable of the party.

      (2) ☐ Bank account statements, canceled checks, and check registers from any and all bank accounts in which the party has an interest.

      (3) ☐ Savings account passbooks and statements, savings and loan account passbooks and statements, and credit union share account passbooks and statements of the party.

      (4) ☐ Stock certificates, bonds, money market certificates, and any other records, documents, or papers concerning all investments of the party.

      (5) ☐ California registration certificates and ownership certificates for all vehicles registered to the party.

      (6) ☐ Deeds to any and all real property owned or being purchased by the party.

      (7) ☐ Other *(specify)*:

3. Good cause exists for the production of the documents or other things described in paragraph 2 for the following reasons:

    My contention is that I returned the books for which the library is suing me. The inventory should back me up on this.

    ☐ Continued on Attachment 3.

4. These documents are material to the issues involved in this case for the following reasons:

    The location of the books at issue is central to this case.

    ☐ Continued on Attachment 4.

I declare under penalty of perjury under the laws of the State of California that the foregoing is true and correct.

Date: May 20, 20xx

John O'Gara	▶	John O'Gara
(TYPE OR PRINT NAME)		(SIGNATURE OF PARTY)

(See proof of service on page three)

| SC-107 [Rev. January 1, 2000] | **SMALL CLAIMS SUBPOENA AND DECLARATION** | Page two of three |

Subpoenaing Police Officers

You normally use the standard subpoena form to subpoena a police officer, firefighter, or other peace officer to testify to anything observed or investigated in the course of duty. Fill the form out, take it to the court clerk for a seal and date stamp, then take it to the relevant police or fire department to comply with any of their additional procedures. (For example, the police department may require two copies of the subpoena instead of one.) Give the witnesses plenty of advance notice. You will have to pay the officer's salary for the time taken off work to appear. You must pay this in advance in the form of a deposit (usually about $150), payable to the agency employing the officer. The subpoena may be served on the officer personally or on the officer's superior.

Depending on the amount of the officer's time that is used, you may eventually get a refund of some of your deposit. Don't hold your breath, however. Many law enforcement offices are seemingly unaware that this is a deposit and not a flat fee, and have no procedure in place for issuing refunds.

Subpoenaing Documents

In addition to witnesses, you can also subpoena documents. This is rarely done in small claims court, but there are times when it may be helpful. An organization (such as a police department, phone company, hospital, or corporation) may have certain books, ledgers, papers, or other documents that can help your case. Unless the organization volunteers to bring the documents to court for you (which is rare), you'll need to prepare a court order, called a "subpoena duces tecum," that directs the person in the organization who is in charge of the records to send them directly to the court. This subpoena is very similar to the standard subpoena form, except for the added space where you describe the papers or other documents you want. Keep in mind that successfully bringing documents before the court does not guarantee that the judge will admit them into evidence. The judge must be convinced that the records are relevant to your case.

To get a subpoena duces tecum issued, you must normally follow a procedure along the following lines: Attach to the completed subpoena form an affidavit stating "under penalty of perjury" why you need the written material. Prepare three copies of all papers and, after you get the clerk to issue the subpoena, serve it on the witness using personal service, as described in Chapter 11. As with a regular subpoena, the witness is entitled to ask for a fee. The Proof of Service is on the back of the subpoena form; it must be filled out and returned to the clerk.

CAUTION

Rules for subpoenas vary from state to state. Technical rules on filing and serving papers, as well as paying witness fees, vary considerably from one state to the next. Make sure you know what will be required. Also, before subpoenaing documents, be sure to ask whether the other side will simply give you photocopies in advance.

A subpoena duces tecum must be directed to the person who is in charge of the documents, books, or records you want produced in court. It may take a few phone calls to find out who this is. Be sure you get this information accurately. If you list someone on the subpoena duces tecum who has nothing to do with the documents, you won't get them. When dealing with a large corporation, public utility, or municipal government, it is wise to list the person who is in overall charge of the department where the records are kept. Thus, if you want records having to do with library fines from a public library, or having to do with business license fees from the city tax and license department, you should not list the city manager or the mayor, but should list the head librarian or the director of the tax and license office.

EXAMPLE: You are being sued by the city on behalf of the public library for $800 for eight rare books that they state you failed to return. You know you did return the books but can't seem to get that across to the library, which insists on treating you like a thief. You learn that each April the library takes a yearly inventory of all books on their shelves. You believe that if you can get access to that inventory, you may be able to figure out where the library misplaced the books, or at least show that a significant percentage of the library's other books are not accounted for, raising the implication that they, not you, lost the books.

Your first step is to ask the library to voluntarily open the inventory to you. If they refuse, you may well want to subpoena it. Here's how:

1. Complete the subpoena form.
2. Prepare a declaration under penalty of perjury. Briefly describe the documents you need and why they are necessary to prove issues involved in the case. If you want the custodian of the records to show up in person, give a reason. Don't argue the merits of your case.
3. Have a subpoena issued by the small claims clerk. Then deliver the subpoena to the head librarian, being sure to properly fill out the Proof of Service (see Chapter 11) and return it to the clerk.

> **TIP**
>
> **Ask to examine documents prior to your court hearing.** The documents you have subpoenaed will be mailed or presented to the court— not to you. You will probably want an opportunity to examine them and should request it from the judge, who may well let you look at them right there in the courtroom while other cases go ahead. Or, if necessary, the judge may postpone the case for a few days and arrange to have you examine the documents at the place of business where the records are normally kept.

Witness Testimony by Letter

In most small claims courts, there are no formal rules of evidence requiring a witness to testify in person (but be sure to check your local rules). It is often preferable to have a witness appear in court, but this isn't always possible, and a judge will accept written statements from both eyewitnesses ("I was there and saw the filthy apartment") and expert witnesses ("I examined the transmission and found that a rebuilt part was installed improperly"). If you do present the written statement of a witness, make sure the witness states the following facts:

For an eyewitness:

- who the witness is
- the date of the event, and
- what she saw, heard, smelled, felt, or tasted, and where and how she did so.

For an expert witness:

- who the witness is
- the witness's work and education credentials, which demonstrate her expertise in the field she is commenting on (if these are lengthy, it's a good idea to attach the person's résumé)
- what he did to be able to render his opinion ("I examined the paint on Mr. Jones's 35-foot Cabin Cruiser and subjected it to the following test....")
- when he did the work
- his conclusion (the paint used was not suitable for salt water immersion)
- if possible, an estimate of the cost to redo the work properly, and
- any other facts that have a bearing on the dispute.

> 💡 **TIP**
>
> **Make sure you establish your expert's experience and training.**
> It's a good idea to attach to an expert's letter a separate list of the expert's credentials. If your expert has a résumé listing credentials, attach it to the letter in which she states her findings. The more distinguished your expert, the more likely the judge is to respect her opinion.

Sample Letter by Eyewitness

Victor Van Cleve
37 Ogden Court
Kansas City, KS
September 30, 20xx

Presiding Judge
Small Claims Court
Kansas City, KS
Re: *John Swift vs. Peter Petrakos*
Small Claims Case No. 11478

Your Honor:

On September 15, 20xx, at approximately 7:30 a.m, I was parked near the corner of South Dora and 7th Streets in Larchville. I was parked on South Dora, about three parking spaces south of the intersection. Just after 7:30, I witnessed an auto accident involving John Swift and Peter Petrakos.

I clearly saw Mr. Petrakos's yellow Toyota, which was heading north on South Dora, go through a red light and hit Mr. Swift's blue van, which was proceeding west on 7th, well inside the 25 MPH speed limit. I noticed that the traffic light facing Mr. Petrakos did not turn to green for ten seconds or so after the accident, so it is clear to me that Mr. Petrakos really did go through the light while it was fully red. In short, this was not a situation where Mr. Petrakos was just a tiny bit early getting into the intersection at a light change.

Sincerely,

Victor Van Cleve

Victor Van Cleve

Sample Letter by Expert Witness

Gail McClosky
47 Penrod Street
Helena, MT
Sept. 30, 20xx

Judge
Small Claims Court
Helena, MT

Re: *James Dills vs. R & B Construction*
Small Claims Case No. 11478

Your Honor:

I am a fully licensed contractor with 20 years' experience here in Helena (Contractor's License 4021B). For the last ten years I've run my own five-person contracting company specializing in building enclosures and buildings to house horses and other large animals. I enclose a résumé outlining my specialized training and experience in this field.

On April 23, 20xx, I was asked by James Dills to inspect several new stalls he had contracted to be built in the main barn of his Lazy T Riding Stable by R&B Construction.

In my opinion these stalls are seriously below normal industry standards, for three reasons.

1) They are too small for the animals intended to be kept in them. [*Continue with details.*]

2) Walls and doors are built of plywood too thin to safely contain an agitated animal. [*Continue with details.*]

3) Construction is so rough and unfinished in several places as to pose a danger of injury to an animal intended to be kept there. [*Continue with details.*]

In conclusion, I believe the stalls are so poorly constructed they can't reasonably be upgraded to provide safe habitable housing for horses. Were they mine, I would rip them out and start over.

Sincerely,

Gail McClosky

Gail McClosky

Judges as Witnesses

A small claims judge has great discretion to climb down off the bench to check out an important fact. Asking a judge to check out a key fact in your case can be a valuable technique in some situations. For example, in disputes involving damaged clothing it is routine to bring the damaged or defective garment into court for the judge's examination. Indeed, it normally makes sense to bring physical evidence that meets these three criteria:

- showing it to the judge will help your case

- it will fit through the door, and

- bringing it into the courtroom is not dangerous or inappropriate, as would be the case with an animal, firearm, or extremely dirty or smelly items.

But what if your evidence is impossible to bring into the courtroom (a car with a poor paint job or a supposedly pedigreed puppy that grew up to look as if Lassie were the mother and Rin Tin Tin the father)? Simply ask the judge to accompany you outside the building to the parking lot to examine the car, the dog, or whatever else is important to your case. Many (but not all) judges will cheerfully do so if you make a convincing argument as to why it is necessary to understand the dispute (and especially if it won't take too long). For example, one excellent judge I know was disturbed one morning when two eyewitnesses gave seriously contradictory testimony about a traffic accident. He questioned both in detail and then took the case under submission. That evening, he drove over to the relevant corner. Once there, it was clear that one of the witnesses couldn't possibly have seen the accident from the spot on which she claimed to be standing (in front of a particular restaurant). The judge decided the case in favor of the other party.

CAUTION

Don't waste a judge's time. Never ask a judge to take time to leave her court to view evidence if you can establish or prove the same point by other means, such as by presenting the testimony (or letter) of a witness or by showing the judge a photograph.

JUDGES' TIPS

Small claims court judges may independently consult expert witnesses. Many small claims judges keep lists of "experts" whom they consult from time to time regarding particular issues in medicine, dentistry, plumbing, auto repair—you name it. If a judge is going to do this, she should tell the parties so they have some idea where the decision is coming from. If you think the judge is considering such a step, don't be shy about asking if that is indeed her intention and what expert the judge has in mind. It would not be untoward, for instance, to ask the judge to state in the written judgment the source of any expert advice. The worst the judge can do is say no.
—Commissioner Douglas G. Carnahan

JUDGES' TIPS

A judge may go on a "walkabout." A colleague who was deciding a small claims neighborhood nuisance case went out and walked through the neighborhood in question, getting a stronger understanding of the problem than if he had remained in the courtroom.
—Judge (Ret.) Roderic Duncan

Testimony by Telephone

A surprising number of small claims court judges will take testimony over the phone if a witness cannot be present because she is ill, disabled, out of state, or can't take time off from work. While procedures vary, some courts will do this by setting up a conference call so that the opposing party has the opportunity to hear what is being said and to respond.

Don't assume that a particular judge will allow telephone testimony. If you think you'll need to have a witness testify by phone, explain your problem to the court clerk well in advance. If you get a negative response, don't give up—ask the judge when you get into the courtroom. Be sure you also present a letter from the witness stating what he would testify to if he was present in court (for example, your opponent's car ran a red light and broadsided you) and explaining why it is impossible for him to be there. This letter should look like the first sample letter in "Witness Testimony by Letter," above, except the witness should add:

> *"Mr. Swift has asked me to testify on his behalf, and normally I would be happy to do so. However, I will be in New York City on business during the months of October, November, and December 20xx and cannot be present.*
>
> *"I have asked Mr. Swift to let me know the day and approximate time of the court hearing and have told him that I will give him a phone number where I can be reached. If you think it desirable, I will be pleased to give my testimony by phone."* ●

CHAPTER

15

Your Day in Court

This chapter focuses on how to present your case to the judge. However, we first need to deal with the very real possibility that the other party does a no-show.

If Your Opponent Doesn't Show Up

If one party to a case doesn't appear in court on the proper day at the proper time, the case is normally decided in favor of the other, although the judge will first verify that the defendant was properly served with court papers (see Chapter 11) and that neither party requested a postponement (see Chapter 10).

> **TIP**
>
> **Don't rely on a second chance.** In some states, if neither party appears, the judge may take the case "off calendar," meaning the case is delayed until a future date. Don't count on it, however. Make every effort to show up or notify the court clerk if you are unavoidably detained.

If the Defendant Doesn't Show Up

If you, the plaintiff, appear, but the defendant doesn't, the judge in most states normally will ask you to state briefly the basic facts of your case and present any important written evidence, such as a copy of the written contract you claim the defendant broke. In the few states that require a defendant to file a written answer (see the Appendix), you should be able to find out before the court date whether the other side will appear. The next step is to ask what, if anything, you must do to get your default judgment.

JUDGES' TIPS

Don't expect to win just because your opponent failed to appear. The law requires that you give enough evidence to show that the defendant actually owes you money. —Commissioner Douglas G. Carnahan

Plaintiff Gets a Default Judgment

Because the defendant is not present to contradict anything you say, the judge usually will rule in your favor as long as you state the bare bones of a valid legal claim. The defendant has no right to appeal this judgment in most states (see Chapter 23) unless he first gets the small claims court judge to reopen the case by vacating the default judgment.

EXAMPLE: "Your Honor, I own the Racafrax Auto Repair Shop. On January 11, 20xx, I repaired defendant's 2001 Honda Civic. He paid me $500 and agreed to pay another $500 on March 1. He has not made the second payment. I have copies of the contract defendant signed and of several unpaid bills I sent him. I am asking for a judgment of $500 plus $55 for my court filing fee and the cost of having the papers served."

TIP

No need for a long-winded presentation. If the defendant isn't present, a judge only wants to hear the basic facts necessary to support a judgment in your favor. You do not need to make an extended argument, because in the absence of your opponent the judge will assume your version of what happened is true.

Defendant May Ask Judge to Set Aside the Default Judgment

If the defendant has a good excuse for failing to appear at the hearing, she may ask the judge to retract the judgment against her (this is called "setting aside the judgment" or "vacating the judgment.") Courts are not very sympathetic to setting aside or vacating a default judgment unless you can show that the original papers weren't properly served on you and that you didn't know about the hearing. In some states, this can happen if someone signs your name for a certified letter and then doesn't give it to you. In all states, it can occur when a dishonest process server doesn't serve you, but tells the court otherwise. As soon as you find out that a default judgment has been entered against you, call the court clerk. It doesn't make any difference if the hearing you missed was months before, as long as you move to set it aside immediately upon learning about it.

If you have had a default judgment entered against you after you were properly served, you will face an uphill struggle to get it set aside. A few judges will accept almost any excuse ("I forgot," "I was sick," "I got called out of town"). Generally, however, judges assume that you could have at least called, or had a friend call, no matter what the emergency, and they will not vacate the judgment except for an extremely good cause. However, if you act promptly and if you have a good excuse, you stand a reasonable chance of getting the judge to set the default aside.

⚠ **CAUTION**

No appeal from default judgment. In most states, you can't appeal a default judgment even if you have a great case. Instead, you must promptly try to get the default set aside, or the judgment will be final. To try to set aside a default, go to the small claims court clerk's office and ask for the proper form, which will normally be titled something like Notice of Motion to Vacate Judgment.

Sometimes the defendant files a motion to vacate (set aside) a default judgment only after a "writ of execution" to collect the small claims judgment has already been entered for the plaintiff. In this situation, in most states the writ of execution will be recalled (stayed) by the court until a decision on the motion to vacate the default judgment is made. If the writ of execution has already been served as part of an effort to collect, the defendant must file a motion to suspend the writ of execution (often called a Motion to Stay or Quash the Writ of Execution), pending the court's decision on whether or not to set aside the default judgment and reopen the case. For more information on how to do this, or to find out the exact rules for your state, consult your small claims court clerk.

How to Handle a Motion to Vacate Judgment: Defendant's and Plaintiff's Perspectives

Some judges will routinely vacate defaults on the basis of almost any hard luck story. Others, however, will refuse to vacate a default judgment unless the defendant made a written request for a postponement before the hearing or can show that a real emergency caused her to miss the hearing. An example of an emergency that would persuade the judge is a death in the family the day before the hearing or having never received the original court papers and therefore having had no idea a hearing was scheduled.

Because the judge has great legal discretion as to whether to vacate a default, it's impossible to predict what any particular judge will do. For this reason, defendants should immediately make their motion to vacate the judgment as soon as they realize they missed the original hearing.

Plaintiffs, who benefit from a default judgment and understandably would prefer it to stand, should emphasize that they played by the rules and showed up on the original hearing date, whereas the defendant failed to do so and, assuming it's true, failed to request a postponement. If the plaintiff had witnesses ready to testify at the original hearing, and these people will have a hard time coming to court a second time, plaintiffs should also mention this (and perhaps submit written statements from the witnesses).

If the small claims judge grants the defendant's motion to vacate judgment, then one of two things will happen. If all parties are present and agree, the small claims judge may hear the original case without rescheduling it. If, however, the plaintiff is not present for the hearing on the defendant's motion to vacate judgment, or if the parties do not agree to hear the case then and there, the judge will reschedule the hearing and the clerk will mail written notice of the new hearing date to the parties.

> 💡 **TIP**
>
> **Always be ready to argue your side of the actual case.** If the judge decides to grant the defendant's motion to vacate judgment, the judge will ask the parties whether they are prepared to argue the underlying case. Also, if the small claims court judge denies the defendant's motion to vacate judgment and the defendant appeals to superior court (see below), the superior court judge has the authority to decide the underlying small claims court case if he grants the defendant's motion. For that reason, both parties should always be prepared to argue the case whenever they have a hearing.

If the small claims judge decides not to set aside the default, defendants in most states can appeal the judge's refusal (but not the decision in the case itself) to a higher court. (See Chapter 23 for more on appeals.)

If the higher court judge agrees with the small claims court judge, then the case is over and the plaintiff wins. If, however, the appeals court judge disagrees with the small claims court judge and vacates the default judgment, and if both parties are present and agree, the appeals court judge in most states can hear and decide the case immediately. If both parties aren't present or do not agree, then the appeals court judge will order the small claims court to schedule another hearing.

If the Plaintiff Doesn't Show Up

Occasionally, though less frequently, it is the plaintiff who fails to show up. In this situation, the judge normally will either dismiss the case or decide it based on the defendant's evidence, especially if the defendant filed a Defendant's Claim. The defendant usually will prefer to have the judge decide the case, because if the case is simply dismissed (called a "dismissal without prejudice"), the plaintiff can refile it.

If the Judge Dismisses the Plaintiff's Case

If a plaintiff does not show up at the hearing and did not request a postponement, the judge probably will dismiss the case. If the judge dismisses the case "without prejudice," this means the plaintiff can refile the case as long as the statute of limitations has not run out in the meantime. (See Chapter 5.) Normally, you have to refile quickly (many states have a 30-day limit).

However, if the judge dismisses the case "with prejudice," the plaintiff can't refile the case without first asking the judge to cancel (vacate or set aside) the dismissal. A judge is most likely to dismiss a case with prejudice if the defendant shows up in court and the plaintiff did not file a written request for postponement before the court date. (See Chapter 10.)

The judge is most likely to grant your motion to set aside the dismissal if both of the following are true:

• The plaintiff moves to have the judgment vacated promptly upon learning of his mistake. "Promptly" usually means within 30 days after the day the dismissal was entered and is thought by most judges to be a much shorter time.

• The plaintiff has a good explanation as to why he was unable to be present or call on the day the case was regularly scheduled. A judge might accept something like this: "I had a flu with a high fever and simply lost track of a couple of days. As soon as I felt better, which was two days after my case was dismissed, I came to the clerk's office to try to get the case rescheduled."

To get a dismissal vacated (when allowed), ask the small claims court clerk for the rules and forms you should use.

If the Judge Gives the Defendant a Default Judgment

If the judge enters a default judgment for the defendant, the plaintiff cannot appeal the judgment against her but may appeal the judge's decision to give the defendant a default judgment. (For details on how to do this, see "Defendant May Ask Judge to Set Aside the Default Judgment," above.) Remember, the plaintiff is the one who initiated the case and established the hearing date, so no one is going to have a great deal of sympathy for the plaintiff's failure to show up, and the plaintiff's reason for not appearing must be a very good one and should be supported by written evidence.

Contested Cases

Assume now that both sides show up and step forward when the case is called by the clerk. What happens next? First, the judge will ask everyone's name and who they are (plaintiff, defendant, or witness). Second, she will ask the plaintiff to briefly state his case. After the plaintiff and any witnesses for the plaintiff speak, then the defendant will have her turn.

Tips for Both Parties

Before we focus on the plaintiff's and defendant's presentations, here are a few tips both parties should find helpful. These are not rules written on golden tablets, only suggestions. You may want to follow some and ignore others.

- Stand when you make your initial presentation to the judge. Standing gives most people a sense of presence and confidence at a time when they may be a little nervous. It's fine to sit while your opponent is talking. If the judge interrupts your opponent's presentation to ask you a quick question that requires a short answer, there is no need to leap to your feet to answer it.

- Be as brief as you can while still being sure to explain and document your case thoroughly.

- Start with the end of the story, not the beginning. That is, describe your loss and how much you are asking for. Then go back and tell your story chronologically.

- Don't read your statement. Reading in court is almost always a bore. But you may find it helpful to make a few notes on a card to serve as a reminder in case you get nervous or forget something. If you decide to do this, list the headings of the various points you want to make in an outline form. Be sure your list is easy to read at a glance and that the topics are in the correct order. (See Chapter 13 for a sample list.)

- During your or your witness's presentation, the judge is likely to interrupt to ask questions. Never put the judge off by saying you'll get to the point she is interested in later in your presentation. Far better to directly answer her questions. Just be sure that you and your witnesses eventually get a chance to make all of your key points. If you feel rushed, say so. The judge will normally slow things down a little.

 JUDGES' TIPS

Really, don't interrupt. When I presided over small claims cases, I would start each session by announcing, "Please do not interrupt the other side when they are speaking, no matter how outrageous you think any particular statement might be. I promise you'll have a turn to tell me your side of the case. I don't usually use a point system in deciding a case, but if you interrupt the other side while they are speaking and sing out with something like, 'That's a lie!,' I'd be tempted to subtract a point from any score I was keeping. And you never know, you might need that point later on." I'd smile at the audience, and they'd chuckle, but when the first person violated that rule, there'd be a big groan from the audience.
—Judge (Ret.) Roderic Duncan

- Try to present any portion of your case that is difficult to explain verbally in another way. This often means bringing your used car parts, damaged clothing, or other exhibits, such as photographs or canceled checks, and presenting them to the judge in an organized way. Short videos can be helpful, but call in advance to see whether your court has a VCR.

- Don't act like a lawyer when asking your witnesses to testify; let them tell their story and only ask questions at the end if they've left out an important fact.

- There will be a blackboard in court. If drawings will be helpful, as is almost always true in cases involving car accidents, be sure to ask the judge for permission to use it. You will want to draw clearly and legibly the first time, so it's wise to practice in advance or prepare a small version of the drawing ahead of time to copy from.

- If you are the defendant, don't repeat facts already presented by the plaintiff that you don't dispute (for example, that the two of you had a fender bender at a certain corner in a certain city at a certain time during certain weather conditions). Instead, focus on the facts of your principal disagreement (whether the light facing you was green or red, for example) and introduce evidence to prove that point.

- Ask for a continuance if necessary. The best laid plans can occasionally go haywire. Perhaps a key witness doesn't show up, or maybe, despite careful preparation, you overlook some aspect of the case that the judge feels is crucial. If this occurs, you may want to ask the judge to reschedule the case on another day so that you can prepare better. It is perfectly proper to make this sort of request. Whether or not it will be granted is up to the judge. If she feels that more evidence isn't likely to change the result, or that you are making the request as a stalling tactic, it will not be granted. If, despite the fact that you prepared conscientiously, there is a good reason for a delay, it will usually be allowed.

- Recognize that a judge who is convinced that one side is morally in the right will bend over backward to find a legal reason to rule in that person's favor. For example, if you lent a friend money in an emergency and he is now trying to wriggle out of his obligation based on a legal technicality (claims the loan was really a gift), make sure the judge understands the trouble your opponent's bad act has caused you (you can't afford to pay college tuition).

- If you've done legal research and believe that a statute or court decision supports your position, call it to the attention of the judge as part of your oral presentation. If possible, it's also a good idea to back this up with a brief written memo. (See "Sample Legal Research Memo," below.) Begin with the name and number of your case. Then list the official citation of the statute, ordinance, or court case you think helps your case and briefly explain why. (See Chapter 25 for an explanation of how to cite statutes and cases.) In court, give one copy of the memo to the clerk to hand to the judge and another to your opponent.

 JUDGES' TIPS

Less can be more when you're testifying. If the judge asks you a question like, "Did you have a written lease with the landlord?" the better answer is either "Yes" or "No," as appropriate, not something like: "Well, Your Honor, before I answer that question I need to tell you the background of the case. I first met the landlord in 1967, and then..." You get the idea.
—Commissioner Douglas G. Carnahan

TIP

Practice your presentation early and often. As emphasized throughout this book, it pays to practice making your oral presentation ahead of time. Have a tough-minded friend or family member play the part of judge and be ready to ask questions and try to poke holes in your best points. Run through your presentation several times until you get it right.

Sample Legal Research Memo

MEMO

August 10, 20xx

Lee vs. Yew   Small Claims #127654

To: Small Claims Judge

From: Robert Yew, Defendant

Re: California law on boundary trees

This case involves Mr. Lee, my next-door neighbor, suing me because he claims my Monterey Pine tree drops debris on his roof and yard. Although he is asking for a judgment of $500 for cleanup costs, what he really wants is for me to pay several thousand dollars to remove the 80-foot tree.

There is only one problem with Mr. Lee's argument—because the tree touches our boundary line, the tree is half his. That's because California law, as set forth in Civil Code Section 834, clearly states that "Trees whose trunks stand partly on the land of two or more coterminous owners, belong to them in common."

Mr. Lee will argue that the tree was planted 100% on my property by the person who owned my house before I bought it and that the tree is still 90% on my side of the property line. Both contentions are true, but as you can see under Civil Code Section 834, it makes no difference. As long as the tree touches the boundary line—which the photographs I have presented the court clearly prove—the tree belongs to both of us as co-owners (tenants in common). *(Anderson v. Weiland,* 12 Cal. 2d 730 (1936).)

I have offered to try and mediate the dispute, but so far Mr. Lee says, "No." I hope he will change his mind.

Respectfully submitted,

Robert Yew

Robert Yew

From the Plaintiff's Side

If you are the plaintiff, you should clearly tell the judge what the dispute is about before you start describing the details of what happened.

If your case involves a car accident, you might start by saying:

"This case involves a car accident at Cedar and Rose Streets in which my car suffered $872 worth of damage when the defendant ran a red light and hit my front fender."

That introduction is much better than:

"It all started when I was driving down Rose Street after having a bagel with cream cheese for breakfast."

It's a rare case where the plaintiff's initial presentation should take longer than five minutes. As part of your statement, you should present and explain the relevance of any papers, photos, or other documentary evidence. You should hand these to the clerk, who will pass them on to the judge. You should also be sure to tell the judge if you have any witnesses to present.

Your witness will normally be given a chance to speak after you complete your presentation. The witness should be well prepared to state her key information in an organized way (for example, that she inspected the apartment immediately after you did your final cleanup and found it to be clean). Too often, when a witness is asked to testify, she either leaves out important points or is so disorganized that the force of her testimony is lost. (For information on preparing your witnesses, see Chapter 14.)

JUDGES' TIPS

The judge will probably question your witnesses. Don't count on being allowed to ask your witnesses questions or cross-examine the other party or their witnesses. Most judges will want to do any questioning of witnesses that is going to take place. Hostile feelings often bubble forth

if the parties are allowed to ask questions of opposing witnesses. If one of your witnesses forgets an important point, wait until the judge is about to excuse the witness and then politely suggest that the judge allow the witness to make a further statement, for example, "Your Honor, Ms. Peterson hasn't said anything about the color of the traffic light. Would it be possible for you to ask her to cover that subject?" If your opponent or one of her witnesses skirts an important issue, say something similar, like, "Your Honor, the defendant hasn't said anything about how many beers he drank that night. I would appreciate it if you would ask him to cover that subject."
—Judge (Ret.) Roderic Duncan

From the Defendant's Side

Sooner or later it will finally be the defendant's turn. Defendants often get so angry at something the plaintiff has said that when they get to speak, they attack angrily. This is usually counterproductive. Far better to calmly and clearly present your side of the dispute to the judge. Start with the key point of contention and then fill in the details of what happened from your point of view. If the plaintiff has made significant false or misleading statements, these should definitely be pointed out. But to show the judge how calm and fair-minded you are, wait until after you have made your key points to calmly point out your opponent's misstatements.

> EXAMPLE: "Your Honor, it's true that the bumper of my truck hit the defendant's fender and pushed it in slightly. But the key thing I want you to understand is that this happened because the defendant's pickup entered the intersection before it was clear and therefore the accident was his fault. Here is what happened. I was driving south on Cedar and entered the intersection just as the light first turned yellow. I slowed briefly near the center line behind a car that was turning left and then continued across, at which point the defendant's car darted in front of me...."

A Sample Contested Case

Now let's look at how a contested case might be presented from both the plaintiff's and defendant's perspectives.

Clerk: "The next case is *John Andrews v. Robertson Realty*. Will everyone please come forward?" (Four people come forward and sit at the table facing the judge.)

Judge: "Good morning. Which one of you is Mr. Andrews? Okay, will you begin, Mr. Andrews?"

John Andrews: (stands) "This is a case about my failure to get a $700 cleaning deposit returned, your Honor. I rented a house from Robertson Realty at 1611 Spruce Street in Rockford in March 20xx on a month-to-month tenancy. On January 10, 20xx, I sent Mr. Robertson a written notice that I was planning to move on March 10. In fact, I moved out on March 8 and left the place extremely clean. I know it was clean because I spent eight hours, a lot of them on my hands and knees, cleaning it. In addition, all of my rent was properly paid. A few days after I moved out, I asked Mr. Robertson to return my $700 deposit. He wrote me a letter stating that the place was dirty and he was keeping my deposit.

"I have with me a copy of a letter I wrote to Mr. Robertson on March 15 setting out my position in more detail. I also have some photographs that my friend, Carol Spann, who is here as a witness, took on the day I moved out. I believe the pictures show pretty clearly that I did a thorough cleanup." (John Andrews hands the letter and pictures to the clerk, who hands them to the judge.)

"Your Honor, I am asking not only for the $700 deposit, but also for $1,400 in punitive damages, which the law of this state allows a tenant when a landlord improperly refuses to return a deposit."

Judge: "Mr. Andrews, will you introduce your witness?"

Andrews: "Yes, this is Carol Spann. She helped me clean up and move on March 7 and 8."

Judge: (looking at the pictures) "Ms. Spann, were you in the house the day John Andrews moved out?"

Carol Spann: (standing) "Yes, your Honor, I was—and the day before, too. I helped clean up, and I can say that we did a good job. Not only did we do the normal washing and scrubbing, but we waxed the kitchen floor, cleaned the bathroom tile, and shampooed the rugs."

Judge: (turning to Mr. Robertson) "Okay, now it's your turn to tell me why the deposit wasn't returned."

Harry Robertson: (standing) "I don't know how they could have cleaned the place up, your Honor, because it was filthy when I inspected it on March 9. Let me give you a few specifics. There was mildew and mold around the bathtub, the windows were filthy, the refrigerator hadn't been defrosted, and there was dog—how shall I say it—dog manure in the basement. Your Honor, I have brought along Clem Houndstooth as a witness. Mr. Houndstooth is the tenant who moved in three days after Mr. Andrews moved out. Incidentally, your Honor, the place was so dirty that I only charged Mr. Houndstooth a $200 cleaning deposit, because he agreed to clean it up himself."

Judge: (looking at Clem Houndstooth) "Do you wish to say something?"

Clem Houndstooth: (standing) "Yes, I do. Mr. Robertson asked me to come down and back him up and I am glad to do it because I put in two full days cleaning that place up. I like a clean house, your Honor, not a halfway clean, halfway dirty house. I just don't think that a house is clean if the oven is full of gunk, there is mold in the bathroom, and the insides of the cupboards are grimy. All these conditions existed at 1611 Spruce Street when I moved in. I just don't believe that anyone could think that that place was clean."

Judge: "Mr. Andrews, do you have anything to add?"

John Andrews: (standing up) "Yes, I sure do. First, as to the mildew problem. The house is 40 years old, and there is some dampness in the wall of the bathroom. Maybe there is a leaky pipe someplace behind the tile. I cleaned it a number of times, but it always came back. I talked to Mr. Fisk in Mr. Robertson's office about the problem about a month after I moved in, and he told me that I would have to do the best I could because they couldn't afford to tear the wall apart. As to the cupboards and stove, they are both old. The cabinets haven't been painted in ten years, so, of course, they aren't perfect, and that old stove was a lot dirtier when I moved in than it is now, because I can tell you I personally worked on it with oven cleaner for over an hour."

Judge: "What about the refrigerator, Mr. Andrews? Was that defrosted?"

John Andrews: "No, your Honor, it wasn't, but it had been defrosted about three weeks before I moved out, and I thought that it was good enough the way it was."

Judge: "Okay, if no one else has anything to add, I want to return your pictures and letters. You will receive my decision by mail in a few days."

Now, I have a little surprise for you. The case I just presented is based closely on a real small claims case. As they used to say on *Dragnet*, "Only the names have been changed to protect the innocent." And I have another surprise for you. I spoke to the judge after the court session. Here is how he decided the case.

"This is a typical case in which both sides have some right on their side. What is clean to one person may be dirty to another. Based on what I heard, I would have to guess that the old tenant made a fairly conscientious effort to clean up and probably left the place about as clean as it was when he moved in, but that the new tenant, Houndstooth, had much higher standards and convinced the landlord that it was filthy. The landlord may not have needed too much convincing since he probably would just as well keep the deposit. But I did hear enough to convince me that Andrews, the old tenant, didn't do a perfect job cleaning up. My decision will be that Andrews gets a judgment for the return of $450 of the $700 deposit, with no punitive

damages. I believe that $250 is more than enough to compensate the landlord for any damages he suffered as a result of the house 'being a little dirty.'"

I then asked the judge if he felt that the case was well presented. He replied substantially as follows:

"Better than average. I think I got a pretty good idea of what the problems were. The witnesses were helpful and the pictures gave me a pretty good idea that the place wasn't a total mess. Both sides could have done better, however. Andrews could have presented a witness to testify to the condition of the house when he moved in if, in fact, it was truly a lot dirtier than when he left. Another witness to testify to the fact that the house was clean when he moved out would have been good, too. His friend, Carol Spann, seemed to be a very close friend, and I wasn't sure that she was objective when it came to judging whether or not the place was clean. The landlord, Robertson, could also have done better. He could have presented a more disinterested witness, although I must say that Houndstooth's testimony was pretty convincing. Also he could have had pictures documenting the dirty conditions and an estimate from a cleaning company for how much they would have charged to clean the place up. Without going to too much trouble, I think both sides could have probably done somewhat better with more thorough preparation."

Don't Forget to Ask for Your Costs

Both plaintiff and defendant are entitled to ask that a judgment in their favor include any recoverable costs, such as for filing and serving court papers or subpoenaing essential witnesses. Sometimes defendants have no costs, unless they subpoena a necessary witness. In most states, costs that are recoverable by the winner include:

- The plaintiff's court filing fee (defendants pay no fee to appear unless they file a Defendant's Claim).

- Service of process costs. A plaintiff must always pay this fee, which can vary from a few dollars where certified mail is used to considerably more if a professional process service is required. A defendant will normally only have to pay to serve papers if she files a Defendant's Claim (counterclaim).

- Subpoenaed witness fees, if approved by the judge. Both the plaintiff and defendant can incur this cost if a witness must be subpoenaed and claims a fee. Fees for subpoenaing witnesses and documents are likely to be approved only if the judge believes the presence of the witness in court was necessary to prove the case.

- The cost of obtaining necessary documents, such as verification of car ownership. (Both plaintiffs and defendants can have these costs.)

If you forget to get your costs added to the judgment in court and want to go to the trouble, ask the small claims clerk what to do. Usually you can file a written request for costs within a few days of the judgment. For information on recovering costs incurred after judgment when your opponent won't voluntarily pay the judgment, see "Creating Property Liens" in Chapter 24.

CAUTION

Some costs are not recoverable. You can't recover for such personal expenses as taking time off from work to prepare for or attend court, paying a babysitter, parking your car, or making photocopies of evidence.

Motor Vehicle Repair Cases

magine that you go to the auto repair shop to pick up your trusty old steed after a complete engine overhaul. The bill, which you agreed to pay in advance, is $1,225. This always seemed a little steep, but the mechanic talked you into it by claiming he would do a great job and that the overhauled engine should last another 50,000 miles. At any rate, you write a check and drive out of the garage in something approaching a cheerful mood. As you head up the first hill, you start to hear a funny noise. You drive back to the garage in a sour mood. Not only are you out $1,225, but your car runs worse than it did when you brought it in.

After a bit of foot stomping, you get someone to say that they will look over the car. The next day you call the garage. Nothing has been done. You yell at the garage owner and then call your bank to stop payment on the check, but it already has been cashed. The next day the garage owner tells you the problem is in a part of the engine they didn't work on. "Give us another $500 and we can surely solve this new problem." You pick up your mechanical friend and drive it home—very slowly. You are furious and decide to pursue every legal remedy, no matter what the trouble. How do you start?

First, park your car, take a shower, and have a glass of wine, milk, or whatever seems calming. Nothing gets decided well when you're mad. Now, following the approach I have presented throughout this book, ask yourself these two key questions.

Have You Suffered a Loss?

That's easy. Your car works worse than it did before you paid a lot of money to have it fixed. Unless some divine power has suddenly intervened to create a new mechanical problem, you have suffered a loss.

Can You Prove the Defendant's Negligence Caused Your Loss?

Now we get to the nitty-gritty. The car now works less well than before you had it fixed, and you are doubtless convinced that a lousy repair job caused your problem. But in this type of case, you can almost always expect the garage owner to claim the work was done properly and that the car simply needs more work. For all the judge knows, this may even be true. In short, to win this type of case it's your job to prove that the repair work was not up to a reasonable standard of competence. Doing so will make your case; failing to do so will break it.

Collect Available Evidence

Gather all the relevant evidence, pronto. In this situation, this means getting your used parts (it's a good idea to do this any time you have major work done). If the garage will not give them to you, ask them again by letter, keeping a copy for your file. If you get the parts, fine—if you don't, you have evidence that the garage is badly run or has something to hide.

Have Your Car Checked by an Expert

Before you drive many miles after the disputed work is done, have your car checked by an experienced mechanic. Sometimes it is possible to get a free estimate from a repair shop. In this situation, however, you are probably better off paying for someone to look at the engine thoroughly, with the understanding that if the need arises, the mechanic will testify on your behalf in small claims court—or at the very least, will write a letter stating what's wrong with the engine. A few states require that you present three written estimates in small claims court. Whether this is required or not, it's a good idea to have them.

Try to Settle Your Case

By now you should have a pretty good idea what the first garage did wrong. Call and ask them to redo the job or refund part or all of your money. Often the repair shop will agree to do additional work to avoid a hassle. If they agree to take the car back, insist on a written agreement detailing what they will do and how long it will take. Also, talk to the mechanic who will actually work on the car to be sure you both have the same understanding about what needs to be done. You may be a little paranoid about taking your car back to the garage that just screwed it up. Nevertheless, unless they have been outrageously incompetent, this is probably your best approach because it's usually easier to get work redone than it is to get a big refund. Also, if you sue and the garage owner shows up in court and says he offered to work on the car again but you refused, it may weaken your case.

Write a Demand Letter

If the garage isn't cooperative, it's time to write a formal demand letter. Remember our discussion in Chapter 6. Your letter should be short, polite, and written with an eye to a judge reading it. (See sample letter, below.)

TIP

Be sure to emphasize any promise made by the garage. Most small independent garages don't make a written warranty or guarantee on their work. However, if you were given any promises in writing, mention them in your letter. Also, if you were promised things orally about the quality of the work the garage planned to do and you relied on these statements as part of your decision to authorize the repairs, make sure the letter describes this express oral warranty. (See Chapter 2.)

Sample Car Repair Demand Letter

Haig Mackey
15 Orange Street
Hamden, CT
October 1, 20xx

Happy Days Motors
100 Speedway
New Haven, CT

Dear People:

On August 13, 20xx, I brought my 2000 Ford to your garage. You agreed to do a complete engine rebuild job for $1,525. You told me, "Your car will be running like a watch when we're through with it." The car worked well when I brought it in, but was a little short on power. Two days later, when I picked up my car, it barely moved at all. The engine made such a clanging noise that I've been afraid to drive it.

I have repeatedly asked you to fix the car or to refund my money. You have refused.

I've had two mechanics check out my car since you worked on it. Both agree you did your work improperly and even installed some used parts instead of new ones, which you did not tell me. The work you did on the engine rings was particularly poorly done.

After receiving no response from you, I had the work redone at a cost of $900. My car now works well. Please refund my $1,525. Should you fail to do so within ten days, I will promptly file complaints with the local Better Business Bureau and take this dispute to small claims court. I hope to hear from you promptly.

Sincerely,

Haig Mackey

Haig Mackey

cc: Connecticut Dept. of Consumer Affairs
     Bureau of Automotive Repair
     Hartford, CT

File Your Court Papers

If you still get no satisfactory response from the garage, file your papers at the small claims court clerk's office in the county where the garage is located.

Prepare for Court

If you want the judge to understand your case, you must understand it yourself. Sounds simple, doesn't it? It did to me too, until I got involved with a case involving a botched car repair. All I knew was that after I paid to have the engine fixed, the darn thing was not supposed to belch black smoke and make a disgusting noise. I really wasn't interested in the details.

Fortunately, I realized that for me to argue a case in small claims court with this level of ignorance would likely end in a bad loss. To be able to convince a judge that the mechanic had ripped me off, I needed to do some homework. After all, I could expect the people from the garage to show up in court with a terrific-sounding story about the wonderful job they did with pistons, bearings, and camshaft. I had seen other people unsuccessfully argue car repair cases knowing no more than "the car was supposed to be fixed, Your Honor, and it's worse than ever."

It turned out that a 15-minute conversation with a knowledgeable mechanic was all I really needed to understand what the first mechanic did wrong. (Also, my local library had several car manuals, complete with diagrams of my problem, which were a big help.) In court, armed with my new knowledge, I had no trouble explaining to the judge that the mechanic had done a substandard job. I got a judgment for the full amount I had paid.

> ### 💡 TIP
> **Remember, the judge is probably not a mechanic.** In Chapter 13, I mentioned that it's important to pay attention to the human being to whom you are presenting your case. It's no secret that many, if not most, small claims judges don't understand the insides of cars any better than you do. So be prepared to make a convincing presentation to a person who nods his head but doesn't really understand the difference between the drive shaft and the axle.

Appearing in Court

When you show up in court, be sure that you are well organized. Bring all the letters you have written or received about your car problem, any written warranty, photographs if they are helpful, and your used parts if they aid in making your case. If you have a witness to oral statements made by the garage, be sure to bring that person with you to court. Or if that's impossible, ask her to write a letter explaining what she heard. Also, be sure to present any letter(s) written by an independent expert(s) who has arranged to examine your car. Even one cogent letter from an experienced mechanic, explaining how the repair job was botched, when combined with your own informed presentation, can make you a winner.

If you are well prepared you should win the sort of case outlined here without difficulty. Judges drive cars and have to get them fixed; they tend to be sympathetic with this type of consumer complaint. Simply present your story (see Chapter 15), your documentation, and your witnesses. If you feel that your opponent is snowing the judge with a lot of technical lingo, get things back on track by asking that all jargon be explained in ordinary English. This will be a relief to everyone in the courtroom except your opponent. You will likely find that, once his case is shorn of all the magic words, it will shrink from tiger to pussycat.

TIP

A good drawing can help. In cases involving machinery, people can give effective testimony by presenting a large drawing illustrating the screw up. This approach is most effective when your expert appears in court and authoritatively points to the drawing to detail the problem.

Motor Vehicle Purchase Cases

Occasionally someone buys a vehicle and drives it a short way, only to have it fall apart. And too frequently the seller of the defective vehicle won't stand behind the product. What can you do if you are the victim of this kind of rip-off? There are major differences in how you should approach your problem depending on whether you purchased a new or used vehicle, so let's look at each situation separately.

New Vehicles

It can be especially frustrating to buy a new car and have it break down much sooner than it should. Most states have a law (the "lemon law") that requires the car dealer or manufacturer to give you a new car or a refund if your new car breaks down during the first 18 months or first 18,000 miles of the car's warranty period, whichever ends sooner. Unfortunately, because most new vehicles cost more than the small claims maximum, it is unlikely that you will be able to bring a small claims lawsuit against a car dealer or manufacturer for violating the lemon law.

 RESOURCE

Making lemonade out of your lemon. For more information on lemon laws, see the following websites:

- www.autopedia.com/html/HotLinks_Lemon.html (includes individual summaries of each state's lemon laws)
- www.autosafety.org/lemonlaws.html (includes information on defects common to particular car models).

What if your car breaks down just outside the warranty period? Luckily, you may still have a winnable case: When a relatively new car falls apart for no good reason, many small claims court judges bend over backward to look for a legal way to give you protection over and above the actual written warranty that comes with the vehicle. For example, you still may be able to recover some money under one of the following approaches:

Prove that the defects arose while your car was still under warranty. Often a newish car that suffers serious mechanical problems soon after the warranty period runs out suffered similar problems during the warranty period. If so, you will want to argue that the dealer made inadequate repairs in the first instance and should still be responsible for the subsequent problems.

> **TIP**
>
> **Document your attempts to have your car repaired.** Make sure the judge knows about all the trips you have made to the dealer's repair shop. One way to establish this is by presenting copies of work orders you signed. If you don't have these or other records, request copies from the dealer (see Chapter 14 for instructions on subpoenaing documents), or sit down with a calendar and reconstruct the dates you brought your car in for repair. In court, give the copies or your list to the judge. If you have only your list, explain that it's your best estimate. The judge should accept it as being true unless the car dealer disputes it.

Investigate the possibility of a "secret warranty." After a model has been in production for awhile, a pattern of problems or failures may develop. Manufacturers are extremely sensitive to complaints in "high problem" areas—if for no other reason than to head off a possible federal safety recall. As a result, the manufacturer may have issued a "service bulletin" and created an adjustment program that extends the warranty or offers to pay for repair of conditions that substantially affect the vehicle's durability, reliability, or performance. Here's how you can find out about service bulletins and adjustment programs:

- Dealers must post a notice in the showroom or other areas with information on how to obtain service bulletins.
- You can search the National Highway Traffic Safety Administration's database of technical service bulletins at www-odi.nhtsa.dot.gov (click on "Service Bulletins").
- If you go to the dealer for repair of a condition covered by an adjustment program, the dealer must inform you of the program's terms.
- The manufacturer must notify eligible owners about an adjustment program within 90 days after adopting it.

If your vehicle has a serious problem but the manufacturer hasn't issued a service bulletin or adopted an adjustment program (or you can't find out about either), talk to people at independent garages that specialize in repairing your model. Especially if they tell you the problem is widespread and that the manufacturer has fixed it without charge for some persistent customers, your next step is to write a demand letter to the car dealer and manufacturer. (See Chapter 6.) Mention that if your problem is not taken care of, you will sue in small claims court and you will subpoena all records having to do with this defect. This may well cause the manufacturer to settle with you. If not, follow through on both threats.

EXAMPLE: Bruno bought an expensive European car that repeatedly had engine problems while under the manufacturer's written warranty. Each time, Bruno brought it into the dealer's repair shop and adjustments were made that seemed to fix the problem. A few months after the written warranty ran out, the engine died. Even though the car was only a little over a year old and had gone less than 50,000 miles, both the dealer and the parent car company refused to repair or replace it. Their refusals continued even though the owner repeatedly wrote to them, demanding action. How does Bruno deal with his problem?

First, because he needed his car, he had the repairs made. Second, although the repairs cost slightly more than the small claims limit, he decided he would scale down his claim and sue for the small claims maximum to save the extra expense and hassle of finding a lawyer and suing in regular court.

At the hearing, both Bruno and his wife testified about their trials and tribulations with the car. They gave the judge copies of the several letters they had written to the dealer, one of which was a list of the dates they had taken the car to the dealer's shop while it was still under warranty. They also produced a letter from the owner of the independent garage that finally fixed the engine, stating that when he took the engine apart, he discovered a defect in its original assembly. The new car dealer testified only that his mechanics had done their best to fix the car when it was under the written warranty. He then contended that, once the written warranty had run out, he was no longer responsible. The dealer made no effort to challenge the car owner's story, nor did he bring his own mechanics to court to testify to how they had repaired the car while it was still under warranty. Bruno won and the dealer was ordered to reimburse him for the repair costs.

Used Vehicle Dealers

Successfully suing used vehicle dealers can be tricky. Unlike new vehicle dealers, who are usually somewhat dependent upon their reputation in the community for honesty, a fair percentage of used vehicle dealers don't have a good reputation to start with and survive by becoming experts at self-protection.

The principal self-protection device employed by used vehicle dealers is the "as is" designation in the written sales contract. The salesperson may praise a car to the sky, but when you read the contract, you will see it clearly stated that the seller takes absolutely no responsibility for the condition of the vehicle and that it is sold "as is."

To successfully sue a used car dealer, you must be able to prove that:

• you suffered a financial loss (this is not hard if you had to pay for repairs), and

• the dealer is legally responsible for your damages.

This second point is often harder to prove. Almost surely, the used car dealer will testify that she had no way of knowing how long a ten-year-old Dodge would last and that, for this very reason, she sold the car "as is." She will then show the judge the written contract that not only contains the "as is" designation, but also "this written contract is the entire agreement between the parties and no oral statements or representations made by the dealer or any salesperson are part of the contract."

How can you fight this sort of cynical semi-fraud? It's difficult to do after the fact. The time for self-protection is before you buy a vehicle, when you have the opportunity to have it checked by an expert and to get a vehicle history report through an online service (search the Internet for "vehicle history"). In addition, you have the opportunity to refuse to close the deal unless the salesperson's claims about the great condition of the car are put in the contract. Of course, after the damage has been done, good advice such as this isn't worth much. If you have just been cheated on a used car deal, you want to know what, if anything, you can do now. Here are some suggestions.

Your state's lemon law may apply to used vehicles. If you reside in Alabama, Arizona, Hawaii, Maine, Massachusetts, Minnesota, New Jersey, New York, or Rhode Island, your state's lemon law applies to used as well as new cars. Check to see if your situation is covered.

Argue fraud. If the car broke almost immediately after you took it out of the used car lot, you can file in small claims court and argue that you were defrauded. Your theory is that, no matter what the written contract said, there was a clear implication that you purchased a car, not a junk heap. When the dealer produces the "as is" contract you signed, argue that it is no defense to fraud. (For more discussion of fraud, see Chapter 2.)

Did the dealer make promises? If the dealer made any promises, either in writing or orally, about the good condition of the vehicle, he may be required to live up to them. Why? Because, as noted in Chapter 2, statements about a product that you rely on as part of deciding whether to purchase the product constitute an express warranty that the dealer breaches if the promise turns out to be a lie. This is true even if the seller had you sign a contract with an "as is" statement that disclaims all warranties, because an "as is" statement does not disclaim an express warranty if one is made. The key to winning this sort of case is to produce a witness to the dealer's laudatory statements about the vehicle, copies of ads that state the car is in good shape, and anything else that will back up your story.

There also may be an implied warranty. There are two types of implied warranties. One type—the implied warranty of fitness—means that the vehicle is warranted to work for a particular purpose (say, consistency). The more common implied warranty is for merchantability. Here, you would argue that the car you bought was so defective that it didn't meet the reasonable standards expected of even a used car. (See Chapter 2 for more on warranties.)

A radical remedy: Give the car back and stop payment. You may consider having the car towed back to the lot and then refusing to make future payments. This option should be considered only in an extreme situation, but it does shift the burden of taking legal action to the other side, at which point you can defend on the basis of fraud (see above). If you take this approach, be sure you have excellent documentation that the car was truly wretched. And be sure to write a letter detailing the circumstances surrounding your extreme difficulties with the dealer, along with a convincing statement that, taken as a whole, the dealer's conduct amounts to consumer fraud. Send copies to the dealer and the bank or finance company to whom you pay your loan. Of course, you will probably have already made a down payment, so even in this situation you may wish to initiate action in small claims court to try to recover it.

> **CAUTION**
>
> **Your credit rating will suffer.** If you stop making payments, it will appear as a default on your credit report and will affect your credit score significantly, so think very carefully before choosing this course of action.

> **TIP**
>
> **How to find signs of fraud.** If you really suspect that you have been defrauded, have your car checked by an experienced mechanic who will be willing to write a letter explaining what she finds. If this person can find affirmative evidence that you were cheated, you will greatly improve your small claims case. The mechanic might, for example, find that the speedometer had been tampered with in violation of state law, or that a heavy grade of truck oil had been put in the crankcase so that the car wouldn't belch smoke. Also, this is the sort of case where subpoenaing documents might help. (See Chapter 14.) Specifically, you might wish to subpoena the car dealer's records, including any that indicate the dealer's purchase price and the condition of the car when he purchased it. It might also be helpful to learn the name of the car's former owner, with the idea of contacting him. You can also check the car's history through an online service (search the Internet for "vehicle history"), which can tell you whether the car was stolen or salvaged, or was used as a rental or a taxi. (See Chapter 2 for more on fraud.)

Consider other remedies besides small claims court. These can include checking with your state department of consumer affairs or the local department of motor vehicles to see if used car lots are regulated. In many states, the department of motor vehicles licenses used car dealers and can be very helpful in getting disputes resolved, particularly where your complaint is one of many against the same dealer for similar practices. Also, contact your district attorney's office. Most now have a consumer fraud division, which can be of great help. If you can convince them that what happened to you smells rotten, or if your complaint happens to be against someone they have already identified as a borderline criminal, they will likely call the used car dealer in for a chat. In theory, the D.A.'s only job is to bring a criminal action, which will be of no direct aid in getting your money back; but in practice, negotiations can often result in restitution. In plain words, this means that the car dealer may be told, "Look, buddy, you're right on the edge of the law here (or maybe over the edge). If you clean up your act, which means taking care of all complaints against you and seeing that there are no more, we will close your file. If you don't, I suggest you hire a good lawyer, because you are going to need one."

Used Vehicles From Private Parties

Normally it is easier to win a case against a private party than against a used vehicle dealer. This often runs counter to both common sense and fairness, as a private party may be more honest than a dealer. But fair or not, the fact is that a nondealer is usually less sophisticated in legal self-protection than is a pro. Indeed, in most private party sales the seller does no more than sign over the title slip in exchange for the agreed-upon price without any formal contract.

Too often, trouble develops soon after you purchase the vehicle and you must pay money for unexpected repairs. As is true with a used vehicle purchased from a dealer, your problem usually is not with proving that you suffered a loss. Instead, the key to winning is usually to show the judge that the seller of the vehicle is responsible for making your loss good. To do this, you normally must prove that the seller claimed that the vehicle was in better shape than, in fact, it was, and that you relied on these promises when you purchased it. The seller will almost certainly claim that she told you she was selling the car "as is." Remember, however, that an "as is" statement does not invalidate an express promise she made about the car's condition.

EXAMPLE: Barbara, a 20-year-old college student, bought a used BMW motorcycle from John. She sued John for $2,150 in repair costs, claiming that the motorcycle was in far worse shape than he had advertised. In court, she ably and convincingly outlined her conversations with John about the purchase of the motorcycle, testifying that he repeatedly told her that the cycle was "hardly used." She hadn't gotten any of John's promises in writing, but she did a creative job of developing and presenting what evidence she had. This included:

- A copy of her letter to John that clearly outlined her position, such as the letter below.

- Copies of repair bills (and estimates) dated within two weeks of her purchase of the cycle, the lowest of which came to $2,150.

- A copy of John's newspaper ad, which read: "BMW 500 c.c., almost new— hardly used—excellent condition—$7,500."

Sample "Lemon" Demand Letter

14 Stockton Street
Moline, IL
January 27, 20xx

John Malinosky
321 South Zaporah
Moline, IL

Dear Mr. Malinosky:

This letter is a follow-up to our recent phone conversation in which you refused to discuss the fact that the 2002 BMW motorcycle I purchased from you on January 15 is not in the "excellent condition" that you claimed.

To review: On January 12, I saw your ad for a motorcycle that was "almost new—hardly used—excellent condition" in the local flea market newspaper. I called you, and you told me that the cycle was a terrific bargain and that you would never sell it except that you needed money for school. I told you that I didn't know much about machinery.

The next day, you took me for a ride on the cycle. You told me specifically that:

1. The cycle had just been tuned up.

2. The cycle had been driven less than 30,000 miles.

3. The cycle had never been raced or used roughly.

4. If anything went wrong with the cycle in the next month or two, you would see that it was fixed.

Relying on these statements, I bought the cycle from you for $7,500.

I had the cycle less than a week when the brakes went out. When I had them checked, the mechanic told me that the transmission also needed work (I confirmed this with another mechanic—see attached estimate). The

Sample "Lemon" Demand Letter (cont'd.)

mechanic also told me that the cycle had been driven at least 75,000 miles (perhaps a lot more) and that it needed a tune-up. In addition, he showed me caked mud and scratches under the cycle frame that indicated to him that it had been driven extensively off the road in rough terrain and had probably been raced on dirt tracks.

The lowest estimate to do the repairs was $2,150. Before having the work done, I called you to explain the situation and to give you a chance to arrange for the repairs to be made, or to make them yourself. You laughed at me and said, "Sister, do what you need to do—you're not getting one dime from me."

Again I respectfully request that you make good on the promises you made to me on January 15. I relied on the truth of your statements when I decided to buy the bike. I enclose a copy of the mechanic's bill for $2,150, along with copies of several higher estimates that I received from other repair shops.

Sincerely,

Barbara Parker

Barbara Parker

- Finally, Barbara presented the judge with this note from the mechanic who fixed the cycle:

Sample Letter from Witness

February 3, 20xx

To Whom It May Concern:

It's hard for me to get off work, but if you need me, please ask the judge to delay the case a few days. I have been in the motorcycle-repair business for 20 years, and have repaired hundreds of BMWs. The BMW that Barbara Parker brought to me was in fair shape at best. It's impossible to be exact, but given that the brakes and transmission were completely shot, I would conservatively guess it had been driven at least 75,000 miles. And given the damage to the underside of the bike, it was definitely driven a lot of those miles on dirt.

Respectfully submitted,

Honker Green

Al "Honker" Green

Barbara quickly outlined for the judge what happened and emphasized that she had saved for six months to get the money to buy the motorcycle. True, testimony about financial hardship isn't relevant, but a quick tug on the judge's heartstrings never hurts. Next, John had his turn. He helped Barbara make her case by acting like a weasel. His testimony consisted mostly of a lot of vague philosophy about machinery. He kept asking, "How could I know just when it would break?" When the judge asked him specific questions about the age, condition, and previous history of the cycle, he clammed up as if he were a Mafia don called to testify by a Senate antiracketeering committee. When the judge asked him if he had, in fact, made specific guarantees about the condition of the bike, John began a long explanation about how when you sell things, you "puff them up a little" and that "women shouldn't be allowed to drive motorcycles anyway." Finally, the judge asked him to please sit down.

> **TIP**
>
> **Even a little tangible evidence is better than none.** In this type of case, without a written warranty such as an ad that states the vehicle is in great shape, it's often one person's word against another's. Any shred of tangible evidence that the seller really did make an express oral warranty as to the condition of the car and that the seller relied on those statements to make the purchase can be enough to shift the balance to your side. Of course, if you have a friend who witnessed or heard any part of the transaction, her testimony will be extremely valuable. Getting a mechanic to check over a vehicle and then testify for you is also a good strategy. Sometimes you can get some help from publications that list wholesale and retail prices for used cars. Some people bring these publications into court to back up their assertion that they paid above the "Blue Book" price for a used car "because the car was represented to be in extra good shape." This type of evidence doesn't constitute much in the way of real proof that you were ripped off, but it is helpful to at least show the judge that you paid a premium price for unsound goods.

Bad Debts: Initiating and Defending Cases in Which Money Is Owed

Small Claims Court Is a Good Place to Sue on Bad Debts

Many small claims cases involve a claim that the defendant owes the plaintiff money. Usually this means a bill for goods or services hasn't been paid, but it also can involve failure to pay a promissory note (for example, a loan from a friend or relative) or even a civil fine for something as simple as the failure to return a library book. The plaintiff wins the vast majority of these cases, often because the defendant defaults. This illustrates how effective small claims court can be as part of any business's collection strategy.

But paradoxically, small claims court can also work well for a defendant who puts on a spirited defense because he believes he owes no money or the plaintiff is asking for too much. In large part this is because, unlike formal court, in small claims, a defendant doesn't need to file complicated paperwork or jump through other legal hoops to present her side of the story. Indeed, all a defendant has to do is show up on the appointed day and make a convincing, well-documented presentation.

Some businesspeople, and especially professionals like doctors, dentists, and lawyers, don't use small claims court to collect unpaid bills because they think it takes too much time or is "undignified." You will have to worry about your "dignity" yourself, but realize that small claims court actions can be handled with very little time and expense once you get the hang of them. And, in many states, the job of actually appearing in court can often be delegated. By contrast, businesspeople who don't use small claims court as part of a self-help debt collection strategy must normally either write off the loss or turn the bill over to a collection agency.

TIP

Unincorporated businesses can often send a representative to small claims court. As discussed in Chapter 7, a bookkeeper, financial manager, or other employee of a sole proprietorship or partnership can appear and present a case in small claims court if the case can be proved by presenting a business record (showing that a bill hasn't been paid, for example), and if there is no other issue of fact involved in the case. And, of course, a corporation or limited liability company has the right to send any authorized representative to court.

Who Should Appear in Court?

Small claims courts vary from state to state in terms of who can sue to collect unpaid bills. As listed in the state-by-state Appendix, some states:

- allow bill collectors (called "assignees") to use small claims court
- ban bill collectors, but let lawyers carry out much the same task by representing multiple creditors, or
- ban both bill collectors and lawyers, only allowing businesses to sue on their own behalf.

Even among the states where businesses can't hire third parties but must represent themselves to sue on bad debt claims, there are important differences. For example, a few states entirely prohibit corporations from suing in small claims court, while others make it difficult for unincorporated businesses to send anyone but an owner or partner to court. By contrast, most states allow corporations to sue and make it reasonably easy for both incorporated and unincorporated businesses to designate a bookkeeper or other employee to handle court appearances. (See Chapter 7 for more on who can sue in small claims court.)

After first checking the summary of rules in the Appendix and on your state's website, contact your small claims court clerk and find out exactly what rules govern bill collection activities in your state. Then talk to other businesspeople (or business associations, such as the chamber of commerce) to learn practical strategies to cope with any rules that hinder using small claims as part of a cost-efficient bill collection strategy. Also, if you are in a state where bill collectors or lawyers do small claims collection work, you will want to find out how much they charge and how efficient they are and then compare this information to the time and energy it would take for you to do it yourself. Because bill collectors and lawyers typically charge from 30%–50% of any money they collect, you'll probably conclude that you can do this work yourself.

> **TIP**
>
> **A bookkeeper or other representative is often, but not always, a good choice to appear in small claims court.** In many states, a business owner does not have to personally appear in court but can send an employee. Where money is owed, a bookkeeper or financial manager is normally a good choice, because the person can testify that a valid contract existed and the defendant has not paid the promised amount. However, if the defendant shows up and defends on the basis that the goods or services were defective, delivered late, or otherwise not acceptable, the bookkeeper is likely to be at a serious disadvantage; he or she probably has no firsthand knowledge of anything except that the check was not in the mail. For example, if you own a graphics business and are suing on an unpaid bill in a situation where you expect the defendant may show up in court and falsely claim you did lousy work, you will need to have someone in court who knows the details of the particular job. Typically, this should be the employee(s) who dealt with the customer and did the work.

Bad Debt Cases From the Plaintiff's Point of View

The job of the plaintiff who sues for nonpayment of a debt is often easy. That's because in the majority of cases, the debtor doesn't show up. In the absence of a defendant, the plaintiff needs only to introduce evidence that a valid debt exists and it has not been paid. To accomplish this, present written proof of the debt in the form of a contract, work order, promissory note, or purchase order signed by the defendant. Even if a debt is based on an oral contract, it's usually easy to get a judgment because the defendant isn't present to contradict the plaintiff's version of events.

Here are a few suggestions for plaintiffs who plan to sue to collect a debt.

Don't Bother Suing on Some Types of Debts

Although using small claims court as part of your debt collection process often makes sense, there are exceptions. Here are the principal ones:

When there isn't enough money at stake. For disputes involving a few hundred dollars or less, the costs of filing, preparing, and presenting a small claims case are likely to be unacceptably high relative to what you are likely to recover. Of course, this is doubly true if you doubt that a court judgment will be collectible.

When the defendant is a deadbeat. As discussed in more detail in Chapters 3 and 24, most court judgments are fairly easy to collect, because the defendant usually has a job, bank account, investments, or real estate. However, some people are broke and unemployed and are likely to stay that way. People who have so little money or property that they can effectively thumb their noses at creditors make up only between 10%–20% of the U.S. population and undoubtedly run up a disproportionate share of bad debts. One thing is sure—you don't want to spend your time and energy taking to court people who are never likely to have enough money to pay the resulting judgment. Better to write off the debt and tighten up your credit-granting procedures.

When you want or need to get along with the person in the future. Any court action, even a small claims lawsuit, tends to aggravate a dispute, with the result that the parties become angrier at one another. This isn't a big problem when dealing with people or businesses you don't plan to have future contact with. But in other circumstances, such as where a relative or local business owes you money, it's possible that your ongoing relationship with a debtor may be more important than collecting all that you are owed. It may make sense to try to minimize conflict by trying to work out your dispute through mediation. (See Chapter 6.)

Ask for Your Money Before You Sue

Chapter 6 explains techniques for settling your case without going to court. Because writing an effective letter demanding payment frequently produces a check by return mail, you should always do this before filing in small claims court. Unfortunately, instead of doing this many businesses rely on fill-in-the-blank past-due notices and dun letters purchased from commercial sources. While sending one of these is better than doing nothing, it's far more effective to write your own, more personal letter (see the sample in Chapter 6)—or at least to customize a form letter enough so the debtor can see it's really aimed at him. But realize that whenever you demand payment of a debt, a number of laws protect the debtor from overzealous collection techniques. For the legal dos and don'ts of collecting bills, see *Legal Guide for Starting & Running a Small Business,* by Fred Steingold (Nolo).

 TIP

Plan in advance to counter any claim that your bill wasn't paid for a good reason. If you provide goods or services, it's wise to include a statement on all your bills and collection letters requesting that the debtor notify you if goods are defective or services are substandard. Bring copies of these notices to court. Then if the debtor shows up and, for the first time, claims he didn't pay because the goods or services were somehow defective, you will be prepared to counter his claim. Do this by first showing the judge your many notices asking that any problem be brought to your attention and then testifying that the defendant never made a complaint. This should go far toward convincing the judge that the defendant is fabricating, or at least exaggerating, his current complaint in an effort to avoid paying you.

Bring Your Debt Collection Case Promptly

For maximum success in collecting on bad debts, file suit as soon as you conclude that informal collection methods are unlikely to work. You'll be pleasantly surprised that a small but significant number of debtors will quickly pay up—or call you to work out a payment plan—to avoid having a court judgment appear in their credit records. Fast action is also advisable for other reasons, the most important being that people who owe you money are likely to have other debts as well and may be considering bankruptcy. The quicker you act, the faster you'll get a judgment and be eligible to start collection activities, like wage garnishment or property attachment.

In addition, if you file promptly, you will avoid having to worry about whether you are within the legal filing deadline, called the "statute of limitations." Depending on the state and the type of debt, this usually is anywhere from one to four years. (You will find a discussion of the statutes of limitations applicable to different sorts of debts in Chapter 5.)

Judges tend to be skeptical of old claims. If you wait three years to sue over a $1,000 debt, the judge may wonder why you waited so long—are you honestly convinced your suit is valid? Did you and the defendant recently get into a spat over something else and you're trying to get even? You could end up answering a lot of questions you weren't prepared for.

Special Rules for Installment Debts

If you lend money or sell an item with payments to be made in installments, and a payment or two is missed, you normally are entitled to sue only for the amount of the missed payments, not the whole debt. Before you can sue for the entire amount, you must wait until all payments are missed. But there is a major exception to this rule: You can immediately sue for 100% of the debt—plus any interest—if your contract contains an "acceleration clause." This is a statement that if one payment is missed, the whole debt is due. To see whether this type of provision is present, carefully read your installment sales contract and consider rewriting it to include such a clause.

Written Contracts—Bring Documentation to Court

Most debts are based on written contracts. The contract may be a purchase order, credit agreement, lease, or formal contract. It normally makes no difference what your document is called, as long as you have something in writing with the defendant's signature.

Always bring your written documentation to court on the day your case is heard and be ready to show it to the judge. Also, bring any ledger sheets, computer printouts, or other business records documenting the payments that have been made or missed.

Take your responsibility to be organized seriously. Sometimes I have seen otherwise sensible-looking businesspeople show up with botched records and become flustered when closely questioned by the judge. The courtroom is not the place to straighten out a poor accounting system.

How to Prove Debts Covered by Oral Contracts

Generally, a debt based on an oral contract is legal as long as the contract was (or could have been) carried out in one year and is not for the sale of real estate or of goods (personal property) worth more than $500. (See Chapter 22 for more on written documentation requirements for the sale of goods.) Of course, it may be hard to prove the debt exists if the defendant flat out denies that he borrowed the money or bought the goods or services. Your best bet is to attempt to come up with some written documentation that your version of what occurred is true. For example, even if there is no written agreement, the defendant may have written you a down payment check or a letter asking for more time to pay. Either would be a huge help in convincing the judge that a debt exists. Or, when you write a letter demanding payment before you sue (see Chapter 6), include a description of the oral agreement and existing debt along with a phrase like "If my understanding is incorrect in any way, please contact me in writing or by phone by [date]." If the debtor doesn't dispute your version of events, then bring a copy of your letter to court and tell the judge you never got a reply, if that's truly the case.

If you can't come up with anything in writing, try to think of a person who has firsthand knowledge of the debt and who is willing to testify. For example, if you asked the defendant to pay you and he said in the presence of a friend, "I know I owe you $1,000. I'll pay you next month," or even, "Too bad you will never get your money back," or anything similar that indicates that the loan existed, bring your witness to court or have the witness write a letter explaining what he heard, and show the letter to the judge.

If you don't have a witness, consider whether you can establish the debt's existence by looking at the debtor's actions. It is often particularly easy to do this when you haven't been paid for services you provided in a commercial context. After all, if the other party accepted your labor, there is almost always an implication that payment is expected.

EXAMPLE: Jane, a commercial illustrator, works as a freelancer for a number of ad agencies, publishers, and other clients. One day she gets a call from Harold, a dress designer, asking her to do a series of drawings of his new line of evening wear. Jane does the drawings and submits her bill for $2,000. Harold refuses to pay, claiming both that payment was conditional on the drawings being published in a fashion magazine (they weren't) and that even if a contract did exist, Jane is charging too much. Jane files in small claims court. The judge has no trouble finding the existence of an oral contract based on Harold's admission that he asked Jane to do the work. However, the judge only awards Jane $1,400, because she can't document her claim that she was to be paid $100 an hour, and Harold made a convincing presentation that illustrators with similar qualifications customarily charge no more than $70 per hour.

 CROSS-REFERENCE

More on contract cases. See "How to Approach a Breach of Contract Case," in Chapter 2, for more on oral and implied contracts.

Debt Cases From the Debtor's Point of View

There's a tendency to start out somewhat biased in debt collection cases. Especially where individuals are being sued by businesses, we assume they do owe the money. We might even wonder why most defendants bother to show up if they know in advance that they have no realistic defense.

But many debtors do not fit the stereotyped deadbeat role. Instead of shuffling in with heads down, saying something like, "I didn't pay that bill because I'm short of money right now," they often present well-thought-out, convincing defenses, with the result that the judge would reduce the amount the plaintiff asked for, or occasionally even rule that no debt exists.

A prominent study of small claims court cases found that when a defendant shows up to contest a case, the plaintiff's chance of winning 100% of the amount asked for declines substantially. ("Small Claims and Traffic Courts," by John Goerdt (National Center for State Courts).) In fact, defendants win outright in 26% of debt cases and pay half or less of what the plaintiff asked for in an additional 20%.

Here are some examples of cases in which the defendant succeeded in whole or part:

EXAMPLE 1: A local hospital sued an unemployed man for failure to pay an emergency room bill for $678. It seemed like an open and shut case—the person from the hospital had all the proper records, and the defendant hadn't paid. Then the defendant told his side of it. He was taken to the emergency room suffering from a superficial but painful gunshot wound. Because it was a busy night and he was not about to die, he was kept waiting four hours for treatment. When treatment was given, it was minimal, and he suffered later complications that might have been avoided if he had been treated more promptly and thoroughly. He said he didn't mind paying a fair amount, but that he didn't feel he got $678 worth of care in the 20 minutes the doctor spent with him. The judge agreed and gave judgment to the hospital for $250, plus court and service of process costs. After the defendant explained that his only income was his unemployment benefits, the judge ordered that he be allowed to pay the judgment at the rate of $25 per month.

EXAMPLE 2: A large local tire retailer sued a woman for not paying the balance on a tire bill. She had purchased eight light truck tires manufactured by a major tire company and still owed $612. The tire company representative presented the judge with the original copy of a written contract along with the woman's payment record, and then waited for judgment. The woman, who ran a small neighborhood gardening and landscaping business, produced several advertising flyers from the tire company that strongly implied that the tires would last at least 40,000 miles. She then testified and presented a witness to the fact that the tires had lasted less than 25,000 miles before wearing out. The defendant also had copies of four letters she had written over the past year to the headquarters of the tire company in the Midwest complaining about the tires. Both in the letters, and in court, she repeatedly stated that the salesperson at the tire company told her several times that the tires were guaranteed for 40,000 miles. Putting this all together, the judge declared the total price of the tires should be prorated on the basis of 25,000 miles and, after figuring what the defendant had already paid, gave the tire company a judgment for only $350, instead of the $612 requested. The woman wrote out a check on the spot and departed feeling vindicated.

EXAMPLE 3: A rug company sued a customer for $1,486 and produced all the necessary documentation to show that the carpet had been installed and that no payment had been received. The defendant testified that the rug had been poorly installed, with a seam running down the center of the room. He brought pictures that left little doubt that the rug installer was either incompetent or completely thoughtless. The defendant also presented drawings that illustrated that there were several better ways to cut the carpet to fit the room. The rug company received nothing.

Of course, the real point of these examples is not to be found in their individual fact situations—yours will surely differ. Rather, they illustrate the fact that if you can convince the judge that goods or services were substandard, chances are good that you'll win at least a partial victory.

Kinds of Defenses Common to Debt Cases

As discussed in more detail in Chapter 2, defenses in cases where a bill was not paid include:

Breach of contract. The other party failed to live up to (perform) the terms of the contract within the correct period of time, with the result that you are no longer obligated to keep your payment obligation. For example, you contracted to have your kitchen counter remodeled using white ceramic tile, and ended up with beige plastic tile. Or, you ordered a cake from a website and it arrived looking nothing like the picture.

! **CAUTION**

Trivial defects won't void a contract. To succeed with a breach of contract defense, you must show that the other party's breach was significant enough that it prevented you from receiving all or at least a substantial amount of the benefits that you wanted from the contract. For example, if you order light yellow flowers for a wedding and refuse to pay the bill because cream-colored flowers are delivered, you can be pretty sure the judge will decide in favor of the flower vendor, especially if you used the flowers. By contrast, if you order yellow flowers and receive dark red ones that obviously clash with your color scheme, your chances of winning would be much better.

Fraud. The other party intentionally lied to you about a key fact in a transaction. For example, you purchased a used car with 75,000 miles on the odometer. Later, you meet the vehicle's first owner who says it really had gone 125,000 miles and that the odometer said so when he sold it to the used car dealer who sold it to you.

Breach of warranty. An express or implied warranty (assurance) made by the seller of goods is breached. For example, a roofer claims in writing that your new roof will last 20 years. In fact, it leaks in the first big storm.

Violation of statute. Many federal and state laws require the seller of a particular type of goods or services to comply with specific rules. For example, the Federal Trade Commission provides that a door-to-door seller of goods and services that cost more than $25 must give you notice of your right to cancel within three days, along with a cancellation form. If he fails to do so, your right to cancel continues indefinitely. For example, if you buy an expensive vacuum cleaner from a door-to-door salesperson and ask to cancel the deal the next day, you have a good defense if the vacuum cleaner company sues you for nonpayment.

EXAMPLE: TopHat Models, a New York modeling agency, sued Mary P., claiming she had not paid its $1,000 fee for creating a portfolio of "professional quality photographs." The photos were designed to help Mary obtain employment as a model. In her defense, Mary claimed that TopHat had violated New York State's employment agency licensing law (N.Y. Gen. Bus. L. § 170 and following) by falsely claiming it would help her find modeling jobs and in fact making no effort to do so. After concluding that TopHat was primarily a scheme designed to get consumers to overpay for photographs and that it had not attempted to find Mary modeling work, the court agreed and ruled that Mary owed nothing.

Evidence to Defend Your Case

To successfully defend a suit claiming you owe money, you'll normally need to document a very good reason why the goods or services you received were inadequate or some other reason why you are not legally required to pay for them. This means you'll need to do more than tell the judge a sad story. If shoddy goods are involved, show them to the judge or bring a picture or written report from an expert. (See Chapter 14.) If you received truly bad service, bring a witness or other supporting evidence to court. For example, suppose the new paint on your recently refinished boat immediately began to chip and peel and, as a result, you notified the boat yard that you would not pay for the job. In case you are later sued, you will want to take pictures clearly showing the problem and get a written opinion from another boat refinisher stating the work was substandard as well as an estimate to fix or redo the job.

Appearing in Court

You may have a tactical advantage at the hearing if the person who appears in court on behalf of the creditor is not the same person with whom you dealt. For example, if you state that a salesperson told you X, Y, and Z, the salesperson probably won't be present to state otherwise.

This may tilt a closely balanced case to you. It is perfectly appropriate for you to point out to the judge that your opponent has only books and ledgers, not firsthand knowledge of the situation. The judge may sometimes postpone the case until another day to allow the creditor to present the testimony of the employee(s) you dealt with, but often this is impossible because the person in question has moved on.

> **TIP**
>
> **You can always ask for a little more time to pay.** In some states, the judge has considerable discretion to order that a judgment be paid in installments. If you are financially pressed, installment payments can obviously be extremely helpful, because as long as you meet the payment schedule, the creditor can't initiate a wage levy (garnishment) or other collection activity. So don't be shy about asking the judge to establish time payments—she won't know that you want them if you don't ask. Even if you don't make your request in court, it may not be too late. Some courts allow you to file a request to pay a judgment in installments after the hearing. ●

Vehicle Accident Cases

I t is a rare small claims session that does not include at least one fender bender. Unfortunately, these cases are often badly prepared and presented, with the result that the judge commonly makes a decision at least partially by guesswork.

> **TIP**
>
> **File personal injury cases in formal court.** Cases involving all but very minor personal injuries don't belong in small claims court, as they will involve claims for far more money than the small claims maximum. And in states that have no-fault insurance, personal injury cases may not be allowed in court at all unless you've first complied with the requirements of your state's no-fault insurance law.

The average vehicle accident case that ends up in small claims court doesn't involve personal injury but is about damage to one or both parties' vehicles. Many are extremely hard fought. Because of some quirk deeply embedded in our overgrown monkey brains, it is apparently almost impossible for most humans to admit that they are even occasionally bad drivers or could possibly be at fault in a car accident. Out of fantasies such as these are lawsuits made.

Chapter 2 explains the legal concept of negligence. Please reread this material. To recover in a vehicle accident case, you have to prove either that the other person was negligent (careless) and you were driving safely or, if both of you were negligent, that you were less so. Normally, dealing with concepts of negligence in a vehicle accident is a matter of common sense; you probably have a fairly good idea of the rules of the road and whether you or the other driver screwed up. One key is whether you or the other party was cited for breaking a law having to do with highway safety. (See "Determining Fault," below.) When a safety-related law is broken, negligence is usually presumed.

CAUTION

Check rules in no-fault states. States with no-fault insurance laws generally require that auto accident disputes—especially those involving less serious injuries—be submitted to the no-fault administrative system, not to the court. Check your state's rules.

CAUTION

Don't assume you will lose if you were partially at fault. You can still win, or at least partially win, a case involving negligence even if you were not completely in the right. Under the doctrine known as "comparative negligence," if the other person was significantly more at fault than you were, you may still have a good case. (See Chapter 2 for more on comparative negligence.)

Who Can Sue Whom?

The owner of a vehicle is the person who should file a claim for damage done to the vehicle, even if that person wasn't driving when the accident occurred. The lawsuit should be brought against the negligent driver and—if the driver is not also the vehicle's owner—against the registered owner as well. To find out who owns a car, contact the state Department of Motor Vehicles. As long as you can tell them the license number, they can tell you the registered owner. (See the discussion in Chapter 8.)

Was There a Witness to the Accident?

Because the judge has no way of knowing what happened unless one or more people tell her, a good witness can make or break your case.

It is better to have a disinterested witness than a close friend or family member, but any witness is far better than none. If the other guy is likely to have a witness who supports his point of view (even though it's wrong) and you have none, you will have to work extra hard to develop other evidence. Reread Chapter 14 for more information on witnesses. If you do have an eyewitness but can't get that person to show up in court voluntarily, try to get him to give you a written statement of what he saw, and present that as evidence.

Police Accident Reports

When you have an accident and believe the other person was more at fault than you were, it is almost always wise to immediately call the police so that a police report can be prepared. (In some areas, however, accident reports are only prepared if someone claims to be injured.) A police report is admissible as evidence in small claims court. The theory is that an officer investigating the circumstances of the accident at the scene is in a better position to establish the truth of what happened than is any other third party. So, if an accident report was made, buy a copy for a few dollars from the police station. If it supports you, bring it to court. If it doesn't, be prepared to refute what it says. This can best be done with the testimony of an eyewitness. If both an eyewitness and a police report are against you, you might want to rethink this whole lawsuit thing.

Determining Fault

Chapter 2 explains the general concept of negligence. That discussion is fully applicable to motor vehicle cases. Negligence can also be determined by showing that the other driver caused the accident (in whole or in part) as a result of safety-related violations of driving laws.

For instance, if Tommy runs a red light (prohibited by driving laws) and hits a car crossing the intersection, Tommy is presumed to be negligent unless he can offer a sufficient excuse for his action. On the other hand, if Tommy is driving without wearing his seatbelt (also prohibited) and has an accident, the violation cannot be said to have caused the accident and therefore can't be used to presume negligence.

If there is a police report, the reporting officer will have noted any driving law violations that occurred during the accident. The report may even conclude that a driving violation caused the accident. Obviously, if the police cited the other driver, this is terrific evidence that you'll want to show to the judge. If there is no police report, you may wish to do a little research on your own. Your state's vehicle code is available online at www.nolo.com/statute/state.cfm, in most large public libraries, and in all law libraries. You can use its index to review dozens of driving rules that may have been violated by the other driver. If you discover any violations that can fairly be said to have contributed to the accident, call them to the attention of the judge. (For more tips on legal research, see Chapter 25.)

CAUTION

Beware! Professional drivers have an incentive to bend the truth. Be particularly on your guard when you are opposing a bus or truck driver. Many of these people will suffer job problems if they are found to be at fault in too many accidents. As a result, they often deny fault almost automatically. Judges usually know this and are often unsympathetic when a bus driver says that there has never been a time when he didn't "look both ways twice, count to ten, and say the Lord's Prayer" before pulling out from a bus stop. Still, it never hurts to ask the driver in court whether his employer has any demerit system or other penalty for being at fault in an accident.

Diagrams

With the exception of witnesses and police accident reports, the most effective tool in presenting an accident case is a good diagram. Many good cases have been lost because the judge never properly visualized what happened, and several iffy cases won because plaintiffs made persuasive drawings. All courtrooms have blackboards, and it is an excellent idea to draw a diagram of what happened as part of your presentation. If you are nervous about your ability to do this, prepare your diagram in advance and bring it to court. Use crayons or magic markers and draw on a large piece of paper about three feet square. Do a good job with attention to detail. When it's your turn to speak, ask the judge for permission to display your drawing (this will be easy if you have attached it to a piece of cardboard or similar stiff surface).

For example, suppose you're involved in an intersection accident—you collide with another car coming from the right. You'd want to draw the intersecting streets, showing the lane separators and any stop signs or signals, and use arrows to indicate the lines of travel. Draw any obstructions, such as trees and other vehicles.

Photos

Photographs can sometimes be helpful in auto accident cases. This is especially true if they back up your story about how an accident occurred. For example, if you claim that you were sideswiped while you were parked, a photo showing a long series of scratches down the side of your car is likely to be convincing. Assuming they help you tell a convincing story, it can also be effective to show the judge pictures of the defendant's car (if you can manage to get them).

Estimates

Whenever you attempt to recover money for damage done to your vehicle, it is important to show the judge several estimates for the cost of repairs. Three is usually a good number. If you have already had the work done, bring your canceled check or receipt from the repair shop along with the estimates you didn't accept. Be sure to get your estimates from reputable shops. If, for some reason, you get an estimate from someone you later think isn't competent, simply ignore it and get another. You have no legal responsibility to get your car fixed by anyone suggested to you by the person who caused the damage. Indeed, common sense often dictates that you don't. Unfortunately, you can't recover money from the other party to cover the time you put in to get estimates, take your car to the repair shop, or appear in court.

In addition to damage to your car, you can also recover money for the fair market value of anything in your car that was destroyed. You must be prepared to establish both the fact of the damage and the dollar amount of the loss. (See Chapter 4 for a discussion of how to do this.) You can also recover money for the cost of alternate transportation while your car is disabled. However, a judge will usually only allow car rental fees for the minimum period of time it reasonably should have taken to get your car fixed. Thus, if you could reasonably have arranged to get a fender fixed in two days, you are only entitled to be reimbursed for renting a car for that time, not the days it took for an overworked body shop to get around to it.

! **CAUTION**

Defendants should be on their guard against plaintiffs who try to pad their repair bill. Although it's a nasty practice, sometimes plaintiffs dishonestly try to fix existing damage to their car as part of getting legitimate accident work done. If you think the plaintiff is asking for too much money, try to develop evidence to support your belief. For example, if you can present evidence that the plaintiff's car was already damaged at the time of your accident, but that she is suing you for 100% of her repair costs, the judge should award her less—maybe a lot less—than the amount she is demanding. Also, remember that the plaintiff is only entitled to get repairs made up to the total value of the car before the accident. If the car was worth only $1,500 and the repairs would cost $2,500, the plaintiff is only entitled to $1,500. (See Chapter 4.)

Your Demand Letter

As in almost every other type of small claims court case, you should write a letter to your opponent, with an eye to the judge reading it, that proposes settlement. See the sample letters in Chapter 6. Here is another:

Sample Demand Letter After Auto Accident

18 Channing Way
Eugene, OR
August 27, 20xx

R. Rigsby Rugg
27 Miramar Crescent
Eugene, OR

Dear Mr. Rugg:

On August 15, 20xx, I was traveling eastbound on Rose Street in Eugene, Oregon, at about 3:30 on a sunny afternoon. I stopped at the stop sign at the corner of Rose and Sacramento and then proceeded to turn right (south) on Sacramento. As I was making my turn, I saw your car going southbound on Sacramento. You were about 20 feet north of the corner of Rose. Instead of stopping at the stop sign, you proceeded across the intersection and struck my car on the front left fender. By the time I realized that you were coming through the stop sign, there was nothing I could do to get out of your way.

As you remember, after the accident the Eugene police were called and cited you for failure to stop at a stop sign. I have a copy of the police report, and it confirms the facts as I have stated them here.

I have obtained three estimates for the work needed to repair the damage you caused to my car. The lowest is $612. I am proceeding to get this work done because I need my car fixed as soon as possible.

I will appreciate receiving a check from you as soon as possible. If you wish to talk about any aspect of this situation, please don't hesitate to call me, evenings at 486-1482.

Sincerely,

Sandy McClatchy

Sandy McClatchy

Appearing in Court

Here's how a motor vehicle accident case can be presented in court:

Clerk: "Next case, *McClatchy v. Rugg*. Please come forward."

Judge: "Please tell me what happened, Ms. McClatchy."

Sandy McClatchy: "Good morning. This dispute involves an auto accident that occurred at Rose and Sacramento Streets on the afternoon of August 15, 20xx. I was coming uphill on Rose (that's east) and stopped at the corner. There is a four-way stop sign at the corner. I turned right, or south, on Sacramento Street, and as I was doing so, Mr. Rugg ran the stop sign on Sacramento and crashed into my front fender. Your Honor, may I use the blackboard to make a quick diagram?"

Judge: "Please do, I was about to ask you if you would."

Sandy McClatchy: (makes a drawing as suggested in "Diagrams," above, points out the movement of the cars in detail, and answers several questions from the judge): "Your Honor, before I sit down, I would like to give you several items of evidence. First, I have a copy of the police accident report from the Fullerton police, which states that Mr. Rugg got a citation for failing to stop at the stop sign in question. Second, I have some photos that show the damage to the front fender of my car. Third, I have my letter to Mr. Rugg trying without success to settle this case. Finally, I have several estimates as to the cost of repairing the damage to my car. As you can see from my canceled check, I took the lowest one (hands copies of each piece of evidence to bailiff to give to judge)."

Judge: "Thank you, Ms. McClatchy. Now, Mr. Rugg, it's your turn."

R. Rigsby Rugg: "Your Honor, my case rests on one basic fact. Ms. McClatchy was negligent because she made a wide turn into Sacramento Street. Instead of going from the right-hand lane of Rose to the right-hand or outside lane on Sacramento Street, she turned into the center lane on Sacramento Street. (Mr. Rugg moves to the blackboard and points out what he says happened.) Now it might be true that I made a rolling stop at the corner. You know, I really stopped, but maybe not quite all the way—but I never would have hit anybody if she had kept to her own side of the road. Also, your Honor, I would like to say this—she darted out; she has one of those little foreign cars and instead of easing out slow like I do with my Lincoln, she jumped out like a rabbit being chased by a red fox."

Judge: "Do you have anything else to say, Ms. McClatchy?"

Sandy McClatchy: "I am not going to even try to argue about whether Mr. Rugg can be rolling and stopped at the same time. I think the policeman who cited him answered that question. I want to answer his point about my turning into the center lane on Sacramento Street, instead of the inside lane. It is true that, after stopping, I had to make a slightly wider turn than usual. If you will look again at the diagram I drew, you will see that a car was parked almost to the corner of Sacramento and Rose on Sacramento. To get around this car, I had to drive a little farther into Sacramento before starting my turn than would have been necessary otherwise. I didn't turn into the center lane, but as I made the turn, my outside fender crossed into the center lane slightly. This is when Mr. Rugg hit me. I feel that since I had the right of way and I had to do what I did to make the turn, I wasn't negligent."

Judge: "Thank you both—you will get my decision in the mail."

(The judge decided in favor of Sandy McClatchy and awarded her $612 plus service of process and filing costs.) ●

Landlord-Tenant Cases

By using small claims court, tenants in most states can sue for money damages over a whole host of landlord violations—failure to return a cleaning or damage deposit, invasion of the tenant's privacy, violation of the duty to provide safe and habitable premises, and rent control violations, to name but a few. In addition, a group of tenants or neighbors can individually (but simultaneously) sue a landlord who tolerates an illegal or even legal but highly annoying situation on the rental property. For example, if ten tenants sue a landlord who tolerates drug dealing for $7,500 each, the landlord would face $75,000 worth of lawsuits.

Although the majority of cases are initiated by tenants, landlords also can and do use small claims court—for example, to sue a current or former tenant for unpaid rent or for damages done to the rental property. In some states, it is also possible for a landlord to use small claims court to evict a tenant. (See the Appendix for state-by-state information.) This is an exception to the general rule that only money damage cases can be handed down by small claims court—but it's an exception landlords may find hard to take advantage of, as discussed in "Evictions," below.

Further Reading on Landlord-Tenant Law

To minimize your chances of ending up in small claims court and to more effectively fight your case if a dispute ends up in court, we highly recommend the following Nolo books. These provide detailed state-specific information on landlord-tenant law and checklists and forms to avoid disputes involving security deposits, housing code violations, late rent and rent withholding, inspections (tenants' privacy rights), discrimination, illicit tenant activity, and more.

- For tenants: *Every Tenant's Legal Guide,* by Janet Portman and Marcia Stewart.

- For property owners and managers: *Every Landlord's Legal Guide,* by Marcia Stewart, Ralph Warner, and Janet Portman.

Security Deposit Cases

Disagreements about whether a landlord properly withheld all or part of a tenant's security deposit account for a large percentage of the landlord-tenant disputes that end up in small claims court.

Problems involving security deposits often arise like this:

- The tenant moves out, making what the tenant considers to be a reasonable effort to clean the place.

- The landlord keeps all or part of the deposit, stating that the place was left damaged or dirty.

- The tenant is furious, claiming the landlord is illegally withholding the deposit.

If the tenant and landlord can't reach a compromise, the tenant's best remedy is to sue the landlord for the money withheld, leaving it up to the small claims court judge to decide who is telling the truth.

Whether you're a tenant filing a case or a landlord defending one, it's important to understand state law on security deposits.

State Deposit Laws

State law often dictates how large a deposit a landlord can require, how it may be used, when and how it must be returned, and more. In most states, it is up to the landlord to prove that dirty or damaged conditions justified keeping all or part of a deposit. Often state law also provides that if a deposit is not returned within a specified time after the tenant moves out (usually somewhere between 14 and 30 days, depending on the state), the tenant is entitled to receive the entire deposit back. If a judge decides that the landlord's failure to follow the law was deliberate, the judge may make the landlord pay an additional monetary penalty.

If the landlord acted in bad faith in retaining the deposit (by deliberately withholding the deposit despite repeated requests to follow the law), the tenant may be entitled to extra ("punitive") damages over and above the actual amount of the withheld deposit. Whether the tenant actually gets these extra damages is up to the judge, but after checking your state's rule (which you can do using our website at www.nolo.com/statute/state.cfm), it never hurts to bring your small claims suit for an amount that includes these extra damages.

Deposit Cases From the Tenant's Point of View

How should a tenant prepare a case involving a landlord's failure to return a deposit? Ideally, preparation should start when you move in. Any damaged or dirty conditions should be noted as part of the lease or rental agreement, which should be signed by both you and the landlord. You should also take photographs of substandard conditions and have neighbors or friends look the place over. When you move out and clean up, you should do much the same thing—take photos, have friends (or another tenant in the building) check the place over, keep receipts for cleaning materials, and, once the place is cleaned up, try and get the landlord to agree in writing that it is in satisfactory condition or that the noted areas of damage are all there is.

Now let's assume that you are a tenant, and your former landlord has not returned your $900 security deposit even though you moved out more than three weeks ago, having paid all your rent, given proper notice, and "passed" the pre-move out inspection. Start by writing the landlord a letter like this:

Sample Letter Demanding Security Deposit

October 25, 20xx

Adam Anderson
Anderson Realty Co.
10 Rose Street
Costa Mesa, CA

Dear Mr. Anderson:

As you know, until September 30, 20xx, I resided in Apartment #4 at 1700 Walnut Street and regularly paid my rent to your office. When I moved out, I left the unit cleaner than it was when I moved in. During the pre-move-out inspection, the only issue you identified was the cleanliness of the drapes, which I then had dry-cleaned in accordance with your instructions.

As of today, I have received neither my $900 security deposit nor any accounting from you for that money. Please be aware that I know my rights under California Civil Code § 1950.5. If I do not receive my money within the next week, I will regard the retention of this deposit as showing "bad faith" on your part and shall sue you, not only for the $900 deposit plus interest, but also for the $1,800 punitive damages allowed by Section 1950.5 of the California Civil Code. May I hear from you soon?

Sincerely,

Farrah Shields

Farrah Shields
456 Main Street
Costa Mesa, CA

> ⓘ **CAUTION**
>
> **Be specific when requesting the return of a deposit.** If your landlord has returned only part of your security deposit, deducting more for cleaning or damages than you thought was reasonable, your demand letter should detail exactly why you believe the deductions were improper. For example, if the landlord says a door was damaged and cost $200 to fix, you might claim that the work could have been done competently for $75. If you get no satisfactory response from your landlord, file your case.

Whom Should Tenants Sue in Security Deposit Cases?

A tenant who knows who owns the building should sue this person or business. However, sometimes it is hard to know who to sue, because rent is often paid to a manager or other agent instead of the owner. In most states, multiple occupancy buildings with two or more units must have ownership information posted on the premises, or list the name of the owner (or the owner's agent for purposes of suit) on the rental agreement. If you are in doubt as to who owns your unit, you are probably safe if you sue both the person to whom you pay your rent and the person who signed the rental agreement, unless you have received notice that the building has been transferred to a new owner, in which case you would sue that person.

On court day, a well-prepared tenant should show up in court with as many of the following pieces of evidence as possible:

- Photos or a video of the apartment showing how it looked when you moved in, including any dirt or damage that already existed. (If you don't have these, it's not fatal; if you do, it helps.)
- A copy of the pre-move-out inspection report, if one was done.

- Photos or a video of the apartment showing clean conditions when you moved out.

- A copy of an inventory of conditions upon moving in and moving out, signed by the landlord and tenant, if one or both was prepared.

- Receipts or canceled checks for any cleaning supplies used in the final cleanup.

- A copy of your written lease or rental agreement.

- A copy of a demand letter to the landlord, such as the sample set out above, showing that you made the required demand before suing.

- One or, preferably, two witnesses who were familiar with the property, saw it after you cleaned up, and will testify that it was in good shape. Incidentally, the testimony or written statements of people who actually scrubbed an oven or toilet are particularly effective. If you also have a witness who saw the place when you moved in and who will say that it wasn't perfectly buffed (or that damage already existed), so much the better.

Proceedings in court should go something like this:

Clerk: "*Shields v. Anderson Realty*. Please step forward."

Judge: "Good morning. Please tell me your version of the facts, Ms. Shields."

Farah Shields: "I moved into the apartment at 1700 Walnut Street in Costa Mesa in the spring of 2006. I paid Mr. Anderson, here, my first and last months' rent, a total of $2,000. I also paid him a $2,000 'security deposit.' I moved out on September 30 of this year. Because my tenancy began in 2006, I was entitled to a pre-move-out inspection, which we did on September 20. Mr. Anderson pointed out that the drapes were dirty, so I had them dry-cleaned at the place he recommended. Three weeks after I moved out, Mr. Anderson had not yet returned my $2,000 deposit, so I wrote him a letter asking for my money back. I have yet to hear from him. As I believe this constitutes a willful denial of my rights under Civil Code Section 1950.5, I am asking for the $2,000 Mr. Anderson owes me, but also $6,000 in punitive damages, for a total of $8,000 plus my court costs. Because the total is above the $7,500 limit in this court, I'm willing to trim my demand to $7,500. Here is a copy of the rental agreement (hands it to the clerk), which specifically states my deposit is to be returned to me if the apartment is left clean and undamaged.

"When I moved into #4 at 1700 Walnut, it was a mess. It's a nice little apartment, but the people who lived there before me were sloppy. The stove was filthy, as was the bathroom, the refrigerator, the floors, and just about everything else. In addition, the walls hadn't been painted in years. But I needed a place to live and this was the best available, so I moved in despite the mess. I painted the whole place—everything. Mr. Anderson's office paid me for the paint, but I did all of the work. And I cleaned the place thoroughly, too. It took me three days. I like to live in a clean home.

"Here are some pictures of what the place looked like when I moved in (hands photos to clerk, who gives them to the judge). Here is a second set of photos that were taken after I moved out and cleaned up (again hands pictures to clerk). Your Honor, I think these pictures tell the story—the place was clean when I moved out. I also have receipts (hands to clerk) for cleaning supplies and a rug shampooer that I used during the cleanup. They total $45.25. I have also brought two people who saw the place the day I left and can tell you what it looked like when I moved out."

Judge: (looking at one of the witnesses) "Do you have some personal knowledge of what this apartment looked like?"

John DeBono: "Actually, I helped Farah move in and move out. I simply don't understand what the landlord is fussing about. The place was a smelly mess when she moved in, and it was spotless when Farah moved out."

Judge: (addressing the second witness) "Do you have something to add?"

Puna Polaski: "I never saw 1700 Walnut when Farah moved in because I didn't know her then. But I did help her pack and clean up when she moved out. I can tell you that the windows were washed, the floor waxed, and the oven cleaned, because I did it. And I can tell you that the rest of the apartment was clean, too, because I saw it."

Judge: "Mr. Anderson, you may now tell your side of the story. I should remind you that you have the burden of proving that the amounts you withheld were reasonable."

Adam Anderson: "Your Honor, I am not here to argue about whether or not the place was clean. Maybe it was cleaner when Miss Shields moved out than when she moved in. The reason I withheld the deposit is that portions of the walls were all painted odd, bright colors and I have had to paint them all over. I couldn't see these during the inspection, because she had posters and cloth hangings over them. Here are some color pictures of the walls taken just after Miss Shields moved out. They show pink and purple walls, two of which are adorned with rainbows. And in one of the bedrooms, there were even animals painted on the walls. I ask you, your Honor, how was I going to rent that place with a purple bulldog painted on the wall? It cost me more than $500 to have the place painted over white."

Judge: (looks at the pictures and gives up trying to keep a straight face, which is okay, as everyone in the courtroom is laughing except Mr. Anderson) "Let me ask a few questions. Was it true that the place needed a new coat of paint when you moved in, Ms. Shields?"

Farah Shields: "Yes."

Judge: "Do you agree, Mr. Anderson?"

Adam Anderson: "Yes, that's why my office paid her paint bills, although we never would have if we had known about that bulldog, not to mention the rainbows."

Judge: "How much did the paint cost?"

Adam Anderson: "$125."

Judge: "I normally send decisions by mail, but today I am going to explain what I have decided. First, the apartment needed repainting anyway, Mr. Anderson, so I am not going to give you any credit for paying to have the work done. However, Ms. Shields, even though the place looked quite—shall I say, cheerful—when you moved out, Mr. Anderson does have a point in that you went beyond what is reasonable. Therefore, I feel that it's unfair to make Anderson Realty pay for paint twice. My judgment is this: The $125 for the paint that was given to Ms. Shields is subtracted from the $2,000 deposit. This means that Anderson Realty owes Farah Shields $1,875 plus $32 for costs (the filing fee plus service by certified mail). I am not awarding any punitive damages because I do not believe that Anderson Realty acted in bad faith in retaining the deposit."

The Landlord's Perspective: Defending Deposit Cases

Your best protection against spending hours haggling over security deposits is to follow the law scrupulously when a tenant moves out. It is your responsibility to return the deposit within the number of days legally required or explain why you are withholding some or all of it. But no matter how meticulous you are about properly accounting for your tenants' deposits, sooner or later you may be sued by a tenant who disagrees with your assessment of the cost of cleaning or repairs.

This section shows landlords how to defend themselves in tenant-initiated small claims court cases. The sections that follow cover the occasional necessity of taking a tenant to small claims court for unpaid rent, damage, or cleaning bills not covered by the deposit.

Within the time limit set by your state's law, after inspecting the premises and documenting any dirty or damaged conditions, send the tenant a written itemization of deductions for repairs, cleaning, and unpaid rent. Include details on the costs of any cleaning or damage repair, including a reasonable hourly charge if you or your employees do any necessary cleaning or repainting, and an itemization if work is done by an outside firm. Keep receipts for costs of repairs such as new carpets or repainting. If you use an outside cleaning service, ask the service whether they will testify in small claims court, if necessary, or at least write a letter describing what they did in detail if the tenant contests your deposit deductions.

Before your court hearing, you should gather all the evidence you have that the premises needed cleaning or were damaged. It's important to understand that you, the landlord, have the legal burden of proving one or both of these facts. If you fail to do that, the tenant will win. In other words, all a former tenant needs to prove to win is that a residential tenancy existed, that she paid you a deposit, and that you didn't return all of it.

To make a winning case, a landlord should show up in court with as many of the following items of evidence as possible:

- Photos or a video of the premises before the tenant moved in, showing how clean and undamaged the place was.

- Photos or a video taken at the pre-move-out inspection, if any, and then after the tenant left, that show a mess or damage.

- Copies of inventory sheets (if they were prepared) detailing the condition of the rental unit when the tenant moved in and out, signed by the landlord and tenant. (These are particularly valuable if they show that an item that is now broken was in good shape when the tenant moved in.)

- A copy of your written lease or rental agreement.

- An itemization of hours spent by you, or your repair or cleaning people, working on the unit, complete with the hourly costs for the work.

- A copy of the written security deposit itemization(s) (pre-move-out and post-move-out) you sent the tenant with details about the deductions.

- Any damaged items to be brought into the courtroom (for example, a curtain with a cigarette hole would be effective evidence).

- Receipts for professional cleaning or repair services.

- One, or preferably two, witnesses who were familiar with the property, saw it just after the tenant left, and who will testify that the place was dirty or that certain items were damaged. People who helped in the subsequent cleaning or repair or the new tenant who saw the place before you cleaned it are likely to be particularly effective witnesses. Written statements or declarations under penalty of perjury can be used, but they aren't as effective as live testimony. A sample written statement is shown below.

Sample Declaration

Declaration of Paul Stallone

I, Paul Stallone, declare:

1. I am employed at A & B Maintenance Company, a contract cleaning and maintenance service located at 123 Abrego Street, Tucson, Arizona. Gina Cabarga, the owner of an apartment complex at 456 Seventh Street, Tucson, Arizona, is one of our accounts.

2. On May 1, 20xx, Gina asked me to go to the premises at 456 Seventh Street, Apartment 8, to shampoo the carpets. When I entered the premises, I noticed a strong odor, part of which seemed like stale cigarette smoke. An odor also seemed to come from the carpet.

3. When I began using a steam carpet cleaner on the living room carpet, I noticed a strong smell of urine. I stopped the steam cleaner, moved to a dry corner of the carpet, and pulled it from the floor. I then saw a yellow color on the normally white foam-rubber pad beneath the carpet. I also smelled a strong urine odor, apparently caused by a pet (probably a cat) having urinated on the carpet. On further examination of the carpet, I noticed similar stains and odors throughout the carpet and pad.

4. In my opinion, the living room carpet and foam-rubber pad underneath need to be removed and replaced and the floor should be sanded and sealed.

5. I declare under penalty of perjury under the laws of the State of California that the foregoing is true and correct.

DATED: June 15, 20xx

SIGNATURE: _____
                         Paul Stallone

Unpaid Rent, Rent Withholding, and Other Money Damage Cases

In most states, landlords can initiate small claims actions to sue for unpaid rent. Typically, the tenant breaks the lease early or skips out on a month-to-month tenancy without providing adequate notice. If the tenant stops paying rent but stays on the premises, it's usually better to request damages as part of an eviction action in formal court.

If you are a landlord who decides that it is worthwhile to go after your tenant for money owed, your first step is to write a letter asking the tenant to pay the amount of your claim. Itemize how you applied the tenant's security deposit to the charges for cleaning and damage repair, and request payment of the balance.

If the tenant has no good reason for withholding rent, then your small claims case as a landlord should be relatively simple. However, if the tenant claims that she withheld rent because the rental unit was in an unlivable condition, then you will have to prepare to refute that claim at your hearing.

! CAUTION

Take care of your reputation. If you are a landlord with many rental units and regularly use a local small claims court, make particularly sure that every case you bring is a good one. You do not want to lose your credibility with the court in the future by ever appearing to be unfair or poorly prepared.

When the Tenant Has No Defense

Often the tenant has already moved out and doesn't bother to show up in court. If this happens, the landlord briefly states her case and, assuming it's credible, will win by default. (See "If Your Opponent

Doesn't Show Up," in Chapter 15.) Sometimes the tenant does show up but presents no real defense (often he is there only to request the judge to allow him to pay the judgment in installments). (See Chapter 24.) Again, the landlord should easily prevail.

The landlord should bring the lease or rental agreement to court and simply state the time periods for which rent is due but unpaid. Nothing else is required unless the tenant presents a defense, as discussed below. Sometimes a landlord will sue for more than the amount of rent owed under a lease or rental agreement that states that the landlord is entitled to a high "holdover rent" when the tenant fails to pay rent but stays in the rental unit. Doing this will almost guarantee that the tenant will put up a fight. Landlords are not guaranteed more than the regular rent, even if their lease calls for it, and for tactical reasons the landlord is often better off ignoring a holdover rent provision and suing only for the regular rent.

When a Tenant Breaks a Lease

A tenant who leaves before the expiration of a fixed-term lease (whether or not she notifies the landlord that she's leaving) and refuses to pay the remainder of the rent due under the lease is said to have "broken the lease." This means the tenant is liable for the rent for the entire lease term (except where the landlord breaches an important lease provision first). However, the tenant's responsibility for paying all rent still due under the lease when she leaves early is limited in most states by the landlord's duty to "mitigate damages." Stated in plain English, the landlord has a legal duty to try to find a new tenant as soon as reasonably possible to limit the financial loss.

What all this adds up to is that a landlord whose tenant breaks a lease with no good reason is entitled to:

• the remaining rent due under the lease, minus

- any portion of that amount that the landlord can reasonably obtain by rerenting the unit, plus

- any reasonable advertising expenses incurred in finding a new tenant, plus

- charges for necessary repair and cleaning after the tenant moves out.

A landlord can deduct the total cost of these items from the tenant's security deposit (see "Security Deposit Cases," above) and sue for the remainder in small claims court. (See Chapter 4 for a discussion of the "mitigation of damages" concept.)

When the Rent-Withholding Tenant Claims the Unit Is Uninhabitable

Now let's look at small claims suits where a tenant stops paying rent based on a claim that the rental unit is seriously defective (uninhabitable). Although this issue most often comes up in the context of an eviction ("unlawful detainer") lawsuit (see "Evictions," below), occasionally a landlord brings a separate small claims suit for unpaid rent.

From the Tenant's Point of View

Tenants have several valid defenses to a landlord's suit based on a tenant's failure to pay rent. The principal defense is to claim that you withheld rent because the condition of the premises was "uninhabitable." This amounts to saying to the landlord: "I won't pay my rent until you make essential repairs or provide essential services."

This defense is based on the fact that, under all but two states' laws, every landlord makes an implied promise that a dwelling will be fit for human habitation—whether or not the promise is written down in a lease or rental agreement. If the landlord does not keep the place in a habitable condition at all times, he is said, in legalese, to have "breached the implied warranty of habitability." That breach justifies the tenant's

withholding of rent. For a tenant to withhold rent legally, all of the
following must be true:

- you must not have caused the problems
- the defects must be serious ones that threaten your health or safety,
  and
- you must have given the landlord reasonable notice of the problem
  and of your intention to withhold rent if the problems are not fixed.

The important thing for a tenant to understand is that rent
withholding is not legal where the landlord is slow (or refuses) to fix
some minor defect. For rent to be legally withheld, the condition
needing repair must be sufficiently serious as to make the home
"uninhabitable," unhealthy, or unsafe. Thus, a broken furnace that a
landlord refuses to fix in February would qualify as a condition making
a home uninhabitable, but lack of heat in the summer for a few days
probably would not.

As a tenant living in a rental unit with serious defects, you may end up
in small claims court one of two ways: Either your landlord sues you for
failing to pay rent (in which case you may end up defending an eviction
lawsuit), or you sue your landlord for failing to repair serious defects.
In either case, your job is to prove—with pictures, witnesses, and other
evidence—that the condition that caused you to withhold rent is indeed
serious. Thus, you might call the building inspector or an electrician to
testify that the wiring was in a dangerous state of decay. The landlord,
of course, will probably testify that the rental unit is in fundamentally
sound shape, even though there may be some minor problems.

Keep in mind that the landlord will likely claim that you caused the
damage. Be prepared to prove that's not true. Most state laws require
tenants to use rented premises properly, refrain from damaging or
defacing the premises, and keep them clean. Standard lease and rental
agreements usually make the tenant financially responsible for repair
of damage caused by the tenant's negligence or misuse. For example,

if a refrigerator no longer works because the tenant defrosted it with a carving knife, it's usually the tenant's responsibility to make the repairs or to reimburse the landlord for doing so. If a tenant refuses to repair or pay for the damage he caused, the landlord can sue the tenant in small claims court for the cost of the repairs.

How much rent can you withhold? Theoretically, a tenant can withhold an amount of rent equal to the dollar amount by which the unfixed defect lowers the value of the property. As a practical matter, however, the tenant can withhold as much rent as the landlord—or a judge, if the matter gets to court—will allow under the circumstances. A judge will make a decision based on what she thinks is the rental value of the premises, in light of the seriousness of the defect.

A landlord who fails to maintain property can be sued by a tenant for failing to provide a habitable dwelling. The tenant, whether or not he remains in the property, can sue the landlord for the following:

- Partial or total refund of rent paid while conditions were substandard.

- The value, or repair costs, of property lost or damaged as a result of the defect—for example, furniture ruined by water leaking through the roof.

- Compensation for personal injuries, including pain and suffering, caused by the defect. Landlords may be liable for physical injuries caused by faulty premises, such as a broken step, inadequate lighting, or substandard electrical wiring. Tenants can sue for medical bills, lost earnings, and pain and suffering in small claims court. (See Chapter 2, "How to Approach a Personal Injury (and Mental Distress) Case," and Chapter 4, "How to Calculate the Exact Amount of Your Claim," for more on this.)

CAUTION

In many states, landlord retaliation is illegal. For example, a rent increase or termination notice is often illegal if done in response to a tenant's complaints to authorities about conditions in the property or a tenant's lawsuit. Unfortunately, some states offer no such protections.

CAUTION

Laws concerning habitability, repairs, and other landlord-tenant issues are slightly different in every state. See Chapter 25 for tips on legal research, or go straight to Nolo's website at www.nolo.com/statutes/state.cfm.

From the Landlord's Point of View

If you are a landlord involved in a rent withholding case, you're probably either responding to a tenant's suit based on claimed substandard conditions or, more likely, suing the tenant for the portion of the rent withheld because he claims that the rental unit was uninhabitable. Either way, be prepared to prove one of the following:

- The claimed defect was not so serious or substantial as to render the property legally uninhabitable and, therefore, to justify the tenant's decision to withhold rent. One good way to establish that the problem was not serious (for example, a hot water heater was noisy but still functioning), is to have the repairperson who eventually corrected the problem write a letter or testify in person.

- Even if the defect was substantial, the tenant didn't give you adequate notice and a chance to fix it. Especially if you regularly solicit and respond quickly to tenant complaints about potential safety problems, install and maintain basic security features, and have a detailed complaint procedure for tenants to report potential safety hazards or maintenance problems, you'll want to explain your system to the judge to convince him that if the tenant had made a timely complaint, the problem surely would have been taken care of.

- Assuming there was a substantial defect that you didn't fix within a reasonable time, this defect justifies only the withholding of a small amount of rent (not the amount the tenant withheld) because it didn't inconvenience the tenant much.

Tenants Suing Cotenants for Unpaid Rent

When two or more people rent property together and all sign the same rental agreement or lease, they are cotenants. Each cotenant shares the same rights and responsibilities under the lease or rental agreement. For example, all cotenants, regardless of agreements they make among themselves, are liable to the landlord for the entire amount of the rent. But being cotenants together does not establish one cotenant's legal right to sue the other cotenant for his share of the rent. In order to do that, the cotenants need to have an agreement between them that specifies how much each will contribute to the total rent. A cotenant who doesn't pay his share, as specified in the agreement, may be sued by the other cotenant(s) in small claims court.

EXAMPLE: James and Helen sign a month-to-month rental agreement for an $800 apartment. They agree between themselves to each pay half of the rent. After three months, James moves out without notifying Helen or the owner, Laura. As one of the two cotenants, Helen is still legally obligated to pay all the rent and may be able to recover James's share by suing him in small claims court. In the same way, Laura, the owner, may sue Helen, the tenant, for the full amount of the rent in small claims court.

Rent Control Cases

In the cities in New York and California that have rent control laws, a landlord who charges illegally high rent can be sued by the tenant not only for the excess rent charged, but for a punitive amount as well (often several times the overcharge).

Foreclosed-Upon Tenants

The mortgage industry crisis that started in 2006 has resulted in millions of foreclosed homes—some of which are occupied by renters who find themselves at the short end of an eviction notice from the bank that now owns the property.

Most tenants will lose their leases upon foreclosure. The rule in most states is that if the mortgage was recorded before the lease was signed, a foreclosure will wipe out the lease (this rule is known as "first in time, first in right"). Because most leases last no longer than a year, it's all too common for the mortgage to predate the lease and destroy it upon foreclosure.

That doesn't always mean the lease-holding tenants have to leave immediately—but those who remain join the ranks of month-to-month renters, all of whom can be terminated with proper notice, usually 30 days. And the new owners tend to move quickly to terminate, giving as little notice as is legally possible (sometimes no more than three days). Tenants who refuse to leave face an eviction lawsuit, for which they usually have no legal defense.

There are some notable exceptions, however, to this grim scenario. Tenants who participate in the federally financed Section 8 program will see their leases survive, as will tenants in New Jersey, New Hampshire, and the District of Columbia. In these states, new owners cannot evict lease-holding tenants unless the tenants have failed to pay the rent or violated any other important lease term or law. Tenants in other states who live in cities with rent control "just cause" eviction protection may also be protected.

Tenants whose states follow the "first in time, first in right" rule will not be able to convince a court to change that rule. But tenants who learn that their new landlord is a bank can at least lessen the financial consequences by suing the former owner. Here's how it works.

After signing a lease, the landlord is legally bound to deliver the rental for the entire lease term. In legalese, this duty is known as the "covenant of quiet enjoyment." A landlord who defaults on a mortgage, which sets in motion the loss of the lease, violates this covenant, and the tenant can sue for the damages it causes. Small claims court is a perfect place to bring such a lawsuit. The tenant can sue for moving and apartment-searching costs, application fees, and the difference, if any, between the new rent for a comparable rental and the rent under the old lease. Though the former owner is probably not flush with money, these cases won't demand very much, and the judgment and award will stay on the books for many years. A persistent tenant can probably collect what's owed eventually.

Drug Dealing and Other Crimes

Your landlord has some degree of legal responsibility to provide secure housing. This means he must take reasonable steps to:

- protect tenants from would-be assailants, thieves, and other criminals
- protect tenants from the criminal acts of fellow tenants
- warn tenants about dangerous situations they are aware of but cannot eliminate, and
- protect the neighborhood from their tenants' illegal activities, such as drug dealing.

When landlords don't live up to this responsibility, they may be liable for any injuries or losses that befall you as a result.

A tenant or neighbor also may sue the landlord for maintaining or allowing a "nuisance"—a serious and persistent condition that adversely affects the tenant's (or neighbor's) enjoyment of the property—even if no physical injury occurs. For example, a tenant plagued by the stench of a pile of garbage because the landlord hasn't provided enough garbage cans for the apartment building can sue the landlord for the annoyance and inconvenience of putting up with the smell.

Tenants Band Together

Increasingly, tenants have gotten together to hold landlords accountable for failing to fulfill their legal responsibility to maintain rental property in a habitable condition. For example, tenants and homeowners have extended this group action approach to sue landlords for failing to protect tenants and neighbors from drug dealers, neighborhood gangs, or other tenants who are creating excessive noise, running an illegal business, or throwing trash in common areas. Similarly, homeowners have filed multiple suits to collect damages from neighbors who allow their teenage children to create disturbances that keep the neighborhood awake all night.

As noted in "Class Actions" in Chapter 7, this technique of using small claims court for groups of individual actions became popular after a neighborhood group successfully banded together to bring hundreds of small claims suits against the City of San Francisco to recover damages for the nuisance created in their neighborhood from the noise from the city airport (*City & Co. of S.F. vs. Small Claims Division, San Mateo Co.,* 190 Cal.Rptr. 340 (1983)).

Despite the fact that this approach is legal and effective, some judges have greeted the filing of many simultaneous lawsuits with verbal disapproval. Nonetheless, a number of claimants in such cases have been successful in obtaining a quick and inexpensive resolution of their neighborhood disputes when other channels for solving their problems had failed. It appears that unless society or the legal system creates another efficient, economic alternative for dealing with neighborhood problems such as these, small claims court judges will be facing a growing number of this type of claim whether they like it or not.

One problem that often arises in this type of case is how much to sue for. Assuming the annoyance is serious and persistent and the landlord or other source of the problem does not take reasonable steps to reduce or eliminate it after receiving a written demand to do so, it often makes sense for each claimant to sue for the small claims maximum and let the judge scale this back if she feels that a lower amount is appropriate.

Drug-Dealing Tenants

Trafficking in illegal drugs, most notably cocaine, has turned some formerly placid neighborhoods into battle zones. Drug dealing has hurt law-abiding landlords and tenants alike. It causes lower rents and property values for landlords and reduces safety and security for tenants and neighbors. To combat this seemingly intractable problem, the law is making landlords who rent to dealers liable for the interference with neighbors' enjoyment of their property.

The legal theory boils down to this: Landlords have a responsibility to keep their properties law-abiding. That means it's up to the landlord to keep dealers out or, failing that, to kick them out pronto when they are discovered. When landlords allow drug-dealing tenants to annoy, frighten, or prey upon other tenants and neighbors, law-abiding tenants may start withholding rent, and neighbors or the government may bring costly lawsuits against the landlord.

Rent Withholding

If your rented home becomes truly dangerous, it may be legally considered uninhabitable—which means that you might be justified in withholding rent. Because this is a relatively drastic step, consider it carefully—if you withhold rent and trigger an eviction lawsuit for nonpayment of rent, you stand to lose your rental. Here are some guidelines that you must meet if you intend to withhold rent or sue your landlord for a rent refund because you claim that your rental unit is uninhabitable because of high crime danger.

- Make sure the problem is truly serious, not merely annoying or a potential problem. For example, having to walk past drug dealers on your way through the hall is unavoidable, frightening, and loaded with potential for violence. On the other hand, unverified stories regarding prostitution in your neighborhood or even in your building are less compelling.

- Document the problem and get your facts straight. Keep a list of threatening or dangerous encounters you have; ask neighbors to do the same. Take photographs *only* if you can do so safely. Report criminal activity to the police and get a copy of the police report. If you believe certain individuals are causing trouble or breaking the law, be sure you have your facts straight before telling other people. Otherwise, you might find yourself on the wrong end of a slander lawsuit.

- Don't act until you've given the landlord notice of the problem and time to respond by fixing the problem or informing the legal authorities (police or district attorney), who are better equipped to deal with it. For example, if drug dealers have moved in next door, you must alert the landlord and allow him time to begin eviction procedures; if gangs have invaded your neighborhood, you must complain to the landlord and give the police time to act.

Lawsuits Against Landlords

Tenants and others who become victims of the crime that surrounds a drug dealer's home may also sue a landlord who does nothing to stop drug dealing on his property. In recent years, exasperated neighbors have brought individual lawsuits against such landlords in small claims court—and won. Clusters of such claims can quickly add up to tens of thousands of dollars.

In 1989, 19 neighbors plagued by the crime, noise, and fear generated by a crack house in Berkeley, California, won small claims court judgments of $2,000 each (then the California small claims maximum) against an absentee owner who had ignored their complaints for years. In San Francisco, California, a similar rash of small claims suits cost one landlord $35,000. Soon after the verdicts, both landlords evicted the drug-dealing tenants. In the years since, dozens of other neighborhood groups have filed similar small claims suits, many of which have succeeded.

If you want to sue a landlord for allowing drug dealing on his property, first take the steps described above. Most importantly, inform the landlord in writing about the problem and give him an opportunity to take whatever steps are within his power to remedy the situation.

The Obnoxious Landlord

Occasionally a particular landlord can get pretty obnoxious. This is also true of plumbers, physics teachers, and hair stylists, but because this chapter is about landlord-tenant disputes, we will concentrate on these folks.

Typically, tenants have problems with landlords who cannot stop fidgeting and fussing over their property. Smaller landlords tend to develop this problem to a greater extent than do the larger, more commercial ones. Nosy landlords are always hanging around or coming by, trying to invite themselves in to look around and generally being pests. In addition, a tenant may also run into a manager or owner who sexually harasses tenants or is on a power trip.

A landlord or manager who is difficult or unpleasant to deal with can make a tenant's life miserable. There are no laws that protect a tenant from a landlord's disagreeable personality, and when tenants have no lease, they are especially unprotected from all but the most outrageous invasions of privacy, sexual harassment, or trespass (discussed just below). However, if the landlord or manager's conduct is truly obnoxious, courts in some states recognize that tenants have a right to sue for the intentional infliction of emotional distress. (See Chapter 4 for advice on determining the dollar amount of a suit for emotional or mental distress.)

The Landlord's Right of Entry and the Tenant's Right of Privacy

Tenants are easily and understandably upset when they feel their privacy is invaded. Landlords, on the other hand, have a legal right to enter their rental units in certain situations. Sometimes a tenant's need to be left alone and a landlord's need to enter conflict. If they do, it is extremely important that both parties understand their rights.

About half the states have access laws specifying when and under what circumstances landlords may enter tenants' premises. Typically, there are only four broad situations in which a landlord may legally enter while a tenant is still in residence. They are:

- to deal with an emergency
- to make needed repairs (or assess the need for them)
- to show the property to prospective new tenants or purchasers, or
- when the tenant gives permission (for example, invites the landlord to enter).

In most instances (emergencies and invitations by tenant excepted), a landlord can enter only during "normal business hours" (usually considered to be 9 a.m. to 5 p.m. Monday through Friday, though some people claim that Saturday should be a business day) and then only after "reasonable notice," which is presumed to be 24 hours.

If a landlord does not follow these rules, a tenant's first step is to politely ask him to do so. If violations persist, a follow-up letter is in order. If this doesn't help, it is possible to sue in small claims court if the landlord's conduct is persistently outrageous. The specific claims that a tenant might make against a landlord in such a situation include: invasion of privacy, trespass, harassment, violation of the tenant's right to enjoy his home free from the landlord's unreasonable interference, or intentional or negligent infliction of emotional distress.

A tenant who sues a landlord for entering the tenant's unit without permission (lawyers call this "trespass") may have a hard time proving much in the way of money damages. (A judge will want to know why the landlord's improper entry justifies a good-sized monetary award.) However, if a tenant can show a repeated pattern of trespass (and the fact that he asked the landlord to stop it) or even one clear example of outrageous conduct, he may be able to get a substantial monetary recovery.

As a tenant who feels you've been trespassed upon, how much do you sue for? There is no easy answer, but one approach is to keep or reconstruct a list (or diary) of each incident, complete with a fair amount of detail about the distress it caused you. Then read it over and assign a reasonable dollar value to each hour of distress. For example, if a landlord's repeated illegal entries into your house caused you 75 hours of serious upset, and you value your time at $25 per hour, you would sue for $1,875.

If you are a landlord being sued, but believe that your entry or conduct was legal, you should be able to document this. For example, if a tenant claims that you entered his apartment without 24-hour notice, then you should be able to show a copy of a formal 24-hour notice to enter to make needed repairs that you sent him (notes you took documenting related phone conversations would also be useful). You could also ask a repairperson or cleaning service to testify (either in person or in writing; see Chapter 14) as to the date and time that he or she entered the rental unit, which should be at least 24 hours after you delivered the notice. Or, you may be able to explain that the urgent nature of the repair required you to enter sooner. If there is a good reason—for example, a repairperson is available to make urgently needed repairs on a few hours' notice—you can legally give a reasonable but shorter notice.

But what if you are a landlord whose tenant repeatedly refuses to let you or your employees enter during normal business hours for one of the legitimate reasons cited above? In such a situation, you can legally enter anyway, provided you do so in a peaceful manner. Bring someone along who can later act as a witness in case the tenant claims some of her property is missing.

Discrimination

Federal laws make it illegal for a landlord to refuse to rent to a tenant, or to engage in any other kind of discrimination (such as requiring higher rent or larger deposits), on the basis of any group characteristic such as race, color, religion, national origin, familial status (includes families with children younger than 18 and pregnant women), disability, and sex (includes sexual harassment). In some states and localities, additional characteristics, such as gender identity, are protected. A landlord who attempts to or actually terminates someone's tenancy for a discriminatory reason, or who discriminates in providing services such as the use of a pool or other common area, is also acting illegally.

The discriminated-against tenant can use the landlord's behavior as a defense to an eviction lawsuit as well as a basis for suing the landlord for monetary compensation and an order directing the landlord to stop the discriminatory behavior. Even an innocent owner whose agent or manager discriminates without the owner's knowledge can be sued and found liable. A landlord who unlawfully discriminates against a tenant or prospective tenant may end up in federal or state court, including small claims court, or before a state or federal housing agency facing a tenant's allegations of discrimination.

Most of these cases involve amounts in excess of the small claims maximum. If you've experienced discrimination, your most effective remedy is to sue the offending landlord in formal court. For more information on how to spot and prove discrimination, see *Every Tenant's Legal Guide,* by Janet Portman and Marcia Stewart (Nolo). To find a lawyer who handles this type of lawsuit, contact a tenants' rights or civil rights organization in your area.

Evictions

In some states, it is legal to do some types of evictions (known technically as "unlawful detainer," "summary dispossess," or "forcible entry and detainer," depending on the state) in small claims court. A few larger cities even have separate "landlord-tenant" courts that amount to small claims courts for this specific purpose.

Landlords should have a simple and cheap way to free themselves of tenants who don't pay their rent. But in states that don't have special "landlord-tenant" courts, the only practical method is to file an "unlawful detainer" action in formal court. Traditionally this has required the expense of a lawyer, though more and more landlords are learning to handle their own eviction actions.

Formal court, though less friendly to nonlawyers than small claims court, may actually be preferable when you have a choice. The small claims court rules, even in those states where evictions are allowed, tend to limit a landlord's rights when it comes to getting the tenant out in the minimum time and getting a judgment for the maximum amount of rent and other damages. In a few states' small claims courts, a losing tenant even has an automatic right to appeal the eviction judgment and to stay in the rental unit while the appeal is pending, despite the fact that the tenant isn't paying rent and hasn't posted bond.

So before you bring an eviction action in small claims court, find the answers to the following questions by reviewing your state's small claims court rules (see Chapter 25 for tips on painless legal research):

- If you win an eviction order, can you get the sheriff or marshal to enforce it immediately?

- If the defendant appeals, can he or she stay in the dwelling while the appeal is pending?

- Can you sue for enough damages to fully or at least mostly cover your legitimate claim for back rent and damages to the premises?

- If the defendant can stay in the dwelling during an appeal, is there a requirement that he or she must post some money in the form of a bond that will go to you to cover lost rent if the appeal fails?

If you decide to go ahead with an eviction in small claims court, you must prove that the rent was not paid and that a correct notice was properly served. Bring a copy of this notice to court along with an appropriately completed Proof of Service form. The fact that a tenant is suffering from some hardship, such as illness, poverty, birth of a child, and so on, is not a defense to failure to pay rent. Possible tenant defenses are discussed above. In most states, the tenant may claim, as a defense, that the rental property was uninhabitable. But remember, a tenant cannot legally raise the existence of a defect for the first time on the day of the court hearing. The landlord must be given reasonable notice that a defect exists before the tenant withholds rent or makes repairs. ●

Miscellaneous Cases

B y now you should have a pretty clear idea of how a small claims case should be researched and presented. The facts of each situation will vary, but the general approach will not. This chapter will very briefly discuss a few of the common types of cases not covered in the previous few chapters. Unfortunately, given the huge number of fact situations that commonly result in small claims disputes, it still may not cover your situation in detail. It will be up to you to adapt the approaches outlined in Chapters 13–20.

Clothing (Alteration and Cleaning)

It's surprising how often you'll encounter people in small claims court clutching an injured garment. We humans really must view our clothing as an extension of ourselves because so many of us react with a level of indignation out of proportion to our monetary loss when a favorite item is damaged.

Unfortunately—no matter how much we love a favorite coat, dress, or sweater—winning a significant amount of money in a case involving clothing is difficult. That's because—as also discussed in Chapter 4— while it's often fairly easy to prove that the defendant mutilated your garment, most used clothing simply isn't worth much. Remember: in theory, at least, you are only legally entitled to the fair market value of the item of clothing just before it was damaged or destroyed, not to its replacement value. To get more, you'll normally need to engage the sympathies of the judge. Here are some possible ways to do this:

- Bring the damaged clothing to court. It's hard for a tailor to say much in his own defense when confronted with a coat two sizes too big or featuring three sleeves.

- Be ready to prove the original purchase price with a canceled check, newspaper ad, or credit card statement. If the item was purchased at a pricey store, let the judge know where. Most judges at least occasionally shop at stores like Nordstrom, Saks, or Macy's, and may be sympathetic if an item you just paid top dollar for was destroyed.

- If you only wore the damaged or destroyed item a few times, make sure the judge knows it. For example, if you paid $500 for a good-quality suit you planned to wear to work 50 to 100 times over the next three years and a dry cleaner screwed it up after just five wearings, try to get the judge to value it at close to $500.

- Be sure that the person you are suing (tailor, cleaner, seamstress) really caused the problem. As noted in the example of the suede coat in Chapter 2, some problems that develop during cleaning or alterations may be the responsibility of the manufacturer.

TIP

Don't let the cleaners take you to the laundry! Cleaners are particularly apt to offer "proof" from "independent testing laboratories" that the damage caused to your garment during cleaning was really the fault of its manufacturer. Because these labs work almost exclusively for the dry-cleaning industry, the idea that they are independent is a joke. If you are faced with one of these reports, ask the defendant:

- "How much did you pay the testing lab for the report?"
- "How many times have you used the same testing lab before?"
- "How did you know about the testing lab (for example, does it place ads in dry cleaners' trade journals that say, 'Let us help you win in court')?"

Dog-Related Cases

No question, dogs can be frustrating, especially to people who don't own dogs. As a result, lots of dog-related cases end up in small claims court. Because many of these involve neighbors who will benefit by maintaining or establishing a pleasant relationship, trying to work out the dispute through mediation is almost always a good first step. (See Chapter 6.)

Dog Bites (and Other Injuries)

Many states have dog-bite statutes that make dog owners completely liable for injuries their dogs cause—no ifs, ands, or buts. Some statutes cover only injuries occurring off the owner's property. Also, some statutes cover only bites, whereas others apply to any injury (for example, the dog jumps on you, scratches you, or knocks you over) or property damage (for example, the dog digs up your rose garden). Do some legal research (see Chapter 25) to find out whether your state has a dog-bite statute. If it does, your task in court could be a lot easier.

If your state doesn't have a dog-bite statute, the old "common law" rule probably applies. This means you'll have to prove that the owner was aware of, or should have been aware of, the fact that the dog was vicious. So, if you're bitten by a dog and can show that the dog had snarled, snapped, and lunged at people before and the owner knew about it but let the dog run free anyway, the owner is probably liable (unless you provoked the dog or offered the dog your hand). If the dog is mean-looking, a photo will be a great help in court; a video is even better.

Also be ready to prove the extent of the injury, the location where it occurred, and the amount of your money damages. As discussed in Chapter 4, this consists of the value of any uncompensated time you took off from work, out-of-pocket medical expenses, property damage (for example, your chewed-up coat), and the value of your pain and suffering.

Barking Dogs

The problem of barking dogs is often regulated by city or county ordinance. Sometimes there is a separate ordinance involving animals; other times dogs are covered by a general noise ordinance. Look up the law to find out the specifics (see Chapter 25) and whether your city or county government will help enforce it. In addition, the owner of a barking dog that interferes with your ability to enjoy your home has committed a civil wrong (tort) called a nuisance. As with any other tort, the dog's owner is responsible for compensating people harmed by the nuisance. (For more information about suing someone for causing a nuisance, generally, see Chapter 2.)

If you can't work something out through negotiation or mediation and you file in small claims court, you will face two main challenges:

1. Establishing that the barking dog really has damaged your ability to enjoy your property. One good way to do this is to get a number of neighbors to write letters or, better yet, testify in court to the fact that the dog is truly a noisy menace. (Don't forget to bring a copy of the local dog-barking ordinance to establish that the dog is also a law breaker.) Also, if your city has cited the dog's owner for violating the noise ordinance, make sure the judge knows about it.

2. Proving money damages. Establishing money damages caused by a noisy dog is obviously a subjective task. One approach is to try to put a money value on each hour of your lost sleep. For example, if you can convince the judge that each hour you lie awake is worth a certain amount (perhaps $10 or even $20), your damages will quickly add up. As a backup to your oral testimony about how miserable it is to be denied sleep by a howling canine, keep a log of the dates and times you are awakened and present it to the judge. In one case, six neighbors kept a log for 30 days detailing how often a particular dog barked after 10 p.m. The number, which was over 300, was influential in convincing the judge to give the plaintiffs a good-sized judgment.

 RESOURCE

More on dog problems. *Every Dog's Legal Guide: A Must-Have Book for Your Owner*, by Mary Randolph (Nolo), answers common legal questions about biting, barking, leash laws, problems with veterinarians, and other common dog-related problems. You will also find a number of interesting dog law-related articles on Nolo's website (www.nolo.com).

Damage to Real Estate (Land, Buildings, and So On)

There is no typical case involving damage to real property, because individual fact situations vary greatly. So instead of trying to set down general rules, here's an example of how one person (let's call her Babette) coped with a property damage problem. Hopefully some of the legal lessons Babette learned will apply to your situation.

EXAMPLE: Babette owns a cinder-block building that houses two retail stores. One morning she noticed water pouring in through the back of her building. Because the building was set into a hill, it abutted about eight feet of her uphill neighbor's land (let's call her neighbor Boris). After three days of investigation involving the use of green dye in Boris's plumbing system, it was discovered that the water came from an underground leak in Boris's sewer pipe. At this point, Babette had spent considerable effort and some money to pay helpers to get the water mopped up before it damaged anything in the stores.

Instead of fixing the leak promptly, Boris delayed for four days. All of this time, Babette and her helpers were mopping frantically and complaining loudly to Boris. Finally, when Boris did get to work, he insisted on digging the pipe out himself, which took another four days. (A plumber with the right equipment could have done it in one.) In the middle of Boris's digging, when his yard looked as though it was being attacked by a herd of giant gophers, it rained. The water filled the holes and trenches instead of running off, as it normally would have. Much of it ran through the ground into Babette's building, bringing a pile of mud with it.

When the flood was finally over, Babette figured out her costs as follows:

First three days (*before the source of the water was discovered*)	$148 (*for help with mopping and cleaning*)
Next four days (*while Boris refused to cooperate*)	$188 (*for help with mopping and cleaning*)
Final four days (*including the day it rained*)	$262 (*for help with mopping and cleaning*)
One secondhand water vacuum purchased during rainstorm	$200
Her own time, valued at $8.00 per hour.	$600

Assuming that Boris is unwilling to pay Babette's mopping and cleanup costs, how much should she sue for and how much is she likely to get? Remembering the lessons taught in Chapter 2, before Babette can get compensation for her very real loss, she must show that Boris was negligent or caused her loss intentionally. Probably, she can't do this for the first three days when no one knew where the water was coming from. It's also likely to be difficult to convince a judge that Boris was negligent for failing to replace a pipe that, up until then, had worked fine. (But Babette might try to show that the pipe was so old it was likely it would break and Boris should have anticipated this by replacing it.) However, once the problem was discovered and Boris didn't take steps to fix it as fast as possible, he was clearly negligent, and Babette will probably get at least her out-of-pocket expenses ($450 for labor costs and $200 for the water vacuum). Can Babette also recover for the value of her own time? The answer to this question is "maybe." If Babette could show she had to close her store or take time off from a job to stem the flood (and as a result she lost income), she probably could recover. But if she was retired and lost no pay as a result of her efforts to stem the flood, it would be more difficult. If I were Babette, I would sue for about $1,250 ($450 for labor she paid for, $200 for the vacuum, and $600 for the value of her own labor) and expect to get most of it.

Police Brutality/False Arrest Cases

Now and then individual actions alleging false arrest or brutality by the police end up in small claims court. Usually, the plaintiff tried and failed to get an attorney to represent him in a larger suit and, as a last resort, filed for the maximum amount small claims court will allow. Unfortunately, most of these cases end up losers. Why? Because the police and jailers have excellent access to legal advice and (unfortunately) may not be afraid to bend the truth to back each other up. It's no secret that few police officers are going to tell the whole truth if doing so means collecting a black mark on their (or a buddy's) service record. What's more, most law enforcement people have testified many times and know how to handle themselves in court.

The reason many plaintiffs use small claims court to sue law enforcement personnel pretty much tells the story. Private lawyers normally won't invest their time and money in these sorts of cases because they find them almost impossible to win. Does this mean that people bringing false arrest, police brutality, and similar types of cases are wasting their time? If you're going it alone, and your primary goal is monetary compensation, then the answer is usually yes.

But, given the attention police misconduct has recently been receiving, you may get some form of justice (or at least bring attention to the problem) by combining your efforts with those of other victims or groups in your area. An Internet search for "police brutality" or "police misconduct" may bring up the names of local organizations that help victims of police brutality. It's possible you'll even link up with others willing to join you in filing a number of small claims cases on the same day, a strategy that is likely to focus media attention on your claims. However, realize that even if you win in small claims court, the police can and probably will appeal the case to superior court, where they can be represented by a lawyer. (See Chapter 23 for more on appeals.)

If, despite the above, you are still brave enough to drag a police officer, jailer, or anyone else with a badge into small claims court on your own, be sure that you have several witnesses or other evidence to back you up. Never, never rely on one officer to testify against another; they will almost never do it. You would also be wise to spend a few dollars and talk to a lawyer who specializes in criminal cases. For a small fee, you can probably pick up some valuable pointers on how to convince the judge that you were treated in an illegal and unreasonable way.

> **TIP**
> **Sue the city or county as well as the officer.** In most cases where you claim police misconduct, you will want to sue the city, county, or state government that employs the officer, as well as the individual involved. But remember, before you can sue a government entity, you must first promptly file an administrative claim. (See Chapter 8.)

Defamation

In California, you can bring libel and slander cases in small claims court. However, many states have placed an outright ban on bringing such cases in small claims court. Even in states where you can bring a defamation case in small claims court, oftentimes judges don't take them seriously, because most untrue statements don't really result in serious damage.

To prevail, you need to show that the statement made about you was false, that others saw or heard it and understood that it was about you, and most importantly, that the statement really did significantly harm your reputation. In addition, if you are a public figure (politician, actor, media celebrity), you not only need to show that the statement was false, but also that the defendant either knew it was false or made it in reckless disregard of whether or not it was true. In short, the fact that the defendant's statement was just plain wrong isn't enough to make you a winner if you are a public figure.

EXAMPLE: Your nutty neighbor tells everyone on the block you are an idiot. You wonder if you have grounds to sue. Probably not, because chances are you haven't been harmed—after all, everyone in the neighborhood knows your neighbor is a kook, so it's probable that no one has taken his comments seriously. However, if he writes and distributes a leaflet all over town that falsely accuses you of having sex with minors, your chances of winning are much better. One reason is that at least some people who receive the flyer won't know that the writer isn't very reliable and therefore may take it seriously, which damages your reputation.

 RESOURCE
To learn more about the many intricacies of defamation law. Start with a law student course outline on torts (a negligent or intentional "wrong" that results in damage). These are carried by all law bookstores (usually located near law schools) and most public law libraries.

Internet Purchases

We love the Internet, don't we? We shop at home and have packages delivered to the front door. We create websites for our families or small businesses. And some of us do much of our work over the Internet, as well. Technology has definitely made things more convenient.

But what about when something goes wrong? The package doesn't arrive or is different than advertised. Or perhaps you agree via email to write a restaurant review for a local magazine, and you email the article on time to the editor, but never receive payment. Are these types of problems any different from the face-to-face disputes we've discussed in the rest of this book? Can you use small claims court to get compensation from a person or business you've dealt with only over the Internet?

The answer is, maybe. As with face-to-face disputes, your ability to sue in small claims court for a wrong you suffered via an Internet transaction depends on where the person or business you want to sue is located. As you recall from Chapter 9, you cannot automatically sue someone in small claims court when you have suffered an economic loss. The court has to have power over that particular party, which basically depends on where the person or business lives, works, or has an office. If your Internet-related dispute is with a person or business located in your state, then you shouldn't have a problem. However, only under specific circumstances can you sue a nonresident in your state's small claims court.

If the person or business does not regularly do business with state residents over the Internet (in other words, if the transaction at issue is a one-time event), then you will not be able to sue in your local small claims court, because that person does not live, work, or regularly do business in-state; it is therefore fundamentally unfair to ask that party to travel to your state to defend itself from a lawsuit.

If, however, the person or business regularly does business over the Internet in your state, then you should be able to bring your lawsuit in your local small claims court. In the context of Internet transactions, what does it mean to "regularly do business" in a state? The courts are actively discussing this issue, and different judges have different opinions, but here are some basic guidelines:

- When you made the transaction, did the person or business know what state you were a resident of—for example, did you fill out a form with your address or have a package shipped to you?

- Does the person or business do a lot of business with state residents?

- Does the person or business have any offices or employees in-state, even though its main "location" is on the Internet?
- Does the person or business send employees or agents into your state to conduct business?
- Does the person or business advertise or solicit business in your state?
- Does the person or business have a registered agent for service of process in your state? (See Chapter 11 for instructions on finding out if a business has a registered agent.)

If your answer to all or most of these questions is yes, then you will probably be successful in bringing your case against the party in your local small claims court.

EXAMPLE 1: Mary Mallone lives in Vermont and sells handmade jewelry to customers around the world via her Internet website. She designed the website herself, and the computer files are stored on a web hosting company, Web-R-Us, located in Colorado. She signed a contract with Web-R-Us to provide her with this service and regularly uploads new files for her website to Web-R-Us's computers in Colorado from her computer in Vermont. When customers visit her website, they can make purchases online, and that information is temporarily stored on Web-R-Us's computers until it is transmitted to Mary. One day, due to the carelessness of a Web-R-Us employee, the office floods and the computers are ruined. As a result, Mary loses 15 jewelry orders that were stored on Web-R-Us's computers. Can Mary sue Web-R-Us in Vermont for losing $2,000 worth of jewelry orders even though its offices are in Colorado?

Yes. Web-R-Us knows that Mary lives in Vermont and has repeatedly done business with her in Vermont by transmitting computer files back and forth. (See *Zippo Manufacturing Co. vs. Zippo Dot Com, Inc.*, 952 F. Supp. 1119 (WD Pa. 1997)).

EXAMPLE 2: James buys new gears for his brand new $3,000 bicycle at an Internet auction house. The gears are delivered to him from Will Wheely, who lives in Nevada and advertised the gears at the auction house. The gears are defective and James crashes, ruining the bicycle. James finds out that Will Wheely bought the gears from BigGear, Inc., a bicycle parts manufacturer in Florida that does no business in Texas, where James lives. Can James sue either Will Wheely or BigGear in Texas small claims court to get compensation for his busted bike?

No. Neither potential defendant is a Texas resident. Will Wheely does not do regular business in Texas, nor did he actively seek a Texas purchaser for the gears he advertised online. Rather, he was required by the auction house to sell the gears to the highest bidder, no matter where the bidder lived. Nor does BigGear have anything to do with Texas. It sold the gears to Will Wheely, who lives in Nevada, and didn't have anything to do with the resale of the gears to James in Texas. If James wants to pursue his case, he'll have to do it in a different state.

CAUTION

Nonresidents will fight your attempt to sue them in your state's small claims court. It's a tremendous hassle for a nonresident to travel to defend a lawsuit, which is why the courts have strict rules stating that a person must already do regular business in a state in order to be sued there. (See Chapter 9 for information on how a nonresident defendant might challenge such a lawsuit.)

Consumer Complaints About Internet Transactions

If an Internet transaction goes wrong, you might consider filing an official complaint against the person or business, either in addition to or instead of filing a lawsuit. The Federal Trade Commission accepts complaints about consumer Internet transactions. Visit www.consumer.gov and click "File a Complaint."

Disputes Between Small Businesses

More and more small business owners are turning to small claims court to settle business disputes when they have been unable to reach an acceptable compromise through negotiation or mediation. Small claims court offers them speed and cost efficiency. In several states, business-friendly changes in the law are making it easier for businesses to use the court efficiently. For example, New York state has established a separate commercial small claims court in Manhattan and other areas. Unfortunately, other states still block businesses' efforts to use small claims courts to resolve their disputes. For example, in California a business may not bring more than two lawsuits for more than $2,500 in a 12-month period. And in some other states—including Pennsylvania—incorporated businesses are required to be represented by an attorney under certain circumstances, which prevents incorporated businesses from saving money by handling their own legal affairs.

This chapter focuses on how to handle substantive disputes between businesses in small claims court. Typically, these center on a claim that one party's work for the other was done poorly, late, or not at all. (Cases involving the simple failure to pay a bill are covered in Chapter 18.) Although many disputes between small businesses involve a simple failure to pay money, a significant number are more complicated. Commonly these more complex disputes involve people who have had a continuing business relationship and find themselves in the midst of a major misunderstanding that goes beyond the refusal to pay a bill. Often both parties are in court because they feel badly used—perhaps even ripped off or cheated—by the other.

A surprising variety of businesspeople use small claims court for small business disputes. They include:

- A dentist who was furious at a dental equipment wholesaler who passed off slightly used equipment as new.
- An architect who wasn't paid for drawing preliminary plans for a small retail complex when the development failed to get financing.

- A phototypesetter who refused to pay her former accountant because she disputed the value of the latter's services.

- A landscape designer who tried to enforce an oral agreement, which he claimed allowed him to increase his fee when he accommodated a client by making changes to final plans.

- An author who claimed that her publisher had taken too long to publish her book.

- A client who claimed that his lawyer's incompetence was a prime reason he had to pay too much to settle a case.

Remember: You Didn't Always Hate the Other Guy

Although the disputes listed above seem very different, they all have one thing in common: In each situation, the disputing parties previously enjoyed a friendly business or personal relationship. And in each case, at least part of the reason the plaintiff brought the dispute to court was that he was just plain mad at the defendant.

Disappointment is a significant factor driving many small business disputes. But feeling let down by the other party doesn't help you evaluate whether you have a good case. Nor does it help you prepare for court or collect your money should you win. In fact, aside from its value in goading you to take action, disappointment often gets in the way of the clear thinking necessary to make good decisions. It follows that your first job is to try to cool your emotions. If you are having trouble doing this, enlist another businessperson as your mentor. Carefully explain both sides of the dispute. Then ask your mentor for a frank evaluation of both the merits of the argument and whether there really is enough at stake to warrant taking the case to court.

> ⊙ **TIP**
>
> **Mediation may offer the best way to settle your dispute.**
> Assuming you really do have a good case and the defendant is solvent, going
> to small claims court is a quick and cost-effective way to put dollars in your
> pocket. But like all courts, small claims court tends to polarize disputes and
> deepen enmities. In some circumstances—especially where businesspeople
> will benefit from working together, or from at least being civil to each other
> in the future—attempting to arrive at a compromise settlement through
> mediation is a better initial choice. (See Chapter 6 for more on mediation.)

Organizing Your Case

When it comes to preparing for court, small business owners normally
have two advantages over run-of-the-mill mortals. First, as a matter of
course, they maintain a recordkeeping system. Depending on the type
of business, this typically includes a good filing system to maintain
bids, contracts, and customer correspondence, as well as a bookkeeping
system that tracks payables and receivables. Taken together, these
resources normally contain considerable raw material helpful to proving
a small claims case. The second advantage is more subtle but no less
real. It involves the average businessperson's organizational skill—that
is, the ability to take a confused mess of facts and organize them into a
coherent and convincing narrative. Of course, when one businessperson
sues another, those advantages often cancel out, meaning that both sides
are likely to be well organized and prepared.

Other sections of this book explain how to decide whether you have
a good case (Chapter 2) and, assuming you do, how to prepare and
present it in court (Chapters 13–21). There is no point in repeating this
information, so instead the rest of this chapter will supplement it with
material of particular interest to small businesses.

Most Business Disputes Involve Contracts

In the majority of business cases one business claims that the other has broken a contract. (See Chapter 2 for more on contract law.) If you're facing this issue, take a close look at any contract involved in your case. Specifically, ask yourself what were your obligations and expected benefits from the deal? What was the other person supposed to do and how was he going to benefit?

Oral Contracts Are Usually Legal
Most oral contracts—except those for the sale of real estate or goods (tangible property) worth $500 or more, or those that can't be carried out in one year—are legal and enforceable if they can be proven. But when nothing has been written down, proving that a contract existed can sometimes be difficult. An exception to this rule applies when you did work for someone and weren't paid (for example, you are a commercial photographer and spend a day taking pictures of a hat designer's new creations), because the judge is likely to agree with your contention that, by implication, the designer must have noticed what you were doing, and you wouldn't have done the work unless she had promised to pay you.

What is a written contract? It need not be a formal negotiated document with both parties' signatures at the end. Under the Uniform Commercial Code (UCC)—which has been adopted in all states and applies to the sale of goods but not services—a contract can be a letter or other written document that doesn't even state the price or time of delivery, only that the parties agree on the sale of goods and the quantity of goods sold. If it meets this modest requirement, any letter, fax, or other writing can constitute a contract. (See "The Sale of Goods," below.)

EXAMPLE: Hubert, a pest control operator, sends a fax to Josephine, the business manager of a company that manufactures rodent traps, saying, "I would like to order 1,000 gopher traps at $14 per trap." Josephine faxes back, "Thank you for your order. The traps will be sent next week." There is a contract. Indeed, even if Josephine didn't reply but instead promptly sent the traps, a contract would be formed based on the circumstances of the transaction.

Usual business practices and customs in a particular field are also commonly viewed as being part of a contract and can be introduced as evidence in small claims court to support or thwart your case. Thus, if Hubert ordered rodent traps in February and Josephine didn't send them until September, Hubert could present evidence to the judge that everyone in the rodent control business knows that traps are only saleable in the summer when rodents attack crops, and that Josephine's failure to deliver the traps in the correct season constituted a breach of contract.

Finally, keep in mind that contracts can be, and often are, changed many times as negotiations go back and forth and circumstances change. The important agreement is the most recent one.

The Sale of Goods

The Uniform Commercial Code (UCC), adopted by all states, contains special rules affecting contracts for the sale of goods. It requires you to produce something in writing if you want to enforce a contract for a sale of goods and the price is $500 or more, but it also provides that this writing can be very brief—briefer than a normal written contract. Under the UCC, the writing need only:

- indicate that the parties have agreed on the sale of the goods, and
- state the quantity of goods being sold.

If terms such as price, time, and place of delivery, or quality of goods are missing, the UCC fills them in based on customs and practices in the particular industry. And where specially manufactured goods are ordered, the UCC doesn't require any writing at all once a party makes a significant effort toward carrying out the terms of the contract.

EXAMPLE: A restaurant calls and orders 200 sets of dishes from a restaurant supply company. The dishes are to feature the restaurant's logo. If the supply company makes a substantial beginning on manufacturing the dishes and applying the logo, the restaurant can't avoid liability on the contract simply because it was oral.

Presenting Your Evidence in Court

In addition to the normal techniques of efficiently presenting evidence in court (discussed in Chapters 14 and 15), this section reviews additional approaches of special interest to small business owners.

In business disputes, the problem is often having *too much* evidence, rather than too little. Your job is to separate the material that is essential to proving your case from that which is less important. Organize both your oral presentation and the backup written evidence around the heart of the dispute, rather than trying to first fill in all the background information.

> EXAMPLE: Alice, the owner of Ames Country Inn, hires Ted, an interior decorator, to freshen up the decor of her bed and breakfast. Ted submits an estimate, which Alice verbally accepts by telephone. Later, Alice stops by Ted's office to drop off a set of detailed architectural drawings. Ted works for three days on the new decor plan before Alice suddenly calls and cancels the deal because, "on second thought, I don't like the colors you are proposing." After Ted's bills are not paid and his demand letter is ignored, Ted files in small claims court, asking for three days' pay plus the money he spent on supplies. In court, Ted very sensibly begins his presentation like this: "Your Honor, the defendant hired me to prepare a detailed plan to redecorate the Ames Country Inn. I worked on the job for three days and bought $200 worth of supplies before she canceled our contract. Today, I'm asking for a judgment for my normal rate of pay of $80 per hour for the 24 hours I worked, plus the $200 for supplies. The total is $2,120."

Of course, there is more to Ted's story, which means, after stating the crux of his claims, he will need to fill in the key points. Ted should next make these points:

- He and Alice had worked together before, and his work had always been acceptable and paid for.
- He really did the 24 hours of work he claimed, as documented by drawings and worksheets he brings to court.
- He has canceled checks covering an itemized list of supplies he purchased for the job ready to show the judge.

This should be enough to make Ted a winner. But as is true of all small claims litigants, Ted should also try to anticipate and deflect what he thinks will be the other side's key points. For example, in this instance, if Ted is pretty sure Alice is going to claim she canceled because Ted was using a design theme and colors she had specifically ruled out, he would be wise to make it clear that no such restrictions were contained in their contract.

Many businesspeople have employees, partners, or business associates who have intimate knowledge of the dispute. By all means, bring them to court as witnesses. A witness who is knowledgeable about the transaction is almost always worth more than a stack of documentary evidence.

EXAMPLE: Assume Ted's assistant, Doris, attended a preliminary meeting with Alice at which Ted asked Alice for a list of her suggestions. Also assume Doris can truthfully testify that when the subject of color came up, Alice just waved her hand and said, "You know I don't like purple too much, but it's really up to you—you're the designer." Aided by Doris's testimony, Ted should be a winner, even if Alice claims he violated their agreement not to use purple.

In some situations, having a witness testify as to the normal business practices in an industry field can also be helpful. Thus, if in your industry goods are normally shipped within five to 15 days after an order is received (unless written notice of a delay is sent), but the person you are having a dispute with claims you still must pay for goods that were shipped 90 days after your order was received, it would be a good idea to present an "expert" witness—or a letter from someone knowledgeable about relevant business practices—who could testify that unfilled orders are never good for more than 30 days.

The Drama of the Distraught Designer

Now let's review a typical small business case with an eye toward identifying good strategies. Don Dimaggio is a successful architect and industrial designer who heads his own small company, which specializes in designing small manufacturing buildings. He prides himself on doing highly innovative and creative work. Recently Don did some preliminary design work for an outfit that wanted to build a small candle factory. When they didn't pay, he was out $8,500. In Don's view, the dispute developed like this:

"Ben McDonald, who makes custom candles, had a good year and wanted to expand. He called me and asked me to rough out a preliminary design. McDonald claims now that we never had a contract, but that's simply not true. What really happened is that McDonald authorized me to do some preliminary work before his company got their financing locked down. When interest rates went through the roof, the whole deal collapsed. I had already completed my work, but they refused to pay. My next step was to get Stephanie Carlin, a lawyer who has done some work for me, to write McDonald a letter demanding payment. When that didn't do any good, I took Stephanie's advice and filed a small claims court suit against McDonald. True, I had to scale my claim back to $7,500, the small claims maximum. But I obviously couldn't afford to pay Stephanie $200 an hour to file in formal court, so it seemed like the best approach."

Don's most immediate problem was that he had never used small claims court before. He wasn't sure how he needed to prepare, but knew, at the very least, he had to develop a coherent plan—if for no other reason than to overcome his anxiety. Here is how I coached him to do this:

RW: "Your first job is to establish why McDonald owed you money. Presumably it's because he violated an agreement that he would pay you for your work."

DD: "True, but unfortunately, nothing was written down."

RW: "Oral contracts to provide services are perfectly legal if they can be proven, and judges typically bend over backward to see that freelancers get paid. But don't be so sure you have nothing in writing. Tell me, how did McDonald contact you?"

DD: "Mutual friends recommended me to him. He phoned me and we talked a couple of times. There was some back and forth about how much I would charge for the whole job and how much for parts of it. After a little garden-variety confusion, we decided that I would start with the preliminary drawings and be paid $8,500. If the whole job came through and we felt good about one another, I would do the entire thing. On big jobs, I always insist on a written contract, but this one was tiny and I couldn't see wasting the time. McDonald just stopped by with someone else from his business, and we hashed out the whole thing in person."

RW: "Did you make notes?"

DD: "Sure. In fact, I made a few sketches, and they gave me specifications and sketches they had already made."

RW: "Do you still have those?"

DD: "Of course, in a file along with a couple of letters they sent later thanking me for my good ideas and making a few suggestions for changes. And of course, I have copies of the detailed drawings I made and sent them."

RW: "Well, that's it."

DD: "What do you mean, that's it?"

RW: "You've just told me that you can prove a contract exists. The combination of the sketches McDonald provided and the letters someone at his company wrote to you pretty convincingly prove they asked you to do the work. Of course, it helps your case that the law presumes that when a person is asked to do work in a situation where compensation is normally expected, he must be paid when the work is completed." (In legalese, this presumption is called "quantum meruit." See Chapter 2.)

DD: "That's all there is to it? I just tell the judge what happened and I win?"

RW: "Not so fast. First, let me ask if you are sure you can present your case coherently. After you make your opening statement, you need to back it up with the key facts that show that McDonald hired you, that you did the work, and that he broke the contract by failing to pay you. (As discussed throughout this book, because so many people do a poor job making their oral presentation, make sure that you practice ahead of time.) Ask a savvy friend to serve as your pretend judge. Then present your case as if you were in court. Encourage your friend to interrupt and ask questions, since that's what a judge will likely do. Finally, be sure you have organized all your evidence, especially the plans and letters, so you are ready to present them to the judge at the appropriate time."

DD: "What about McDonald? Is he likely to show up?"

RW: "Many cases involving money being owed result in defaults, meaning the person being sued ignores the whole proceeding. (See Chapter 15.) But you know that McDonald claims he doesn't owe you the money, so it's my guess he will probably show up and claim no contract existed. Therefore, you should be prepared to counter the points he is likely to make."

DD: "You're right. Although it's a total crock, he will probably claim I agreed to do the work on speculation that he would get financing and that since the job fell through, he doesn't owe me anything."

RW: "And if your case is typical, McDonald will also probably try to claim your work was substandard. That way, even if you prove that a contract existed, the judge may award you less than you asked for."

DD: "But they wrote me that my design was of excellent quality."

RW: "Great, but don't wait until they raise the issue. Because you are pretty sure this point will come up, emphasize in your opening statement how pleased McDonald was with your work and present the letter to the judge. Now, what about McDonald's argument that there was no deal in the first place? Do you ever do preliminary work without expecting to be paid unless the deal goes through? And is that a common way to operate in your business?"

DD: "Me? Never! I don't have to. I suppose some designers do, or at least prepare fairly detailed bid proposals without pay, but I have so much work coming my way these days, I'm turning jobs down right and left, so when I do submit a bid, I make it clear to all potential clients that I charge for preliminary drawings. In this situation, as I said, we agreed on the price in advance."

RW: "What about witnesses to that conversation?"

DD: "Well, Jim, my partner, sat in on one of the early discussions. We hadn't agreed on the final price yet, but we weren't too far apart."

RW: "Was it clear to Jim that you intended to charge for your work and that McDonald knew you did?"

DD: "Yes, absolutely."

RW: "Great, bring Jim to court with you as a witness. Here is how I would proceed. Organize your statement as to what happened so it takes you no longer than five minutes to present it to the judge. Bring your sketches, and most important, the sketch that McDonald made, along with the letters they sent you, and show them to the judge. (See Chapter 15.) Then introduce your partner and have him state that he was present when money was discussed."

This little scenario is a simplified version of a real case. What happened? The small claims court judge awarded Don the entire amount he requested, and McDonald paid it.

Old Friends Fall Out

Finally, let's review another typical small claims dispute. Toni, a true artist when it comes to graphics, is an ignoramus when it comes to dollars and cents. Recognizing this, she never prepares her own tax returns. For the past several years, she has turned all of her tax affairs over to Phillip, a local C.P.A. They discussed price the first year, but after that Toni just paid Phillip's bill when the job was done.

One spring, things went wrong. As usual, Toni's records weren't in great shape, and she was late in getting them to Phillip. By this time Phillip, who was overly busy, put Toni's tax return together quickly, without discussing it with her in detail. When Toni saw the return, she was shocked by the bottom line. She felt that she was being asked to pay way too much to Uncle Sam.

She called Phillip and reminded him of a number of deductions that she felt he had overlooked. There was some discussion of whether Phillip should have known about these items or not. Things began to get a little edgy when Phillip complained about Toni's sloppy records and her delay in making them available, and Toni countered by accusing Phillip of doing a hurried and substandard job. But after some more grumpy talk back and forth, Phillip agreed to make the necessary corrections. In a week this was done and the return was again sent to Toni.

While her tax liability was now less, Toni was still annoyed, feeling that not all of the oversights had been corrected. Toni called Phillip again and this time they quickly got into a shouting match. When Phillip finally and reluctantly agreed to look at the return a third time, Toni replied, "Hell no, I'm taking my business to an accountant who can add."

True to her word, Toni did hire another accountant, who made several modifications to her return, resulting in a slightly lower tax liability. The second accountant claimed that because he needed to check all of Phillip's work to satisfy himself that it was correct, he ended up doing almost as much work as if he had started from scratch. As a result, he billed Toni for $2,300, saying that this was only $500 less than if he had not had the benefit of Phillip's work.

Phillip billed Toni $3,000. Toni, still furious, refused to pay. Phillip then sent Toni a demand letter asking to be paid and stating that most of the problems were created by Toni's bad records. He added that he had already made a number of requested changes and had offered to make relatively minor final changes at no additional charge. Phillip also suggested in his letter that he was willing to try to mediate the claim using a local community mediation center that charged very low fees.

When Toni didn't answer the letter, Phillip filed suit. Here is how Phillip should prepare the case:

Phillip's Case

Step 1. Phillip has already written a clear demand letter (see Chapter 6 for a discussion of how to do this) and suggested mediation—a good idea, as both he and Toni work in the same small city and Phillip has an obvious interest in not turning Toni into a vocal enemy. Unfortunately, Toni didn't bite on Phillip's suggestion of mediation.

Step 2. Phillip knows that Toni's business makes money, so he is pretty sure he can collect if he wins, which of course should be a big consideration in deciding whether to file any small claims case. (See Chapter 3.)

Step 3. In court, Phillip's main job will be to prove that he did a job that was worth $3,000 and to refute Toni's likely contention that his work was so bad it amounted to a breach of their contract. Bringing copies of the tax returns he prepared for Toni as well as his own worksheets is probably the simplest way for Phillip to accomplish this. He should not present the returns to the judge page by page, but as a package. The purpose is to indicate that a lot of work has been done, without going into details.

Step 4. Phillip should then testify as to his hourly rate and how many hours he worked. He should emphasize that extra hours were required because Toni did not have her records well organized. To illustrate his point, Phillip should present to the judge any raw data Toni gave him that he still has (for example, a shoebox full of messy receipts). If he no longer has Toni's material, he might create something that looks like it, carefully pointing out to the judge that this is a simulation of Toni's data, not the real thing.

Step 5. By testifying that he was hired to do a job, that he did it, and that he wasn't paid, Phillip has presented facts necessary to establish a breach of contract case. However, he would be wise to go beyond this and anticipate at least some of Toni's defenses, which will almost surely involve the claim that Phillip broke the contract by doing poor quality work and doing it late. In addition, Phillip should anticipate Toni's backup claim that he charged too much and that the judge should award him less than $3,000. Phillip could attempt to take the sting out of Toni's likely presentation by saying something along these lines:

"Your Honor, when I finished my work, my client pointed out that several deductions had been overlooked. I believed then and believe now that this was because the data she provided me with was disorganized and inadequate, but I did rework the return and correct several items that were left out. When my client told me that she felt the revised draft needed additional changes, I again told her that I would work with her to make any necessary modifications. It was at this point that she refused to let me see the returns and hired another accountant. In my professional opinion at this stage, very little work remained to be done—certainly nothing that couldn't be accomplished in an hour or two.

"Now, as to the amount charged—it took me ten hours to reconstruct what went on in the defendant's business from the mess of incomplete and incoherent records I was given. At $90 per hour, this means that $900 of my bill involved work that had to be done prior to actually preparing the return. Taking into consideration the difficult circumstances, I believe I charged fairly for the work I did and that I did my work well."

Toni's Case

Okay, so much for looking at what happened from the point of view of the indignant accountant. Now let's see how Toni, the upset graphic artist, might deal with the situation.

Step 1. For starters, Toni made a mistake by refusing to negotiate or mediate with Phillip. Especially since this is the sort of dispute over the quality of work where a judge is likely to enter a compromise judgment, it would have saved time and anxiety for both her and Phillip to at least try to arrive at a compromise outside of court. (See Chapter 6.)

Step 2. Once Toni has decided not to try to settle the case, she should write a letter of her own, rebutting Phillip's demand letter point by point. (See Chapter 6.) She should bring a copy of this letter to court and give it to the judge as part of her presentation. The judge doesn't have to accept Toni's letter (it's not really evidence of anything but the fact that she rejected Phillip's request for payment), but more often than not, the judge will look at both parties' letters.

Step 3. Next, Toni should testify that she refused to pay the bill because she felt that Phillip's work was so poor that she didn't trust Phillip to finish the job. To make this point effectively, Toni should testify as to the details of several of the tax issues Phillip overlooked. For example, if Toni provided Phillip with information concerning the purchase of several items of expensive equipment for which Phillip didn't claim depreciation, this would be important evidence of poor work. But Toni should be careful to make her points about tax law in a relatively brief and understandable way. She won't gain anything by a long and boring rehash of her entire return. One good approach might be for Toni to submit pertinent sections of IRS publications or a privately published tax guide outlining the rules that require equipment to be depreciated.

Step 4. Toni should next present more detailed evidence that supports her claim that Phillip did poor work. The tax return as correctly prepared by the new accountant would be of some help, but it would be even better to have the second accountant come to court to testify about the details of Phillip's substandard work. Unfortunately for Toni professionals are commonly reluctant to testify against one another, so this may be difficult to arrange. But Toni should at the very least be able to get a letter from the new accountant outlining the things that he found it necessary to do to change the return as prepared by Phillip.

Step 5. Toni should also present to the court her canceled checks, establishing the amounts she paid Phillip for the last several years' returns—assuming, of course, that Phillip's previous bills were substantially less. For example, if Toni had been billed $1,700 and $1,900 in the two previous years, it would raise some questions as to whether Phillip's bill of $3,000 for the current year was reasonable.

TIP

Both Toni and Phillip should be prepared to answer the judge's questions. Especially in a case like this one involving a technical subject, the judge is almost sure to interrupt both Toni's and Phillip's presentations and ask for details. So in addition to preparing and practicing presenting their cases before a critical friend, both Phillip and Toni should be prepared to answer likely questions and then smoothly return to presenting their cases.

Because this little story is based on a real case, I can tell you what happened. The judge gave Phillip a judgment for $1,800. The judge didn't explain his reasoning but apparently felt that there was some right on each side. He split the difference with a little edge to Phillip; probably because Toni hired Phillip in the first place and had worked with him for several years, she was on somewhat shaky ground claiming he was incompetent. This sort of compromise decision, where each side is given something, is common in small claims court and again illustrates the wisdom of the parties' negotiating or mediating their own compromise. Even if Toni and Phillip had arrived at a solution where one or the other gave up a little more than the judge ordered, there would have been a savings in time and aggravation that probably would have more than made up the difference.

Judgment and Appeal

The Judgment

In most states, the decision in your case will be mailed to the address on record with the clerk any time from a few days to a few weeks after your case is heard. The exception to this rule is when one side doesn't show up and the other wins by default. Default judgments are normally announced right in the courtroom.

CROSS-REFERENCE
See Chapter 15 for information on how to set aside a default. For information on how to get a court judgment after a mediated settlement isn't carried out, see Chapter 6.

The truth is that in the vast majority of contested cases, the judge has already made a decision at the time the case is heard and jots down the decision before the parties leave the courtroom. Decisions are sent by mail because the court doesn't want to deal with angry, unhappy losers in court, especially those few who might get violent. However, despite the fact that an occasional person may be upset, some judges are willing to announce and explain their decisions in court, on the theory that both parties are entitled to know why a particular decision was reached. One progressive judge explained his policy in this regard as follows: "The only time I don't announce my decision in court is when I have phoning or research to do before finalizing it, or if I feel that the losing party will be unnecessarily embarrassed in front of the audience."

JUDGES' TIPS
Don't be flummoxed by the judge who takes everything under submission and sends the results by mail. If, when you receive the decision, you have questions about it, consider writing to the judge (send a copy to your opponent) with a respectful request for a further explanation of the judge's reasoning. Most judges will respond.
—Commissioner Douglas G. Carnahan

> **TIP**
>
> **Legal jargon note.** Now that a judgment has been entered, we need to expand our vocabulary slightly. The person who wins the case (gets the judgment) now becomes "the judgment creditor," and the loser is known as "the judgment debtor."

Often when a judgment is entered the losing party feels that the judge would surely have made a different decision if he hadn't gotten mixed up, overlooked a crucial fact, or failed to understand an argument. On the basis of my experience on the bench, I can tell you that in the vast majority of cases this is not true. Even if you had an opportunity to argue the whole case over, there is little likelihood that the judge would change his mind. Or put another way, chances are good the judge did understand your side of the case but simply didn't agree that you were in the right. (See "The Appeal" below, for information about your appeal rights.)

If you sued more than one person, the judgment should indicate who the judgment is against and for how much. Some defendants may not owe anything, or their financial liability may be limited to a stated amount. If so, this is the maximum you can collect from them. However, in most instances where a judgment is against two or more defendants, they will be "jointly and severally liable." This means that each defendant is 100% on the hook for the entire amount. For example, if you receive a $1,000 judgment against two defendants, you may collect it in any proportion from either defendant (for example, you could collect $800 from one defendant and $200 from another). If you collect a disproportionate amount from one defendant, she is left with the task of evening things out. (In this example, the defendant who paid the $800 could sue the other for $300.)

> **TIP**
>
> **The words "joint and several liability" may not appear on the judgment.** A judgment against two or more defendants will often simply list the names of the judgment debtors. This means they are jointly and severally liable for the entire amount. In cases where one defendant's judgment debt liability is limited (say to $200), the judgment will make that clear.

Installment Payments

In most states, the judge may order that the loser—usually the defendant but sometimes the plaintiff if the defendant filed a Defendant's Claim— be allowed to pay the winner over a period of time, rather than all at once. But the judge normally won't make this sort of order unless you request it. So, be sure the judge knows that if you lose, you wish to pay in installments. You might put your request this way:

- "In closing my presentation, I would like to say that I believe I have a convincing case and should be awarded the judgment, but in the event that you rule for my opponent, I would like you to allow me time payments of no more than [*an amount convenient to you*] per month."

Or, if you have no real defense:

- "Your Honor, I request that you enter the judgment against me for no more than [*an amount convenient to you*] per month."

If you neglect to ask for time payments in court and wish to make this request after you receive the judgment, first contact the other party to see whether the person will voluntarily agree to accept the money on a schedule under which you can afford to pay. If the other party agrees, it is wise to write your agreement down and each sign it. Some courts also have a form for you to fill out. (See "Sample Letter to Judge Requesting Installment Payments," below.)

If your opponent is an all-or-nothing sort of person and refuses payments, promptly contact the court clerk and ask that the case again be brought before the judge—not as to the facts, but only to set up a payment schedule you can live with. The clerk should arrange things for you, but if there is a problem, write a letter like this one to the judge:

Sample Letter to Judge Requesting Installment Payments

October 17, 20xx

Honorable Felix Hamburg
Judge of the Small Claims Court
111 Center Street
New York, NY

Re: *Elliot v. Toller*

Index No. _____

Dear Judge Hamburg:

I recently appeared before you in the case of *Elliot v. Toller* (Index No. _____). Mr. Elliot was awarded a judgment in the amount of $526. Paying this amount all at once would be nearly impossible because of _____
[*state reason, such as lack of employment or illness*]. I can pay $25 per month.

Please change the order in this case to allow for a $25 per month payment. If it is necessary for me to make this request in court, please inform me of the time I should be present.

Sincerely,

John Toller
John Toller

Paying the Judgment Directly to the Court

In some states the judgment debtor may pay the amount of the judgment directly to the small claims court, which will then notify the judgment creditor. This procedure is helpful for a judgment debtor who doesn't want to deal directly with the prevailing party or doesn't know the person's current address. Contact your small claims clerk to find out whether your court has a direct pay procedure.

> **TIP**
>
> **Notify the court when you move.** It's important to keep your current address on file if you've won a lawsuit but haven't yet been paid. That way, you won't miss out on your money in a situation where the losing party pays the court and the court can't find you.

File Satisfaction of Judgment After Payment

Once a judgment is paid, whether in installments or a lump sum, a judgment creditor (the person who won the case, remember) must acknowledge that the judgment has been paid by filing a Satisfaction of Judgment form with the court clerk. Doing this makes it clear to the world (and especially credit rating agencies) that the person who lost the case (the judgment debtor) has met her obligation. (See sample form, below.)

If the judgment creditor has also recorded a lien on real property (see Chapter 24), she must make sure the lien is removed. Ask the small claims clerk for more information about how to do this.

If a judgment creditor receives payment in full on a judgment but fails to file a Satisfaction of Judgment form, the judgment debtor will want to send a written demand that this be done. A first-class letter is adequate. If, after written demand, the judgment creditor still doesn't file within the required number of days of the request (usually between

Sample Acknowledgment of Satisfaction of Judgment

EJ-100

ATTORNEY OR PARTY WITHOUT ATTORNEY *(Name, State Bar number, and address):*
After recording return to:

Andrew Printer, Judgment Creditor
1800 Marilee Street
Fremont, CA 94536

TELEPHONE NO.:
FAX NO. *(Optional):*
E-MAIL ADDRESS *(Optional):*
ATTORNEY FOR *(Name):*

SUPERIOR COURT OF CALIFORNIA, COUNTY OF   Alameda
STREET ADDRESS: 600 Washington Street, 3rd Floor
MAILING ADDRESS:
CITY AND ZIP CODE: Oakland, CA 94607
BRANCH NAME:

FOR RECORDER'S OR SECRETARY OF STATE'S USE ONLY

PLAINTIFF: Andrew Printer

DEFENDANT: Acme Illusions, Inc.

CASE NUMBER:
002006

ACKNOWLEDGMENT OF SATISFACTION OF JUDGMENT	*FOR COURT USE ONLY*

[X] FULL   [ ] PARTIAL   [ ] MATURED INSTALLMENT

1. Satisfaction of the judgment is acknowledged as follows:
   a. [ ]   Full satisfaction
     (1) [X] Judgment is satisfied in full.
     (2) [ ] The judgment creditor has accepted payment or performance other than that specified in the judgment in full satisfaction of the judgment.
   b. [ ]   Partial satisfaction
     The amount received in partial satisfaction of the judgment is $
   c. [ ]   Matured installment
     All matured installments under the installment judgment have been satisfied as of *(date):*

2. Full name and address of judgment creditor:*
   Andrew Printer
   1800 Marilee Street, Fremont, CA 94536

3. Full name and address of assignee of record, if any:
   N/A

4. Full name and address of judgment debtor being fully or partially released:*
   Acme Illusions, Inc., 100 Primrose Path, Oakland, CA 94602

5. a. Judgment entered on *(date):*   7/21/20xx
   b. [ ] Renewal entered on *(date):*

6. [X] An [X] abstract of judgment [ ] certified copy of the judgment has been recorded as follows *(complete all information for each county where recorded):*

COUNTY	DATE OF RECORDING	INSTRUMENT NUMBER
Alameda County	8/14/20xx	21

7. [ ] A notice of judgment lien has been filed in the office of the Secretary of State as file number *(specify):*

NOTICE TO JUDGMENT DEBTOR: If this is an acknowledgment of full satisfaction of judgment, it will have to be recorded in each county shown in item 6 above, if any, in order to release the judgment lien, and will have to be filed in the office of the Secretary of State to terminate any judgment lien on personal property.

Date: 8/14/20xx

▶   *Andrew Printer*
(SIGNATURE OF JUDGMENT CREDITOR OR ASSIGNEE OF CREDITOR OR ATTORNEY**)

Page 1 of 1

*The names of the judgment creditor and judgment debtor must be stated as shown in any Abstract of Judgment which was recorded and is being released by this satisfaction. ** A separate notary acknowledgment must be attached for each signature.

Form Approved for Optional Use
Judicial Council of California
EJ-100 [Rev. January 1, 2005]

ACKNOWLEDGMENT OF SATISFACTION OF JUDGMENT

Code of Civil Procedure, §§ 724.060, 724.120, 724.250

15 and 30—check your local rules) and without just cause, many states allow the judgment debtor to recover all actual damages he or she suffers as a result of the failure (for example, denial of a credit application). In addition, some states will penalize the judgment creditor by requiring him or her to pay a set amount of money to the judgment debtor.

Here is a sample Satisfaction of Judgment form used in California. Again, it should be signed by the judgment creditor when the judgment is paid, and then filed with the court clerk. Don't forget to do this; otherwise, you may have to track down the other party later.

TIP

It's easy to get a copy of a Satisfaction of Judgment form. If either party ever needs it (for example, to correct an out-of-date credit report), the court clerk will provide a certified copy of a filed Acknowledgment of Satisfaction of Judgment. This form proves that the judgment was paid.

Sometimes judgment debtors forget to get the judgment creditor to sign the Satisfaction of Judgment form when they pay a judgment, only to find that they can't locate the judgment creditor later. If this happens and you need the form to clean up your credit record or for some other reason, you can get it if you present the court clerk with proof the judgment was paid. The following documents will help:

1. A canceled check or money order written subsequent to the date of the judgment by you, the judgment debtor, for the full amount of the judgment, or a cash receipt for the full amount of the judgment signed by the judgment creditor after the date the court awarded judgment.

2. A statement signed by you under penalty of perjury stating all of the following:

    • The judgment creditor has been paid the full amount of the judgment and costs.

- The judgment creditor has been asked to file an Acknowledgment of Satisfaction of Judgment form and refuses to do so or can't be located.
- The document attached (for example, the check or money order) constitutes evidence of the judgment creditor's receipt of the payment.

Sample Statement

My name is John Elliot. On January 11, 20xx , a judgment was awarded against me in small claims court in Ithaca, New York (Case # 1234). On March 20, 20xx, I paid Beatrice Small, the prevailing party, $1,200, the full amount of this judgment [*or, if payments were made in installments—* *"I paid Beatrice Small, the prevailing party in this action, installments of the following amounts on the following dates: _____ , concluding with a final payment of $_____ on March 20, 20xx."*]

I attach to this statement a canceled check [*or other proof that the judgment was paid*] for the full amount of the judgment endorsed by Beatrice Small. [*If payment was made by money order or cash (with a receipt), modify this statement as needed. If payment was made in installments, modify this statement as needed and enclose copies of all canceled checks.*]

Beatrice Small did not voluntarily file a Satisfaction of Judgment. When I tried to contact her, I learned that she had moved and had left no forwarding address. [*If the judgment creditor refuses to sign a Satisfaction of Judgment form, or is otherwise not available to do so, modify this statement as necessary.*]

I declare under penalty of perjury under the laws of the State of _____ that the foregoing is true and correct.

DATED: June 4, 20xx. _____

John Elliot

The Appeal

Unlike small claims court itself, where rules and procedures are remarkably the same throughout the United States, the rules that cover appeals from small claims court judgments vary greatly from one state to the next. A few allow no appeal. New York allows an appeal of a judge's decision but not an arbitrator's. California, Massachusetts, and a few other states allow a losing defendant to appeal but do not permit the person who brought the suit (the plaintiff) to do so, except to appeal from counterclaims initiated by the defendant. In the Appendix you will find a very brief summary of the appeal procedures of every state.

> **CAUTION**
>
> **You can't appeal if you didn't show up in small claims court.** Appeal rights are almost always restricted to those who showed up in small claims court, argued their case, and lost. If you defaulted (didn't show up), you normally can't appeal unless and until you get the default set aside. Normally you must file paperwork to do this almost immediately, or the small claims judgment will become final and unappealable. (See Chapter 15.) Filing a request to set aside a default judgment normally *does not* extend the time allowed to appeal.

> **TIP**
>
> **Don't assume the deck is stacked against you just because you lost in small claims court.** You may have heard that some higher court judges consider small claims appeals to be a nuisance and try to discourage them by routinely upholding the original judgment. There's very little truth to this. Most judges will give you a fair hearing on appeal if you are well prepared and able to present a convincing case. Therefore, if you believe you were victimized by a bad decision in small claims court and your case

involves enough money to make a further investment of time and energy worthwhile, go ahead and appeal if your state's rules allow it.

Determining whether you are eligible to appeal is important, but it is only part of the information you need. It is just as important to determine what kind of appeal is permitted in your state. Some states allow an appeal only on questions of law, while others allow the whole case to be replayed from scratch. Let's pause for a moment and look at some of the differences.

New Trial on Appeal

In several states, either party can appeal and have the case heard over from scratch. In other states, only the defendant can appeal (in most cases), but if the defendant does file an appeal, the whole case is presented again by both sides as if the first hearing hadn't occurred.

When a whole new hearing is allowed on appeal (it's called a trial de novo, in legalese), you simply argue the case over, presenting all necessary witnesses, documents, and testimony. Starting from scratch is required because records usually aren't kept at small claims court hearings. However, in a few courts, judges now tape-record hearings, and these recordings are available to the judge who considers the appeal as part of the reargument of the case.

Appeal on Questions of Law Only

In many states, appeals can be based only on questions of law, not on the facts of the case. (See the Appendix.) What's the difference between "law" and "facts"? It's best illustrated with a couple of examples.

EXAMPLE 1: You sue your mechanic in small claims court, claiming that he botched a repair job on your car. After listening to both sides, the judge rules for the mechanic, concluding that the repairs were made properly and something else was wrong with your car. You disagree, contending that the repairperson really did mess up the job. Too bad—you are not eligible to appeal, because this is a factual dispute.

EXAMPLE 2: You are a tenant suing for the return of a cleaning deposit withheld by the landlord. The court agrees with you and awards you the amount of the deposit plus $500 in punitive damages. The landlord appeals, claiming that under the law of your state, the judge only has the power to award punitive damages in the amount of $250. Because this appeal claims a mistake was made in applying the law, it is proper and will be considered.

In most states, appeals made on the basis of a mistake of law must be supported by a written outline of what the claimed mistakes are. This can put nonlawyers at a disadvantage, because they are unfamiliar with legal research and legal writing techniques. Start by contacting the court clerk and requesting all forms and rules governing appeals. Although it's important to take these seriously and do your best to comply, the good news is that most appellate judges will consider any well-reasoned written statement you submit claiming the small claims judge made a legal error.

CROSS-REFERENCE

Painless legal research tips. Check out Chapter 25 for pointers on how to learn about the laws that apply to your appeal.

Here is a brief example of appropriate paperwork:

Sample Appeals Statement

Appeal from Small Claims Judgment #_____ ,
Based on Legal Error

Under the laws of the state of _____ , a small claims judgment
may be set aside if it is based on a legal error or mistake. In my personal injury
case, the court incorrectly applied the statute of limitations, because it did not take
into consideration the fact that I was a minor when the accident occurred.

My case is based on a personal injury I suffered on January 23, 2001, when I was
17 years and two months old. The small claims judge dismissed my case because
it was not filed within one year after my injury, as is required by the statute of
limitations. This was an incorrect application of the law.

It's true that under the terms of Code of Civil Procedure Sec. 340, a personal
injury case must normally be filed within one year of the date of the injury, which
in my case occurred on January 23, 2001. However, Sec. 352 of the Code of
Civil Procedure also states: "If a person entitled to bring an action, mentioned in
Chapter 3 of this title, be, at the time the cause of action occurred, ... under the
age of majority ... the time of such disability is not a part of the time limited for
the commencement of the action."

Because I was still a minor until November 23, 2002 (when I turned 18), under
the terms of Code Civ. Proc Section 352, it was from this date (not from January
23, 2001) that the court should have begun counting the one-year statute of
limitations for personal injury actions. Therefore, I was entitled to file my case
until November 22, 2003. In fact, because I filed on June 27, 2003, I was well
within the allowed time.

In conclusion, I request that the judgment in this case be vacated and that I be
granted a new small claims court hearing.

Filing and Presenting Your Appeal

If you haven't already done so, it is absolutely essential that you obtain and study a copy of your state's small claims appeal rules. They vary considerably, especially between those states where you can only appeal questions of law and those where you are entitled to a completely new trial.

File Your Appeal Promptly

In all states, appeals must be filed promptly (usually within 10 to 30 days), so wherever you are, don't delay. In many states, you must file a notice of appeal within 30 days after the court clerk mails the judgment to the parties (or hands it over, if a decision is made in the courtroom). This means that if the decision was mailed, there will be less than 30 days to file an appeal from the day that the defendant receives the judgment. In a number of states, appeals must be filed within 10 days.

> **CAUTION**
>
> **Don't oversleep in Washington, DC, or Rhode Island!** You'll have only two days to appeal your small claims court decision in Rhode Island, and three days in Washington, DC. Luckily, weekends and holidays don't count.

You'll need to consult your state statute to find out when to start counting your time to appeal. Because many states start counting from the date the judgment was mailed, this date, which should appear on the judgment, is critical. If for some reason your judgment doesn't show up within the number of days in which you are allowed to appeal, call the small claims clerk immediately and request help getting an extension of time to file your appeal.

Appeals must usually be filed using a form supplied by the small claims court.

Appeal Fees

The appeal fee is often higher than the original filing fee. If you ultimately win your appeal (that is, get the original decision turned around in your favor), you can add these court costs to the judgment. In many states, the party filing an appeal must post a cash bond (or written guarantee by financially solvent adults) to cover the amount of the judgment if he or she loses.

Arguing Your Appeal Without a Lawyer

You are entitled to have an attorney in the appeals court. By definition, your small claims case is not worth big bucks, so you will probably decide it is not cost-efficient to hire one. Indeed, there should be little practical reason for an attorney, as you probably have an excellent grasp of the issues by this time.

> **JUDGES' TIPS**
> **It doesn't take a lawyer to make a good impression in an appeal.** A prepared, respectful, and self-represented litigant can often make just as impressive a showing at a small claims appeal as a lawyer would.
> —Commissioner Douglas G. Carnahan

But what if your opponent hires a lawyer? Aren't you at a disadvantage if you represent yourself? Not necessarily. As noted in "Presenting Your Appeal," below, in many states the appeals court must follow informal rules similar to those used in small claims court. This puts you on a relatively equal footing, even if your opponent has a lawyer. If you have prepared carefully, you may even have an advantage: You carry with you the honest conviction that you are right. If, despite this commonsense view of the situation, you still feel a little intimidated, the best cure is to go watch a few small claims appeals. Ask the court clerk when they are scheduled. Watching the process should persuade you that you are perfectly capable of handling your own appeal.

Presenting Your Appeal

On appeal, both sides should give careful thought to how their presentation can be improved. This is particularly true if you are the person who lost. Ask yourself: Did the judge decide against me because I presented my case poorly or because I didn't support my statements with evidence? Or did the judge simply misapply the law? To answer these questions, you may have to do some additional legal research. (See Chapter 25 for some tips on how to do this.)

JUDGES' TIPS

Read the case file before your appeals hearing. The file is a public record, and you have a right to see it (ask the small claims clerk how to get a copy). You'll be better prepared if you know what material the appeals judge has read. Sometimes the trial judge will leave notes in the file that the appeal judge will be reading. If so, you'll want to know that and adjust your case accordingly. —Commissioner Douglas G. Carnahan

Once you have decided how to improve your case, practice presenting it to an objective friend. When you are done, ask your friend which parts of your presentation were convincing and which need more work.

CAUTION

Jury trials. A few states, including Massachusetts and Virginia, permit jury trials on appeal. Most states don't. Check with your court clerk and the Appendix.

In some states, small claims appeals can be presented to the judge just as informally as any small claims court case. At the other extreme, however, some states' small claims court appeal rules require that an appeal be conducted with all the pomp and circumstance of a regular trial court case. Because procedures can differ even within the same state, this book can't tell you exactly what type of hearing you will face. So, again, it is important to take the time to check out exactly what type of appeal hearing rules you will encounter. For example, you may learn you'll need to be prepared to present your testimony while sitting in the witness box. You may also have to question your witnesses using the formal lawyer style you have seen so often on TV, and introduce evidence according to a strict, step-by-step script.

Some Cures for Prehearing Jitters

What should you do if you see that your appeal will be conducted in a style you find intimidating?

- Read *Represent Yourself in Court: How to Prepare & Try a Winning Case*, by Paul Bergman and Sara Berman Barrett (Nolo). This book beautifully explains how to conduct a contested civil trial in a formal courtroom setting, including how to present testimony and cross-examine witnesses. It should quickly increase your comfort level.

- Ask the judge, in advance, to conduct your appeal as informally as possible. You can do this on the day of your hearing or, better yet, by writing a brief, polite letter to the court ahead of time. Explain that, as a nonlawyer, you are thoroughly prepared to present the facts of your case, but because you are unfamiliar with formal rules of evidence and procedure, you would appreciate it if your small claims appeal could be conducted so that a citizen who has not spent three years at law school is given a fair opportunity to be heard.

- During your small claims appeal, if there is some procedure you don't understand, politely ask the judge for an explanation. If necessary, remind the judge that, as a taxpayer and a citizen, you are entitled to understand the rules and procedures that control the presentation of your case.

Further Appeals

If a defendant loses the appeal, there is usually no right to file a second appeal. However, it is sometimes possible to file an extraordinary writ (a special request for review based on extraordinary circumstances) to a court of appeal claiming that either the small claims court or first appeals court made a serious legal mistake in handling the case (for example, the court had no power to consider the issues involved in your case). In some states, the lower court judge may have the power to recommend that the court of appeal hear your case. But because of the relatively small amounts of money involved, extraordinary writs based on small claims judgments are almost never filed. And when they are, they are seldom granted. For these reasons, I do not cover this procedure here.

Collecting Your Money

Y ou won. Congratulations! You undoubtedly want to collect every penny from the opposing party, pronto. If the other party is cooperative that won't be much trouble. But some defendants have figured out that there's not much the court will do to make them pay. That's where this chapter comes in, explaining when you can start your collection efforts and how to enforce your judgment. With a little patience and some careful planning, you should be able to collect—by garnishing wages, attaching the defendant's bank account, or taking other legal steps.

(!) **CAUTION**
Don't harass the debtor. Now that you are a creditor, you are subject to the laws that protect debtors from abusive or unfair conduct. Basically, the rules require that you don't call the debtor at odd hours or bad-mouth her in the community. (Of course, it's fine to talk about the judgment to officials who are helping with the collection process.)

The Timing of Collecting Your Money

Wait until the dust settles before beginning your collection efforts. This means different things in contested cases and default cases.

Contested Cases

If the defendant appeared in court, fought the case, and lost, you must wait to see whether she appeals the loss before you start trying to collect the judgment amount. (Learn about appeals in Chapter 23.) After all, the money isn't rightly yours while there's still a chance that the case could be reversed in the defendant's favor. Depending on your state's rules, an appeal must normally be filed within 10 to 30 days. (See the Appendix.)

CAUTION

Exception. In a few states, no appeals are allowed, and in several more, only a losing defendant can appeal. (See the Appendix.) If the other party can't appeal, you can begin collection activities immediately.

After the allowed time to appeal has passed, check with the small claims court clerk to make sure that the defendant hasn't appealed. If the defendant has appealed, then you will get notice in the mail of the appeals hearing date. (Learn more about appeals in Chapter 23.) After the appeals court makes its decision, it will notify the small claims court. If the appeal was decided in your favor, you can proceed to enforce the judgment immediately.

Default Judgments

If you got your judgment because the defendant defaulted (that is, didn't show up), the defendant usually can't appeal without first asking the court to set aside the default. Most defendants who didn't show up in the first place don't bother to do this. Nevertheless, in some states, such as California, you must wait out the time period during which the losing party is allowed to ask the court to set aside the default judgment. (See Chapter 15 for more on setting aside default judgments.) And even if waiting isn't required, it's always a good idea if you are in a state that allows defendants a certain number of days in which to petition the court to set aside the default judgment. The reason is simple: If you move to collect your judgment immediately, you may alert the defendant to try to set it aside.

> **CAUTION**
>
> **Let sleeping defendants lie.** It is not illegal to ask the defendant to voluntarily pay you your money during the 30-day period after a judgment is entered. However, it is unwise. Why? Because if you make your request for money, you may remind the defendant to take advantage of the right to appeal, or, in the case of a default judgment, to ask the judge to reverse the decision. If the defendant does appeal, you can no longer enforce the original small claims judgment until the appeal is decided or dismissed.

How to Collect

Once the relevant waiting period is up, what should you do? There are a few possibilities.

Ask the Debtor for Payment

Start by asking politely for your money. This works in many cases, especially if you have sued a responsible person or business. If you don't have personal contact with the party who owes you money, try a note like the sample below.

Sample Request For Payment

P.O. Box 66
Bangor, Maine
February 15, 20xx

Mildred Edwards
11 Milvia Street
Bangor, Maine
Re: *Toller vs. Edwards* (Small Claims Case No. 200600)

Dear Mrs. Edwards:

As you know, a judgment was entered against you in small claims court on January 15 in the amount of $1,457.86. As the judgment creditor, I will appreciate your paying this amount within ten days.

Thank you for your attention to this matter.

Very truly yours,
John Toller
John Toller

The Debtor May Pay the Judgment to the Court

Your judgment debtor may be willing to pay up—but may not want to deal directly with you. In some states, the judgment debtor can pay the judgment to the court instead. Contact your small claims court clerk to find out whether this is an option in your state. If so, it might make sense to write a short note explaining that payment can be made to the court. (See the sample letter, below.) The court may charge the debtor for this service. Once the court receives payment, it will notify you. If you fail to claim the payment within a certain amount of time, the state gets to keep the money—which is an important reason to keep your current address on file with the court.

Sample Payment Request With Information on Making Payments to the Court

P.O. Box 18-C
Bangor, Maine
July 2, 20xx

Donald Lee
Donald Lee Industries
14 Western Avenue, S.W.
Bangor, Maine

Re: *Andrews vs. Lee* (Small Claims Case No. 200600)

Dear Mr. Lee,

As you know, a judgment was entered against you in small claims court on June 25 in the amount of $4,112.87. If you would prefer to pay the small claims court rather than pay me directly, you can do so. However, please be aware that the court may charge a small fee for processing your payment. To arrange payments directly to the court, contact the small claims clerk at _____ [*name and address of court where small claims case was decided*] .

As an alternative, you can send the payment directly to me. I would appreciate your handling this matter within ten days.

Thank you for your consideration.

Very truly yours,
Alice Andrews
Alice Andrews

Collect the Money Yourself

If you receive no payment after sending a polite note, you will have to get serious about collecting your money—or forget it. The emphasis in the previous sentence should be on the word "you." Much to many people's surprise, the court will not enforce your judgment and collect the money for you—you have to do it yourself.

Fortunately, a few of the ways to legally collect money from a debtor are relatively easy—if the debtor has any money in the first place. Hopefully you gave some thought to collection before you brought your case. If you only now realize that your opponent doesn't have the money to buy a toothbrush, let alone pay off your judgment, you are better off not wasting more time and money trying to get her to pay up, at least for the present. In some situations, you may want to sit on your judgment with the hope that your judgment debtor will show signs of economic life sometime in the future. But if the debtor owns real estate, you'll want to immediately put a lien on the property so that money from a sale will go to pay your judgment, even if the only property she currently owns is a residence that is exempt from being sold. (See "Creating Property Liens," below.)

TIP

Collection rules are getting tighter. A few states, such as New York, are putting teeth into their collection rules. In New York, if a judgment debtor who has the ability to do so doesn't pay three or more small claims court judgments, a judgment creditor can get triple the judgment as damages, plus attorney fees. If you are in New York, contact the small claims court clerk for details.

When the Debtor Pays by Check

Always make copies of any checks the debtor sends you as partial payment on your judgment. If the debtor fails to pay the entire judgment, you'll need to find a collection source for the unpaid portion—and the debtor's bank account is a great place to start. (See "How to Levy on Wages or Bank Accounts," below.) Your copy of the check will show the debtor's bank, branch, and account number.

If the debtor's check bounces, you may, depending on your state's law, be entitled to:

- Sue in small claims court for the original amount of the bounced check plus damages. First, you must follow your state's detailed procedures, usually including sending a demand letter to the debtor (often by certified mail).

- See whether your county's district attorney's office has a check diversion program. To avoid prosecution, the person who wrote a bad check must make the check good and comply with other rules. You cannot seek damages if you enlist the district attorney's help— but you'll be spared the hassle of another lawsuit.

If Installment Payments Aren't Made

When a court orders a judgment to be paid in installments and the judgment debtor misses one or more payments, the person holding the judgment (the judgment creditor) has the right to collect the missed payments immediately. But here is the problem: The judgment creditor can't collect the rest of the judgment (the part that hasn't come due yet) unless the court first sets aside the installment payment provisions and makes the entire judgment due and payable.

EXAMPLE: Phoebe gets a judgment against Ted for $3,000. The judge grants Ted's request to pay the judgment in installments of $300 per month. Ted misses the first payment, and Phoebe hears he plans to move out of state. She can immediately move to collect the $300. But to collect the rest, Phoebe must either wait until each subsequent payment is missed (and then try to collect each one) or go back to court and ask the judge to set aside the installment payments portion of the judgment so that she can collect it all.

To set aside an installment judgment, call the small claims clerk's office and find out whether they have a form for this purpose. Below is a sample form you can copy if your court doesn't have its own form. File the original form with the small claims clerk, have a copy served on the debtor, and follow up with a Proof of Service form. (See Chapter 11.)

Sample Request to Set Aside Payment Terms

CITY OF _____, SMALL CLAIMS COURT

[Plaintiff's name] , PLAINTIFF VS. _[Defendant's name]_ , DEFENDANT

CASE NO. _____

PETITION OF JUDGMENT CREDITOR

TO SET ASIDE TERMS FOR PAYMENT OF JUDGMENT

The undersigned hereby declares the following:

1. The judgment was entered in the above-entitled action on ___ _[date]_ ___ against the judgment debtor(s) _____ _[name(s)]_ _____ in the amount of: $_____ principal, $_____ interest, and $_____ costs.

2. The judgment bore terms for payment of the above amount as follows: $_____ to be paid on ___ _[date]_ ___ and $_____ to be paid on ___ _[date]_ ___ . (Complete the applicable item below.)

❏ No "grace period" for late payments was stated on the judgment.

❏ If payment is (specify): _____ days late, the entire balance is due and owing.

3. The judgment debtor(s) has defaulted in payment of the judgment, and the balance owing is $_____, including interest and costs awarded at the time of judgment. The last payment by the judgment debtor(s) was made on ___ _[date]_ ___ in the amount of $_____.

4. The judgment creditor therefore petitions the court for an order setting aside the terms for payment of the judgment so that execution on the entire balance of the judgment may issue forthwith.

5. I, the undersigned, am ___ _[specify: "the judgment creditor," or "the agent for the judgment creditor"]_ ___ .

I declare under penalty of perjury under the laws of the State of _____ that the foregoing is true and correct.

Date: _____

_____
Signature of Declarant

_____ _[print name of declarant]_ _____

NOTICE TO THE JUDGMENT DEBTOR(S):

If you dispute any allegation made on this petition, you must file a declaration in opposition to the petition with the small claims court within 10 days of the mailing of this petition.

Collecting a Judgment Against a Government Agency

If you have a small claims judgment against a government agency, you can't use any of the enforcement procedures outlined in the rest of this chapter. Instead, you'll need to follow special procedures to collect. Public entities include your state government, counties, cities, school districts, public authorities, and any other political subdivisions in the state.

Procedures differ slightly from state to state. As soon as you are awarded a judgment against a government agency, contact the agency to get information about its payment procedures. In many states, you must take the following steps to collect a judgment from a government agency:

1. Prepare a written declaration under penalty of perjury stating the following:
   - the fact that you have a judgment in your favor
   - the name of the government agency
   - that you desire payment, and
   - the amount of the judgment.

   The sample declaration below contains all the required information.

2. Get a certified copy of the judgment from the small claims court clerk.

3. Contact the agency that owes you money and find out its fee to collect the judgment.

4. Take or send the declaration, copy of the judgment, and the fee to the auditor of the agency you have the judgment against.

5. You're then supposed to deliver a notice to the judgment debtor (the same government agency) that you filed a request for payment, even though doing so is redundant. To play it safe, have a friend mail photocopies of the declaration, the judgment, and a completed Proof of Service form to the government agency.

6. Keep the original Proof of Service and your copies of the declaration and judgment in a safe place.

The government agency will notify its treasurer or controller, who will deposit the money with the court. Make sure that you have your current address on file with the court—otherwise, you may never get paid.

Sample Declaration

I, Steven Nakamura, declare as follows:

1. I have a judgment against the City of Los Angeles (Los Angeles Small Claims Court case #11212).

2. I desire payment according to the terms of the judgment.

3. The exact amount required to satisfy the judgment is $2,312, plus interest at the rate allowable by law from February 16, 20xx, until the judgment is paid in full.

I declare under penalty of perjury under the laws of the State of California that the foregoing is true and correct.

Dated: February 16, 20xx   _____

Steven Nakamura

Finding the Debtor's Assets

Collecting your small claims judgment isn't too difficult if the judgment debtor has some money or property and you know where it is. But what do you do if you suspect that money or other assets exist but you have no idea how to find them? For example, you may know a person works, but not where, or that he has money in the bank, but not which one.

Judgment Debtor's Statement

Wouldn't it be nice to simply ask the judgment debtor a few questions about his assets? Well, in many states the loser (judgment debtor) must

Sample Judgment Debtor's Statement of Assets

<table>
<tr><td>**MAIL TO THE JUDGMENT CREDITOR**
DO NOT FILE WITH THE COURT</td><td>SC-133</td></tr>
</table>

JUDGMENT CREDITOR (the person or business who won the case) *(name):*

JUDGMENT DEBTOR (the person or business who lost the case and owes money) *(name):*

SMALL CLAIMS CASE NO.:

NOTICE TO JUDGMENT DEBTOR: You *must* (1) pay the judgment or (2) appeal or (3) file a motion to vacate. If you fail to pay or take one of the other two actions, you must complete and mail this form to the judgment creditor. If you do not, you may have to go to court to answer questions and may have penalties imposed on you by the court.	**AVISO AL DEUDOR POR FALLO JUDICIAL: Usted debe (1) pagar el monto del fallo judicial, o (2) presentar un recurso de apelación o (3) presentar un recurso de nulidad.** Si usted no paga el fallo o presenta uno de estos dos recursos, deberá llenar y enviar por correo este formulario a su acreedor por fallo judicial. Si no lo hace, es posible que deba presentarse ante la corte para contestar preguntas y pagar las multas que la corte le pueda imponer.

INSTRUCTIONS

The small claims court has ruled that you owe money to the judgment creditor.

1. You may appeal a judgment against you only on the other party's claim. You may *not* appeal a judgment against you on *your* claim.
   a. If you appeared at the trial and you want to appeal, you must file a *Notice of Appeal* (form SC-140) within 30 days after the date the *Notice of Entry of Judgment* (form SC-130) was mailed or handed to you by the clerk.
   b. If you did not appear at the trial, before you can appeal, you must first file a *Notice of Motion to Vacate Judgment and Declaration* (form SC-135) and pay the required fee within 30 days after the date the *Notice of Entry of Judgment* was mailed or handed to you. The judgment cannot be collected until the motion is decided. If your motion is denied, you then have 10 days after the date the notice of denial was mailed to file your appeal.
2. Unless you **pay the judgment or appeal the judgment or file a motion to vacate, you must fill out this form and mail it to the person who won the case** within **30 days** after the *Notice of Entry of Judgment* was mailed or handed to you by the clerk. Mailing this completed form does not stay enforcement of the judgment.
3. If you lose your appeal or motion to vacate, you must pay the judgment, including postjudgment costs and interest. As soon as the small claims court denies your motion to vacate and the denial is not appealed, or receives the dismissal of your appeal or judgment from the superior court after appeal, the judgment is no longer suspended and may be immediately enforced against you by the judgment creditor.
4. Unless you have paid the judgment, complete and mail this form to the judgment creditor within **30 days** after the date the clerk mails or delivers to you (a) the denial of your motion to vacate, or (b) the dismissal of your appeal, or (c) the judgment against you on your appeal.

If you were sued as an individual, skip this box and begin with item 1 below. Otherwise, check the applicable box, attach the documents indicated, and complete item 15 on the reverse.

   a. ☐ *(Corporation or partnership)* Attached to this form is a statement describing the nature, value, and exact location of all assets of the corporation or the partners, and a statement showing that the person signing this form is authorized to submit this form on behalf of the corporation or partnership.

   b. ☐ *(Governmental agency)* Attached to this form is the statement of an authorized representative of the agency stating when the agency will pay the judgment and any reasons for its failure to do so.

JUDGMENT DEBTOR'S STATEMENT OF ASSETS

EMPLOYMENT

1. What are your sources of income and occupation? *(Provide job title and name of division or office in which you work.)*

2. a. Name and address of your business or employer *(include address of your payroll or human resources department, if different):*

   b. If not employed, names and addresses of all sources of income *(specify):*

3. How often are you paid?
   ☐ daily   ☐ every two weeks   ☐ monthly
   ☐ weekly   ☐ twice a month   ☐ other *(explain):*
4. What is your gross pay each pay period? $
5. What is your take-home pay each pay period? $
6. If your spouse earns any income, give the name of your spouse, the name and address of the business or employer, job title, and division or office *(specify):*

Page 1 of 2

Form Adopted for Mandatory Use
Judicial Council of California
SC-133 [Rev. January 1, 2004]

JUDGMENT DEBTOR'S STATEMENT OF ASSETS
(Small Claims)

Code of Civil Procedure,
§§ 116.620(a), 116.830

Sample Judgment Debtor's Statement of Assets (cont'd.)

CASH, BANK DEPOSITS

7. How much money do you have in cash? . . . . $

8. How much other money do you have in banks, savings and loans, credit unions, and other financial institutions either in your own name or jointly *(list):*

Name and address of financial institution	Account number	Individual or joint?	Balance
a.			$
b.			$
c.			$

PROPERTY

9. List all automobiles, other vehicles, and boats owned in your name or jointly:

Make and year	License and vehicle identification (VIN) numbers	Value	Legal owner if different from registered owner	Amount owed
a.		$		$
b.		$		$
c.		$		$
d.		$		$

10. List all real estate owned in your name or jointly:

Address of real estate	Fair market value	Amount owed
a.	$	$
b.	$	$

OTHER PERSONAL PROPERTY (*Do not list household furniture and furnishings, appliances, or clothing.*)

11. List anything of value not listed above owned in your name or jointly *(continue on attached sheet if necessary):*

Description	Value	Address where property is located
a.	$	
b.	$	
c.	$	

12. Is anyone holding assets for you? ☐ Yes. ☐ No. If yes, describe the assets and give the name and address of the person or entity holding each asset *(specify):*

13. Have you disposed of or transferred any asset within the last 60 days? ☐ Yes. ☐ No. If yes, give the name and address of each person or entity who received any asset and describe each asset *(specify):*

14. If you are not able to pay the judgment in one lump sum, you may be able to make payment arrangements with the person or business who won the case (the judgment creditor). State the amount that you can pay each month: $, beginning on *(date):* . If you are unable to agree, you may also ask the court for permission to make installment payments by filing a *Request to Pay Judgment in Installments* (form SC-106).

15. I declare under penalty of perjury under the laws of the State of California that the foregoing is true and correct.

Date:

▶

(TYPE OR PRINT NAME)   (SIGNATURE)

Mail or deliver this completed form to the judgment creditor at the address shown on the Notice of Entry of Judgment *form.*

SC-133 [Rev. January 1, 2004]   **JUDGMENT DEBTOR'S STATEMENT OF ASSETS**   Page 2 of 2
(Small Claims)

fill out a form entitled the Judgment Debtor's Statement of Assets. (See "Sample Judgment Debtor's Statement of Assets," above.) The judgment debtor must send a completed copy of this form to the person who won the case (the judgment creditor) within a certain number of days after the judgment is mailed out by the clerk—unless the judgment debtor pays off the judgment, appeals, or asks the judge to reverse a default judgment. If the judgment debtor fails to complete the statement (which, unfortunately, is all too common), the judgment creditor may ask the court to hold the debtor in contempt of court, and even issue a bench warrant for his arrest. Ask a small claims advisor how to ask the court to hold the debtor in contempt.

Order of Examination

If the judgment debtor doesn't fill out the Statement of Assets form when required to do so (or if no such form exists), the judgment creditor can ask the court clerk to issue an order requiring the judgment debtor to appear in court in person to be questioned. In some states, this is called an order of examination or judgment debtor's examination. This order, which must be properly served on the judgment debtor, requires the debtor to show up in court and provide the information personally. If the debtor fails to show up, the judge can issue a bench warrant for the person's arrest.

There are usually some limits to your use of this procedure. You can't require the judgment debtor to travel too far to participate, for example.

TIP

Ask for relevant documents. You may want the judgment debtor to bring certain documents to the examination. Bank statements, vehicle records, and documents regarding property ownership may be helpful in trying to collect. To do this, you must ask the clerk to issue a Subpoena for Production of Documents. (See Chapter 14 for more information.)

> **TIP**
>
> **At the debtor's examination, in many states the judgment creditor can ask whether the debtor has any cash in his possession.** If so, the judge may issue a "turnover order," authorizing you to take the cash right then and there to satisfy at least a portion of the debt.

Collecting Judgments Across State Lines

What if your judgment debtor moves to another state, or you discover that he or she owns property or assets elsewhere? Collecting on the judgment will become less convenient, but it is still possible. The majority of U.S. states have enacted what's called the Uniform Enforcement of Foreign Judgments Act, creating standard procedures for going after a debtor's assets or property across state lines.

Here's how it ordinarily works: Say you file your small claims case in Illinois and get a judgment for $2,500. When you try to collect, you discover that the debtor has moved to Florida. In order to start your collection efforts, you will need to file your judgment in Florida, the new state. The procedure there, as in most states, is that you mail a certified copy of the original judgment to the Florida court clerk, along with an affidavit showing your and the judgment debtor's names and addresses. (Some states vary this routine, so check with the court clerk first.)

Once the court receives the certified copy and affidavit, your filing becomes a valid part of the court record. The court will also notify the judgment debtor of your filing. Now you can proceed with your collection efforts, following the collection laws of the new state.

Levying on Wages, Bank Accounts, Business Assets, and Personal Property

This section discusses a number of ways to collect a court judgment. One or more may work easily and quickly. However, some judgment debtors hide assets or are otherwise difficult to collect from. If you face this situation and believe the judgment debtor may own or buy real property, your best bet may be to establish a lien against that property and wait until the judgment debtor pays you. (See "Creating Property Liens," below, for details on how to do this.)

> Ⓘ **TIP**
>
> **Think twice before using a collection agency.** If you don't want to bother pursuing the debtor, you can turn your debt over to a real collection agency. However, this probably doesn't make much sense, as the agency will often take up to 50% of what it can collect as its fee. And unless you are a regular customer, the agency probably won't treat your debt with much priority unless it believes your judgment will be easy to collect. Of course, if the debt is easy for them to collect, you should be able to do the job yourself and pocket the collection fee.

If you know where the judgment debtor works, you are in good shape. In most states, you are generally entitled to get approximately 25% of a person's net wages to satisfy a debt. (But if a person has a very low income, the amount you may recover can be considerably less than 25% and possibly nothing at all.)

Wage garnishments are not allowed in Texas and are limited to 10% of a debtor's wages in New York. Some other states make it difficult to garnish the wages of a head of family if the family has a low income and needs all of it to survive. The sheriff's or marshal's office in your area can supply you with the rules in your state.

Knowing where a judgment debtor banks can also be extremely valuable, as you can order a sheriff, marshal, or constable to levy on a bank account and get whatever it contains at the time of the levy, subject to several exceptions. (See "Some Money Is Protected From Attachment," below.) Of course, a bank account levy will only work once at a given bank, because the debtor is pretty sure to move the account when he realizes that you are emptying it.

Other types of property are normally much more difficult to grab. Why? Because all states have debtor's exemption laws that prohibit creditors from taking certain types of property to satisfy a debt. Items protected typically include a portion of or all equity in a family house, furniture, clothes, and much more. (*Solve Your Money Troubles: Get Debt Collectors Off Your Back & Regain Financial Freedom,* by Robin Leonard and John Lamb (Nolo), includes a list of the exempt property laws of all 50 states.)

Practically speaking, the only types of personal property (as opposed to real estate) other than wages and bank accounts that are normally worth going after to satisfy a small claims judgment are business receipts and property, and motor vehicles in which the judgment debtor has equity that's greater than your state's exemption amount. Theoretically, there are many other assets that you could reach—boats and planes, for example—but in most cases they are not worth the time and expense involved, considering that your judgment is for a modest amount.

Real estate is different. Even if the judgment debtor doesn't have much equity in the property, you will still want to record a judgment lien. Most people refinance or sell within a three-year period, at which time your lien will probably be paid in order to clear title to the property. (See "Creating Property Liens," below.)

Writ of Execution

Before you can levy on a person's wages or other property, you must get court permission, usually in the form of a writ of execution, writ of garnishment, writ of attachment, or similarly titled document. (See "Sample Writ of Execution," below.) Some courts also require that you complete a short application for the writ. If you have a small claims judgment, you are entitled to this writ. In most states, you get your writ from the small claims court clerk, who will help you fill it in. There is often a small fee, which is a recoverable cost. (See "Recovering Collection Costs and Interest," below.)

Deliver the Writ to the Sheriff (or Marshal or Constable)

Once your Writ of Execution form is issued by the court, take or send it to the sheriff, marshal, or constable in the county where the assets are located. The small claims court clerk will do this for you if you request it. Give the officer or small claims clerk the following:

- The original Writ of Execution and one to three or more copies, depending on the asset to be collected. Keep a copy of the Writ of Execution for your files.

- The required fees for collecting, which will vary as to the type of asset. Call ahead to inquire or check the county's website—many post information on collection procedures and fees.

- Instructions on what type of asset to collect and where it is located. The sheriff, marshal, constable, or small claims clerk may have a form to use when providing these instructions. Normally, however, they will accept a letter if it contains all the necessary information.

Sample Writ of Execution

EJ-130

ATTORNEY OR PARTY WITHOUT ATTORNEY *(Name, State Bar number and address):*	FOR COURT USE ONLY

TELEPHONE NO.:   FAX NO. *(Optional):*

E-MAIL ADDRESS *(Optional):*

ATTORNEY FOR *(Name):*

[ ] ATTORNEY FOR   [ ] JUDGMENT CREDITOR   [ ] ASSIGNEE OF RECORD

SUPERIOR COURT OF CALIFORNIA, COUNTY OF

STREET ADDRESS:

MAILING ADDRESS:

CITY AND ZIP CODE:

BRANCH NAME:

PLAINTIFF:

DEFENDANT:

WRIT OF	[ ] **EXECUTION (Money Judgment)** [ ] **POSSESSION OF** [ ] **Personal Property** [ ] **Real Property** [ ] **SALE**	CASE NUMBER:

1. **To the Sheriff or Marshal of the County of:**

   You are directed to enforce the judgment described below with daily interest and your costs as provided by law.

2. **To any registered process server:** You are authorized to serve this writ only in accord with CCP 699.080 or CCP 715.040.

3. *(Name):*

   is the [ ] judgment creditor [ ] assignee of record   whose address is shown on this form above the court's name.

4. **Judgment debtor** *(name and last known address):*

   [ ] Additional judgment debtors on next page

5. **Judgment entered** on *(date):*

6. [ ] **Judgment renewed** on *(dates):*

7. **Notice of sale** under this writ
   a. [ ] has not been requested.
   b. [ ] has been requested *(see next page).*

8. [ ] Joint debtor information on next page.

   [SEAL]

9. [ ] See next page for information on real or personal property to be delivered under a writ of possession or sold under a writ of sale.

10. [ ] This writ is issued on a sister-state judgment.

11. Total judgment . . . . $

12. Costs after judgment (per filed order or memo CCP 685.090) . . . . $

13. Subtotal *(add 11 and 12)* . . . . $

14. Credits . . . . $

15. Subtotal *(subtract 14 from 13)* . . . . . $

16. Interest after judgment (per filed affidavit CCP 685.050) (not on GC 6103.5 fees). . . $

17. Fee for issuance of writ . . . . $

18. **Total** *(add 15, 16, and 17)* . . . . $

19. Levying officer:
    (a) Add daily interest from date of writ *(at the legal rate on 15)* (not on GC 6103.5 fees) of . . . . . . $
    (b) Pay directly to court costs included in 11 and 17 (GC 6103.5, 68511.3; CCP 699.520(i)) . . . . $

20. [ ] The amounts called for in items 11–19 are different for each debtor. These amounts are stated for each debtor on Attachment 20.

Issued on *(date):*   Clerk, by _____ , Deputy

NOTICE TO PERSON SERVED: SEE NEXT PAGE FOR IMPORTANT INFORMATION.

Page 1 of 2

Form Approved for Optional Use
Judicial Council of California
EJ-130 [Rev. January 1, 2006]

WRIT OF EXECUTION

Code of Civil Procedure, §§ 699.520, 712.010,
Government Code, § 6103.5
www.courtinfo.ca.gov

> CAUTION
>
> **Don't delay in serving a writ of execution.** A writ of execution expires if it is not served on the debtor by the sheriff, marshal, or constable within 180 days of the date it was issued by the court. If this time runs out, you will have to go back to the small claims clerk and get another writ of execution issued.

How to Levy on Wages or Bank Accounts

To seize a person's wages, you will probably have to provide an official copy of the Writ of Execution form to the sheriff, marshal, or constable in the county where the assets are located, and a letter of instruction (see "Sample Letter Containing Wage Levying Instructions," below). The sheriff or marshal will serve a wage withholding order on the debtor's employer, and you should get some money soon. An earnings withholding order lasts until the judgment is satisfied or expires.

To levy on a bank account, first contact the sheriff, marshal, or constable's office to be sure they handle this work (if not, contact a process server). Assuming they do, you'll need the original and one copy of the Writ of Execution, a letter of instruction, and the correct fee. If a bank account is in the name of the defendant and someone else, you may have to post a bond, depending on your state's laws.

TIP

Timing is key. The amount of money in most of our bank accounts fluctuates over the course of a month or year. If the debtor is employed, her bank account is probably ripest for the picking around the first of the month. If the debtor has seasonal employment, certain times of the year are probably best for the levy. Before you write your instructions to the levying officer, think about when you are most likely to find the money.

Some Money Is Protected From Attachment

Not all money in a debtor's bank account is up for grabs. California's debtor protection laws prohibit you from taking exempt funds, and if you do take exempt funds the judgment debtor can force you to return them. Most importantly, approximately 75% of wages placed in a bank account are exempt (100% if there has been a previous wage attachment involving the same money) for 30 days after payment. Social Security, certain retirement accounts, and financial aid for school are also exempt.

Sample Letter Containing Wage Levying Instructions

P.O. Box 66
Jackson, Wyoming
March 1, 20xx

Sheriff (Civil Division)
Mapleville, Wyoming

Re: *John Toller vs. Mildred Edwards*
Small Claims Court No. 81-52

Dear Sheriff:

Enclosed you will find the original and one copy of a Writ of Execution issued by the small claims court in the amount of $ _____ . I also enclose a check for your fee in the amount of $_____.

I hereby instruct you to levy on the wages of Mildred Edwards, who works at the Graphite Oil Co., 1341 Chester Street, Mapleville, Wyoming. Please serve the Writ on or before March 15, 20xx. [*For a bank account, you would simply substitute* "all monies in the accounts of Mildred Edwards, located at [*address*]." *You generally do not need to know the account number—although some counties may require it—only the bank and branch.*]

Very truly yours,
John Toller
John Toller

How to Levy on Business Assets

In many states, it is possible to have someone from the sheriff's, marshal's, or constable's office sent to the business of a person who owes you money to collect it from the cash on hand. It is done with a "till tap" or a "keeper." You will want to ask your court clerk about your local rules.

A till tap consists of a one-time removal of all cash and checks from the business. The fees are reasonable. For a "keeper," a deputy from the sheriff's, marshal's, or constable's office goes to the place of business, takes all the cash and checks in the cash register, and then stays there for a set period of time (an "eight-hour keeper," a "24-hour keeper" or a "48-hour keeper") to take more money as it comes in. Because you must pay the deputy to stay at the collection site, keepers' fees are relatively high. It is also possible for the business's property to be seized and sold. But the costs of doing so are usually prohibitive.

Talk to the sheriff, marshal, or constable in your area to get more details. He will want an original and copies of your Writ of Execution, as well as instructions telling him where and when to go. You can get the judgment debtor to reimburse you for money you spend on collection processes, if enough money comes in to cover it.

How to Levy on Motor Vehicles (Including Planes, Boats, and RVs)

Seizing a person's motor vehicle tends to be difficult for several reasons, including the following:

- A portion of the equity in a car is exempt from your levy in many, though not all, states. The exempt amount ranges widely, from $1,000 to $20,000.

EXAMPLE: A judgment debtor in Oregon has a car worth $4,000 on which he owes $3,000 to a bank. This means his equity is $1,000—the bank owns the rest. Equity of up to $1,700 is exempt under Oregon law, so you would end up with nothing.

- The car must be parked in an accessible place, such as a street or driveway, unless you obtain a court order allowing entry into a garage or other private place.
- You can't always be sure that the judgment debtor owns the car he drives. It may be in someone else's name, or he may be leasing it.

Finding out whether a judgment debtor owns the car he drives can be tricky. You might get this information from the judgment debtor's Statement of Assets or by conducting an order of examination (see "Finding the Debtor's Assets," above). In addition, for a small fee, you may be able to find out from the department of motor vehicles who owns the car, including whether or not a bank or finance company has an interest.

Once you have this information, you can determine whether the car is worth enough to levy against. If the car is sold, will the sale price be enough to pay off any car loan the debtor has, give the debtor her exemption, cover the costs of the sale, and leave enough to pay all, or at least a substantial part, of your judgment? If you are convinced that the vehicle is worth enough to cover these costs, as would be the case if it is relatively new and owned free and clear by the debtor, then have the sheriff pick up the car and sell it. But remember, the sheriff's fees to do this are relatively high and must be paid in advance. Also, the sale price at a public auction will fetch far less than at a private sale. You can get back the money spent on sheriff's fees when the vehicle is sold.

Call the sheriff, marshal, or constable of the county in which the car is located to find out how much money is required as a deposit and how many copies of the writ you'll need. Then write a letter like the one below.

Sample Letter to Sheriff Requesting Levy

P.O. Box 66
Jackson, WY
March 1, 20xx

Sheriff (Civil Division)
Cheyenne, WY

Re: *John Toller vs. Mildred Edwards*
No. SC 81-52

Dear Sheriff:

You are hereby instructed, under the authority of the enclosed Writ of Execution, to levy upon and sell all of the right, title, and interest of Mildred Edwards, judgment debtor, in the following motor vehicle:

[*Enter the description of the car as it appears on the DMV report, including the license number.*]

The vehicle is registered in the name(s) of Mildred Edwards, and is regularly found at the following address(es):

[*List home and work address of owner. Remember that the car must be in a public place, such as parked on a street.*]

Enclosed is my check for $_____ to cover your costs of levy and sale.

Very truly yours,
John Toller
John Toller

CAUTION

Some states have no exemption for motor vehicles, and some exempt a higher amount of equity. Check your state's laws, call your local sheriff's or marshal's office, or consult *Solve Your Money Troubles: Get Debt Collectors Off Your Back & Regain Financial Freedom,* by Robin Leonard and John Lamb (Nolo), which contains an up-to-date list of all states' exemptions.

How to Levy on Stocks, Bonds, Mutual Funds, and Other Securities

If the judgment debtor owns stock or other securities that are not exempt as part of a retirement plan (see below), you may be able to force the debtor to sell these assets to pay your judgment. Your collection method will depend on whether the debtor personally holds the stock certificates or whether they're held by a stockbroker.

If the judgment debtor personally holds the certificates, you can levy against the certificates themselves as tangible personal property. However, you will first need to get a court order allowing you to reach property in a private home.

If, as is common, the certificates are held for the judgment debtor by a broker, you can initiate a third-party levy against the branch office of the stock brokerage firm. The sheriff, marshal, or constable will require a writ of execution, written instructions, and fee to handle the levy.

Sometimes stock or mutual fund ownership is not manifested in certificates but is recorded in the computers of the company issuing the securities. In this case, it is possible to make a third-party levy at a company's in-state headquarters. If the company's headquarters are out of state, you will need to obtain a court order assigning you the right to the securities. For assistance with this, ask the small claims court.

How to Levy on Other Personal Property

Normally, it isn't worth the trouble to try to levy on small items of personal property, such as furniture or appliances, because they are commonly covered by one or another debtor's exemption laws. Even if property isn't exempt, selling it is usually more trouble (and produces less cash) than it's worth. If you identify valuable nonexempt property, you will need a court order to allow a levying officer access to property in a private home.

How to Levy on Pensions and Retirement Benefits

In many states, you can get at money in the judgment debtor's individual or self-employment retirement plans held in banks or savings institutions. You'll need to check your state laws to find out whether retirement accounts are fair game. If you're entitled to go after this money, you can do so just as you would with any other money kept in a bank. Of course, you need to know where the money is.

Private company retirement plans and state or local government retirement plans generally can't be touched until the money is paid over to the employee. Even then, the judgment debtor might claim those amounts as exempt.

Federal government pension and retirement benefits may not be garnished to satisfy any debts, except those for alimony and child support.

Judgments Stemming From Auto Accidents

In certain circumstances, a judgment debtor's driver's license may be suspended by the department of motor vehicles if the debtor doesn't pay a judgment stemming from an auto accident. Check with your department of motor vehicles for information.

> ⓘ **TIP**
>
> **First, try negotiation.** If the debtor needs to drive to work, license suspension may make her lose her job. To get rid of the debt and therefore avoid the suspension, the debtor might decide to declare bankruptcy. If you are a creditor and intend to ask the department of motor vehicles to suspend the debtor's license, first negotiate with the debtor. You may be able to work out a payment plan, which is a win-win result: You get your money, and the debtor doesn't have to declare bankruptcy.

Creating Property Liens

Another way to collect money from a person or business against whom you have a small claims judgment is by putting a lien on real estate owned by the debtor. In just under half of the states, the entry of a court judgment automatically creates a lien on any real property the debtor owns in the county where the judgment was obtained. In the rest of the states, you must record the judgment with the county to create a lien on the debtor's real property.

Once you have a lien on the judgment debtor's property, especially real property, there is a good chance you'll eventually be paid. It usually works like this: When the judgment debtor wishes to sell his real estate, the title will be clouded by your lien and he will probably pay you off to be able to transfer clear title to a third party. Likewise, if he wishes to refinance, it almost certainly will be contingent on all liens being paid off. Thus, sooner or later, you should get your money. Remember, however, that a portion of the debtor's equity in the home is exempt from collection.

Before you record your lien, make sure you wait until the time to appeal has passed (see above). In many states, here's how to record a property lien against all the debtor's real estate that you know about:

1. Get an Abstract of Judgment form from the small claims clerk's office at the court where your case was heard (a small fee is required).

2. Take or mail the Abstract of Judgment form to the County Recorder's office in each county where property is located or you think the debtor might buy property, and pay the required fee. The recorder's office will record your lien and notify the judgment debtor.

Recovering Collection Costs and Interest

Using formal collection methods like wage garnishments and property liens to get a judgment debtor to cough up the money she owes you can be expensive. You will want to make the judgment debtor pay you back for these costs, if possible. You can be compensated for many—but not all—costs of collecting a judgment. Generally speaking, you can get your direct costs of collecting, which include costs like:

- sheriff, marshal, or constable fees
- costs to get copies of required court papers, like a Writ of Execution or Abstract of Judgment, and
- fees to file a lien against a debtor's real estate.

However, you won't be able to get compensated for indirect costs such as:

- babysitting costs
- lost wages
- transportation costs, or
- postage or photocopying.

You are entitled to collect interest on your judgment according to your state's law. Interest begins to accrue on the date the judgment was entered. If the judge has entered a judgment to be paid in installments, you can charge interest on the unpaid balance. Apply any payments you receive first toward interest and then to the unpaid balance of the judgment. You cannot claim interest on accrued unpaid interest.

Renew Your Judgment

Judgments expire after a certain number of years—usually between five and 20, depending on the state. To find out your state's rule, see "Time Limits to Collect Court Judgments," below. Be aware that the expiration periods may differ if you are collecting on a judgment that was originally entered in another state.

Fortunately, most states allow you to renew your judgment—and any liens based on it—if you do so before the expiration date. For information on how to renew a judgment, contact your small claims court clerk's office.

Time Limits to Collect Court Judgments

State	Statute	Time Limit
Alabama	Ala. Code § 6-2-32	20 years
Alaska	Alaska Stat. § 09.10.040	10 years
Arizona	Ariz. Rev. Stat. § 12-1551	5 years
Arkansas	Ark. Code Ann. §§ 16-56-114, 16-19-1002	10 years (5 years in justice of peace courts)
California	Cal. Civ. Proc. Code § 683.020	10 years
Colorado	Colo. Rev. Stat. § 13-52-102	20 years
Connecticut	Conn. Gen. Stat. Ann. § 52-598	20 years (10 years if small claims court judgment)
Delaware	Del. Code Ann. tit. 10, § 4711	10 years
District of Columbia	D.C. Code Ann. § 15-101	12 years
Florida	Fla. Stat. Ann. § 95.11(1)	20 years
Georgia	Ga. Code Ann. § 9-12-60	7 years
Hawaii	Haw. Rev. Stat. § 657-5	10 years
Idaho	Idaho Code § 5-215	6 years
Illinois	735 Ill. Comp. Stat. § 5/12-108	7 years
Indiana	Ind. Code Ann. § 34-11-2-11	10 years
Iowa	Iowa Code § 614.1(6)	20 years
Kansas	Kan. Stat. Ann. § 60-2403	5 years
Kentucky	Ky. Rev. Stat. Ann. § 413.090	15 years
Louisiana	La. Civ. Code art. 3501	10 years
Maine	Me. Rev. Stat. Ann. tit. 14, § 864	20 years
Maryland	Md. Code Ann., [Cts. & Jud. Proc.] § 5-102(a)(3)	12 years
Massachusetts	Mass. Gen. Laws ch. 260, § 20	20 years
Michigan	Mich. Comp. Laws § 600.5809(3)	10 years
Minnesota	Minn. Stat. Ann. § 541.04	10 years
Mississippi	Miss. Code Ann. § 15-1-43	7 years
Missouri	Mo. Rev. Stat. § 511.370	10 years

Time Limits to Collect Court Judgments (cont'd)

State	Statute	Time Limit
Montana	Mont. Code Ann. § 27-2-201	10 years
Nebraska	Neb. Rev. Stat. § 25-1515	5 years
Nevada	Nev. Rev. Stat. Ann. § 11.190(1)(a)	6 years
New Hampshire	N.H. Rev. Stat. Ann. § 508:5	20 years
New Jersey	N.J. Stat. Ann. § 2a:14-5	20 years
New Mexico	N.M. Stat. Ann. § 37-1-2	14 years
New York	N.Y. C.P.L.R. Law § 211(b)	20 years
North Carolina	N.C. Gen. Stat. § 1-47	10 years
North Dakota	N.D. Cent. Code § 28-01-15(1)	10 years
Ohio	Ohio Rev. Code Ann. § 2325.18	10 years
Oklahoma	Okla. Stat. Ann. tit. 12, § 735	5 years
Oregon	Or. Rev. Stat. § 12.070	10 years
Pennsylvania	42 Pa. Cons. Stat. Ann. § 5525(5)	4 years
Rhode Island	R.I. Gen. Laws § 9-1-17	20 years
South Carolina	S.C. Code Ann. § 15-3-600	10 years
South Dakota	S.D. Codified Laws Ann. § 15-2-6(1)	20 years
Tennessee	Tenn. Code Ann. § 28-3-110(2)	10 years
Texas	Tex. Civ. Prac. & Rem. Code Ann. § 34.001	10 years
Utah	Utah Code Ann. § 78-12-22	8 years
Vermont	Vt. Stat. Ann. tit. 12, § 506	8 years
Virginia	Va. Code Ann. § 8.01-251	20 years
Washington	Wash. Rev. Code Ann. § 4.16.020(2)	10 years
West Virginia	W. Va. Code § 38-3-18	10 years
Wisconsin	Wis. Stat. Ann. § 893.40	20 years
Wyoming	Wyo. Stat. § 1-17-307	5 years

Current as of October 2007

Legal Research

W hen you're involved in a dispute, there may come a time when you need to know more about the relevant law. No deep or mysterious powers are required. Usually, all you'll need to know is how to find the local ordinances, state statutes, or judicial opinions that speak to your particular problem. Sometimes researching the law doesn't even mean a trip to the local library: City and county agencies and offices can often give you good advice and information. For example, a zoning or planning office may answer questions about fence height restrictions or building permits. Also, all state laws are available on the Internet for free, and you can also use the Internet to read many cities' local laws and some judicial decisions.

Where's the Law Library?

Public law libraries are usually located in or near the main county courthouse. You can check the white pages' government listing under "Law Library" or visit www.publiclawlibrary.org/find.html to search for your nearest public law library. If that fails, call the clerk of the local court for information.

This chapter gives basic guidelines for using the Internet and libraries to find answers to legal questions that frequently arise in small claims disputes. If you wish to delve more deeply into the law, Nolo publishes a comprehensive book called *Legal Research: How to Find & Understand the Law,* by Stephen Elias and Susan Levinkind.

Local Laws

Most cities' and towns' official websites contain a large body of helpful information, including local ordinances available for searching and downloading. Most cities' and counties' websites follow these formats:

- County: www.co.<county name>.<state postal code>.us

  Example: www.co.hennepin.ca.us

- City: www.ci.<city name>.<state postal code>.us

  Example: www.ci.boulder.ca.us.

Your state website also may have links to cities and counties.

If your city's website does not include the text of local ordinances, you may be able to find local laws on one of these sites:

- State and Local Government on the Net (www.statelocalgov.net), and

- the Municipal Code Corporation (www.municode.com).

If you don't have success with the Internet, your local laws may be available at your local public library or the city or county law library (usually located near the courthouse). You can also try getting a copy of local ordinances from the relevant city or county office or special district. For example, the zoning board may give you a copy of your town's zoning ordinances; your regional water district may have copies of local water usage ordinances. These departments usually charge a small fee to cover photocopying costs.

Once you've found a copy of your town's local laws, look for your topic in the index, if there is one, or in the table of contents. Be prepared to look under several different terms. Some indexes are not as helpful as they should be. For instance, if you're quarreling with neighbors about the excessive height of their new fence, you might start by looking under "height" and "fence." If you are unsuccessful, try "zoning laws."

Once you've found the law you need, make sure it hasn't been changed or repealed. If you're reading an ordinance online, the source will tell you what year's version of the law you're looking at. If you're not sure it's current, you can call the city or county clerk's office and ask when the law was last amended. At the library, check the front or back of the book of ordinances for updates, and ask the librarian when the library received its most recent update.

State Laws

The easiest way to find a copy of a state law (also called a statute) is if you already know its citation—that is, the number of the specific statute. For example, some chapters of this book list citations to state statutes on issues that commonly arise in small claims court. If you don't know the statute's citation, there are both Internet and print resources to help you find statutes on a particular subject.

If You Know the Citation

Citations to state statutes normally refer to the title (or volume) and section numbers. The three examples shown in Figure 1 are typical.

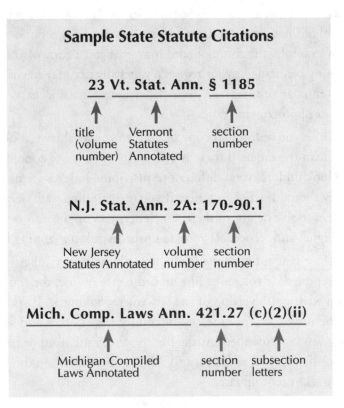

Sample State Statute Citations

23 Vt. Stat. Ann. § 1185

title (volume number)   Vermont Statutes Annotated   section number

N.J. Stat. Ann. 2A: 170-90.1

New Jersey Statutes Annotated   volume number   section number

Mich. Comp. Laws Ann. 421.27 (c)(2)(ii)

Michigan Compiled Laws Annotated   section number   subsection letters

Figure 1

Some states' laws are divided up into several different topical sections. In states such as New York and California, citations look like those shown below.

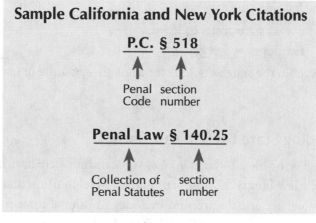

Figure 2

When you know the statute's citation, then you can use the Internet or a local law library to get a copy.

Finding State Laws on the Internet

Every state now maintains its statutes on the Internet. The websites vary in their format, but almost all of them allow you to search for statutes by topic, keyword, or citation. Start your search with Nolo.com's legal research pages (www.nolo.com/statute/index.cfm), which will guide you to your state's website containing laws and other legislative materials.

If your state's official website does not allow you to search by topic or keyword, then try one of the following websites:

- FindLaw (www.findlaw.com).
- The Cornell Legal Information Institute (www.law.cornell.edu) lets you search for statutes by topic as well as by name. The "search by topic" feature is under the "Law by Source or Jurisdiction" section of the website.

Finding Your State's Website

Every state has its statutes on the Internet. State websites usually use the following format:

www.<state postal code>.gov

Example: www.tx.gov

Within the state's site, look for a link to legislature or laws.

Finding State Laws in the Library

If you don't have Internet access, you can find state laws in your local public law library. Use the "annotated" version of the statute book if possible, because that version includes additional information that will help with research. These books also have subject indexes or tables of contents that you can use to find statutes on particular topics. For example, if someone has cut down your tree, you'd look under "trees." Nothing useful there? Try "timber" or "trespass"—anything you can think of. Sometimes finding a particular state statute is easy. But sometimes, depending on the subject and the particular state, it can take quite a bit of time and patience. A few states have pretty bad indexes.

Make Sure the Law Is Current

Once you've found the law you need, make sure it hasn't been changed or repealed. If you're reading an ordinance online, the source will tell you what year's version of the law you're looking at. At the library, check the front or back of the book of statutes for updates. Just look for the number of the law in the update material. If nothing is there under that number, it means there has been no change. If you find a change, it replaces the law printed in the hardbound volume. If there is nothing but the word "repealed" after the number of the law, the law printed in the hardbound volume is no longer in effect.

Reading and Interpreting a Statute

When you find a statute on your subject, read it carefully. Remember that the laws are written by lawyers, many of whom seem unable to write in plain English. (How wonderful it would be if other states could learn from North Dakota. That state not only has a good index, but the laws are clearly written in a style that puts other state statutes to shame.)

Figure 1 shows a page from a volume of state statutes. This state law on spite fences is from the annotated laws of Massachusetts. Let's look at the different pieces of information on the page:

❶ the topic of the statute

❷ the section number of the statute

❸ the name of the statute

❹ the text of the statute

❺ historical information including when the statute was enacted (1887), and when it was modified

❻ a listing of reference materials that discuss the statute

❼ a subject index of cases interpreting the statute

❽ a citation to a case discussing the statute, and

❾ the page number of the book in which the statute appears.

Sometimes you'll want to read a judicial decision interpreting a particular statute—for example, if the phrasing of the statute is unclear or if you want to know how the court applied the statute in a particular situation. To find cases interpreting a statute, check the listings after the text of the statute in an "annotated" version of your state's statutes in the law library.

In the annotated code, one-sentence summaries of court cases that interpret the statute directly follow the notes on the statute's history. (See number 8 in Figure 3.) Some statutes have been interpreted by the courts so many times that the publisher includes a little index to the case summaries, which are organized by issues raised by the statute.

❶

❸

SPITE FENCES

❷

❹

§ 21. Definition; remedy of injured occupant

A fence or other structure in the nature of a fence which unnecessarily exceeds six feet in height and is maliciously erected or maintained for the purpose of annoying the owners or occupants of adjoining property shall be deemed a private nuisance. Any such owner or occupant injured in the comfort or enjoyment of his estate thereby may have an action of tort for damages under chapter two hundred and forty-three.

❺

❻

Historical Note

St.1887 c. 348.   R.L.1902 c. 33 § 19.

Library References

Nuisance ⬤3(12).   Comment. Damnum absque injuria,
C.J.S. Nuisance § 39.   see M.P.S. vol. 14, Simpson, § 1373.

Notes of Decisions

❼

Constitutionality 1
Distance from boundary line 3
Motive in erecting fence 2
Persons liable 4
Subsequent proceedings 5
Validity 1

tutional. Rideout v. Knox (1889) 19 N.
E. 390, 148 Mass. 368, 2 L.R.A. 81, 12
Am.St.Rep. 560; Smith v. Morse (1889)
19 N.E. 393, 148 Mass. 407.

2. Motive in erecting fence

Under St.1887, c. 348, purpose of annoyance must be dominant motive for erecting and maintaining fence. Rideout v. Knox (1889) 19 N.E. 390, 148 Mass. 368, 2 L.R.A. 81, 12 Am.St.Rep. 560.

❽

1. Validity

St.1887, c. 348, declaring fences unnecessarily exceeding six feet in height for annoyance of adjoining owner to be private nuisances, applies to existing structures subsequently maintained as well as those afterward erected and is consti-

3. Distance from boundary line

Where defendant maliciously erected fence unnecessarily more than 6 feet

5A M.G.L.A.—29

449

❾

Figure 3

(See number 7 in Figure 1.) It is often difficult to tell from such a brief summary whether or not a case is in fact relevant to your problem. Fortunately, the summaries also contain a case citation that allows you to look up the case and read it for yourself. It is essential that you read the case itself and not just rely on what it says in the annotation.

Annotated statutes are not available online except for a fee. At Westlaw (www.westlaw.com), you can pay a fee by credit card and then enter the citation for a statute and receive a list of all court cases discussing the law.

Case Law

A judicial "opinion," "decision," or "case" is a written opinion of a court, ruling on one or more issues of a particular lawsuit. These opinions are called case law. Often they interpret the laws created by the legislature, which is why you may need to read them. Even if your state laws address a particular topic, the language of the law may not give you a clear-cut answer to your dilemma. If you find a particular statute that looks as if it will help you, it's always helpful to know how courts have actually interpreted the law.

You may need to read a judicial decision for another reason, too. Although most common small claims court issues are addressed either by local law or state statute, some issues are governed entirely by the courts. When there are no state statutes or local ordinances to help you, you may find help in what's called the "common law." The common law is the body of law that is entirely developed by the courts through their written decisions.

Finding Cases on the Internet

Unfortunately, the full text of many judicial decisions is not available online unless you're able to pay a (usually reasonable) fee.

Understanding Case Citations

A case's "citation" is like its address: It tells you exactly where to locate the published opinion. A citation will tell you the name of the case, the book it is published in, which court decided the case, and the year in which it was published.

Court cases are published in books called "reporters." There are two kinds of reporters: One, called a state reporter, publishes just the court cases from a particular state; the second, called a regional reporter, includes cases from a group of states in the same book. A case's citation will usually give you information about where to find the case in either the state or the regional reporter.

Let's take an example: You find a citation for a case stating that a tree owner may have to pay for damage caused to his neighbor's property by his tree. The case citation is *Israel v. Carolina Bar-B-Que, Inc.*, 292 S.C. 282, 356 S.E.2d 123 (Ct. App. 1987). This tells you the name, the two different reporters the case is published in, plus the court and the date. Here's how to decode the information.

- The case name: Israel versus Carolina Bar-B-Que, Inc. (who sued whom).
- The first reporter information, 292 S.C. 282, means the case is published in volume 292 of the South Carolina Reporter, at page 282. Abbreviations for particular reporters are listed in the front of the volumes of reporters.
- The second reporter information, 356 S.E.2d 123, tells us the case is in volume 356 of the Southeastern Reporter, 2nd Series, at page 123.
- The court that published the opinion: We know the case is from South Carolina, because the South Carolina Reporter publishes only cases from that state. We can see that the case comes from a Court of Appeals of South Carolina from the "Ct. App." language in the parentheses.
- The date: 1987.

Free Research Sites

The best free resource for finding state cases online is FindLaw (www
.findlaw.com). Even FindLaw, however, has cases from only a small
number of states, and it only has cases published since September
1990. FindLaw's database consists of case summaries, not the text
of the actual decision. However, a FindLaw search may give you the
names and citations of cases you want to read, and you can then use
another resource (a fee-based website or your local law library) to read
the entire case.

FindLaw allows you to search by state and by topic (including property
law), or you can search the text of FindLaw's summaries for keywords of
your choosing.

Another free resource for finding cases online is the court website for
your state. Most state courts have their current or recent cases available
online free of charge, but often you'll only find cases decided in the past
two to 12 months. Another limitation is that most court websites allow
searches only by party name; keyword or topical searches are not usually
available.

The best way to find your state's court website is to use one of the
following sites, which provide direct links to state cases:

- Cornell Legal Information Institute (www.law.cornell.edu), and
- FindLaw (www.findlaw.com).

Fee-Based Research Sites

If you can't find what you need for free, you'll need to try a site that
charges for access to cases. A good place to start is VersusLaw, a fee-based
system for finding both current and past (archived) state and federal
cases. VersusLaw (www.versuslaw.com) offers state and federal court
opinions that range from the most recent to those decided 75 years ago.

At $13.95 a month, VersusLaw is the most reasonably priced of all the
online sources of archived cases. You don't have to subscribe for more

than a month at a time, so if you are a one-time researcher, you can buy just one month of solid online research.

You can get a good sense of how VersusLaw works by using its "Guest Research" utility. Just provide some basic personal information and you will be able to browse the search facilities and create a search. If your search brings up some links to cases that meet your search criteria, you'll have to subscribe to go further. So, no free lunch here, but an opportunity to familiarize yourself with this service.

One of the great features of VersusLaw is its online help. The research manual and FAQs are written in plain English and provide some of the best research support we've encountered on the Internet.

Other fee-based legal research sites include Westlaw (www.westlaw .com) and LexisNexis (www.lexis.com).

Finding Cases in the Library

Even if you start your legal research on the Internet, you may find yourself needing a law library, especially if you're looking for case law and are unable or unwilling to pay a fee for searching. In the law library, you can read the full text of court cases once you know the citation (see "Understanding Case Citations," above), or use reference materials to find cases on particular subjects.

Ask the librarian to point you to some reference books or to a general legal encyclopedia. These books can give you background information and may also mention cases that will bear on your situation.

Legal encyclopedias. Some states have their own; if yours doesn't, use a national one, such as *American Jurisprudence* (called "Am. Jur." for short). Like regular encyclopedias, these books are arranged alphabetically by topic. The encyclopedia articles discuss how courts have ruled in actual court cases.

12 Am Jur 2d   BOUNDARIES   § 88

mutual acquiescence and recognition by the adjoiners is essential to practical location, provided that there is, at the time of the location, a disputed, indefinite, or uncertain boundary line between the adjoining owners.[11] A practical location of a boundary line has been said to be simply an actual designation on the ground, by the parties, of the monuments and bounds called for by the conveyances,[12] and it has also been said that when a disputed or uncertain boundary line is fixed by practical location it is binding, not by way of transfer of title, but by way of estoppel.[13]

§ 88. Erection of fence.

Where there is doubt and uncertainty as to the location of the true boundary line[14] between adjoining landowners, they may agree that a fence may be the division line between their lands.[15] To constitute the fence the boundary line it is not necessary that the agreement be express; it may be inferred from or implied by the conduct of the parties, especially where the fence is acquiesced to as the boundary line for the period of the statute of limitations.[16] It has

11. Drury v Pekar, supra, quoting Kincaid v Peterson, 135 Or 619, 297 P 833.

The practical location of a boundary line can be established in any one of three ways: (1) the location relied upon must have been acquiesced in for a sufficient length of time to bar a right of entry under the statute of limitations; (2) the line must have been expressly agreed upon between the parties claiming the land on both sides thereof and afterward acquiesced in; or, (3) the parties whose rights are to be barred must have silently looked on, with knowledge of the true line, while the other party encroached upon it or subjected himself to expense in regard to the land which he would not have done had the line been in dispute. Fishman v Nielson, 237 Minn 1, 53 NW2d 553.

12. Wells v Jackson Iron Mfg. Co. 47 NH 235.

Boundary lines may be determined by physical indications of the lines on the ground accepted by the parties over a period of time. Fallone v Gochce, 9 App Div 2d 569, 189 NYS2d 363, app den 9 App Div 2d 699, 191 NYS2d 560.

The actual location of a deed may be satisfactorily established, not only by the natural objects found on the ground, but by the fact that all the parties who knew the facts and were interested in the land located the deed in a certain way. Kenmont Coal Co. v Combs, 243 Ky 328, 48 SW2d 9 (holding that location of deed by grantor and his grantee, subsequently acquiesced in for more than 30 years, could not be disputed).

13. Adams v Warner, 209 App Div 394, 204 NYS 613, quoted with approval in Drury v Pekar, 224 Or 37, 355 P2d 598.

14. Uncertainty of or dispute as to the location of the true boundary line is essential in order that a fence built on a line agreed as the boundary line may operate to preclude the parties from later claiming a different boundary line. Vowinckel v N. Clark & Sons,

217 Cal 258, 18 P2d 58; Pederson v Reynolds, 31 Cal App 2d 18, 87 P2d 51; Blank v Ambs, 260 Mich 589, 245 NW 525; Talbot v Smith, 56 Or 117, 107 P 480, 108 P 125. Annotation: 170 ALR 1146.

But it is not necessary that there should be an actual dispute between the parties regarding the true division line; it is sufficient if it appears that they were uncertain as to the true line and therefore agreed to a designated and certain boundary upon which they constructed a fence and occupied and cultivated or improved their respective portions to that division fence for more than the statutory period. Martin v Lopes (Cal App) 164 P2d 321, superseded 28 Cal 2d 618, 170 P2d 881.

When the real boundary line between contiguous landowners is known to them, neither of them may acquire title by acquiescence beyond such line by merely building a fence upon the other's property and cultivating and claiming the land to that point, since title to land by acquiescence is founded on an agreement when an uncertainty exists as to the true line. Martin v Lopes, supra.

15. An oral agreement fixing an uncertain and disputed dividing line of lands, and execution thereof by the building of a fence thereon, is not in violation of the statute of frauds, since the parties do not thereby undertake to acquire and pass title to real estate, but merely fix the location of the boundary of the land that they already own, the purpose being to identify their several holdings and make certain that which they regard as uncertain. Holbrooks v Wright, 187 Ky 732, 220 SW2d 524.

Generally as to oral agreements fixing boundary lines, see §§ 78 et seq., supra.

16. Hannah v Pogue, 23 Cal 2d 849, 147 P2d 572; Roberts v Brae, 5 Cal 2d 356, 54 P2d 698; Kandlick v Hudek, 365 Ill 292, 6 NE2d 196.

Annotation: 170 ALR 1145.

Figure 4

Some encyclopedias have more than one series; you want the most recent. For instance, the current series of Am. Jur. is Am. Jur. 2d. Also be sure to check the back of the books for more recent updates (called pocket parts).

Figure 4 shows a page from Am. Jur. 2d, discussing uncertain boundary lines—in this example, neighbors setting a boundary by building a fence. You can see the short summaries of court decisions that follow each issue that is raised. Let's look at the different sections of the page:

❶ the volume you're currently reading

❷ the topic

❸ the section number within that topic

❹ the name of the section

❺ explanatory text

❻ citation to a relevant case

❼ the page number, and

❽ a cross-reference to A.L.R., a set of volumes whose full name is *American Law Reports*, where you'll find another article about this topic.

American Law Reports is another national compilation of court decisions, books, and articles published concerning all areas of the law. *A.L.R.* also comes in several series—the 6th is the latest—and has updated material in the back. *A.L.R.* has separate index volumes that list the topics in alphabetical order.

Reading a Case

A court case contains a lot of information before you even get to the court's actual opinion. Let's look at an example. You find a case that says that a neighbor was not able to collect money for damage caused by a neighbor's healthy tree. The case is *Turner vs. Coppola*, 102 Misc. 2d

864   424 NEW YORK SUPPLEMENT, 2d SERIES

"8. The instruction and supervision given * * * were so negligently given as to result in the * * * injuries sustained."

No other factual averment was made by plaintiff which in any way indicates a basis for his conclusion of negligence (*Koppers Co. v. Empire Bituminous Products, Inc.*, 35 A.D.2d 906, 316 N.Y.S.2d 858); and, such is not satisfied by a mere repetition of the complaint without factual evidence upon which to impose liability upon the movant (*Golding v. Weissman*, 35 A.D.2d 941, 316 N.Y.S.2d 522).

Defendant, Senior's motion is granted.

102 Misc.2d 1043

Barbara G. TURNER, Plaintiff,

v.

Caroline COPPOLA, Richard Petersen, Minna Petersen and Freda Amster, Defendants.

Supreme Court, Special Term, Nassau County, Part I.

Feb. 13, 1980.

Plaintiff, who alleged that branches on defendants' trees encroached on plaintiff's property, caused cosmetic damage to her garage and prevented her lawn from receiving adequate sunlight and that twigs, branches and buds from the trees constantly fell on her property, brought action for omnibus relief. On defendants' motion to dismiss complaint for failure to state cause of action, the Supreme Court, Nassau County, Special Term, B. Thomas Pantano, J., held that: (1) the trees were not a "nuisance per se," in such a sense as to sustain an action for relief; (2) complaint did not state cause of action for relief from private nuisance; (3) plaintiff did not have a cause of action in trespass; (4) plaintiff did not

have a cause of action in negligence; but (5) plaintiff could protect herself by self-help consisting of a reasonable cutting of branches to extent that they invaded her property.

Motion to dismiss complaint granted.

1. Nuisance ⟐1

Essence of a "private nuisance" is interference with the use and enjoyment of land amounting to an injury in relation to a right of ownership in that land.

 See publication Words and Phrases for other judicial constructions and definitions.

2. Nuisance ⟐3(1)

In light of fact that defendants' trees, whose branches allegedly encroached on plaintiff's property and from which twigs, branches and buds were alleged to have constantly fallen onto such property, were not poisonous or noxious in their nature, the trees were not a "nuisance per se," in such a sense as to sustain an action for relief.

 See publication Words and Phrases for other judicial constructions and definitions.

3. Nuisance ⟐42

Right to recover damages from overhanging branches depends on presence of actual injury to plaintiff or plaintiff's property.

4. Nuisance ⟐48

Complaint, in which it was alleged that branches on defendants' trees encroached on plaintiff's property, caused cosmetic damage to her garage and prevented her lawn from receiving adequate sunlight and that trees, branches and buds from the trees constantly fell on plaintiff's property, did not state cause of action for relief from private nuisance. RPAPL § 871.

5. Nuisance ⟐3(1)
 Trespass ⟐10

If an invasion of plaintiff's interest in exclusive possession of his land also deprives him of use and enjoyment of the land, trespass and nuisance would jointly arise, so long as the interference causes

Figure 5

1043, 424 N.Y.S.2d 864 (N.Y. Sup. Ct. 1980). Figure 5 shows a copy of this page. Let's look in depth at what you see there:

❶ the name and volume of the reporter (collection of cases) you're reading

❷ the page number

❸ the official citation for the case

❹ the name of the case

❺ the name of the court

❻ the date the opinion was decided

❼ a summary of the case, including what this court ruled, and

❽ a topic and key number.

The West Publishing Company has given thousands of discrete issues of law their own "key numbers," ordered under topic headings. The topic and key number of a particular rule can be used to find other cases on the same point.

All published cases begin with this kind of introductory information. Once you have gone over the introduction, it is time to read the opinion itself. Never depend on what a reference book, or even the case summary, tells you an opinion says. The people doing the research for these books are only human, and occasionally summaries are very misleading.

Make Sure the Case Is Still Valid

Once you've located a case that addresses the issue you're interested in, you'll want to make sure the case is still valid (that is, hasn't been overturned or reversed by another court decision) before you use the case in your small claims dispute. You can make sure a case is still good law by using an online service called KeyCite, which is available from Westlaw (www.westlaw.com). KeyCite requires you to register and use a credit card to pay approximately $3.75 for each search, which will tell you whether the case has been overturned. For your money, you also get a complete list of all cases that refer to the case, which may lead you to additional cases on the subject you're interested in.

You can check a case's validity using books in the law library—it's an arcane process called Shepardizing. For instructions, see Nolo's book *Legal Research: How to Find & Understand the Law*, by Stephen Elias and Susan Levinkind. ●

Small Claims Court Rules for the 50 States (and the District of Columbia)

> **CAUTION**
>
> **Please read this.** The following summary of state-by-state small claims rules is for general reference only. Because laws may change after this book goes to press and local court rules may vary from one county to the next, be sure to check your local small claims court rules before making any legal decisions. Whether you are a plaintiff or a defendant, you should either call your local small claims court clerk or see if the information you need is on the Web. This Appendix lists websites for each state's small claims information. (All links are accurate at the time of publication.) You will also find links to small claims courts at Nolo's Small Claims Center (www.nolo.com).

Alabama

Court: Small Claims Docket (district court).

Statutes: Ala. Code §§ 6-3-2; 6-3-7; 12-12-31; 12-12-70; 12-12-71.

Court rules: Alabama Small Claims Rules, Rules A to N; Alabama Small Claims Forms, 1 to 5.

Court information: www.alsp.org (click "Consumer Issues/Small Claims Actions")

Dollar limit: $3,000.

Where to sue: County or district where any defendant resides or where injury or property damage occurred. Corporation, where injury or property damage occurred, where principal place of business is located, or where plaintiff resides (if defendant does business there).

Service of process: Sheriff or other person approved by court; or certified mail, if requested.

Defendant's response: Defendant must file written answer within 14 days of service to avoid default.

Transfer: No provision.

Attorneys: Allowed; required for assignees (collection agencies).

Appeals: Allowed by either party within 14 days. Heard in circuit court as a new trial.

Evictions: No.

Jury trials: Not allowed.

Alaska

Court: Small Claims Procedure (district court or magistrate).

Statutes: Alaska Stat. § 22.15.040.

Court rules: Alaska District Court Rules of Civil Procedure, Rules 8 to 22.

Court information: www.state.ak.us/courts

Dollar limit: $10,000.

Where to sue: Court nearest to defendant's residence or place of employment, district in which injury or property damage occurred, district where defendant does business, or a place that will not cause unnecessary expense or inconvenience for defendant.

Service of process: Peace officer or registered or certified mail sent by court clerk. Certified or registered mail service is binding on defendant who refuses to accept and sign for letter. If defendant refuses service, clerk will send by regular first-class mail, and service is assumed.

Defendant's response: Defendant must file written answer within 20 days of service to avoid default.

Transfer: Defendant (or plaintiff against whom a counterclaim has been filed) or judge may transfer case to regular district court.

Attorneys: Allowed; required for assignees (collection agencies).

Appeals: Allowed by either party; heard in superior court on law, not facts.

Evictions: No.

Jury trials: Not allowed.

Arizona

Court: Justice of the Peace Court.

Statutes: Ariz. Rev. Stat. Ann. §§ 22-501 to 22-524.

Court information: www.supreme.state.az.us/info/brochures/smclaims.htm or www.jp.co.pima.az.us

Dollar limit: $2,500.

Where to sue: Precinct where any defendant resides, transaction or injury occurred, or obligation was to be performed. Corporation, wherever it does business.

Service of process: Authorized officer or process server approved by court, or registered or certified mail with return receipt requested.

Defendant's response: Defendant must answer in writing within 20 days to avoid default.

Transfer: To justice court, if defendant in small claims division counterclaims over $2,500 or objects at least 10 days before hearing (for right of appeal and jury). For counterclaims over $5,000, transfer is allowed to superior court.

Attorneys: Allowed only if both parties agree in writing.

Appeals: Not allowed.

Evictions: No.

Jury trials: Not allowed.

Notes: Justice Courts, similar to small claims court but with more procedures, have a limit of $10,000. Rules can be found at Ariz. Rev. Stat. Ann. §§ 22-201 to 22-284.

Arkansas

Court: Small Claims Division (district court).

Statutes: Ark. Const. amend. 80, § 7.

Court rules: Arkansas District Court Rule 10; Administrative Order 18.

Court information: http://courts.state.ar.us/pdf/small_claims_info.pdf or http://courts.state.ar.us/courts/districtcourt/index.cfm

Dollar limit: $5,000.

Where to sue: County where any defendant resides, transaction or injury occurred, or obligation was to be performed. Corporation, wherever it does business.

Service of process: Certified mail sent by the court, unless plaintiff requests otherwise.

Defendant's response: Defendant must file written answer within 20 days of service if in-state, within 30 days if out-of-state.

Transfer: If defendant counterclaims for more than $5,000; judge learns that any party is represented by attorney, case will be transferred to regular district court.

Attorneys: Not allowed.

Appeals: Allowed by either party within 30 days. Heard in circuit court as new trial.

Evictions: No.

Jury trials: Not allowed.

California

Court: Small Claims Division (superior court).

Statutes: Cal. Civ. Proc. Code §§ 116.110 to 116.950.

Court information: www.courtinfo.ca.gov/selfhelp/smallclaims or http://www.dca.ca.gov/publications/smallclaims/index.shtml

Dollar limit: $7,500, except that a plaintiff may not file a claim over $2,500 more than twice a year and plaintiff must be an individual (limit local public entity or for businesses is $5,000). $4,000 is the limit for suits involving a surety company or a licensed contractor.

Where to sue: Judicial district where any defendant resides (or resided when promise or obligation was made), transaction or injury occurred, or obligation was to be performed. Corporation, wherever it does business.

Service of process: Certified or registered mail, return receipt requested, sent by court clerk; sheriff or disinterested adult.

Defendant's response: No written answer required.

Transfer: If defendant counterclaims over $5,000, case will be heard in higher court if the small claims court agrees to the transfer.

Attorneys: Not allowed.

Appeals: Allowed by defendant (or plaintiff who lost on a counterclaim) within 30 days. Heard in superior court as a new trial. Plaintiff may not appeal on a judgment but may make a motion to correct a clerical error or a decision that is based on a legal mistake.

Evictions: No.

Jury trials: Not allowed.

Note: Transfer provision will likely change so that counterclaims over $7,500 will be heard in higher court.

Colorado

Court: County Court (Small Claims Division).

Statutes: Colo. Rev. Stat. §§ 13-6-401 to 13-6-417.

Court rules: Colorado Rules of County Court Civil Procedure, Rule 411; Colorado Rules of Civil Procedure for Small Claims Courts, Rules 501 to 521.

Court information: www.courts.state.co.us (click "Self Help Center")

Dollar limit: $7,500.

Where to sue: County in which any defendant resides, is regularly employed, is a student at an institution of higher education, or has business office.

Service of process: Sheriff or disinterested adult; or certified mail sent by court clerk.

Defendant's response: Defendant must file written and signed response on or before trial date.

Transfer: Allowed by defendant who has a counterclaim over $7,500.

Attorneys: Allowed only if attorney is full-time employee or general partner (partnership), officer (corporation), or active member or full-time employee (association). If attorney does appear as permitted above, other party may have attorney also.

Appeals: Allowed by either party within 15 days.

Evictions: No.

Jury trials: Not allowed.

Connecticut

Court: Small Claims (superior court).

Statutes: Conn. Gen. Stat. Ann. §§ 47a-34 to 47a-42; 51-15; 51-345; 52-259

Court rules: Connecticut Superior Court Procedure in Civil Matters, Rules 24-1 to 24-33.

Court information: www.jud.state.ct.us (click "Self-Help," then "Small Claims")

Dollar limit: $5,000 (except in landlord-tenant security deposit claims).

Where to sue: If plaintiff is corporation or company, county or geographical area where defendant resides or does business or where transaction or injury took place. If plaintiff is individual, where plaintiff resides, where defendant resides, or where transaction or injury took place.

Service of process: Proper officer or disinterested adult, registered mail, or regular first-class mail.

Defendant's response: Must file answer on or before "Answer Date" that appears on "Notice of Suit."

Transfer: Allowed by either party to regular superior court procedure upon counterclaim over $5,000, or upon defendant's request for jury trial.

Attorneys: Allowed; required for corporations.

Appeals: Not allowed.

Evictions: No.

Jury trials: Not allowed; case will be transferred to regular superior court.

Delaware

Court: Justice of the Peace Court (no small claims system).

Statutes: Del. Code Ann. tit. 10, §§ 9301 to 9640.

Court rules: Delaware Rules, Justice of the Peace Courts, Rules 1 to 72.1.

Court information: http://courts.delaware.gov

Dollar limit: $15,000.

Where to sue: County where defendant resides; in eviction cases, county where property is located.

Service of process: Court serves by certified mail return receipt requested; or first class mail with certificate of mailing; sheriff, constable, or by special process server.

Defendant's response: In all debt or trespass claims, defendant must file written answer within 15 days after service is made to avoid default. If defendant files counterclaim above $15,000, can still pursue the counterclaim in justice of the peace court. (There is no provision for transfer to higher court.) If defendant wins counterclaim, there are two options: (1) the court will note the outcome on the record and defendant may take the case to a higher court, or (2) defendant may waive the excess over $15,000 and accept $15,000 as the judgment.

Transfer: No provision.

Attorneys: Allowed.

Appeals: Allowed by either party within 15 days. Heard in superior court as new trial.

Evictions: Yes.

Jury trials: Generally not allowed. Permitted in eviction cases; defendant must make request within 10 days of being served.

District of Columbia

Court: Small Claims and Conciliation Branch (superior court).

Statutes: D.C. Code Ann. §§ 11-1301 to 11-1323; 16-3901 to 16-3910; 17-301 to 17-307.

Court rules: District of Columbia Superior Court Rules of Procedure for Small Claims and Conciliation Branch, Rules 1 to 19.

Court information: www.dccourts.gov/dccourts (click "Superior Court," then "Small Claims")

Dollar limit: $5,000.

Where to sue: District of Columbia Superior Court.

Service of process: U.S. Marshal or adult approved by court; or by registered or certified mail, return receipt requested; sent by court clerk. Certified or registered mail is binding on defendant who refuses to accept letter.

Defendant's response: No written response required.

Transfer: Transferable to regular superior court if justice requires, if defendant's counterclaim affects interest in real property (land or housing), or if either party demands jury trial.

Attorneys: Allowed; required for corporations. (Certified law students may also appear.)

Appeals: To court of appeals by either party within 3 days; reviewed on law, not facts.

Evictions: No.

Jury trials: Either party may demand one, but then case will transfer to regular branch of superior court.

Florida

Court: Small Claims Procedure or Summary Procedure (county court).

Court rules: Florida Small Claims Rules, Rules 7.010 to 7.350; Florida Rules of Appellate Procedure, Rules 7.070, 9.110.

Court information: http://orangeclerk.onetgov.net/ (click "Civil," then "Small Claims Court")

Dollar limit: $5,000.

Where to sue: County where a defendant resides, transaction or injury occurred or property is located, or contract entered into.

Service of process: Peace officer or adult approved by court; or (for Florida residents only) certified mail, return receipt requested, sent by court clerk or attorney of record.

Defendant's response: Must appear personally or by counsel at pretrial conference. No answer required, but must file any counterclaim in writing at least 5 days before pretrial conference.

Transfer: Allowed to regular county court if defendant counterclaims over $5,000.

Attorneys: Allowed; if attorneys are involved, parties are subject to discovery.

Appeals: Appeals may be filed by either party within 30 days. Heard in circuit court on law, not facts.

Evictions: Yes.

Jury trials: Either party may demand jury trial; plaintiff must make demand when filing suit; defendant must make demand within 5 days after service or notice of suit or at mediation/pretrial conference.

Georgia

Court: Magistrate Court.

Statutes: Ga. Code Ann. §§ 15-10-1; 15-10-2; 15-10-40 to 15-10-53; 15-10-80; 15-10-87.

Court information: www.georgiacourts.org/councils/magistrate/faq.html (click "Courts," then "Magistrate Court")

Dollar limit: $15,000 (no limit in eviction cases).

Where to sue: County where defendant resides.

Service of process: Constable or person authorized by judge. Personal service only.

Defendant's response: Defendant must answer within 30 days (either in writing or in person) to avoid default.

Transfer: To appropriate court if defendant's counterclaim over $15,000; or defendant submits a written request for a jury trial.

Attorneys: Allowed.

Appeals: To county superior court for new trial; no appeal if party fails to appear in magistrate court.

Evictions: Yes.

Jury trials: Not allowed.

Hawaii

Court: Small Claims Division (district court).

Statutes: Haw. Rev. Stat. §§ 604-5; 633-27 to 633-36.

Court rules: Hawaii District Court Rules, Small Claims Division, Rules 1 to 13.

Court information: www.courts.state.hi.us (click "Self-Help," then "Small Claims")

Dollar limit: $3,500; no limit in landlord-tenant residential security deposit cases. For return of leased or rented personal property, the property must not be worth more than $3,500.

Where to sue: Judicial district in which defendant resides, where transaction or injury occurred or, in security deposit cases, where rental property is located.

Service of process: Certified or registered mail restricted delivery, return receipt requested; sheriff, disinterested adult, or by either party personally.

Defendant's response: No formal written answer required. Counterclaims up to $20,000 are allowed.

Transfer: If either party demands jury trial or if a counterclaim is filed for more than $5,000. Otherwise, only if plaintiff agrees.

Attorneys: Allowed (except in landlord-tenant security deposit cases).

Appeals: Not allowed. Losing party may not appeal on a judgment but may seek to correct a mistake made in computing amount of judgment or present new evidence discovered after time of trial.

Evictions: No.

Jury trials: Not allowed. Cases that involve a counterclaim for more than $5,000 for jury trial upon timely request and presiding judge's approval will be transferred to circuit court.

Idaho

Court: Small Claims Department of the Magistrate Division.

Statutes: Idaho Code §§ 1-2301 to 1-2315.

Court information: www.isc.idaho.gov (click "Court Assistance Offices," then "Materials & Publications," then look for "Small Claims")

Dollar limit: $5,000.

Where to sue: County where the defendant resides or where claim arose. Corporation, wherever it does business.

Service of process: Personal service; or certified or registered mail, return receipt requested, sent by court clerk.

Defendant's response: Must file written answer within 20 days and sign, complete, and file it with the court clerk to avoid default.

Transfer: No provision.

Attorneys: Not allowed.

Appeals: Allowed by either party within 30 days.

Evictions: No.

Jury trials: Not allowed.

Illinois

Court: Small Claims.

Statutes: 735 Ill. Comp. Stat. §§ 5/2-101 to 5/2-208; 705 Ill. Comp. Stat. § 205/11.

Court rules: Illinois Supreme Court Rules, Rules 281 to 289.

Court information: www.ag.state.il.us/consumers/smlclaims.html

Dollar limit: $10,000.

Where to sue: County in which any defendant resides, or transaction or injury occurred. Private corporation, where it does business; public corporation, where its principal office is located.

Service of process: Sheriff, other law enforcement officer, licensed detective, or court-approved adult; or certified or registered mail, restricted delivery, return receipt requested, by court clerk.

Defendant's response: No formal written answer required. Must appear by date on court summons.

Transfer: No provision.

Attorneys: Allowed; required for corporations.

Appeals: Allowed by either party within 30 days. Heard in appellate court on law, not facts.

Evictions: Yes.

Jury trials: Either party may demand jury trial.

Notes: An alternative procedure exists for claims of $1,500 or less in Cook County only. Called the Pro Se Court, it forbids attorneys. See www.cookcountyclerkofcourt.org.

Indiana

Court: Small Claims Docket (circuit court, superior court, and county court); Marion County Small Claims Court.

Statutes: Ind. Code Ann. §§ 33-28-3-2 to 33-28-3-10 (circuit court); 33-29-2-1 to 33-9-2-10 (superior court); 33-30-5-1 to 33-30-5-10 (county court); 33-34-3-1 to 33-34-3-15 (Marion County Small Claims Court).

Court information: www.in.gov or www.small-claims-court.com/infomenu .html [Marion County]

Dollar limit: $6,000.

Where to sue: County in which any defendant resides or is employed, where transaction or occurrence took place, or where obligation arose or was to be performed by defendant. For landlord-tenant disputes, in county or town where property is located.

Service of process: Sheriff or registered or certified mail, sent by court clerk. Marion County: Personal service or registered or certified mail.

Defendant's response: No formal written answer required.

Transfer: No.

Attorneys: Allowed.

Appeals: Within 30 days. Marion County: All appeals taken to superior court of the county and tried as a new trial.

Evictions: Yes, if total rent due does not exceed $6,000.

Jury trials: Defendant may request jury trial within ten days following service of complaint upon submitting an affidavit stating questions of fact that require a jury trial. Once requested, transferred from small claims to formal court. Marion County: Defendant must file a jury duty request at least three calendar days before the trail date that appears on the complaint. Once filed, transferred from small claims to superior court.

Iowa

Court: Small Claims Docket (district court).

Statutes: Iowa Code §§ 631.1 to 631.17.

Court information: www.judicial.state.ia.us (click "Self Help," then "Civil Law," then "Small Claims")

Dollar limit: $5,000.

Where to sue: County in which any defendant resides or if resident is out of state, where resident can be found, transaction or injury occurred, or obligation was to be performed.

Service of process: Peace officer or disinterested adult; or certified mail restricted delivery, return receipt requested, sent by court clerk. For eviction cases, must be served personally.

Defendant's response: The defendant must appear within 20 days after service is made to avoid default.

Transfer: At judge's discretion if defendant counterclaims over the dollar limit.

Attorneys: Allowed.

Appeals: Allowed by either party upon oral notice at end of hearing or by written notice within 20 days of judgment. Heard in district court; no new evidence on appeal.

Evictions: Yes.

Jury Trials: Not allowed.

Kansas

Court: Small Claims (district court).

Statutes: Kan. Stat. Ann. §§ 61-2701 to 61-2714.

Court information: www.kscourts.org/dstcts/smallclaims.htm or www.kscourts.org/dstcts/4claims.htm

Dollar limit: $4,000.

Where to sue: County in which defendant lives, or county where plaintiff resides if defendant is served there, or defendant's place of business or employment or county where the cause of action arose only if defendant was a resident of that county at the time the cause of action arose.

Service of process: Sheriff or adult approved by court; or certified mail.

Defendant's response: No formal written answer required.

Transfer: If the defendant counterclaims over $4,000 but still within dollar limit of the regular district court, judge may either decide claim or allow defendant to bring claim in court of competent jurisdiction. The court is allowed to hear it or not; court has to allow defendant to file in the proper court or have court hear case up to small claims limit and sue in proper court for remaining amount.

Attorneys: Generally not allowed, but if one party has attorney, all other parties are entitled to attorney.

Appeals: Allowed by either party within 10 days. Heard in district court as new trial.

Evictions: No.

Kentucky

Court: Small Claims Division (district court).

Statutes: Ky. Rev. Stat. Ann. §§ 24A.200 to 24A.360.

Court information: http://courts.ky.gov (search "small_claims2.pdf")

Dollar limit: $1,500.

Where to sue: Judicial district in which defendant resides or does business, or if corporation, county of corporate headquarters.

Service of process: Certified or registered mail by court clerk first; if that fails, then by sheriff or constable.

Defendant's response: Must appear for hearing (20 to 40 days from service of process). Must file counterclaim within five days of hearing.

Transfer: Allowed to regular district court or circuit court if defendant's counterclaim is over $1,500, if defendant demands jury trial, or if judge decides the case is too complex for small claims division.

Attorneys: Allowed.

Appeals: Allowed by either party within ten days. Heard in circuit court.

Evictions: Yes.

Jury trials: Only if defendant makes a written request at least seven days before hearing date. Case is then transferred to regular district court.

Notes: Professional moneylenders and collection agents cannot sue in small claims court.

Louisiana

Court: Rural: Justice of the Peace; Urban: Small Claims Division (city court).

Statutes: La. Rev. Stat. Ann. §§ 13:5200 to 13:5211 (city court); La. Code Civ. Proc., Art. 4831, 4832, 4845, 4901 to 4925, and Art. 42 (justice of the peace court).

Court information: http://brgov.com (click "Departments") or www.la-law.org (click "Resources")

Dollar limit: $3,000 (city court); $3,500 (justice of the peace).

Where to sue: Parish in which defendant resides. Corporation or partnership, in parish or district in which business office located.

Service of process: Certified mail with return receipt requested; or sheriff, marshal, or constable, if certified mail is unclaimed or refused.

Defendant's response: Must file written answer within ten days of service (15 days if served by secretary of state) to avoid default.

Transfer: Small claims may be transferred to regular city court if defendant files written request within ten days of service of process, or if counterclaim ("reconventional demand") is over dollar limit. In justice of the peace court, if demand in amended or supplemental pleading ("incidental demand") exceeds jurisdictional amount, case will be transferred to court of appropriate jurisdiction.

Attorneys: Allowed.

Appeals: In justice of the peace courts, allowed by either party within 15 days; heard in parish court, or if there is no parish court, district court, as new trial. No appeal from small claims division of city court.

Evictions: No.

Jury trials: Not allowed.

Maine

Court: Small Claims Proceeding (district court).

Statutes: Me. Rev. Stat. Ann. tit. 14, §§ 7481 to 7487.

Court rules: Maine Rules of Small Claims Procedure, Rule 1 to 18.

Court information: www.courts.state.me.us (click "Maine Courts," then "Small Claims Court")

Dollar limit: $4,500.

Where to sue: District court division in which defendant resides or has place of business, where the transaction occurred, or where registered agent resides if corporation.

Service of process: By first-class mail with two acknowledgment forms and prepaid envelope for the defendant; if acknowledgment not returned within 20 days, by registered or certified mail or personal service. Can arrange for court clerk to serve.

Defendant's response: No formal written answer required.

Transfer: No provision.

Attorneys: Allowed.

Appeals: Allowed by either party within 30 days. Heard in superior court. Plaintiff's appeal on questions of law only; defendant may request a new trial.

Evictions: Yes.

Jury trials: No provision.

Maryland

Court: Small Claims Court (district court).

Statutes: Md. Code Ann. [Cts. & Jud. Proc.] §§ 4-405; 6-403.

Court rules: Maryland Court Rules, Rules 3-701, 7-104, 7-112.

Court information: www.courts.state.md.us (click "FAQs," then "Small Claims")

Dollar limit: $5,000.

Where to sue: County in which any defendant resides, is employed, or does business; if multiple defendants from different counties, where injury to person or property occurred. Corporation may also be sued where it maintains principal office.

Service of process: Sheriff, constable, or disinterested adult, personally or by certified mail.

Defendant's response: Defendant has 15 days from receipt of summons to file "Notice of Intention to Defend" in order to avoid default (out-of-state defendant has 60 days).

Transfer: To regular civil docket if counterclaim exceeds $5,000 or if defendant demands jury trial.

Attorneys: Allowed.

Appeals: Allowed by either party within 30 days. Heard in circuit court as a new trial.

Evictions: Yes, as long as the rent claimed does not exceed $5,000

Jury trials: Allowed if demand is filed; transferred to regular civil docket.

Massachusetts

Court: Small Claims Division, Boston Municipal Court; elsewhere, Small Claims Section (district court).

Statutes: Mass. Gen. ch. 218, §§ 21 to 25; ch. 223, § 6; ch. 93A, § 9 (consumer complaints).

Court rules: Massachusetts Rules of Court, Uniform Small Claims Rules, Rules 1 to 10; Small Claims Standards, 1:00 to 9:05.

Court information: www.mass.gov/courts

Dollar limit: $2,000; no limit for property damage caused by motor vehicle.

Where to sue: Judicial district in which plaintiff or defendant resides, is employed, or does business. Actions against landlords can also be brought in district in which property is located.

Service of process: First-class mail sent by court clerk for in-state defendants. For out-of-state defendants, sheriff or registered or certified mail.

Defendant's response: Written answer is optional, not required.

Transfer: Allowed only at court's discretion to regular civil docket.

Attorneys: Allowed.

Appeals: Allowed by defendant within ten days. Heard in superior court as new trial; jury allowed on appeal.

Evictions: No.

Jury trials: Not allowed except on appeal.

Notes: Consumer complaint small claims: (1) plaintiff must make written demand for relief at least 30 days before filing suit; (2) attorneys' fees available; (3) triple damages available.

Michigan

Court: Small Claims Division (district court).

Statutes: Mich. Comp. Laws §§ 600.8401 to 600.8427.

Court information: www.courts.michigan.gov (type "Small Claims" in the search box)

Dollar limit: $3,000.

Where to sue: County where defendant resides or is employed, or where transaction or injury occurred.

Service of process: Court clerk shall serve defendant; otherwise, by certified mail, return receipt requested, or personal service.

Defendant's response: No formal written answer required.

Transfer: Either party may transfer to regular district court. If defendant's counterclaim is over $3,000 or if defendant wants attorney, case will be transferred.

Attorneys: Not allowed.

Appeals: Not allowed. Exception: If action is heard by district court magistrate, parties can appeal to small claims division for new trial within seven days.

Evictions: No.

Jury trials: Not allowed.

Minnesota

Court: Conciliation Court (district court).

Statutes: Minn. Stat. Ann. §§ 491A.01 to 491A.03.

Court rules: Minnesota General Practice Rules, Rules 501 to 525.

Court information: www.mncourts.gov/selfhelp (click "Conciliation Court")

Dollar limit: $7,500 ($4,000 for claims based on a personal or household consumer credit transaction).

Where to sue: County in which any defendant resides. Corporation, any county in which it has resident agent, place of business, or office. Landlord-tenant disputes (other than evictions), county where rental property is located.

Service of process: Court clerk shall arrange service by first-class mail; or, if claim is over $2,500, certified mail or personal service. If defendant is out-of-state, plaintiff must arrange service.

Defendant's response: No formal written answer required. Must file counterclaim within five days of the trial date. If defendant counterclaims over jurisdictional limit and files in another court, clerk will strike small claims case from calendar; plaintiff who is not served with counterclaim may reinstate small claims action after 30 days.

Transfer: To county court on demand for a jury trial or defendant's counterclaim above jurisdictional limit.

Attorneys: Allowed.

Appeals: Filed within 20 days. Heard in district court as new trial; jury trial permitted upon appeal.

Evictions: No.

Jury trials: Not allowed except on appeal to district court.

Notes: Educational institution may bring actions to recover student loans, if loans were originally awarded in the county in which it has administrative offices, even though the defendant is not county resident.

Mississippi

Court: Justice Court.

Statutes: Miss. Code Ann. §§ 9-11-9 to 9-11-33; 11-9-101 to 11-9-147; 11-25-1; 11-51-85.

Court information: www.mississippi.gov

Dollar limit: $2,500.

Where to sue: County in which any defendant resides or where transaction or injury occurred; if nonresident, where transaction or injury occurred. Corporation, where registered office is located.

Service of process: Sheriff, constable, or disinterested adult (only in emergency with court's permission).

Defendant's response: No formal written answer required.

Transfer: No provision.

Attorneys: Allowed.

Appeals: Allowed by either party within ten days.

Evictions: Yes.

Jury trials: Either party may demand jury trial.

Missouri

Court: Small Claims Division (circuit court).

Statutes: Mo. Rev. Stat. §§ 482.300 to 482.365.

Court rules: Missouri Supreme Court Rules of the Small Claims Division of Circuit Court, Rule 140.01 to 152.

Court information: www.mobar.org/ (type "small claims court handbook" in the search box) or www.courts.mo.gov (type "small claims" in the search box)

Dollar limit: $3,000.

Where to sue: County in which at least one defendant resides, or in which one plaintiff resides and at least one defendant may be found, or where transaction or injury occurred.

Service of process: Certified mail, return receipt requested. May be served personally by court if plaintiff requests.

Defendant's response: No formal written answer required. Must file counterclaim in person within ten days after service of process and any time before hearing.

Transfer: Allowed to regular circuit court if defendant counterclaims over $3,000, unless all parties agree to stay in small claims court. (Parties must be informed of right to consult attorney before giving consent.)

Attorneys: Allowed.

Appeals: Allowed by either party within ten days for new trial in circuit court.

Evictions: No.

Jury trials: Not allowed.

Montana

Court: Small Claims Court (district court); Small Claims Division (justice court).

Statutes: Mont. Code Ann. §§ 25-2-118; 3-12-101 to 3-12-107 (district court); 25-33-101 to 25-33-306 (appeals); 25-35-501 to 25-35-807; 3-10-1001 to 3-10-1004 (justice court).

Court information: www.montanacourts.org (click "How Do I File a Small Claims Case?") or http://doj.mt.gov/consumer/consumer/smallclaimscourt.asp

Dollar limit: $3,000.

Where to sue: County or judicial district in which any defendant resides; if defendant does not live in state, where transaction or injury occurred.

Service of process: Sheriff or constable (justice court only: other process server).

Defendant's response: No formal written answer required. Defendant must serve counterclaim on plaintiff at least 72 hours before hearing. Counterclaims can't exceed $2,500 or if the court finds against plaintiff, defendant can pursue excess in justice court.

Transfer: Allowed by defendant to regular justice court if request filed within ten days of receipt of complaint.

Attorneys: Not allowed, unless all parties have attorneys.

Appeals: Allowed by either party within ten days. Heard in district court on law, not facts.

Evictions: No.

Jury trials: Not allowed. Defendant may request transfer to regular justice court for jury trial.

Nebraska

Court: Small Claims Court (county court).

Statutes: Neb. Rev. Stat. §§ 25-505.1; 25-2801 to 25-2807; 25-2734 (appeals).

Court information: http://court.nol.org (click "Small Claims Court")

Dollar limit: $2,700.

Where to sue: County in which any defendant resides or works, or where injury or property damage occurred. Corporation, wherever it regularly conducts business.

Service of process: Personal service by disinterested adult or certified mail; return receipt requested.

Defendant's response: Written answer not required. Counterclaim: must file and deliver to plaintiff at least two days prior to trial.

Transfer: Transferable to regular civil court on defendant's request or counterclaim over $2,700.

Attorneys: Not allowed.

Appeals: Allowed by either party within 30 days. Heard in district court as new trial; jury trial not permitted.

Evictions: No.

Jury trials: Not allowed in small claims court. Defendant may request transfer to regular docket of county court and demand jury trial by giving notice at least two days before hearing.

Nevada

Court: Small Claims Action (justice court).

Statutes: Nev. Rev. Stat. Ann. §§ 73.010 to 73.060.

Court rules: Nevada Justice Court Rules of Civil Procedure, Rules 88 to 100.

Court information: www.co.clark.nv.us [Las Vegas]; www.co.washoe.nv.us [Reno]

Dollar limit: $5,000.

Where to sue: Township in which defendant resides, does business, or is employed.

Service of process: Court determines method. Either registered or certified mail, return receipt requested; or personal service by sheriff, constable, disinterested adult, or other person approved by court.

Defendant's response: No formal written answer required.

Transfer: No provision.

Attorneys: Allowed.

Appeals: Allowed by either party within five days.

Evictions: No.

Jury trials: No provision.

New Hampshire

Court: Small Claims Actions (district or municipal court).

Statutes: N.H. Rev. Stat. Ann. §§ 503:1 to 503:11.

Court rules: New Hampshire District Court Rules, Rules 4.1 to 4.28.

Court information: www.courts.state.nh.us/district/claims.htm

Dollar limit: $5,000.

Where to sue: Municipal court of town in which defendant or plaintiff resides; if no municipal court, in the district court in district in which either party resides. If defendant is not a state resident, where defendant does business or owns property, or transaction or injury occurred.

Service of process: Certified mail sent by court, return receipt requested; if not delivered, or defendant does not respond, plaintiff must serve personally according to court clerk's instructions.

Defendant's response: Must respond to claim in writing within 30 days of return date that is given on summons to avoid default.

Transfer: To superior court if defendant requests a jury trial (claim must be more than $1,500).

Attorneys: Allowed.

Appeals: Allowed by either party within 30 days.

Evictions: No.

Jury trials: Not allowed, must transfer to superior court. Defendant must file request for jury trial within five days of plaintiff's claim, but only permitted for claims over $1,500.

New Jersey

Court: Small Claims Section (Superior Court, Special Civil Part).

Court rules: New Jersey Rules of Court, Rules 6:1 to 6:12-2; Rule 2:4-1.

Court information: www.judiciary.state.nj.us

Dollar limit: $3,000 ($5,000 for claims relating to security deposits).

Where to sue: County in which any defendant resides or, if defendants do not reside in New Jersey, county where transaction or injury occurred. For security deposit claims, county where property is located. Corporation, wherever it does business.

Service of process: Certified and regular mail by the court; if service not made, court officer or other adult approved by the court.

Defendant's response: No written answer required. Defendant must file counterclaim within 35 days of service of the complaint.

Transfer: Allowed to special civil part if defendant's counterclaim is more than $3,000 or if defendant demands jury trial.

Attorneys: Allowed.

Appeals: Allowed by either party within 45 days. Heard in appellate division of superior court.

Evictions: No.

Jury trials: Defendant must submit demand at least five days before return of summons (case is then transferred to special civil part).

Notes: The Special Civil Part, like the small claims court but with more procedures, has a limit of $15,000. See www.judiciary.state.nj.us.

New Mexico

Court: Metropolitan Court (Bernalillo County); Magistrate Court.

Statutes: N.M. Stat. Ann. §§ 34-8A-1 to 34-8A-10 (metropolitan court); 35-3-3, 35-3-5, 35-8-1 and 35-8-2 (magistrate court); 35-11-2, 35-13-1 to 35-13-3 (appeals).

Court rules: New Mexico Rules of Civil Procedure for the Magistrate Courts, Rules 2-101 to 2-804; New Mexico Rules of Civil Procedure for the Metropolitan Court, Rules 3-101 to 3-804.

Court information: www.metrocourt.state.nm.us/pdfs/beginlawsuit.pdf or www.nmcourts.com/othercourts/nmmagistratecourts.html

Dollar limit: $10,000.

Where to sue: County in which defendant resides or may be found, or where transaction or injury occurred.

Service of process: Personal service or service by mail to defendant's attorney or if unrepresented, to defendant.

Defendant's response: Must file answer on or before appearance date in summons.

Transfer: No provision.

Attorneys: Allowed.

Appeals: Allowed by either party within 15 days; heard in district court as new trial.

Evictions: Yes.

Jury trials: Allowed at either party's request. Plaintiff must make jury trial request in the complaint, and defendant must make request in the answer.

New York

Court: Small Claims Part (civil court, cities—including New York City; district court, Nassau and Suffolk counties; justice court, rural areas). Commercial Small Claims (city courts and district courts).

Statutes: New York Unif. Cty. Ct. Act §§ 1801 to 1815, 1801-A to 1814-A (commercial claims); N.Y. Unif. Dist. Ct. Act §§ 1801 to 1815, 1801-A to 1814-A (commercial claims); N.Y. Unif. Just. Ct. Act §§ 1801 to 1815; N.Y. Cty. Civ. Ct. Act §§ 1801 to 1815; 1801-A to 1814-A (commercial claims).

Court rules: N.Y. Uniform Trial Court Rules, Rule 208.41; 208.41-A; 210.41; 210.41-A; 212.41; 212.41-A; 214.10.

Court information: www.courts.state.ny.us (click "Litigants")

Dollar limit: $5,000 (town and village justice courts, $3,000).

Where to sue: Political subdivision in which defendant resides, is employed, or has business office.

Service of process: Certified mail, return receipt requested or ordinary first-class mail by court clerk. If after 21 days not returned as undeliverable, then notice presumed.

Defendant's response: No written answer required. Defendant to file counterclaim within five days of receiving plaintiff's claim. If in excess of $5,000, cannot be brought in small claims court.

Transfer: Allowed by court's discretion.

Attorneys: Allowed.

Appeals: Allowed only on the ground that "substantial justice" was not done. Must file appeal within 30 days. Heard in county court or appellate division of supreme court (for NYC) on law, not facts. There is no appeal from arbitrator's decision.

Evictions: No.

Jury trials: Defendant may request jury trial at least one day prior to hearing. Must file affidavit stating issues that require jury trial.

Notes: Corporations and partnerships cannot sue in small claims court, but may appear as defendants. (Does not apply to municipal and public benefit corporations and school districts.) Instead, they can bring commercial claims, which have similar rules to small claims courts but are subject to these additional restrictions: (1) Same limits and procedures as regular small claims except claim is brought by corporation, partnership, or association. (2) Business must have principal office in NY state. (3) Defendant must reside, be employed, or have a business office in the county where suit is brought.

North Carolina

Court: Small Claims Court (district court).

Statutes: N. C. Gen. Stat. §§ 7A-210 to 7A-232; 42-29.

Court information: www.nccourts.org or www.aoc.state.nc.us/www/public/html/cvmforms.html

Dollar limit: $5,000.

Where to sue: County in which defendant resides. Corporation, where it maintains place of business.

Service of process: Personal service or registered or certified mail. (Alternate method is permitted in eviction cases; see N.C. Gen. Stat. § 42-29.)

Defendant's response: Defendant has option to file written answer any time before trial; no particular form required. If answer is not filed, general denial of all claims is assumed. Counterclaims over $5,000 not allowed.

Transfer: No provision; but defendant can bring separate action in proper court.

Attorneys: Allowed.

Appeals: Allowed by either party within ten days. Heard in district court as new trial; jury trial allowed if request within ten days of appeal notice.

Evictions: Yes.

Jury trials: Not allowed. If case is not assigned to magistrate, treated as regular civil case. Plaintiff may request jury trial within five days of receiving notice of nonassignment, and defendant may make request either before or at same time as filing answer.

North Dakota

Court: Small Claims Court (district court).

Statutes: N. D. Cent. Code §§ 27-08.1-01 to 27-08.1-08.

Court information: www.agstate.nd.us/Brochures/SmallClaim.pdf; www.ndcourts.com (click "Forms")

Dollar limit: $5,000.

Where to sue: County where defendant resides. For bad checks or less than $1,000 owed on credit: county where defendant resides, has place of business, or where act or transaction occurred. For claims related to defendant's lease of property, where defendant resides or property is located. Corporations, LLCs, or partnerships, where place of business located or where the subject of the claim arose.

Service of process: Disinterested adult or certified mail.

Defendant's response: Defendant must return form requesting hearing within 20 days of service. Defendant must file and serve counterclaim at least 48 hours before hearing.

Transfer: Defendant may transfer case to regular civil court procedure if request made within 20 days of service.

Attorneys: Allowed.

Appeals: Not allowed.

Evictions: No.

Jury trials: Not allowed.

Notes: Plaintiff may not discontinue once small claims process is begun; if plaintiff seeks to discontinue, claim will be dismissed with prejudice (plaintiff cannot refile claim).

Ohio

Court: Small Claims Division (municipal and county courts).

Statutes: Ohio Rev. Code Ann. §§ 1925.01 to 1925.18.

Court rules: Ohio Rules of Civil Procedures, Rule 3 and 4.1; Ohio Rules of Appellate Procedure, Rule 4.

Court information: www.agstate.oh.us/citizen/pubs/smallclaimscourtWEB.pdf

Dollar limit: $3,000.

Where to sue: County in which defendant resides or has place of business, or obligation arose.

Service of process: Sheriff; or certified mail by clerk, return receipt requested.

Defendant's response: No written answer required. Must file and serve counterclaim at least seven days before trial date.

Transfer: To regular civil court upon defendant's counterclaim over $3,000 or court's motion. Defendant (or plaintiff if counterclaim is made) may request transfer, but must file affidavit stating grounds of defense.

Attorneys: Allowed.

Appeals: Must be filed within 30 days. Heard in court of appeals.

Evictions: No.

Jury trials: Not allowed.

Oklahoma

Court: Small Claims Procedure (district court).

Statutes: Okla. Stat. Ann. tit. 12, §§ 131 to 141; 1751 to 1773.

Court information: www.okbar.org or www.oklahomacounty.org (click "Site Map")

Dollar limit: $6,000.

Where to sue: County in which defendant resides, or if defendant is nonresident, where defendant can be found. In automobile or boat accident cases, where one or more party resides or where accident occurred. For open account or collection on a note cases, can also sue where contract was entered into. Corporations, in a county in which it has principal office or place of business or where transaction or injury occurred.

Service of process: Certified mail by clerk, return receipt requested. Plaintiff may request personal service by sheriff or other disinterested adult.

Defendant's response: No formal written answer required. Defendant must file counterclaim at least 72 hours before appearance date.

Transfer: Allowed to regular district court on a defendant's request or counterclaim over $6,000, unless both parties agree in writing to stay in small claims court. Defendant must make transfer request at least 48 hours before time ordered for appearance and answer.

Attorneys: Allowed.

Appeals: Allowed by either party within 30 days. Heard by Oklahoma Supreme Court on law only, not facts.

Evictions: No.

Jury trials: Not allowed unless claim or counterclaim is more than $1,500. Then either party may demand jury trial at least two working days before time set for defendant's appearance.

Notes: Collection agencies may not sue in small claims court.

Oregon

Court: Small Claims Department (circuit or justice court).

Statutes: Or. Rev. Stat. §§ 46.405 to 46.570; 55.011 to 55.140.

Court information: www.osbar.org or www.ojd.state.or.us

Dollar limit: $7,500.

Where to sue: County where defendant resides or can be found, where injury or damage occurred, or where contract or obligation was to be performed.

Service of process: Certified mail or sheriff or court-approved adult. (In justice court, if claim is over $50, must use personal service.)

Defendant's response: Defendant must answer within 14 days of service to avoid default, and must request hearing. If counterclaim is over $7,500, must file motion to transfer to regular circuit court or counterclaim will be ignored. Plaintiff must reply to defendant's counterclaim within 20 days of service.

Transfer: To regular docket or other appropriate court if counterclaim is more than $7,500 and defendant requests transfer; or if defendant demands jury trial and counterclaim is for more than $750.

Attorneys: Not allowed without judge's consent.

Appeals: From circuit court, no appeal. From justice court, allowed by defendant (or plaintiff, on counterclaim) within ten days. Heard in circuit court.

Evictions: No.

Jury trials: If claim is over $750, defendant may request jury trial. Request must be made at same time as answer, within 14 days of service. Case is then transferred to appropriate court.

Pennsylvania

Court: District Justice Court; Philadelphia Municipal Court.

Statutes: 42 Pa. Cons. Stat. Ann. §§ 1123; 1515.

Court rules: Pennsylvania Rules of Civil Procedure, Rules 400 to 405, 1002, 1006, 2179; Pennsylvania Rules of Civil Procedure Governing Actions and Proceedings Before Magisterial District Judges, Rules 201 to 324; Philadelphia Municipal Court Rules of Civil Practice, Rules 101 to 144.

Court information: http://courts.phila.gov [Philadelphia]

Dollar limit: $8,000. $10,000 in Philadelphia Municipal Court.

Where to sue: Individual, wherever defendant can be served or where act or transaction occurred. Corporation or partnership, where it regularly conducts business or has principal place of business or where act or transaction occurred.

Service of process: Sheriff or first-class mail, with returned acknowledgment from defendant.

Defendant's response: Defendant must file counterclaim at least five days before hearing (district justice court); at least 10 days before trial (Philadelphia Municipal Court), but defendant's counterclaim can't exceed court's dollar limit.

Transfer: If defendant's counterclaim is over $10,000, must bring suit in court of common pleas within 30 days or anything over $10,000 is considered waived and case will proceed as small claim (Philadelphia Municipal Court). There is no provision for transfer from district justice court.

Attorneys: Allowed. Defendant corporations, required if claim is above $2,500 (Philadelphia Municipal Court).

Appeals: Allowed by either party within 30 days (ten days in eviction cases). Heard in court of common pleas as a new trial.

Evictions: Yes.

Jury trials: Either party can request jury trial and case will be transferred (district justice court). Not allowed except on appeal (Philadelphia Municipal Court).

Notes: If claiming more than $2,000 personal injury or property damage, must submit statement of claim signed under oath (Philadelphia Municipal Court).

Rhode Island

Court: Small Claims Court (district court).

Statutes: R.I. Gen. Laws §§ 10-16-1 to 10-16-16; 9-4-3; 9-4-4; 9-12-10 (appeals).

Court rules: Rhode Island District Court Rules of Small Claims Procedure, Rules 1.00 to 7.01; Rhode Island District Court Rules of Civil Procedure, Rule 73.

Court information: www.courts.state.ri.us/district/smallclaims.htm

Dollar limit: $2,500.

Where to sue: District where either party resides or where defendant can be found; if plaintiff is corporation, where defendant resides or can be found.

Service of process: If plaintiff is represented by an attorney, attorney shall serve by registered or certified mail. Otherwise, court clerk shall serve by mail. If defendant does not claim notice, plaintiff must serve with process server. Defendant's refusal of certified mail is still valid service.

Defendant's response: Defendant must file written answer, defense, or counterclaim either before or on date set for answering.

Transfer: If defendant's counterclaim is for over $1,500 and judge finds for defendant, defendant can still file claim in district court. Alternatively, judge can dismiss both claims to be refiled in district court.

Attorneys: Allowed; required for public corporations and private corporations with assets of $1 million or more.

Appeals: Defendant has right to appeal on plaintiff's claim (plaintiff has right to appeal on defendant's counterclaim). Must file within two days. Heard in superior court as new trial. Exception: In consumer plaintiff claim, if manufacturer or seller defendant loses by default, no appeal allowed.

Evictions: No.

Jury trials: No provision.

Note: Transfer provision will likely change so that counterclaims over $2,500 will be heard in higher court.

South Carolina

Court: Magistrates Court.

Statutes: S.C. Code Ann. §§ 22-3-10 to 22-3-320; 15-7-30; 18-7-10 to 18-7-30.

Court rules: South Carolina Administrative and Procedural Rules for Magistrates Court, Rules 1 to 19.

Court information: www.scbar.org/pdf/public/magbook.pdf or www3.charlestoncounty.org/docs/magistrates/summfaq.htm

Dollar limit: $7,500.

Where to sue: County where defendant resides. Corporation or insurance company, county where it has business office.

Service of process: Sheriff or disinterested adult; certified or registered mail with acknowledgement of receipt.

Defendant's response: May answer in writing or orally any time within 30 days after service (five days for claims of $25 or less). Must file counterclaim within 30 days (five days for claim of $25 or less).

Transfer: Counterclaims over $7,500 will be dismissed; defendant can refile in court of common pleas.

Attorneys: Allowed.

Appeals: Must be filed within 30 days. Heard in county or circuit court on law, not facts.

Evictions: Yes.

Jury trials: Either party may request jury trial in writing at least five days before trial date.

South Dakota

Court: Small Claims Procedure (Circuit or Magistrates Court).

Statutes: S.D. Codified Laws Ann. §§ 15-39-45 to 15-39-78; 16-12B-6; 16-12B-12; 16-12B-16; 16-12C-8; 16-12C-13 to 16-12C-15.

Court information: www.sdjudicial.com (click "Public Information")

Dollar limit: $8,000.

Where to sue: County in which any defendant resides, or transaction or injury occurred. Corporation, partnership, or LLC, any county where defendant has place of business.

Service of process: Certified or registered mail first, return receipt requested (service is binding on defendant who refuses to accept and sign for the letter). If undeliverable, then service must be made by another method, determined by court.

Defendant's response: No formal written answer required.

Transfer: Allowed at judge's discretion on defendant's petition for regular civil or jury trial. (Plaintiff may request transfer in response to counterclaim.) Must make petition at least five days before appearance date and provide affidavit giving reasons that justify transfer. Appeals are allowed by both plaintiff and defendant if case transferred.

Attorneys: Allowed.

Appeals: Not allowed.

Evictions: No.

Jury trials: Not allowed. Defendant must apply for transfer to circuit court five days before trial date.

Tennessee

Court: Court of General Sessions.

Statutes: Tenn. Code Ann. §§ 16-15-501 to 16-15-505; 16-15-710 to 16-15-735; 16-15-901 to 16-15-905; 20-4-101; 20-4-103.

Court rules: Tennessee Rules of Civil Procedure, Rule 38.03.

Court information: www.co4.shelbycountytncourt_clerks/gen_sessions_court/ or www.knoxcounty.org/gsjudges/jurisdiction

Dollar limit: $25,000. No limit in eviction suits or suits to recover personal property.

Where to sue: District where defendant resides or can be found or transaction or injury occurred. If both parties reside in the same county, county of residence.

Evictions: Where property is located.

Service of process: Disinterested adult, plaintiff's attorney, or certified mail, with return receipt.

Defendant's response: No formal written answer required.

Transfer: Defendant may request transfer to circuit court at least three days before hearing (must provide affidavit that defense is either substantial, complex, or expensive enough to require transfer).

Attorneys: Allowed.

Appeals: Allowed by either party. Heard in circuit court as new trial. May demand jury trial within ten days after appeal filed.

Evictions: Yes.

Jury trials: Not allowed except on appeal or transfer.

Notes: Tennessee has no actual small claims system, but trials in general sessions court are normally conducted with informal rules.

Texas

Court: Small Claims Court (justice court).

Statutes: Tex. Gov't. Code Ann. §§ 28.001 to 28.055.

Court rules: Texas Rules of Civil Procedure, Rule 523 to 574b.

Court information: www.court.state.tx.us

Dollar limit: $10,000.

Where to sue: Precinct in which defendant resides or county where obligation was to be performed.

Service of process: Sheriff, constable, process server, or (with court approval) disinterested adult. Certified mail by court clerk, upon request by plaintiff.

Defendant's response: Defendant must file a written answer on or before 10:00 a.m. on the next Monday after ten days from service of process.

Transfer: Transfer allowed to another precinct in same county upon written motion of defendant, by either party with affidavits of two county residents that the party can't get a fair and impartial trial, or by consent of both parties.

Attorneys: Allowed.

Appeals: Allowed by either party within ten days (amount in controversy must exceed $250). Heard in county court as new trial.

Evictions: No.

Jury trials: Either party may demand jury trial by filing request at least one day before hearing.

Notes: No professional money lenders or collection agents may sue in small claims court.

Utah

Court: Small Claims Department (district court).

Statutes: Utah Code Ann. §§ 78-6-1 to 78-6-15.

Court rules: Utah Rules of Small Claims Procedure, Rules 1 to 12, A to K.

Court information: www.utcourts.gov/howto/smclaims

Dollar limit: $7,500.

Where to sue: County in which defendant resides or debt was incurred.

Service of process: Sheriff, constable, or certified mail or courier service, return receipt requested.

Defendant's response: No answer required. Must file counterclaim at least 15 days before trial; counterclaim cannot exceed $7,500.

Transfer: No provision.

Attorneys: Allowed.

Appeals: Either party may appeal within 30 business days of entry of judgment. Heard in district court as new trial.

Evictions: No.

Jury trials: No provision.

Vermont

Court: Small Claims Procedure (superior court).

Statutes: Vt. Stat. Ann. tit. 12, §§ 5531 to 5541; 402.

Court rules: Vermont Rules of Small Claims Procedure, Rules 1 to 14.

Court information: www.vermontjudiciary.org/courts/superior/smclaims.htm

Dollar limit: $5,000.

Where to sue: County in which either party resides.

Service of process: Court will serve by first-class mail; if defendant does not return form acknowledging receipt, plaintiff must arrange service by sheriff or, if out of state, someone authorized in that state.

Defendant's response: Defendant must give written or oral answer within 20 days of service to avoid default.

Transfer: A claim or counterclaim cannot be transferred.

Attorneys: Allowed.

Appeals: Allowed by either party within 30 days. Heard in superior court on law, not facts.

Evictions: No.

Jury trials: Defendant may request jury trial at least one day prior to appearance.

Virginia

Court: Small Claims Division (district court)

Statutes: Va. Code Ann. §§ 8.01-62; 16.1-76; 16.1-77; 16.1-106; 16.1-113; 16.1-122.1 to 16.1-122.7.

Court information: www.courts.state.va.us

Dollar limit: $5,000.

Where to sue: District in which defendant resides, is employed, or regularly conducts business; where transaction or injury occurred; or where property is located. Corporations, where any chief officer resides or defendant has registered office or agent for service.

Service of process: Court shall serve defendant.

Defendant's response: No formal written answer required. May file counterclaim any time before trial, counterclaim cannot exceed $5,000.

Transfer: To circuit court if defendant wants attorney representation.

Attorneys: Not allowed in small claims division; if defendant wants attorney representation, can request transfer.

Appeals: Allowed by either party within ten days (on cases over $50). Heard in circuit court as new trial; on appeal either party may request jury trial.

Evictions: No.

Jury trials: Not allowed (except on appeal, if requested).

Notes: General district courts, similar to small claims court but with more procedures, can hear claims up to $15,000. See Va. Code Ann. §§ 16.1-77 to 16.1-80.

Washington

Court: Small Claims Department (district court).

Statutes: Wash. Rev. Code Ann. §§ 12.36.010 to 12.40.120; 3.66.040.

Court information: www.courts.wa.gov or www.metrokc.gov [King County]

Dollar limit: $4,000.

Where to sue: County where any defendant resides or, if residence cannot be determined by reasonable efforts, place of employment. Corporation, where it transacts business or has office.

Service of process: Sheriff, deputy, constable, or disinterested adult; or certified or registered mail, return receipt requested.

Defendant's response: No formal written answer required. Defendant with counterclaim over $4,000 may file separate suit in superior court while plaintiff's case proceeds in small claims court.

Transfer: Allowed only upon judge's decision, following a hearing.

Attorneys: Not allowed without judge's consent, unless case transferred from regular civil court.

Appeals: Within 30 days. The party who files a claim or counterclaim can't appeal unless the amount exceeds $1,000; no party can appeal unless amount claimed is $250 or more. Heard in superior court as new trial.

Evictions: No.

Jury trials: No provision.

West Virginia

Court: Magistrate Court.

Statutes: W. Va. Code §§ 50-2-1 to 50-6-3; 56-1-1.

Court rules: Rules of Civil Procedure for Magistrate Courts, Rule 1 to 21.

Court information: www.state.wv.us/wvsca/magistrate.htm or www.state.wv.us/wvsca/prose/guide.pdf

Dollar limit: $5,000.

Where to sue: County in which any defendant resides or can be served, or where transaction or injury occurred. West Virginia corporations, where principal office located; other corporations, where they do business. For eviction suits, county where property is located.

Service of process: Sheriff or disinterested adult; certified or registered mail by court at plaintiff's request, return receipt requested.

Defendant's response: Defendant must appear or file written answer within 20 days of service to avoid default (30 days if service is made on defendant's attorney or agent). Defendant can also file a counterclaim for $5,000 or less.

Transfer: Allowed if all parties agree to remove to circuit court, or by any party for claims over $300. Also allowed at magistrate's discretion if defendant requests transfer to another venue in her answer or within reasonable time.

Attorneys: Allowed.

Appeals: Allowed by either party within 20 days. Heard in circuit court. If original trial was by jury, appeal is on law only, not facts; if original trial was without a jury, appeal is new trial (also without a jury).

Evictions: Yes.

Jury trials: Either party may demand jury trial if claim is over $20 or involves possession of real estate. Must be made in writing within 20 days of service of defendant's answer, or in eviction cases, five days after service of complaint.

Wisconsin

Court: Small Claims Action (circuit court).

Statutes: Wis. Stat. Ann. §§ 799.01 to 799.445; 421.401; 801.50; 808.03.

Court information: www.wicourts.gov/about/pubs/circuit/smallclaimsguide.htm

Dollar limit: $5,000. No limit in eviction suits.

Where to sue: County in which any defendant resides or does substantial business, where transaction or injury occurred, or where property is located. County where contract claim arose or, if claim arose from consumer transaction, county where contract was signed or where purchase or loan took place. For landlord-tenant claims, county where property is located.

Service of process: Sheriff, process server, or disinterested adult; or by certified mail by court clerk, return receipt requested.

Defendant's response: No formal written answer required.

Transfer: Upon defendant's counterclaim over $5,000, case will be tried according to regular circuit court civil procedure.

Attorneys: Allowed.

Appeals: Allowed by either party within 15 days. No appeal from default judgment.

Evictions: Yes.

Jury trials: Either party may request a jury trial.

Wyoming

Court: Small Claims Case (circuit court).

Statutes: Wyo. Stat. §§ 1-21-201 to 1-21-205; 5-9-128; 5-9-136.

Court rules: Wyoming Rules and Forms Governing Small Claims Cases, Rules 1 to 7, Forms 1 and 2.

Court information: www.courts.state.wy.us or www.tetonwyo.org/jc/ (Teton County)

Dollar limit: $5,000.

Where to sue: County in which defendant has an address.

Service of process: Sheriff, deputy, or disinterested adult; or certified mail, return receipt requested (by court clerk if defendant lives in the same county as court).

Defendant's response: No formal written answer required.

Transfer: No provision.

Attorneys: Allowed. If one party appears with an attorney, the other party is entitled to a continuance to obtain one.

Appeals: Allowed by either party. Heard in district court on law only, not facts.

Evictions: No.

Jury trials: Either party may demand jury trial.

Current as of December 2007. ●

Index

CATALOG
...more from Nolo

BUSINESS

	PRICE	CODE
Business Buyout Agreements (Book w/CD)	$49.99	BSAG
The California Nonprofit Corporation Kit (Binder w/CD)	$69.99	CNP
California Workers' Comp: Take Charge When You're Injured on the Job	$34.99	WORK
The Complete Guide to Buying a Business (Book w/CD)	$24.99	BUYBU
The Complete Guide to Selling a Business (Book w/CD)	$34.99	SELBU
Consultant & Independent Contractor Agreements (Book w/CD)	$29.99	CICA
The Corporate Records Handbook (Book w/CD)	$69.99	CORMI
Create Your Own Employee Handbook (Book w/CD)	$49.99	EMHA
Dealing With Problem Employees	$44.99	PROBM
Deduct It! Lower Your Small Business Taxes	$34.99	DEDU
Effective Fundraising for Nonprofits	$24.99	EFFN
The Employer's Legal Handbook	$39.99	EMPL
The Essential Guide to Family & Medical Leave (Book w/CD)	$39.99	FMLA
The Essential Guide to Federal Employment Laws	$39.99	FEMP
The Essential Guide to Workplace Investigations (Book w/CD)	$39.99	NVST
Every Nonprofit's Guide to Publishing (Book w/CD)	$29.99	EPNO
Form a Partnership (Book w/CD)	$39.99	PART
Form Your Own Limited Liability Company (Book w/CD)	$44.99	LIAB
Home Business Tax Deductions: Keep What You Earn	$34.99	DEHB
How to Form a Nonprofit Corporation (Book w/CD)—National Edition	$49.99	NNP
How to Form a Nonprofit Corporation in California (Book w/CD)	$49.99	NON
How to Form Your Own California Corporation (Binder w/CD)	$59.99	CACI
How to Form Your Own California Corporation (Book w/CD)	$39.99	CCOR
How to Run a Thriving Business	$19.99	THRV
How to Write a Business Plan (Book w/CD)	$34.99	SBS
Incorporate Your Business (Book w/CD)—National Edition	$49.99	NIBS
Investors in Your Backyard (Book w/CD)	$24.99	FINBUS

Prices subject to change.

	PRICE	CODE
The Job Description Handbook (Book w/CD)	$29.99	JOB
Legal Guide for Starting & Running a Small Business	$34.99	RUNS
Legal Forms for Starting & Running a Small Business (Book w/CD)	$29.99	RUNSF
LLC or Corporation?	$24.99	CHENT
The Manager's Legal Handbook	$39.99	ELBA
Marketing Without Advertising	$20.00	MWAD
Music Law: How to Run Your Band's Business (Book w/CD)	$39.99	ML
Negotiate the Best Lease for Your Business	$24.99	LESP
Nolo's Quick LLC	$29.99	LLCQ
Patent Savvy for Managers: Spot & Protect Valuable Innovations in Your Company	$29.99	PATM
The Performance Appraisal Handbook (Book w/CD)	$29.99	PERF
The Progressive Discipline Handbook (Book w/CD)	$34.99	SDHB
Small Business in Paradise: Working for Yourself in a Place You Love	$19.99	SPAR
The Small Business Start-up Kit (Book w/CD)—National Edition	$29.99	SMBU
The Small Business Start-up Kit for California (Book w/CD)	$29.99	OPEN
Starting & Building a Nonprofit: A Practical Guide (Book w/CD)	$29.99	SNON
Starting & Running a Successful Newsletter or Magazine	$29.99	MAG
Tax Deductions for Professionals	$34.99	DEPO
Tax Savvy for Small Business	$36.99	SAVVY
The Work from Home Handbook	$19.99	US-HOM
Wow! I'm in Business	$19.99	WHOO
Working for Yourself: Law & Taxes for Independent Contractors, Freelancers & Consultants	$39.99	WAGE
Working With Independent Contractors (Book w/CD)	$29.99	HICI
Your Limited Liability Company: An Operating Manual (Book w/CD)	$49.99	LOP
Your Rights in the Workplace	$29.99	YRW

CONSUMER

	PRICE	CODE
How to Win Your Personal Injury Claim	$29.99	PICL
Nolo's Encyclopedia of Everyday Law	$29.99	EVL
Nolo's Guide to California Law	$24.99	CLAW
Your Little Legal Companion (Hardcover)	$9.95	ANNI

ESTATE PLANNING & PROBATE

	PRICE	CODE
8 Ways to Avoid Probate	$19.99	PRAV
The Busy Family's Guide to Estate Planning (Book w/CD)	$24.99	FAM
Estate Planning Basics	$21.99	ESPN
The Executor's Guide: Settling a Loved One's Estate or Trust	$39.99	EXEC
Get It Together: Organize Your Records (Book w/CD)	$21.99	GET
How to Probate an Estate in California	$49.99	PAE
Make Your Own Living Trust (Book w/CD)	$39.99	LITR
Nolo's Simple Will Book (Book w/CD)	$36.99	SWIL
Plan Your Estate	$44.99	NEST
Quick & Legal Will Book (Book w/CD)	$19.99	QUIC
Special Needs Trust: Protect Your Child's Financial Future (Book w/CD)	$34.99	SPNT

FAMILY MATTERS

	PRICE	CODE
Always Dad: Being a Great Father During & After a Divorce	$16.99	DIFA
Building a Parenting Agreement That Works	$24.99	CUST
The Complete IEP Guide	$34.99	IEP
Divorce & Money: How to Make the Best Financial Decisions During Divorce	$34.99	DIMO
Divorce Without Court: A Guide to Mediation & Collaborative Divorce	$29.99	DWCT
Do Your Own California Adoption: Nolo's Guide for Stepparents & Domestic Partners (Book w/CD)	$34.99	ADOP
Every Dog's Legal Guide: A Must-Have for Your Owner	$19.99	DOG
Get a Life: You Don't Need a Million to Retire Well	$24.99	LIFE
The Guardianship Book for California	$34.99	GB
A Judge's Guide to Divorce (Book w/CD)	$24.99	JDIV
A Legal Guide for Lesbian and Gay Couples (Book w/CD)	$34.99	LG
Living Together: A Legal Guide for Unmarried Couples (Book w/CD)	$34.99	LTK
Nolo's Essential Guide to Divorce	$24.99	NODV
Nolo's IEP Guide: Learning Disabilities	$29.99	IELD
Parent Savvy	$19.99	PRNT
Prenuptial Agreements: Write a Fair & Lasting Contract (Book w/CD)	$34.99	PNUP
Retire Happy	$19.99	US-RICH
Work Less, Live More: The Way to Semi-Retirement	$17.99	RECL
The Work Less, Live More Workbook (Book w/CD)	$19.99	RECW

ORDER 24 HOURS A DAY @ www.nolo.com
Call 800-728-3555 • Mail or fax the order form in this book

GOING TO COURT

	PRICE	CODE
Becoming a Mediator	$29.99	BECM
Beat Your Ticket: Go To Court & Win!—National Edition	$21.99	BEYT
The Criminal Law Handbook: Know Your Rights, Survive the System	$39.99	KYR
Everybody's Guide to Small Claims Court—National Edition	$29.99	NSCC
Everybody's Guide to Small Claims Court in California	$29.99	CSCC
Fight Your Ticket & Win in California	$29.99	FYT
How to Change Your Name in California	$34.99	NAME
Legal Research: How to Find and Understand the Law	$39.99	LRES
Nolo's Deposition Handbook	$34.99	DEP
Represent Yourself in Court: How to Prepare & Try a Winning Case	$39.99	RYC
Win Your Lawsuit: A Judge's Guide to Representing Yourself in California Superior Court	$39.99	SLWY

HOMEOWNERS, LANDLORDS & TENANTS

	PRICE	CODE
Buying a Second Home (Book w/CD)	$24.99	SCND
The California Landlord's Law Book: Rights & Responsibilities (Book w/CD)	$44.99	LBRT
The California Landlord's Law Book: Evictions (Book w/CD)	$44.99	LBEV
California Tenants' Rights	$29.99	CTEN
Deeds for California Real Estate	$27.99	DEED
Every Landlord's Guide to Finding Great Tenants (Book w/CD)	$19.99	FIND
Every Landlord's Legal Guide (Book w/CD)—National Edition	$44.99	ELLI
Every Landlord's Property Protection Guide (Book w/CD)	$29.99	RISK
Every Landlord's Tax Deduction Guide	$34.99	DELL
Every Tenant's Legal Guide—National Edition	$29.99	EVTEN
For Sale by Owner in California (Book w/CD)	$29.99	FSBO
How to Buy a House in California	$34.99	BHCA
Leases & Rental Agreements (Book w/CD)	$29.99	LEAR
Neighbor Law: Fences, Trees, Boundaries & Noise	$29.99	NEI
Nolo's Essential Guide to Buying Your First Home (Book w/CD)	$24.99	HTBH
Renters' Rights: The Basics	$24.99	RENT

IMMIGRATION

	PRICE	CODE
Becoming A U.S. Citizen: A Guide to the Law, Exam and Interview	$24.99	USCIT
Fiancé & Marriage Visas	$34.99	IMAR
How to Get a Green Card	$29.99	GRN
U.S. Immigration Made Easy	$39.99	IMEZ

MONEY MATTERS

101 Law Forms for Personal Use (Book w/CD)	$29.99	SPOT
The Busy Family's Guide to Money	$19.99	US-MONY
Chapter 13 Bankruptcy: Repay Your Debts	$39.99	CHB
Credit Repair (Book w/CD)	$24.99	CREP
How to File for Chapter 7 Bankruptcy	$29.99	HFB
IRAs, 401(k)s & Other Retirement Plans: Taking Your Money Out	$34.99	RET
Lower Taxes in 7 Easy Steps	$16.99	LTAX
The New Bankruptcy: Will It Work for You?	$21.99	FIBA
Nolo's Guide to Social Security Disability (Book w/CD)	$29.99	QSS
Solve Your Money Troubles	$19.99	MT
Stand Up to the IRS	$29.99	SIRS
Surviving An IRS Tax Audit	$24.95	SAUD

PATENTS AND COPYRIGHTS

All I Need is Money: How to Finance Your Invention	$19.99	FINA
The Copyright Handbook: What Every Writer Needs to Know (Book w/CD)	$39.99	COHA
Getting Permission: How to License & Clear Copyrighted Materials (Book w/CD)	$34.99	RIPER
How to Make Patent Drawings	$29.99	DRAW
The Inventor's Notebook	$24.99	INOT
Legal Guide to Web & Software Development (Book w/CD)	$44.99	SFT
Nolo's Patents for Beginners	$24.99	QPAT
Patent, Copyright & Trademark: An Intellectual Property Desk Reference	$39.99	PCTM

	PRICE	CODE
Patent It Yourself	$49.99	PAT
Patent Pending in 24 Hours	$34.99	PEND
Patent Savvy for Managers: Spot & Protect Valuable Innovations in Your Company	$29.99	PATM
Patenting Art & Entertainment: New Strategies for Protecting Creative Ideas	$39.99	PATAE
Profit from Your Idea (Book w/CD)	$34.99	LICE
The Public Domain	$34.99	PUBL
Trademark: Legal Care for Your Business and Product Name	$39.99	TRD
What Every Inventor Needs to Know About Business & Taxes (Book w/CD)	$21.99	ILAX

SENIORS

Long-Term Care: How to Plan & Pay for It	$19.99	ELD
Social Security, Medicare & Goverment Pensions	$29.99	SOA

SOFTWARE

Call or check our website at www.nolo.com for special discounts on Software!

Leasewriter Plus 2.0—Windows	$49.99	LWD2
LLC Maker—Windows	$69.99	LLP1
Patent Pending Now!—Windows	$89.99	PP1
PatentEase 6.0—Windows	$259.00	PEAS
Personal RecordKeeper 5.0—Windows	$39.99	RKD5
Quicken Legal Business Pro 2008—Windows	$79.99	SBQB8
Quicken WillMaker Plus 2008—Windows	$49.99	WQP8

Special Upgrade Offer

Save 35% on the latest edition of your Nolo book

Because laws and legal procedures change often, we update our books regularly. To help keep you up-to-date, we are extending this special upgrade offer. Cut out and mail the title portion of the cover of your old Nolo book and we'll give you 35% off the retail price of the New Edition of that book when you purchase directly from Nolo. This offer is to individuals only. Prices and offer subject to change without notice.

Order Form

Name	
Address	
City	
State, Zip	
Daytime Phone	
E-mail	

Our "No-Hassle" Guarantee

Return anything you buy directly from Nolo for any reason and we'll cheerfully refund your purchase price. No ifs, ands or buts.

☐ Check here if you do not wish to receive mailings from other companies

Item Code	Quantity	Item	Unit Price	Total Price

Method of payment

☐ Check   ☐ VISA
☐ American Express
☐ MasterCard
☐ Discover Card

Subtotal	
Add your local sales tax (California only)	
Shipping: RUSH $12, Basic $6 (See below)	
"I bought 2, ship it to me FREE!" (Ground shipping only)	
TOTAL	

Account Number

Expiration Date

Signature

Shipping and Handling

Rush Delivery—Only $12

We'll ship any order to any street address in the U.S. by UPS 2nd Day Air* for only $12!

* Order by 9:30 AM Pacific Time and get your order in 2 business days. Orders placed after 9:30 AM Pacific Time will arrive in 3 business days. P.O. boxes and S.F. Bay Area use basic shipping. Alaska and Hawaii use 2nd Day Air or Priority Mail.

Basic Shipping—$6

Use for P.O. Boxes, Northern California and Ground Service.

Allow 1-2 weeks for delivery.

U.S. addresses only.

For faster service, use your credit card and our toll-free numbers

Call our customer service group Monday thru Friday 7am to 6pm PST

 Phone
1-800-728-3555

 Fax
1-800-645-0895

 Mail
Nolo
950 Parker St.
Berkeley, CA 94710

Order 24 hours a day @ www.nolo.com

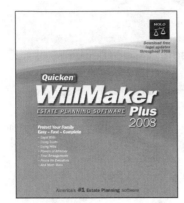

Get the Latest in the Law

Nolo's Legal Updater
We'll send you an email whenever a new edition of your book is published! Sign up at **www.nolo.com/legalupdater**.

Updates at Nolo.com
Check **www.nolo.com/update** to find recent changes in the law that affect the current edition of your book.

Nolo Customer Service
To make sure that this edition of the book is the most recent one, call us at **800-728-3555** and ask one of our friendly customer service representatives (7:00 am to 6:00 pm PST, weekdays only). Or find out at **www.nolo.com**.

Complete the Registration & Comment Card ...
... and we'll do the work for you! Just indicate your preferences below:

Registration & Comment Card

NAME   DATE

ADDRESS

CITY   STATE   ZIP

PHONE   EMAIL

COMMENTS

WAS THIS BOOK EASY TO USE?   (VERY EASY)   5   4   3   2   1   (VERY DIFFICULT)

☐ Yes, you can quote me in future Nolo promotional materials. *Please include phone number above.*

☐ Yes, send me **Nolo's Legal Updater** via email when a new edition of this book is available.

Yes, I want to sign up for the following email newsletters:

    ☐ **NoloBriefs** (monthly)
    ☐ **Nolo's Special Offer** (monthly)
    ☐ **Nolo's BizBriefs** (monthly)
    ☐ **Every Landlord's Quarterly** (four times a year)

☐ Yes, you can give my contact info to carefully selected partners whose products may be of interest to me.

NOLO

NSCC12

Nolo
950 Parker Street
Berkeley, CA 94710-9867
www.nolo.com

YOUR LEGAL COMPANION

M[...]TORNEY

"Loves w[...] rain and drawing up prenuptial agreements."

[...] and creating living trusts."

"Spends time gardening and doing trademark searches."

Brent
San Francisco

Juliana
Phoenix

Ron
Seattle

Start a great relationship
(you can skip the walks on the beach)

You don't need just any attorney. You need that "special someone" – someone whose personality puts you at ease, whose qualifications match your needs, whose experience can make everything better.

With Nolo's Lawyer Directory, meeting your new attorney is just a click away. Lawyers have created extensive profiles that feature their work histories, credentials, philosophies, fees – and much more.

Check out Nolo's Lawyer Directory to find your attorney – you'll feel as if you've already met, before you ever meet.

Visit us and get a free eBook!
http://lawyers.nolo.com/book

Meet your new attorney   **NOLO'S LAWYER DIRECTORY**

The attorneys listed above are fictitious. Any resemblance to an actual attorney is purely coincidental.